THE CALIFORNIA NUTRITION BOOK

THE CALIFORNIA NUTRITION BOOK

A FOOD GUIDE FOR THE '90S FROM
FACULTY AT THE UNIVERSITY OF CALIFORNIA
AND THE EDITORS OF *AMERICAN HEALTH*

Paul Saltman, Ph.D.,
Joel Gurin,
and Ira Mothner

LITTLE, BROWN AND COMPANY   Boston   •   Toronto

Second Printing

Library of Congress Cataloging-in-Publication Data
Saltman, Paul.
  The California Nutrition Book.

  Includes index.
  1. Nutrition. 2. Health. I. Gurin, Joel, 1953–   . II.
Mothner, Ira. III. University of California (System) IV. Ameri-
can Health magazine (New York, N.Y.) V. Title. [DNLM: 1.
Nutrition — popular works. QU 145 S178c]
RA784.S335 1987   613.2   87-3086
ISBN 0-316-76964-9

RRD VA

Designed by Patricia Dunbar

*Published simultaneously in Canada
by Little, Brown & Company (Canada) Limited*

PRINTED IN THE UNITED STATES OF AMERICA

Contents

Acknowledgments   vii

Part I Nutrition and You

Chapter 1. No-Nonsense Nutrition   3

Chapter 2. You and Your Diet   9

Part II The Stuff of Life

Chapter 3. What Life Is Made Of   25

Chapter 4. The Water-Soluble Vitamins: B's and C   43

Chapter 5. The Fat-Soluble Vitamins: A, D, E, and K   64

Chapter 6. Minerals: The Big Seven   72

Chapter 7. Microminerals: Iron and Other Trace Elements   84

Part III All About Eating

Chapter 8. Getting Nutrients out of Food   99

Chapter 9. Foodstyle   118

Chapter 10. All About Body Fat   131

Chapter 11. Weight Control   146

Chapter 12. Exercise: Nutrition in Action   159

Chapter 13. Down the Alimentary Canal   169

Chapter 14. When Foods Hate You: Allergies and Sensitivities   178

Chapter 15. Food and Mood   185

Chapter 16. Toxic Pleasures   193

Part IV Diet and Disease

Chapter 17. Preventing Heart Disease   205

Chapter 18. Controlling Hypertension   222

Chapter 19. Can Diet Prevent Cancer?   232

Chapter 20. Diabetes and Diet   247

Chapter 21. Deficiency Diseases of Today: Anemia
              and Osteoporosis   255

Chapter 22. Eating When Ill   270

Part V Nutritional Needs Through Life

Chapter 23. The Pregnancy Diet   277

Chapter 24. Feeding Infants and Toddlers   287

Chapter 25. Eating in Adolescence   299

Chapter 26. Concerns of the Adult Years   307

Chapter 27. Nutrition During the Later Years   310

Chapter 28. Eating for Health and Pleasure   321

Appendix

Table A1. Recommended Dietary Allowances,
            1980   327

Table A2. Estimated Safe and Adequate Daily Dietary Intakes of
            Selected Vitamins and Minerals   328

Table A3. Mean Heights and Weights and Recommended
            Energy Intake   329

Table A4. Nutritive Value of Foods in Average Servings
            or Common Measures   331

Index   359

Acknowledgments

NO BOOK AS COMPREHENSIVE AS this one can possibly be the work of its authors alone, and we have been most fortunate to have had the help and guidance of a great many people. They have generously provided their insight, experience, and imagination at each stage of its development. Major contributions were made by the scientific advisers, from both the University of California and other institutions, who helped formulate the book's approach to nutritional issues.

University of California Scientific Advisers:

Roslyn Alfin-Slater, Ph.D., professor of nutritional science, School of Public Health, UCLA.

George M. Briggs, Ph.D., professor emeritus, Department of Nutrition, UC, Berkeley.

Robert E. Hodges, M.D., professor of family medicine and internal medicine, UC, Irvine.

Lucille S. Hurley, Ph.D., professor of nutrition, Department of Nutrition, UC, Davis.

Jerrold M. Olefsky, M.D., professor of medicine and head of the Division of Endocrinology and Metabolism, UC, San Diego.

Phyllis A. Crapo, assistant professor of medicine, Division of Endocrinology and Metabolism, UC, San Diego.

Judith S. Stern, Sc.D., professor of nutrition and director of the Food Intake Laboratory, UC, Davis.

Other Scientific Advisers:

Russell Merritt, M.D., associate professor of pediatrics, University of Southern California.

David Kritchevsky, Ph.D., associate director, Wistar Institute.

Judith Rodin, Ph.D., professor of psychology and psychiatry, Yale School of Medicine.

Harold H. Sandstead, M.D., Ph.D., chairman, Department of Preventive Medicine and Community Health, University of Texas Medical Branch, Galveston.

Myron Winick, M.D., director of the Institute of Human Nutrition, College of Physicians and Surgeons, Columbia University.

We owe a special debt to Dr. Doris Howes Calloway, provost of the Professional Schools and Colleges of UC, Berkeley. Dr. Calloway has graciously permitted us to use the food composition charts she painstakingly created for *Nutrition and Physical Fitness*, written with Dr. George M. Briggs.

The true parents of *The California Nutrition Book*, whose concept it was and who gave the project their unflagging support, were Mary Lindenstein Walshok, associate vice chancellor, Extended Studies and Public Service, UC, San Diego; and T George Harris, editor-in-chief, *American Health* magazine.

Working closely with the authors: Judith Groch, executive editor, *American Health*, played a major role in development of the book from its initial outline to its final revision; Steven Brewer took responsibility for coordinating research and organizing material. Yvonne Hancher, director of communications and marketing for the UC, San Diego, Extension Division, coordinated the contributions of the University of California advisers. Anne Krueger, managing editor, *American Health*, supervised the transformation of manuscript to page proofs.

Helping enormously to make the book more useful, readable, and concise were Little, Brown editors Fredrica Friedman and Christina Ward, while Fran Collin, literary agent for *American Health*, provided invaluable aid in making the concept a reality.

The difficult and complicated job of preparing, revising, and circulating draft chapters would not have been possible without the dedication and diligence of the staff: *American Health* editorial assistants Donna Behen, Genia Gould, Karoline Harrington, and Cynthia Moekle, and Judith Hyde, special assistant, Office of Special Projects, UC, San Diego.

We also wish to thank The Quaker Oats Company for a generous grant toward "The New Nutrition," a course developed by UC, San Diego, and *American Health*. As the first national nutrition course, its teaching materials will include this book.

Finally, the authors would like to thank three very special women for their patience and forbearance during the time it has taken to complete *The California Nutrition Book*: Barbara Saltman, Carol Duchow Gurin, and Linda Fennimore.

PART I

NUTRITION AND YOU

CHAPTER 1

No-Nonsense Nutrition

Food is fun, and sound nutrition need not diminish the pleasure. More than anything else, it's the nonsense of nutrition — unreasonable food fears and unnecessary prohibitions — that takes the joy out of eating. So no-nonsense nutrition is as much a matter of what you put in your head as what you put in your stomach, and it starts with discarding food prejudices.

No food is devoid of nutritional value, although some are more nutrient-packed than others. And while what we eat can harm us as well as help us, few foods pose the same degree of danger to everyone, and a great many have reputations worse than they deserve.

Chances are that sugar won't kill you and neither will fats. Red meat isn't bad for you, and *no* food can be dismissed as "junk." Even a heavy hand with the saltshaker won't do most of us any harm at all.

Foods with good reputations shouldn't all be taken at face value either. Fresh fruits and vegetables, although they are a fine source for many necessary vitamins and minerals, are poor sources for others. A diet too dependent on complex carbohydrates (like pasta, whole grains, and beans) can leave you lacking some of the basic materials the body needs. There's no particular virtue to getting nutrients from "natural" foods (as long as one gets them), and a high-fiber diet can be a mixed blessing (it's capable of whisking essential nutrients right out of the digestive tract).

Foods are not by their nature alone either bad or good. Even alcohol, in spite of bringing little but calories to the party, can provide certain health benefits when used in moderation.

What makes food good or bad for you is volume, balance, and interaction. What you eat matters less than how much you eat, when you eat

3

it, and what other foods you're also eating. Think of your diet as though it were a football team. You need all kinds of foods, much as your football team needs all kinds of players. You can't crowd the field with speedy running backs, forgetting to add some muscular linemen, and expect to score many touchdowns.

Food is the source of 40 or so essential nutrients (nutritionists still aren't certain exactly how many there are). They are essential because the body needs all of them and cannot provide them for itself. But it needs the right amounts of each, just as your football team can make do with only one quarterback but has to have at least three or four guys who can catch passes. Foods interact. They work together, as football players do; and they are just as likely to get in each other's way.

In practice, it works like this. Suppose you are concerned about avoiding the bone disease called osteoporosis, which strikes many women late in life. To prevent it, you've got to limit the loss of calcium from your bones (the body will withdraw calcium on deposit there for other purposes). The obvious answer is to take in more calcium, which, as you'll discover later in the book, is no easy matter. But even when there is plenty of calcium in your diet, it can get tangled up with other nutrients in the digestive tract and never make it out of the intestines and into the bloodstream.

Even if you do take in all the calcium you need, your body is likely to lose more than it retains unless you have enough vitamin D on hand. You need estrogen, too, to prevent calcium loss. But that's not all, because the calcium you are getting can't build any new bone unless there's enough of the other bone-building minerals — phosphorus and magnesium — on hand. Finally, it takes still other minerals (zinc, copper, and manganese) before the bone builders can get to work. And none of the above will do much good without the kind of exercise that lets the body know that more load-bearing bone is needed.

All this makes it hard to give simple, easy-to-follow advice for preventing osteoporosis other than "get enough calcium." The advice is valid — without an adequate supply of calcium, nothing else will be of much help — but it's not a sufficient safeguard against the disease.

Nutrition is a complicated business and impossible to boil down to a few simple rules that apply to everyone. Nutritional needs and vulnerabilities are strongly influenced by genetics and vary considerably. Just about everyone wants to eat wisely. But we run into trouble when we generalize dietary advice and take as gospel, for example, such notions as "red meat is bad for you."

To be sure, eating *too much* red meat can upset the balance of carbohydrates, protein, and fat in your diet. Moreover, it can raise the amounts of saturated fatty acids and cholesterol you consume to levels that pose health risks for certain men and women — but not necessarily for *you.* By depriving yourself of roast beef, lamb chops, and the like, however, you risk deficiencies of iron, zinc, and other minerals.

By the same token, the idea that "everyone ought to cut down on salt," although it won't lead to nutritional grief, provides no universal benefits. Reduced salt consumption can help certain people to lower high blood pressure. But *high* salt consumption will not cause blood pressure to rise in the rest of us.

There is a high cost for the kind of oversimplification that ignores the great variation in individual nutritional needs and the potent role of heredity. It leaves a great many people with a sizable list of dietary dos and don'ts and very little understanding of them. Thus, it creates baseless food fears and leads to food choices that may make it nearly impossible to get adequate amounts of essential nutrients. It tends to mystify nutrition, so that even the nutritionally aware are often naive, and it creates a climate in which all kinds of fads and frauds become popular and all manner of charlatans thrive.

To some extent, serious nutritionists are as much to blame for this situation as quacks. They too have put a premium on dietary advice that is too simplified to be very useful for thoughtful men and women attempting to deal sensibly and knowledgeably with their dietary needs. Nutrition scientists have tended to separate their research and teaching from the advice they give the public, and one result has been to preserve a kind of nutritional innocence that encourages the very dietary excesses they had hoped to prevent.

This book, with an approach that the authors call "no-nonsense," brings nutritional knowledge and advice together and provides specific dietary strategies for meeting the many needs created by the physical changes, threats of disease, and differences of lifestyle and foodstyle (the way we eat) that occur throughout life. Although individual chapters cover pregnancy, infancy, adolescence, and aging, the book primarily addresses the needs of adults in their early and middle years. It is focused on health rather than on illness but devotes six chapters to dietary means of preventing and dealing with certain diseases.

THE REWARDS OF NUTRITION

Proper nutrition will not let you live forever. Food choice — no matter how right it may be — cannot extend life span beyond the limit heredity determines. But it can help you to live right up to that limit and to live a healthier, more active, and more productive life. In this book you will read that extra vitamin C cannot cure a cold or treat cancer and that extra zinc will not make you more resistant to infections. But the key word here is *extra*. If levels of vitamins A and C in your bloodstream are inadequate, then raising them can indeed help you to shake a cold and to resist cancer, and bringing subnormal zinc levels up to par will give your immune system a boost.

There's nothing magical or mysterious about such effects — that's what nutrition does. It permits the body to reach its maximum genetic potential. It can't expand that potential. Improved nutrition has raised the average height of the Japanese by more than 3 inches since 1900. But the Japanese were always genetically capable of this height. As the average height of all Americans increased during the past century, the average height of Harvard students changed hardly at all. During this period nutrition among Harvard students (unlike nutrition among the general public) was apparently already sufficient for them to grow as tall as their genes permitted.

Although nutrition can help prevent diseases, it has yet to demonstrate much ability to cure diseases — except those created by nutritional deficiencies. But the final word on the use of nutrients for therapeutic purposes isn't in yet.

Nutrition, however, is only one of the factors that contribute to fitness and health. There are also environmental factors (from toxic waste to infectious disease), accidents, and psychological factors. Over all of these we as individuals have only limited control. But over diet we have considerable control. We also can control how much exercise we get, and there is so much interaction between diet and exercise — in terms of weight control, body metabolism, and nutritional needs — that it is most useful to consider exercise an aspect of nutrition. Together, diet and exercise are the most effective means at our disposal to influence fitness and health — but always within the limits of heredity.

THE ROLE OF HEREDITY

It is hard to overestimate the role that heredity plays in our lives, for we are just beginning to recognize how profound genetic influences are. Think about how different we look from one another, and realize that these differences are more than skin deep. Even our internal organs are shaped differently. Inside and out, there is no such thing as a standard human being.

Heredity makes some of us more vulnerable to disease than others, and medicine now recognizes more than 3,000 genetically influenced disorders. Not all are preventable. If you have the genes, there is almost nothing you can do at present to avoid sickle-cell anemia, Tay-Sachs disease, or Huntington's chorea, for example. But the risk of contracting a number of the more common genetic disorders is reducible, and diet appears to be the most potent and accessible risk-reducing mechanism.

Nutrition cannot change an inherited vulnerability to disease. But diet is capable of helping prevent osteoporosis, heart disease, hypertension, certain forms of cancer, and even obesity in some very specific ways, like building bone mass early in life to reduce the threat of osteoporosis.

There is another aspect of heredity that has significant nutritional implications: the great variety in body functions and needs. We all have slender friends who eat far more, and more often, than we do, scarcely exercise at all, and still never seem to gain weight. What may make them different from us is genetic programming that allows them to burn up calories more rapidly than we do. Genetic differences can also cause variations in nutrient requirements. What are safe and adequate levels of vitamin A or C or the B vitamins for you may not be quite enough for your friend. One purpose of this book is to help you to recognize special individual needs and to develop a diet and eating patterns that respond to them.

FASHIONS, FADS, AND FALSE HOPES

Fashion exercises a powerful influence over nutrition. The present widespread interest in fitness has significantly changed eating habits, as has increased consumption of "fast foods." However, a diet based largely on the latest fitness fads can be as nutritionally unreliable as one that is confined to fast-food burgers, chicken, pizza, fish, and fries. As for the growing interest in gourmet cooking and dining, American epicureanism offers just about equal opportunity for sound and unsound nutrition.

The present passion for slenderness has a substantial effect on diet — more, apparently, than it does on weight, for the national waistline is expanding despite our efforts to reduce. But more significant than whether or not dieters succeed in losing weight is the risk of nutritional deficiency that weight-control diets may pose.

In this regard, you should realize that there is a tremendous amount of inaccurate, ineffective, and downright dangerous information about nutrition now on the market. There are costly "nutritional" products and dietary strategies that can do you little good and may well expose you to considerable harm. These are noted throughout the book. Special "Department of False Hopes" sections deal, for example, with weight-reducing pills, the use of vitamins to allay stress or psychological illness, tests for nutritional deficiencies, and regimens for maximum athletic performance. Other sections examine the rarity of true food allergies and hypoglycemia, popular weight-loss plans, and formulas for life extension.

EATING WISELY AND WELL

There are several principles of nutrition that provide basic ground rules for sound dietary decision making. The first is moderation. Overindulgence by dietary excess or by overdoing "toxic pleasures" (see chapter 16) is foolhardy. Even though your body can handle a good deal of toxicity and is equipped to purge itself of poisonous wastes, it can safely cope with only a limited amount of excess.

Next on the list of sound nutritional principles is body conscious-ness. Listen to what your body says, particularly what it has to say about food. Your body is an infinitely resourceful organism, and it is pro-grammed for survival. There will, of course, be times when you will have to overrule it, but it's usually best to heed what your body's hunger, thirst, fatigue, or satiety is telling you.

Finally, and most important, is variety. This means using as wide a selection of foodstuffs as possible and recognizing that even foods with bad reputations can often be good sources of the nutrients you need.

Knowledge is the key to no-nonsense nutrition. The dietary strate-gies suggested throughout this book can best be applied by readers who understand some of the basics covered in the opening chapters — what the essential nutrients are, why they are needed, where they are found, and how they interact with other nutrients.

With this knowledge, it is not difficult to meet nutritional needs in ways well suited to your life stage and foodstyle. Moreover, it is possible to achieve nutritional goals without diminishing the joys of eating in any way. The great variety of new foods now on the market and the growing availability of different ethnic foods have contributed to wider food choice, and eating adventurously is perfectly consistent with eating wisely. An understanding of nutrition frees you from food fears and rigid prohibitions to choose a diet that is not only healthful but exciting and pleasurable as well.

CHAPTER 2

You and Your Diet

W HAT NUTRITION CAN DO for you depends very much on what it is *not* doing now. Remember, nutrition is the primary means of realizing your genetic potential. Without an adequate amount and proper balance of nutrients, you are simply not going to live as long or as healthily, look as good, or work as hard as you are genetically programmed to do. Neither will you be able to run as fast, resist infection as well, or overcome illness as easily.

It's hard to tell how much your present diet may be costing you in health, energy, looks, or performance, because nutritional effects can be subtle. It doesn't take a full-blown deficiency (with readily recognized symptoms) to slow you down, to make it harder to shake a cold, or to delay healing of cuts and scrapes. Lack of sufficient iron in your diet, for example, needn't be severe enough to bring on anemia before it begins to sap energy and lower physical or intellectual productivity.

Although it is difficult to measure positive genetic potential to see if your body is performing as well as it can, it is possible to look at the other factor in the equation and determine your nutritional status. Your body plainly will not function at peak levels if you aren't providing it with proper amounts of everything it needs. Moreover, determining nutritional status can give you early warning of long-term dietary risks. Consuming too little or too much of certain nutrients over prolonged periods of time can increase your vulnerability to disease.

As poor nutrition raises the risk of disease, appropriate nutrition lowers it, both in general ways — by keeping the immune system in tip-top shape and sustaining recuperative powers — and in some very specific ways as well. Dietary intervention can help prevent some of the most common diseases to which heredity makes us vulnerable —

9

diabetes, osteoporosis, heart disease, hypertension, and cancer of the breast and colon. Obesity, too, is a genetically influenced condition, and diet plays no small role in controlling it.

It is possible to tell how vulnerable to a specific disorder you may be by looking at the history of that disorder in your family — the number of family members affected, their ages at the time the condition appeared, and their connections to you. Keep in mind that there are racial and ethnic aspects to genetic diseases as well. Osteoporosis, for example, occurs much more frequently among white than among black Americans, and most frequently among fair, small-boned women of northern European descent.

Diseases vary in their heritability (some are far more readily inherited than others). The more common form of diabetes, for example, which strikes during middle age, is about twice as heritable as the less common (and more severe) form that affects children. If you have the strongest genetic predisposition — if both your parents were overweight and became diabetic in middle age — then there is little chance you will be spared diabetes should you become overweight. What makes prevention so difficult in such a case is the likelihood that you *will* become overweight, for obesity is 80 percent heritable.

Full-strength heritability only applies if you are at maximum genetic risk. In the case of obesity, your chances of becoming substantially overweight drop to 40 percent if only one of your parents was obese. If three of your four grandparents had heart disease, then you are probably at considerable risk unless they all developed the condition late in life. In general, the fewer close relatives affected, and the later the age at which they became ill, the less the risk to you.

If you're genetically vulnerable to a disease, it's wise to be wary and talk with your doctor about how to lower your risk and detect early symptoms. Diet is one means of prevention for many of the genetically influenced life-threatening diseases (discussed at length in later chapters). Lowering a high level of cholesterol in the blood — and with it, the risk of heart disease — can involve a number of strategies, including reducing the amount of fat and controlling the kinds of fat in your diet. Fat and calorie control may also limit your genetic vulnerability to obesity, and also to colon and breast cancer. Adequate levels of calcium and vitamin D are essential to trim the risk of osteoporosis. And it's necessary for some genetically vulnerable individuals to lower salt (sodium) intake to help bring down high blood pressure and control hypertension.

In addition to genetic vulnerabilities, other conditions or aspects of life may affect your nutritional needs. Smoking increases the need for vitamin C. Women during their menstruating years require far more iron than men. Children in early adolescence should be getting extra iron and calcium. Pregnancy and lactation raise nutrient needs across the board. The aging should be sure their diets include not only enough calcium and iron but also sufficient zinc, vitamins C and D, and the B vitamins thiamin, folacin, and B_6.

It is easy to get a good idea of your daily nutrient needs from the Recommended Dietary Allowances (the RDAs), developed by the National Research Council of the National Academy of Sciences (see Appendix Table A1). But how closely does your current diet come to meeting these needs? Do your normal food choices reflect special dietary requirements? Do they provide the balance of major nutrients (proteins, fats, and carbohydrates) your body should have for optimal performance and health? Let's find out by learning how, and precisely what, you are eating now and what this gives you in terms of calories, the major nutrients, and vitamins and minerals.

LEARNING WHAT YOU EAT

There's only one way to learn what you are eating, and that is to keep a record of it — *all* of it. This means recording not only meals but also snacks, drinks (soft and hard), the odd piece of candy or handful of nuts. Don't forget to list the nibbles and licks you consume while cooking or the forkfuls of pasta you taste from someone else's plate. And include any vitamin or mineral supplements you regularly use.

Record intake as strictly as you can (use estimates when you must) without modifying your diet to make the job easier. The point is to come up with a complete picture of what you normally consume, and this should be possible to do by keeping an honest food diary for just three days. You needn't keep track of three *consecutive* days — in fact, you probably shouldn't. If your weekend eating pattern is substantially different from your weekday pattern, and it probably is (no one is likely to eat brunch on Thursday), then keep your diary for two weekdays and one weekend day. Use a form like the one on pages 12–13. Note amounts of foods by weight (in ounces) and volume (cup, half cup, or quarter cup, tablespoonfuls, and teaspoonfuls), but you may record bread, cheese, and the like in slices.

It may help to know that a piece of meat that will cover the palm of your hand weighs 3–4 ounces, and a 1-inch cube of cheese is about half an ounce. When you come to noting how many teaspoonfuls of sugar you use, think about just how high the spoons are heaped. To discover how *your* teaspoonfuls compare with the standard, dump a dozen of your spoonfuls into a mug and see how many flattened measuring spoonfuls it takes to get them all out.

TRANSLATING DIARY TO DATA

When you have completed three days of your food diary, you can find out what your nutrient intake has been during this period. First, record the food items and amounts from your diary in the left-hand columns of a chart like the Diet Analysis Chart on pages 14–15. Next, check Appendix Table A4 to find out what to enter in columns 3–14.

You need not make entries in more than the first nine columns. But to get useful information from your diary you *must* complete these nine. Record for each food item the amount consumed; the number of calories; the amounts of protein, fat, and carbohydrates in grams (g); the amounts of calcium, iron, and vitamin C in milligrams (mg). For a more complete look at nutritional status, you may complete the chart, filling in columns 10–14 for each food item: the amounts of sodium and zinc in milligrams, vitamin A in Retinol Equivalents (RE), vitamin B$_6$ in milligrams, and folacin in micrograms (μg).

When you have completed your entries, total each column. These totals will let you know how many calories you have consumed for the three diary days, plus total intake of protein, fat, carbohydrate, calcium, iron, and vitamin C, as well as any of the other nutrients you have recorded. Next, divide these totals by 3 to get a daily average. From Appendix Table A1, enter the RDAs appropriate for your sex and age in the line provided for them on the Diet Analysis Chart. For calories, use

FOOD DIARY

Date _____   Day of Week _____

Time	Place	Foods Eaten	Amount
7:30 a.m.	Home	1. orange juice	1 cup
		2. rye toast	2 slices
		3. butter, salted	2 pats
		4. grape jelly	2 tbsp
		5. coffee	1 cup
		6. whole milk	1 oz
		7. sugar	2 tsp
10:30 a.m.	Century Diner	8. doughnut	1
		9. coffee	1 cup
		10. whole milk	1 oz
		11. sugar	2 tsp
12:30 a.m.	McDonald's	12. fish filet sandwich	1
		13. fries	1 order
		14. chocolate shake	10 oz
4:15 p.m.	Work	15. apple	1

the mean recommended energy intake (printed in boldface type) from Appendix Table A3, and for sodium, use the maximum safe and adequate intake listed in Appendix Table A2. Since there are no RDAs for carbohydrate or fat, leave these columns blank, and ignore the RDA for protein. Then subtract the RDAs from your averages to discover surpluses and deficits.

WHAT THE DATA SHOW

The results of this diet analysis won't give you the final word on your nutritional status. But they will provide broad indications of how well or how poorly you are helping your body to fulfill its positive genetic potential and guard against its genetic vulnerabilities. To make the most of these results, you should look at the balance of carbohydrates, proteins, and fats in your diet, at the relation of your calorie intake to your weight and level of activity, and at how close you come to meeting recommended nutrient levels.

Time	Place	Foods Eaten	Amount
6:30 p.m.	Home	16. vegetable soup	1 cup
		17. pork chop	1 medium
		18. rice	$1/_2$ cup
		19. gravy	2 tbsp
		20. Brussels sprouts	6 sprouts
		21. sweet pickles	$1/_2$ medium
		22. hard rolls	2
		23. butter, salted	2 pats
		24. Jell-O	$1/_2$ cup
		25. coffee	1 cup
		26. whole milk	1 oz
		27. sugar	2 tsp
9:15 p.m.	O'Neill's	28. beer	24 oz
		29. potato chips	30 chips
10:00 p.m.	Mario's	30. pizza	$1/_8$ 14-in pizza
		31. beer	12 oz

Sample Diet Analysis Chart

(1) Foods Eaten	(2) Amount	(3) Calories	(4) Protein (g)	(5) Fat (g)	(6) Carbo- hydrates (g)
1. orange juice	1 cup	110	1.7	0.5	26.0
2. rye toast	2 slices	130	4.2	1.8	24.0
3. butter, salted	2 pats	70	—	8.0	—
4. grape jelly	2 tbsp	110	0.2	—	28.0
5. coffee	1 cup	4	—	—	1.0
6. milk, whole	1 fl oz	19	1.0	1.0	1.4
7. sugar	2 tsp	30	0	0	8.0
8. doughnut	1	180	2.5	11.0	16.0
91. frankfurters	2	290	10.0	26.0	2.0
92. beer	12 fl oz	150	0.9	0	13.0
93. broiled salmon	1 steak	230	35.0	9.0	0
94. baked potato	1 large	140	4.0	0.2	35.0
95. shredded cabbage, raw	1 cup	17	0.9	0.1	4.0
96. salad dressing	1 tbsp	65	0.2	6.5	2.0
97. lemon juice	1 tsp	5	0.1	—	1.0
98. hard rolls	2	270	8.6	2.0	56.0
99. butter, salted	4 pats	140	—	16.0	—
100. cherry pie	1/8 pie	410	4.0	18.0	60.0
101. coffee	1 cup	4	—	—	1.0
102. sugar	2 tsp	30	0	0	8.0
103. milk, whole	1 fl oz	19	1.0	1.0	1.4
TOTAL:		9,495	307.8	357.7	1,268.6
DAILY AVERAGE:		3,165	102.6	119.2	422.9
RDA or ESA[b]:		2,700	—	—	—
SURPLUS/DEFICIT		+465	—	—	—

Sources: George Briggs and Doris Howes Calloway, *Nutrition and Physical Fitness* (New York: Holt, Rinehart and Winston, 1984), pp. A7–19; National Academy of Sciences, *Recommended Dietary Allowances*, 9th ed. (Washington, D.C., 1980).
Note: g = grams; mg = milligrams; μg = micrograms; — indicates trace only or unknown.

(7) Calcium (mg)	(8) Iron (mg)	(9) Vitamin C (mg)	(10) Sodium (mg)	(11) Zinc (mg)	(12) Vitamin A (R.E.)[a]	(13) Vitamin B_6 (mg)	(14) Folacin (μg)
25	0.5	125.0	2	0.1	50	0.1	110.0
40	1.4	0	350	0.6	0	0.04	20.0
2	—	0	80	—	80	0	0
8	0.4	—	4	0.2	—	0.02	2.0
4	0.1	0	1	0.03	0	—	—
36	0.01	0.3	15	0.1	9	0.01	1.3
0	—	0	—	—	0	0	0
15	0.6	0	100	0.3	8	0.02	4.0
10	1.0	24.0	1010	1.6	0	0.12	2.0
15	0.1	—	18	0.2	—	0.2	20.0
—	1.5	—	150	2.4	60	1.0	30.0
15	1.1	30.0	5	0.4	—	0.3	20.0
35	0.3	35.0	15	0.3	10	0.1	20.0
2	—	0	90	0.08	6	—	—
1	—	5.0	0	—	—	—	1.5
20	1.2	—	570	0.6	—	0.06	60.0
4	—	0	160	—	160	0	0
20	0.5	—	480	0.06	70	—	—
4	0.1	0	1	0.03	0	—	—
0	—	0	—	—	0	0	0
36	0.01	0.3	15	0.1	9	0.01	1.3
1,657	26.1	386.7	11,588	33.6	2,305	6.7	1,126.3
552	8.7	128.9	3,863	11.2	768	2.2	375.4
800	10.0	60.0	3,300[c]	15.0	1,000	2.2	400.0
−248	−1.3	+68.9	+563	−3.8	−232	0	−24.6

[a]RE = Retinol Equivalents (1 retinol equivalent = 1 μg retinol or 6 μg beta-carotene).
[b]RDA = Recommended Dietary Allowance; ESA = Estimated Safe and Adequate amount. Subtract this figure from the daily average figure.
[c]The ESA for sodium is the maximum amount.

Dietary Balance

Check first the balance of carbohydrates, proteins, and fats, since this probably has more impact on the health of most Americans than any aspect of diet today. Convert your daily average consumption from grams into calories. To do this, multiply grams of carbohydrate and protein by 4, and grams of fat by 9; the number of calories is the result. The sum of these three numbers — total calories from carbohydrates, proteins, and fats — should match your daily average for calories. Next, determine the percentage of calories consumed in the form of carbohydrates, proteins, and fats. For instance,

Total Calories = 3,165

Total Carbohydrates = 422 grams × 4
= 1,688 calories from carbohydrates

$\dfrac{1,688}{3,165}$ × 100 = 53% calories from carbohydrates.

ARE YOU OVERWEIGHT OR UNDERWEIGHT?

There are no clear, absolute standards for overweight or underweight. But recently a consensus conference of the National Institutes of Health concluded that treatment for obesity is "strongly advised" for patients whose body mass index (their weight in kilograms divided by the square of their height in meters) is greater than 27.8 for men or 27.3 for women. This degree of overweight comes very close to 20 percent above the midpoint weight for medium frames in the weight-for-height tables constructed by the Metropolitan Life Insurance Company (described in chapter 10). The left-hand table here shows the weights (without clothing) for each height (without shoes) that are 20 percent above the desirable level and that constitute a medically significant degree of obesity. The right-hand table shows weights that are 20 percent *below* the Metropolitan Life standard. If your weight is less than these, you may be too thin for optimal health.

Your weight may affect your health if it *exceeds* these levels			**Your weight may affect your health if it is *below* these levels**		
Risk Weight (pounds)			*Risk Weight (pounds)*		
Height	*Men*	*Women*	*Height*	*Men*	*Women*
4'10"		138	4'10"		92
4'11"		140	4'11"		94
5'0"		143	5'0"		96
5'1"		146	5'1"		98

For optimum health, you should be getting at least 50 percent of your calories from carbohydrates and 15 to 20 percent from proteins, with no more than 35 percent from fats.

Calories and Weight

The need for calories varies, because people burn them (which is how the body generates energy) at different rates. So comparing your daily average intake to the RDA for your sex and age may not produce much useful information. You need to consider three other factors: your weight, whether you are gaining or losing, and the amount of energy you spend on activity each day.

First consider weight. If your weight is greater than that given for adult men or women of your height in the left-hand table below, then the National Institutes of Health considers your weight itself — or the conditions that have made you overweight — a threat to your health. If your weight is less than that given for adult men and women of your height in the right-hand table, it also poses a health threat.

	Risk Weight (pounds)			Risk Weight (pounds)	
Height	Men	Women	Height	Men	Women
5'2"	163	150	5'2"	109	100
5'3"	166	154	5'3"	110	102
5'4"	168	157	5'4"	112	105
5'5"	171	161	5'5"	114	107
5'6"	174	164	5'6"	116	110
5'7"	178	168	5'7"	118	112
5'8"	181	172	5'8"	121	114
5'9"	185	175	5'9"	123	117
5'10"	188	179	5'10"	126	119
5'11"	192	182	5'11"	128	122
6'0"	196	186	6'0"	131	124
6'1"	200		6'1"	134	
6'2"	205		6'2"	137	
6'3"	209		6'3"	140	
6'4"	215		6'4"	143	

Source: Adapted from the 1983 Metropolitan Insurance Company's Height and Weight Tables. Values at left are 20 percent over the midpoint value for medium frame; those at right are 20 percent under.

HOW ACTIVE ARE YOU?

This table shows the number of calories burned per minute by people of different weights performing different activities. (The more you weigh, the more calories you need to move around.) To use the table, find your weight range and multiply the caloric value by the approximate number of minutes devoted to each activity every week. Then divide the total by 7 for your average daily calorie expenditure.

Calories per Minute Used in Activity

Activity	Weight (pounds)				Intensity of Activity
	105–115	127–137	160–170	182–192	
Aerobic dancing	5.83	6.58	7.83	8.58	moderate
Badminton, singles	4.58	5.16	6.16	6.75	moderate
Baseball, fielder	3.66	4.16	4.91	5.41	mild
Basketball					
half-court	7.25	8.25	9.75	10.75	mod/high
full-court	9.75	11.16	13.16	14.50	high
Bicycling					
5.5 mph	3.16	3.58	4.25	4.66	mild
10.0 mph	5.41	6.16	7.33	7.91	moderate
13.0 mph	8.58	9.75	11.50	12.66	high
stationary, 10 mph	5.50	6.25	7.41	8.16	moderate
stationary, 20 mph	11.66	13.25	15.58	17.16	very high
Calisthenics	3.91	4.50	7.33	7.91	moderate
Dancing					
rock	3.25	3.75	4.41	4.91	mild
square	5.50	6.25	7.41	8.00	moderate
Gardening (weeding, digging)	5.08	5.75	6.83	7.50	moderate
Golf, handcart	3.25	3.75	4.41	4.91	mild
Handball, competitive	7.83	8.91	10.50	11.58	mod/high
Hiking, 20-lb pack					
2 mph	3.91	4.50	5.25	5.83	moderate
4 mph	5.91	6.66	7.91	8.75	moderate
Jogging, 5.5 mph	8.58	9.75	11.50	12.66	high
Lawn mowing, power	3.50	4.00	4.75	5.16	mild
Rowing machine					
easy	3.91	4.50	5.25	5.83	moderate
vigorous	8.58	9.75	11.50	12.66	high

Activity	Weight (pounds)				Intensity of Activity
	105–115	127–137	160–170	182–192	
Running					
6.5 mph	8.90	10.20	12.00	13.20	high
8.0 mph	10.40	11.90	14.10	15.50	very high
9.0 mph	12.00	13.80	16.20	17.80	very high
Sawing wood, by hand	5.08	5.83	6.83	7.58	moderate
Sexual intercourse, active partner	3.91	4.50	5.25	5.83	moderate
Skating					
leisurely	4.58	5.16	6.16	6.75	moderate
vigorous	8.08	9.25	10.91	12.00	mod/high
Skiing					
downhill	7.75	8.83	10.41	11.50	mod/high
x-country, 5 mph	9.16	10.41	12.25	13.33	high
x-country, 9 mph	13.08	14.83	17.58	19.33	very high
Snow shoveling					
light	7.91	9.08	10.75	11.83	mod/high
heavy	13.75	15.66	18.50	20.41	very high
Stair climbing					
normal	5.90	6.70	7.90	8.80	moderate
upstairs rapidly (two at a time)	8.70	14.80	17.60	19.30	very high
Swimming, crawl					
20 yd/min	3.91	4.50	5.25	5.83	moderate
40 yd/min	7.83	8.91	10.50	11.58	mod/high
55 yd/min	11.00	12.50	14.75	16.25	very high
Tennis, competitive					
singles	7.83	8.91	10.50	11.58	mod/high
doubles	5.58	6.33	7.50	8.25	moderate
Trampolining	10.33	11.75	13.91	15.33	high
Volleyball, competitive	7.83	8.91	10.50	11.58	mod/high
Walking					
2 mph	2.40	2.80	3.30	3.60	mild
3 mph	3.90	4.50	5.30	5.80	moderate
4 mph	4.50	5.20	6.10	6.80	moderate

Source: Adapted from Charles T. Kuntzleman, *Diet Free* (Emmaus, PA: Rodale Press, 1981) p. 324–339.

If you are underweight or overweight according to these tables, or if you believe you are heavier than you should be, consider whether you are now gaining or losing weight and how many calories you are investing in activity each day. The bathroom scale will tell you if your weight is changing, and the table on pages 18–19 ("How Active Are You?") will let you know what daily activity costs you in calories. You needn't maintain a diary. Simply estimate the time you spend on the listed activities and add up the calories that are burned in the process.

Now look at your average, daily calorie consumption. If you are burning up substantially more than one third of the calories in your diet through activity, then you are reducing the number available for storage as fat. If you are burning up substantially less than one third, you are increasing that number.

If you are underweight, not gaining, and your caloric intake is near the bottom of the recommended range for your age and sex, you are likely to be lacking a substantial number of the nutrients you need.

If, however, you are underweight and your caloric consumption is well within the recommended range for your age and sex, but you are using more than one third of your calories for activity, then it is likely that a low level of body fat — less than 10 percent of body weight for men and 15 percent for women — poses a health risk.

If you are overweight, not losing weight, not using more than one third of your calories for activity, and your caloric intake is near the top of the recommended range for your age and sex, then the kinds of diet modification and increased activity suggested in chapter 11 may help you adopt a weight-control program that will not threaten your nutritional status.

If you are overweight, losing weight, using more than one third of your calories for activity, and your net caloric intake is within the recommended range, you should be particularly careful that your diet contains an appropriate balance of carbohydrates, proteins, and fats, and adequate levels of all essential nutrients.

But, whether you are losing or not, if your net caloric intake is below the bottom of the recommended range, you are likely to be risking nutritional deficiencies that could substantially reduce physical and intellectual performance, compromise your immune system and other body systems, and have long-term health consequences.

Vitamins and Minerals

Now look at vitamins and minerals. Surpluses can be just as harmful as deficiencies. If, for example, you are consuming more than three times the RDAs for vitamins A and D or iron, then you are risking toxicity. In most instances, it serves no purpose to take in amounts any greater than the recommended allowances for these nutrients.

As for deficiencies, they can have very specific effects. These are covered in detail (along with toxic effects) in later chapters, and your diet analysis can help you determine which, if any, you may be risking.

To make the most of your diet without radically changing your foodstyle requires a sense of how nutrients operate in the body and how they get there. It means learning which deficiencies are common and which are rare, where nutrients are found, and how they can be lost on the way to your plate or your bloodstream. These nutritional basics, discussed in Part II, "The Stuff of Life," will allow you to recognize all the implications of your diet analysis and to modify your foodstyle to compensate for any deficiencies or imbalances.

PART II

THE STUFF
OF LIFE

CHAPTER 3

What Life Is Made Of

"Y OU ARE WHAT YOU EAT." It's the catch phrase for the impact of diet on health and the credo of "the new nutrition." It sums up the current awareness that what we eat can alter the length and quality of our lives.

But "you are what you eat" also reflects a far more fundamental relationship between people and food, for we are actually made up of much the same stuff as that which we consume. The chemical composition of men and women isn't all that different from meats or even eggs, and the basic ingredients are the same ones found in vegetables and fruits. Both eaters and eaten consist mostly of water, along with carbohydrates, fats, proteins, and minerals, plus a smattering of vitamins. This chemical compatibility allows us to convert many food molecules into energy and to use the rest to help repair and replace body cells.

It is hardly surprising that we are so like what we eat. After all, we and our food supply were formed out of the same chemical stockpile, and we followed similar evolutionary routes up from the primordial ooze. It all started more than 3 billion years ago, when life on Earth was just getting under way. The planet was cooling. Water condensed into seas, providing a solvent for gases and minerals and forming a rich chemical soup. In this nourishing gruel, complex molecules developed.

Eventually, over millions of years, some of these molecules mastered photosynthesis and were able to claim energy from the sun as well as from the sea. When they did, they released oxygen into an atmosphere that had lacked it, and the pace of life picked up sharply. Single-cell creatures grouped together, and cell clusters developed specialized functions on their way to becoming more complex creatures with specialized organs.

But a funny thing happened to these multicelled organisms on their way up the evolutionary ladder. As they became more elaborate, they lost nutritional self-sufficiency. They could no longer generate for themselves all the substances necessary for life. They became *eaters* (and hunters and foragers as well), dependent upon external sources for many of the same nutrients that humans require today.

The source of our nutrients is food. But let's understand the difference between the two. The bloodstream, which carries nutrients throughout the body, doesn't move along bits of braised beef or quiche. Body cells can't get what they need directly from strands of pasta or morsels of broccoli. So nutrients are not the same as food. They are chemicals found *in* food along with lots of other things. It's up to the digestive system to break out the nutrients from food and convert them into what the rest of the body can cope with.

Although we must consume a relatively large *amount* of nutrients each day, we can get along on a surprisingly small *number* of them. Our bodies are still very effective chemical factories and generate for themselves most of the substances they need. We produce, for example, as many as 50,000 different kinds of protein, and we can manufacture all but 8 of the 22 amino acids we need to make these proteins. It is those substances we *cannot* produce for ourselves, or cannot produce in sufficient quantities, that are the essential nutrients — the basic stuff of life.

The whole business of nutrition would be a lot simpler if we could get our essential nutrients directly and didn't have to depend upon food. Converting food to nutrients is an inefficient, imprecise, and sometimes risky business. The earth, after all, is filled with things that look like food, taste like food, have nutritional value — and can poison us. Even when we eliminate the risk of poisoning, we often must take some bad with the good. If we want the calcium in Camembert or the iron in ground chuck, we may well have to consume more fats than our bodies can healthfully handle.

It is theoretically possible these days to avoid the "food problem" if you really want to. Back at the start of the sixties, in the early days of NASA, nutritionists working for the space agency came up with a food-free diet for astronauts. What they concocted was a liquid full of essential nutrients and just about nothing else. It could sustain an astronaut for weeks and, since it was waste-free, pretty much eliminated elimination. (There was no fecal matter to create the kinds of plumbing problems that have plagued later space travelers.)

What happened to this total-nutrition, waste-free diet was just what you might expect: the astronauts turned it down flat, demanding more natural fare. So instead of nutrient-laden gelatin they got tubes of pureed stew and apple sauce. In time, the space diet came to include the likes of shrimp cocktail, chicken teriyaki, and cauliflower in cheese sauce. Food may be an inefficient vehicle for the nutrients we need, but it adds a pleasure to life that most of us are not willing to give up.

TOTAL PARENTERAL NUTRITION: NUTRIENTS BY THE BAG

Some people, however, have lost the option of eating; they suffer from severe gastrointestinal disorders that make digestion impossible. A few decades ago, they would have starved to death. Now, medical technology makes it possible for them to survive indefinitely without natural sources of food. In developing synthetic formulas for this life-saving process, nutritionists have discovered that many nutrients they had never considered essential are actually critical to life.

The first to experience the long-term benefits of this technology was a young Canadian mother named Judy Taylor. When she entered a Toronto hospital in 1970, surgeons discovered that a blood clot had cut off circulation to her small intestine, and gangrene had invaded it. Since just about all carbohydrates, fats, and proteins are broken down in the small intestine, and most vitamins and minerals are absorbed into the bloodstream from there, the surgeons were afraid that removing the infected organ would condemn the young woman to slow death by starvation.

What saved Judy Taylor and allowed her to lead a more or less normal life was total parenteral nutrition (TPN), a means of delivering all the body's nutrients directly into the bloodstream. (*Parenteral* means "bypassing the intestine.") Patients are fed through a tube implanted in a major vein, most often the vena cava, which leads directly to the heart. Doctors had been working on TPN since the thirties, trying to help undernourished surgical patients meet the energy demands of surgical stress and provide vital protein to patients whose digestive systems couldn't get right back to work after surgery.

Dr. K. N. Jeejeebhoy, professor of medicine at the University of Toronto, was one of the scientists working on TPN in 1970. Called in by Judy Taylor's surgeon, he took charge of what was to become the first lifelong case of total parenteral nutrition.

When Judy Taylor returned home from the hospital, counting on the plastic bagfuls of sterilized chemicals that flowed into her body each night, she had no guarantee that the regimen would keep her alive very long. There were grave concerns about infection, for TPN had only been administered in hospitals until that time. The big question, however, was how *total* parenteral nutrition actually was. Doctors had no way of knowing if it could indeed supply all her nutritional needs for the next 50 or 60 years.

But the experiment worked, and the odds for patients on TPN have improved ever since. We now know a great deal more about human nutritional needs than was known even in 1970, and much of that knowledge has come from the use of TPN.

The growth of nutritional knowledge has accelerated considerably since 1943, when the National Research Council published its first set of Recommended Dietary Allowances (RDAs). Initially used as standards for civilian food rationing and military diets during World War II, the RDAs have been periodically revised ever since to serve as national nutritional guidelines. The 1943 edition listed, along with calorie needs for each age group, only 9 nutrients. But by 1980 the RDAs recommended allowances for 17 nutrients and gave more tentative suggestions for "safe and adequate" amounts of an additional 12.

Considering the popular interest in nutrition, medical science has been relatively slow to recognize nutritional needs. For some time, most information about the physiological effects of diet on humans came from studying people unlucky enough to have limited or unbalanced food supplies. As long ago as 1747 the British physician Dr. James Lind proved that sailors on long voyages could avoid scurvy if they were supplied with enough citrus fruits.

But it was only in the twentieth century that scientists isolated the essential chemicals in food that could overcome deficiency diseases in laboratory animals. In 1911, Norwegian researchers working with guinea pigs first described the dynamics of ascorbic acid (vitamin C) deficiency and showed *why* lemons and limes helped prevent scurvy. Unlike other laboratory animals, guinea pigs turned out to be just as susceptible to scurvy as humans are, since neither species can manufacture its own ascorbic acid.

Despite such discoveries, it was not until quite recently that most physicians began looking for links between diet and disease in the general population or for evidence of nutritional deficiency more subtle than scurvy. Over the years there has probably been more research focused on the dietary needs of livestock than on the needs of human beings. After all, the economic benefits of formulating fast-fattening, low-cost feeds for chickens, pigs, and dairy cows were clearer than any gains to be made by working out better human diets.

Although all 13 known essential vitamins had been discovered by 1948, science had not yet discovered all the ways these vitamins make themselves essential in the body. As for minerals, it was only through the use of highly purified nutrient formulas like TPN that we learned how many of these elements we actually need. In a fascinating set of experiments, conducted during the early seventies at the Veterans Administration Hospital in Long Beach, California, nutritionist Klaus Schwarz discovered that even arsenic—a deadly poison in large amounts—is essential for growth.

Schwarz was working out a diet for laboratory rats that had been born and raised in an absolutely sterile environment. Their purified food was as free from contaminants as the contents of the TPN bag. But instead of thriving on this wholesome regimen, the rats failed to develop as they should. It turned out that they were missing a number of essential minerals we normally get in the dust and other impurities we consume with our food. Indeed, that "peck of dirt" we are said to eat during our lifetimes takes care of many mineral needs, providing us with minuscule amounts of such trace elements as silicon, nickel, vanadium, and tin as well as arsenic.

Because of research like Schwarz's and techniques like TPN, science today has a fairly good understanding of all the various substances we require to survive and thrive. Synthetic diets have become dependable sources of sustenance. Of course, hardly any of us would willingly trade the pleasures of food for more direct access to the essential stuff of life. Even if we wanted to, the cost would be prohibitive; TPN costs about $70,000 a year. But it's useful for us to recognize nutrients for the chemicals they are — separable from food — just as they are found in a TPN bag.

WHAT'S IN THE BAG

To provide the chemical equivalent of a balanced diet, with all the essential nutrients the body cannot produce for itself, the TPN bag must contain what food contains — including a few items we don't usually realize are there, like the tiny amounts of certain minerals that we pick up through dust or in cooking. And TPN must provide them in forms acceptable to the bloodstream. Since digestion normally converts protein to amino acids and fats to fatty acids, these are what TPN patients get.

The exact formula in a particular TPN bag will also reflect individual needs. These, we are learning, vary considerably, even among relatively healthy men and women. Yet while these individual variations are more difficult to predict than we had once imagined, we can say with certainty what it is that *everybody* needs. No matter what the particular TPN formula, the bag is sure to include water, glucose (the primary nutrient in carbohydrates), nine amino acids, and at least two fatty acids. It will have 13 vitamins and as many as 20 minerals.

Water

The TPN bag is filled mostly with water. (So are you — water makes up slightly more than half of normal body weight.) Water carries other nutrients into the body, but it is more than just a means of moving chemicals out of the bag and into the bloodstream. It is essential to all bodily functions: Water is the medium of the nutritional process, transporting nutrients throughout the circulatory system and flushing out waste. It is the major component of all bodily fluids, regulates body temperature (as sweat), maintains the body's acid-alkaline balance, and takes part in every chemical reaction that occurs in body cells.

You can go weeks without food but only five to seven days without water. When the water in your body is reduced by just 1 percent of your body weight, you become thirsty. When water loss amounts to 5 percent of your weight, you feel tired, hot, and achy. When it reaches 10 percent, you may experience delirium and kidney failure, and at 20 percent you will die.

There is nothing the body needs more than water, for we lose 2–3 quarts each day through elimination, perspiration, and evaporation from the lungs. To replace this amount, it isn't necessary to down eight to twelve glassfuls of water. We get water from other beverages and a great deal from food (which is made up mostly of water). In addition, the body gains small amounts of water as a by-product when it breaks down nutrients for energy. However, since TPN patients aren't drinking any beverages or eating any food, they must count on the bag to supply their daily 2–3 quarts.

Glucose

Other than water, what the body depletes most quickly is fuel, for we are constantly drawing on our energy reserves. And our energy needs are measured in calories.

Technically, a calorie is the amount of energy it takes to raise the temperature of 1 gram of water 1 degree centigrade. Our bodies' energy needs, however, are so large that they must be measured in kilocalories (Kcal), equivalent to 1,000 ordinary calories. But in common usage kilocalories have come to be called just calories, and we'll follow that usage in this book. Among healthy adults, men burn an average of 2,700 calories (technically, kilocalories) in a day; women, an average of 2,000.

The body burns those calories and produces energy by chemical reaction. That's how it produces just about everything — by breaking apart complex molecules and putting new ones together. These ongoing processes — digestion, the formation of body cells and tissue, and the use of fuel — are collectively known as *metabolism* (from the Greek word for "change"). Fuel is converted to energy in the body much as firewood is converted to light and heat, by the electron exchange that occurs during oxidation and reduction ("redox") reactions (see "Oxidation and Reduction," page 31).

Carbohydrates, fats, and proteins all provide fuel. But they are not all equal sources of energy: 1 gram of fat yields 9 calories, more than twice as much energy as 1 gram of carbohydrate or protein (4 calories each). Although fats and proteins contribute to the overall fuel supply and provide other vital nutrients as well, it is from carbohydrates that we draw the energy source we most need: glucose, often called blood sugar (see "Carbohydrates, Simple and Complex," page 32).

No short-term nutritional deficit (except lack of water) is more immediately apparent than a drop in blood sugar. When the level of glucose in our blood falls out of the normal range, we feel not only hungry but irritable, sluggish, and depressed as well. There is, of course, good reason for glucose levels to affect our mental state. While all body cells consume some glucose, two thirds of the glucose we need — about 500 calories per day, the amount in slightly more than a quarter pound of carbohydrate — goes to nourish the cells of the brain and the nervous system. These cells depend upon glucose almost exclusively. Without it, they die.

What happens if you decide to shed a few pounds with a low- or no-carbohydrate diet and cut out sweets and starches — bread, potatoes, pasta, pizza, rice, and the like? You may even cut down on vegetables (there are carbohydrates in vegetables too). Well, first you exhaust the glucose that has been stored in the liver. That goes pretty fast, for the body demands glucose 24 hours a day, and the liver's supply will probably run out before you have shed your first pound.

Perhaps you imagine there is surplus glucose tucked away in your fat cells, but there isn't. What you've got in your fat cells is *fat*. Your body can use fat to meet roughly two thirds of its energy needs, but fat cannot directly fuel your central nervous system.

Let's not forget that we are immensely self-sufficient organisms. The body's primary mandate is to preserve the status quo, and it has a substantial ability to manufacture what it needs from materials at hand. So when glucose in the liver runs out, the body looks around for what it needs to make more. It finds the vital ingredients present in fat. But in

OXIDATION AND REDUCTION

Oxidation and its counterpart, reduction, are driving forces in the chemical reactions by which our bodies use fuel. In simple terms, oxidation is what happens to the nutritional fuel the body burns for energy. Reduction is what happens to the oxygen.

The chemical burning of fuel in the body is analogous to more familiar kinds of burning, like the burning of logs in a fireplace. You must have oxygen to burn wood, and our bodies too need oxygen to burn fats, amino acids, and carbohydrates. Through an elaborate series of carefully controlled reactions involving a number of different enzymes, the body takes carbon and hydrogen atoms out of its fuels and adds oxygen to them. This is oxidation. Each carbon atom then goes to form a molecule of carbon dioxide, which we breathe out; each hydrogen atom becomes part of a molecule of water.

Although we may be unaware of it, the more familiar kinds of burning also produce both carbon dioxide and water. The smoke from that log in your fireplace, or from a candle, contains plenty of carbon dioxide and steam — vaporized water. Hold a fireproof dish filled with ice over a candle, and you will see water from the fire condense on the underside of the dish.

The flip side of oxidation, chemically, is reduction. When oxygen joins carbon to make carbon dioxide, chemists say that the carbon has been oxidized and that the oxygen has been reduced.

order to get hold of these substances, vast amounts of fatty acid must be wasted. Since waste is alien to the body's conservative nature, it will use fat sparingly and draw on it to produce only about one tenth of the glucose the brain and the nervous system need.

For the rest, it turns to a better source: the amino acids in bodily protein. To get at them, however, the body must break down protein already in use, destroying muscle and other tissue in the process.

The body can count on protein to supply raw material for emergency glucose production for only a limited time. Were you to continue

CARBOHYDRATES, SIMPLE AND COMPLEX

Carbohydrates (sugars and starch) are the dietary source of glucose. Chemically, that's just about all there is to them, although it may take a transformation or two for them to reach the glucose stage. Carbohydrates are found in all foods, mostly in grains, fruits, and vegetables. But there are tiny amounts even in meat.

Chemically, carbohydrates in food are made up of carbon, hydrogen, and oxygen and come either in simple one- or two-molecule combinations (the simple sugars) or in large 300- to 1,000-molecule compounds (the complex carbohydrates, or starches). The one-molecule sugars, or **monosaccharides**, commonly found in food are glucose, fructose, and galactose. The two-molecule **disaccharides** are sucrose, lactose, and maltose.

Glucose (the same substance we call blood sugar), found in nearly all fruits and vegetables, is not exceptionally sweet tasting. It moves rapidly from the digestive tract to the bloodstream and goes right to work there. **Fructose**, however, which has the same chemical components as glucose but a different structure, and which is also found in plant foods (particularly fruits), moves into the bloodstream more slowly and doesn't have much impact until it reaches the liver and is converted to glucose. As for **galactose**, it is rarely seen on its own and exists primarily as half of the disaccharide lactose.

The **disaccharides**, which are essentially monosaccharides linked together, always contain at least one glucose molecule. The **sucrose** in regular table sugar (made from either cane or beets) consists of glucose and fructose. It is twice as sweet as glucose alone but less sweet than straight fructose. **Lactose** (milk sugar) is composed of glucose and galactose. And **maltose** (malt sugar), which occurs when beer is brewed and which is found in malted milk shakes, is made up of two glucose molecules.

The nutritionally significant complex carbohydrates — the **starches** — contain nothing but glucose molecules. But it takes these compounds longer than simple sugars to come apart in the digestive system. What's more, starches are found in foods that often contain substantial amounts of fiber, which can also impede absorption. So the glucose in most complex carbohydrates moves into the bloodstream more slowly than the glucose in most sugars. But the nutritional advantages that complex carbohydrates have over simple sugars as a source of energy derive not only from the rate at which their glucose is absorbed but also from the amount of fiber they add to the diet and from the other nutrients present in the major sources of starch (grains, beans, tubers, and the like).

breaking down muscle and other tissue to provide 90 percent of the fuel the brain requires, your life expectancy would dwindle to less than a month. So the body adapts after only two or three days of carbohydrate deprivation and begins to produce an alternative energy source (a kind of "mock glucose") from fatty acid. These ketones, as they are called, can fuel *some*, though not *all*, central nervous system cells.

Ketone production — a process called ketosis, which is often seen in diabetics who can't metabolize glucose properly — has substantial risks. Ketones themselves are toxic. They make the blood more acid,

---

SUGAR ISN'T POISONOUS . . . BUT LACK OF SUGAR IS

When the body has enough glucose, it burns it as neatly and efficiently as a self-cleaning oven. But if you take glucose away, the body turns to less desirable fuels, and poisonous by-products quickly build up. A little chemistry makes the problem clear.

Glucose is a clean fuel. Through a series of chemical reactions, it is burned completely in the body, combining with oxygen to produce carbon dioxide, water, and energy. The process leaves no toxic chemical ash, just harmless compounds.

The key to this clean energy is a series of metabolic reactions called the **Krebs cycle**, or the **citric acid cycle**. With the help of several different chemicals, enzymes, and vitamins, glucose breaks down to produce two different compounds: **oxaloacetic acid** and **acetyl-coA**. The combination of these compounds — to form citric acid — starts the Krebs cycle and the series of reactions that produce energy and release carbon dioxide and water.

Acetyl-coA is fairly easy to come by in the body: fats and some proteins produce it when they break down. But to burn in the Krebs cycle, acetyl-coA must team up with oxaloacetic acid, which comes almost exclusively from glucose. No glucose, no oxaloacetic acid — which means the body must find other ways to burn fuel for energy.

What happens then? Two things, both of them bad. First is **ketosis**. When acetyl-coA can't burn properly, it builds up in the body. Some of it is converted to fat or cholesterol, which can accumulate in fat tissue or in the arteries (neither is desirable). Some becomes acetoacetic acid, which raises the acidity of the blood. And some of that acid turns into acetone, familiar as the main ingredient in nail polish remover. This foul-smelling, toxic compound belongs to the chemical family of ketones, and it accounts for the bad breath that's a hallmark of ketosis.

Glucose deprivation poisons the body in a second way: **uremia**, the buildup of ammonia in the blood. Without glucose the body can't easily rid itself of ammonia, a powerful poison. Ammonia is formed when protein, rich in nitrogen, breaks down. Normally ammonia is changed into urea, a harmless compound excreted in the urine, but this requires compounds produced in the Krebs cycle. So no glucose, no Krebs cycle, no urea — and ammonia builds up, sometimes to toxic levels.

upsetting its chemical balance. They cause a pungently bad breath. And by the time the body must resort to ketones to keep brain cells alive, the lack of glucose has also allowed toxic levels of ammonia to build up in the bloodstream. (To understand how this works chemically, see "Sugar Isn't Poisonous . . . But Lack of Sugar Is," page 33).

Glucose, then, is in the TPN bag for good reason. Without it, TPN patients would waste fatty acid and destroy muscles. If they were deprived of glucose for a long enough period, various central nervous system hormones would start to malfunction. Eventually, of course, brain cells would literally starve to death.

Getting too little of an essential nutrient is life-threatening. But getting too much is often just as risky. Although there is no toxic level for carbohydrates, as there is for most vitamins and minerals, loading up on sugar and starch can threaten health. It can lead to dental problems, aggravate a diabetic condition, and — if you eat enough — contribute to obesity.

Amino Acids

The body uses protein in more ways than it does any other nutrient, not only as fuel but in tissues and other bodily parts, in hormones, and in milk for nursing mothers. And it produces for itself all the 50,000 or more forms of bodily protein it needs from a set of 22 amino acids.

It takes hundreds of amino acid molecules, strung together like beads, to make a single molecule of protein. Since these beads can be assembled in an almost limitless number of combinations, the body has no trouble manufacturing the great variety of protein products it requires. But this protein-building capacity depends upon adequate supplies of all 22 amino acids — the 13 the body can produce for itself and the 9 it must get from the proteins in food.

Among the substances amino acids help to build are the nucleic acids DNA and RNA, which in turn help link amino acids together into proteins. The nucleic acids (so named because they are found in the nucleus of every cell) store and transmit genetic information. In the structure of DNA molecules are coded all the data on inherited characteristics necessary for the reproduction of cells, organs, and complete organisms. RNA works both as a messenger, passing along genetic specifications, and as a kind of drill sergeant, lining up amino acids in many thousands of combinations to form proteins for the body.

How does the body use all these proteins? Structurally, they are present in every cell and make up more than half the body's organic matter. Functionally, they handle most of the body's hard and dirty jobs — demolition and construction, self-defense, transportation, and emergency repairs.

Enzymes are a form of protein that direct and accelerate chemical reactions. It is enzymes that do the demolition work, including breaking down nutrients in the digestive system. But enzymes are also involved in construction. They put compounds together, allowing the body to fabricate most of what it needs from the relatively limited range of raw materials available in food.

Antibodies, too, are proteins. These giant molecules travel through the bloodstream to do battle with specific viruses and bacteria or with any other kind of invader. So effective is this self-defense force that disease agents attacking a normally healthy man or woman are usually routed within hours.

Proteins also provide transportation. They do long-distance hauling, carrying hard-to-handle nutrients and other fragile compounds through the bloodstream. They lift and shift nutrients into cells, and help maintain the body's fluid balance, ensuring that excess fluid does not accumulate between cells.

When it comes to emergency repairs, a protein forms clots to seal blood vessels and scar tissue to close wounds. For major reconstruction, like rebuilding bone, the same protein that forms scars, called collagen, provides temporary bonding until the body can lay down crystals of calcium and other minerals. A strong and versatile protein, collagen is the heavy-duty filament in tendons and ligaments and the reinforcing material in artery walls.

What happens when the body is denied the amino acids it needs to produce bodily protein? In many parts of the Third World, where mother's milk is almost the only source of dietary protein for infants, the disease called kwashiorkor is still all too common. Although the literal translation of this name (which comes from the Ga tribe of Ghana) is uncertain, one interpretation is "the evil spirit which infects the first child when the second child is born."

Whether or not this is linguistically accurate, it makes medical sense. To the Africans who gave the disease its name, the decline of a firstborn after the birth of a brother or sister was a familiar phenomenon, for nursing mothers would wean one child as soon as they bore another. Dependent now almost exclusively on a starchy, high-carbohydrate diet, these older children soon began displaying characteristic signs of protein deficiency. They failed to grow as they should. They had sores and ulcers that would not heal. Their arms, legs, and faces were swollen, and their bellies bulged. They became weak, apathetic, and vulnerable to diseases and infections of all kinds.

The symptoms of kwashiorkor reveal yet another aspect of how the body is programmed for survival. When youngsters are denied the amino acids they need, they cease growing normally as their bodies begin breaking down muscle and any other tissue that can be spared to get protein they can use to sustain vital organs. Antibodies become too precious to waste on externals, so surface sores go unhealed.

But without enough bodily protein to control fluid balance, they develop edema (the accumulation of fluid between cells), which causes their extremities to swell. Their swollen bellies are caused not by edema but by excessive amounts of fat stored in the liver, for protein is needed to transport this fat throughout the body. Without it, the liver becomes so fat-filled that it can no longer function and begins to atrophy.

Keep in mind that we make the proteins our bodies need from amino acids in the proteins that we eat. But we can make do with dietary proteins that lack a good many of the 22 amino acids in bodily protein (even though there is at least a bit of each in every one of our protein parts). That marvelous chemical factory which is our body is capable of synthesizing most of the amino acids we need. So we can get along on protein foods that are far from perfect as long as we get enough of the essential amino acids, the ones our bodies either cannot produce at all or cannot produce in sufficient quantities.

Clearly, certain foods are far more satisfactory sources of these essential amino acids than others. What nutritionists call complete proteins contain *all* the essential amino acids. High-quality proteins (eggs are a good example) contain amounts of each essential acid that are roughly proportionate to what our bodies actually use. On the other hand, when a protein food or meal contains a particularly low level of an essential amino acid, it is said to be limiting. No matter how high the level of other essential acids in that food or food combination, its contribution to tissue production is limited to how far the essential acid in shortest supply will stretch.

What are the essential amino acids? Eight definitely fit the bill: isoleucine, leucine, lysine, methionine, phenylalanine, threonine, tryptophan, and valine. That's been clear ever since William C. Rose and his research team at the University of Illinois conducted their experiments in 1938. They fed pure amino acids, much as they appear in the TPN bag, to groups of baby rats and full-grown young men and watched for signs of deficiency when different amino acids were left out. Later research showed that over long periods of time a ninth amino acid, histidine, is also essential.

For any individual, however, other amino acids may also prove essential, particularly if the ability to produce them has been diminished by disease. Alcoholics, for example, and others with damaged livers often need amino acids that more healthy men and women can supply for themselves. Newborn children too have special demands. To produce the protein their rapidly developing bodies demand, they require more of the growth-promoting amino acids taurine and arginine than they can synthesize. They also must have cystine (another growth-promoting amino acid) to develop properly, for they are not yet able to manufacture it from methionine, as older children and adults can do.

If your diet lacks those amino acids that are essential for you, and you can't produce enough new protein, then you risk losing muscle and other tissue when your body starts scavenging for raw material to meet more vital needs. A lack of enough amino acids for a long enough time will result in long-term protein deficiency, like that seen in kwashiorkor.

But there are other, more subtle penalties for failing to provide your body with enough essential amino acids. Lysine is a fragile substance, vulnerable to heat and often damaged in cooking. If you lack lysine, you will start feeling dizzy and nauseated. Methionine plays a major role in transporting fats from the liver to the rest of the body. So one danger of a methionine deficiency is the kind of "fatty liver" that causes the bellies of protein-deprived children to bulge.

As for histidine, which is still not recognized as essential by all nutritionists, this amino acid is a component of the protein globin (which, together with the iron-bearing substance heme, forms the hemoglobin that transports oxygen through the bloodstream). When there is too little histidine in your diet or in your TPN bag, the result is anemia and such lesser complaints as dry and scaly skin, loss of energy, and shortened temper.

Shortages of several amino acids can affect the mind, for they are necessary for the production of certain neurotransmitters, the substances that pass impulses from one nerve cell to the next. The genetic disease phenylketonuria (PKU), which disrupts the breakdown of phenylalanine, can cause severe retardation if untreated. Intake of tryptophan, which is converted to the important neurotransmitter serotonin, appears to affect alertness and response to pain (see chapter 15).

Like tryptophan, histidine is also converted to a neurotransmitter, histamine, which is a key participant in allergic reactions. When amino acids do not go to make protein but instead serve as precursors (parent substances) of biologically active compounds, these active compounds are called bioamines.

While science has yet to find a toxic level for protein, even among Eskimos and other peoples who live on protein-loaded diets, it has found that high levels of certain amino acids like histidine are clearly unsafe. There is a genetic disease, called histidinemia, which allows heavy concentrations of this amino acid to form in the blood, causing speech defects and increasing vulnerability to disease and infection.

Fatty Acids

Fats play a major role in making eating one of life's more rewarding experiences. Take the fats out of food and you strip away much of its taste and flavor as well as its fat-soluble vitamins (which we talk about in chapter 5). Think of the smell of roasting meat or frying onions, the way ice cream glides along your tongue, the crunch of corn and potato chips, the tangy taste of sharp cheeses, or what butter and sour cream do for baked potatoes.

Even if you have little taste for fat, your stomach is still likely to find it the most satisfying of foodstuffs. Fats have what nutritionists call satiety value. Meals that contain a good deal of fat remain in the stomach much longer than meals that do not. So you are likely to stay satisfied quite a bit longer if you dine on fried chicken and buttered biscuits than on chef's salad and melba toast.

Although TPN patients enjoy none of fat's flavor or satiety value, they need fat just as much as anyone else does. Bodily fat keeps skin in good repair. It makes hair healthy-looking and shiny. It provides a layer of insulation beneath the skin and shock absorbers for kidneys and mammary glands. But its major function is meeting the body's constant demand for fuel. Fat supplies two thirds of our ongoing energy needs, and the body's fat mass provides us with a fuel dump of almost infinite capacity.

One of the big problems with TPN was finding a way to put fat in the formula. Since fats are insoluble in water, they tended to glop together in the TPN bag. But without a good dose of fat, it was very difficult for TPN patients to get enough calories. Nutrition researchers finally turned to purified lecithin, a fat that could form a stable emulsion in solution and not a globular mass. That step, perhaps more than any other, made TPN possible.

But fats need to travel by water not only in the TPN formula but also in the bloodstream. In the process of digestion, fats break down into fatty acids (see "The Different Kinds of Fat," page 39), which are transported in the blood in special protein-coated globules (described in greater detail in chapter 17).

Although we count on fats primarily for energy, they have some far more active roles to play in our bodies. They take part in maintaining cell membranes and blood vessels, synthesizing a number of hormones, transmitting nerve impulses, and storing memory.

Nutritionists have only recently discovered a whole new area in which fatty acids are active: the production of prostaglandins. These are hormonelike compounds that regulate a great many bodily processes. About 100 prostaglandins have been identified, and their functions include controlling the expansion and contraction of blood vessels, blood clotting, moderating the response of tissues to certain hormones, contracting smooth muscles (including the uterus), and altering the transmission of nerve impulses. There is even a prostaglandin in mother's milk that protects babies' digestive tracts.

Despite all the ways in which the body uses fats, there has been considerable misunderstanding — and no little uncertainty, even among nutritionists — about the relation between the fats we consume and the fats our bodies produce. Take cholesterol, for example. It is a member of that family of fats present in both our bodies and in our diets that are

THE DIFFERENT KINDS OF FAT

What we call fats, nutritionists call lipids, compounds that won't dissolve in water. Fitting that definition are many different substances with different effects in the body. **Cholesterol**, for example, which helps the liver make bile, is structurally quite different from most other fats. Its complex molecules, built on four linked rings of carbon atoms, follow the same basic form as the steroid hormones, including the sex hormones that cholesterol helps produce.

Most fats, however, have a simple chemical structure: they are made up of linked carbon atoms, strung together like beads in chains up to 20 atoms long. Each chain is a fatty acid. Rather than floating freely, these chains are usually linked, three at a time, to a small organic molecule called **glycerol**. Imagine a coat hanger — the glycerol — from which three ribbons (the fatty acids) are hanging. The package is called a **triglyceride**. (When a special phosphorus-containing compound replaces one of the fatty acids, the package becomes a **phospholipid**, like lecithin.)

Where do saturated and unsaturated fats fit in? To understand what they are, you need to know a little about carbon atoms. Every carbon atom can form chemical bonds with as many as four other atoms. In the long chain that forms a fatty acid, all the carbon atoms except those at the ends are bound to the carbon atoms above and below them. These atoms can also bind two hydrogen atoms, one on each side. The hydrogens hang off the fatty acid chain like legs on a centipede. But by changing its chemical bond structure, the fatty acid can drop some of these hydrogens, two at a time.

A **saturated** fatty acid, or saturate, is one that carries as many hydrogen atoms as it can hold. Saturated acids are more prevalent in meats and dairy products than in vegetables, although a few vegetable oils, like the coconut oil used in nondairy creamers, are among the most saturate-laden lipids.

If one pair of hydrogen atoms is missing from the fatty acid, it is **monounsaturated**, like the predominant fatty acids in olive oil and avocados. If more than one pair of hydrogen atoms is missing, the acid is **polyunsaturated**, like those most often found in vegetable oils.

Fats high in saturates may pose a risk to the heart (as we explain in chapter 17), and unsaturates can help lower that risk. But the polyunsaturates aren't necessarily more risk-lowering than the monounsaturates.

Margarines can be tricky. Although they are made from vegetable oils high in polyunsaturates, they are often hydrogenated to make them more firm at room temperature. This means that hydrogen atoms are added to the fatty acid chains, transforming some polyunsaturates to saturates and others to trans-fatty acids, unsaturates that behave like saturates.

In general, the more liquid a fat at a given temperature, the more unsaturates it contains. Fish oil is often high in unsaturates, because many fish need fat stores that stay liquid, like antifreeze, in extremely cold water.

called sterols because of their chemical structure. What most of us know about cholesterol is that it can clog arteries and increase the risk of heart disease. This has given cholesterol a bad reputation.

Yet our bodies need cholesterol to make bile (which allows us to digest fats), vitamin D, and sex hormones like testosterone and estrogen. Does that mean we must be sure to eat lots of cholesterol-rich foods to be certain we're amply supplied? Not necessarily, because our livers produce the body's own cholesterol at the rate of 50 quadrillion (that's 50 followed by fifteen zeros) molecules every second, or 1–2 grams (between one fifth and one third of a teaspoon) per day. And our livers needn't use *any* fatty acids to do this. They can make cholesterol from the breakdown products of glucose or amino acids.

Since we're producing that much cholesterol ourselves, does it hurt to eat a bit too? It's hard to say how much we can safely eat, for the relation between dietary and bodily cholesterol isn't all that clear, and genetic differences probably have more than a little to do with how it works.

The case of lecithin is much more straightforward, though many people are still confused by it. Lecithin, unlike cholesterol, has a *good* reputation, for bodily lecithin is known to help build strong cell membranes. Because of the "good press" that lecithin enjoys, there is a brisk demand for lecithin supplements.

But no matter how many doses of lecithin you take, none of it will reach your bloodstream intact (unless you take it in the TPN bag). Like any other fat, lecithin is broken down in the digestive tract. The lecithin that helps strengthen cells is made up anew in the liver. So lecithin supplementation is ineffective and unnecessary, since no one has ever been found to have a lecithin deficiency. Nevertheless, do-it-yourself nutritionists will load up on this dietary fat, even though large amounts of it will upset their stomachs, make them sweat heavily, and ruin their appetites.

If we manufacture just about all of our own bodily fats and can make something as complex as cholesterol out of what we get from carbohydrates, is there any unique nutritional requirement for dietary fats? Beyond the need for calories, are there specific reasons to make sure that certain fatty acids are a part of our diets?

These are questions scientists couldn't answer until 1929, when researchers at the University of California, Berkeley, discovered that rats on a fat-free diet either failed to grow or lost weight. The condition of their skins and tails deteriorated, and they eventually died of kidney damage. Other researchers later demonstrated (in a 1937 experiment that would not be sanctioned today) that human infants too would grow poorly and develop skin lesions if their formulas lacked what have since been recognized as the essential fatty acids (often abbreviated EFA).

Nutritionists haven't always been certain — and aren't all that sure even now — just which of the fatty acids are essential. But they did show fairly early that humans can't synthesize linoleic acid, which is vital for growth (and, as we have recently learned, is the source of prostaglandins).

It took TPN to determine whether a related fatty acid, linolenic acid, was essential or not. Although this substance was believed impossible for the body to synthesize, and its chemical derivatives are important to brain function and sight, researchers had been unable to demonstrate a deficiency in either animals or humans. Not long ago, however, a child on TPN began experiencing blurred vision and feelings of numbness, tingling, and pain in the legs — symptoms consistent with how a linolenic acid deficiency could affect vision and the central nervous system. These symptoms disappeared after linolenic acid was added to the the child's TPN bag.

At the moment, only linoleic and linolenic acids are generally recognized as essential fatty acids (although acceptance of linolenic is not unanimous), but bottle-fed infants may also benefit from arachidonic acid and cholesterol, both found in breast milk. (Arachidonic acid is now added to infant formula and, in a few countries other than the United States, so is cholesterol.) But the final word is yet to be said on essential fatty acids. Others may yet be added to the list. Some nutritionists now consider eicosapentaenoic acid (known as EPA) a promising candidate. This fatty acid, found in fish, tends to reduce the ability of blood to clot and may possibly be useful in preventing heart disease and in treating arthritis.

Symptoms of essential fatty acid deficiency are likely to include, along with abnormal skin conditions, a diminished capacity to repair damaged tissue and resist infection. In animal studies, the lack of essential fatty acids has not only arrested growth and damaged the kidneys but also caused sterility, made blood vessels and red blood cells more fragile, deposited cholesterol in the lungs, liver, skin, and adrenal glands, and enlarged the heart.

Few fats are toxic, and you aren't going to overdose on fats even if you consume extraordinarily large amounts (although you may experience considerable gastric distress). Nevertheless, there are many ways in which high-fat diets may threaten your health. There is the danger of heart disease, based on the relation between dietary fat and the cholesterol which can block the arteries (more on this in chapter 17). There are also indications of a link between high fat intake and cancer of the breast, colon, and uterus (discussed in chapter 19).

Although solid clinical evidence is lacking, there is epidemiological evidence, based on statistical associations seen in studies of large population samples.

There is a clear connection, however, between fats and obesity. The more fat in their diets, the greater the likelihood that both human beings and laboratory animals will put on excess weight, raising the risk of disease accordingly. In fact, it's the fats in cookies, cake, and ice cream that make them so fattening. Sugar makes fat more palatable, so we can eat more of it. But it's a high fat intake, even more than a high sugar intake, that usually leads to weight gain.

Water, glucose, amino acids, and fatty acids just about fill up the TPN bag. There isn't room for much more. But micronutrients don't need much room. Our bodies require relatively small amounts of the vitamins and essential minerals described in the next four chapters — but they require *all* of them.

CHAPTER 4

The Water-Soluble Vitamins: B's and C

S LIP THE WORD *nutrition* into a free-association word test and the response from most Americans would probably be *vitamins*. Aggressive promotion and plenty of publicity have created the illusion that vitamins are pretty much what nutrition is all about.

Vitamins have been seen until quite recently as mysterious, almost magical substances, each with its own special powers. If one could clear your skin, others might clear your mind (of depression or even schizophrenia), cure your cold, or boost your energy level. While there was little science to support all this vitamin hype, skillful marketing has made the vitamin trade a $3-billion-a-year industry and made one adult American in three a regular user of vitamin supplements.

Science is catching up with vitamin salesmanship these days. It is now clear that the B vitamins don't help you fight psychological stress and vitamin E won't improve your sex life. Indeed, our fondest hopes for vitamins as a panacea never had much chance of panning out.

Most of these unrealizable expectations, it seems, were based on faulty reasoning that went something like this: If lack of a certain vitamin makes us more vulnerable to a disease, then an extra dose should cure that disease; if low levels of a vitamin cause a loss of some specific physical capacity, then lots of the vitamin should enhance that capacity. However, while a true vitamin E deficiency can reduce sexual potency in rats, this is no reason to conclude that extra vitamin E will boost it in human beings. By the same token, the fact that an inadequate amount of the B vitamin niacin can cause a form of psychosis shouldn't suggest that large doses of niacin will help schizophrenics, although this has been a popular notion in recent years.

Large doses of vitamins have proved definitely helpful only for certain inherited diseases that involve metabolic disorders. And even in those cases doctors warn that vitamins must be prescribed and taken as carefully as any other drugs.

The popularity of the more-is-better approach to vitamins has, if nothing else, taught us that vitamins are not risk-free. People who have experimented on themselves with vitamin megadoses — 10 or more times the amount nutritionists recommend — have dramatically demonstrated the dangers. Even moderately high doses of some fat-soluble vitamins like vitamin A are known to be toxic. And extremely high doses of vitamins long thought to be safe at any level, like B_6, can do damage.

The megadose danger has caused many doctors, few of them big vitamin boosters to begin with, to view widespread use of vitamin supplements with even more disfavor. When more than 1,000 doctors were asked in a recent survey to rank the relative importance of more than 25 different health-related activities (wearing seat belts, quitting smoking, reducing cholesterol consumption, and so on), they put taking vitamin supplements at the absolute bottom of the list.

A similar sample of dietitians, however, revealed far less skepticism. More than 60 percent of the dietitians in this survey took vitamin supplements themselves (generally multivitamin tablets and vitamin C). Thus, these nutrition professionals were nearly twice as likely as the general public to invest in nutritional insurance — and they had good reason to do so. Vitamins, if not magical, are nonetheless essential, and recent research suggests that many of us may not be getting all we need.

In principle, healthy adults on a diet of 2,000 to 3,000 calories per day — the average requirement — should need no extra vitamins. Our food supply certainly has plenty to offer. Many foods, like milk and white bread, are fortified with synthetic forms of those vitamins that are hardest to get from natural sources. And, in fact, clinical vitamin deficiency is rare in the United States today.

But the vitamin intake of many Americans is still less than optimal — not low enough to cause scurvy or beriberi but not as high as it should be. The major problem is that a good number of us simply don't eat enough of the right foods. Malnutrition is common in low-income families (where children are most likely to be affected) and among the elderly. Among middle-income Americans, dieting is most often to blame for nutritional deficits. This is particularly true for women. A federal survey of a few years ago found that the average woman between the ages of 35 and 44 reported eating just 1,439 calories per day.

Some groups, like pregnant or nursing mothers and their infants, have special nutritional needs. Others run special risks of vitamin deficiencies: smokers, alcoholics, patients with certain medical conditions, and users of some prescription or illicit drugs.

These special nutritional needs aren't mysterious. Although we do not know for certain all that can be known about how each vitamin works, we do know exactly what each one does, and we understand a lot about how vitamins are depleted. Later chapters of this book describe the best food sources for different vitamins, special nutritional needs at various life stages, and the role of some vitamins in sickness and health. But first you need to understand what role each vitamin plays in the body, and that starts with the answer to a basic question: What exactly *is* a vitamin?

Vitamins are that "something extra" in food (not carbohydrates, proteins, fats, or minerals) without which we could not survive but which just about no one suspected was there until the early part of this century. Not that a few sharp researchers hadn't picked up a clue. As early as 1880 the Estonian scientist Nikoli Lunin tried feeding mice a synthetic milk, carefully formulated with all the components milk was then known to contain. The mice died. But when he fed real cow's milk to mice, they lived. Lunin concluded that milk must contain "small quantities of unknown substances essential to life."

More than two decades later, a pair of Dutch researchers, working independently, discovered some of Lunin's "unknown substances" in whey from milk and the husks of rice and other grains. In 1907 the Norwegian team that was to show how vitamin C prevented scurvy began their experiments with guinea pigs. But it was a young Polish biologist working in London, Casimir Funk, who gave these mysterious nutrients the name "vitamines" (under the mistaken impression that they were all organic nitrogen compounds called amines).

Funk, who later moved to the United States (where he continued studying his "vital amines" until his death in 1967), suggested in 1914 that a lack of "vitamines" was to blame for scurvy, beriberi, pellagra, and rickets, all the diseases then known to be caused by dietary deficiencies. He was right. But it still wasn't clear if there was just one of these vital nutrients or many.

Then, two years later, researchers at the University of Wisconsin found that these "accessory food substances" came in both fat-soluble and water-soluble forms. They called the fat-soluble substance in buttermilk fat-soluble A and the water-soluble factor in whey water-soluble B. With the acceptance of Funk's name vitamine (soon to lose its final "e") and the University of Wisconsin's alphabetical system (which didn't work out too well), science had decided what to call these elusive dietary components.

Just knowing what they are called doesn't tell us much about what vitamins are, and the truth is that they are hard to describe. Since they are required in tiny amounts, they are not a source of energy like carbohydrates, amino acids, or fatty acids. (In fact, vitamins do contain some calories, but hardly any; there are only 0.24 calories in 60 milligrams of vitamin C.)

Vitamins are organic compounds. As organic matter, they contain carbon atoms from living or once-living matter. As compounds, they are vulnerable and quite unlike essential minerals, which are pure elements that cannot be broken down (see chapters 6 and 7). Vitamins can be broken up, burned up, or otherwise transformed within the body and outside it.

Most important, *all* vitamins are, by definition, essential to health, either because the body can't synthesize them or because it can't make enough of them. For a substance to be designated a vitamin, researchers must prove that a deficiency is created by its absence.

One way nutritional deficiencies have been found in recent years has been through the use of TPN. And extensive use of this procedure has pretty much convinced nutritionists that there are no additional vitamins to be discovered. The 13 now in the bag appear sufficient. Whatever deficiency symptoms TPN patients have developed thus far have turned out to result from either an absent fatty acid or a missing mineral.

For those of us who get our vitamins from food, not from a TPN bag, deficiencies can show up in many different ways. Vitamins are involved in most bodily processes, though not as leading players. They serve more as directors and stage managers, regulating and monitoring the action. Without them, order starts to break down. Normal functions falter, cells are weakened, and various organs start to fail.

When we're adequately supplied with vitamins, however, they do a lot to keep us healthy. Just about every vitamin has a direct impact on growth. A number are vital to reproduction, to digestion, and to the well-being of tissues. Vitamins are involved in setting the rate at which the body taps its energy sources, and they take part in the metabolic conversions of amino acids, fatty acids, and carbohydrates. They help keep you mentally alert and able to ward off bacterial infections.

WATER-SOLUBLE VITAMINS

When researchers at the University of Wisconsin proved that vitamins came in two varieties — fat-soluble and water-soluble — they didn't realize that their water-soluble B belonged to a whole family of related B vitamins. And it was years before anyone discovered that the scurvy-preventing substance identified by a Norwegian team early in the century was also a water-soluble vitamin (the one we call C). Today, nutritionists recognize the need for nine water-soluble vitamins in our diets and in the TPN bag. These include vitamin C, plus eight B vitamins: thiamin, riboflavin, niacin, pantothenic acid, folacin, biotin, and vitamins B_6 and B_{12}.

The B's and C are found in the watery parts of food and do their work in water-filled parts of the body's cells. They are flushed out rapidly by the kidneys and eliminated in the urine. So they don't stay around long enough to provide the long-term protection that fat-soluble vitamins do. But by the same token, they rarely build up to toxic levels.

The way they are metabolized explains why megadoses of water-soluble vitamins aren't effective. You can see colorfully what happens to excess water-soluble vitamins when you load up on riboflavin. Should your body get more of this bright orange-yellow B vitamin than it can use, the excess soon shows up in your urine. However, at very high doses, the body's flushing ability may not be able to keep up with your intake and render megadoses harmless. High doses of some water-soluble vitamins, particularly B_6, which affects nerve function, have recently been shown to be dangerous.

Water-soluble vitamins are much less hardy than their fat-soluble relatives. Vulnerable to heat, they are often broken down in cooking or processing, and some can also be destroyed by light. But they are relatively easy to replace. With few exceptions (like vitamin B_{12}), the water-soluble vitamins are present in a wide variety of foods, either naturally or as synthetic fortifiers.

The eight B vitamins have much in common; that's what makes them a family. They even have a family trade, construction and demolition. All B vitamins are coenzymes: they help the proteins known as enzymes break down old compounds and assemble new ones (see "How Water-Soluble Vitamins Work," page 48). Without the B's, your body could not convert fuel to energy, and your skin and hair would deteriorate.

The B's (like most vitamins) are essential for normal development and can be particularly important during pregnancy. They are necessary for reproduction, help keep the brain, nervous system, and immune system functioning normally, and are vital for maintenance of the blood supply.

THIAMIN

PROFILE

FUNCTION Helps convert carbohydrates and fats to energy.

ADULT RDA Men, 1.4 milligrams; women, 1.0 milligrams.

DEFICIENCY SYMPTOMS *Moderate*: depression, loss of concentration, fatigue, loss of appetite, constipation, muscle cramps. *Severe*: beriberi (nerve damage, paralysis, heart failure).

RISK OF TOXICITY Low.

TOXIC EFFECTS None observed.

First of the B vitamins available in purified form, and originally called B₁ (until nutritionists gave up on identifying the B's numerically), thiamin is best known for preventing beriberi — which may not mean all that much to us. Few Americans worry about beriberi these days, and not many worried about it in the past.

But this disease, which has plagued the peoples of the Far East ever since polishing rice (stripping away its hull) became popular, gives us fair warning of just how destructive a serious thiamin deficiency can be. Beriberi saps energy, diminishes appetite, and paralyzes the legs. In later stages, it attacks a number of different nerves, including those that control the heart.

It was a Dutch naval doctor who first picked up on the link between diet and beriberi when he noted in 1880 that Indian sailors were less likely to die from the disease if they ate European-style rations instead of just white rice. But it was later work done on the island of Java, in the laboratory of the Dutch East India Medical Service, that showed just which nutrient was missing. Physicians there learned that victims of the disease lacked some ingredient present in the germ, or outer coating, of

---

HOW WATER-SOLUBLE VITAMINS WORK

All water-soluble vitamins — the B family and C — work together with enzymes, the proteins that govern metabolism. These proteins are responsible for taking apart and putting together the many compounds the body must have to function. The vitamins and other substances that work with enzymes are called **coenzymes**.

Actually, B vitamins must pick up extra chemical components in the body before they can become working coenzymes. Once they're ready for chemical action, they can work with enzymes in two different ways: either as bound coenzymes or as detachable coenzymes.

Bound coenzymes form what are called prosthetic groups, permanently attached to their coworker enzymes. Think of them as the enzymes' dentures, without which they cannot chew.

Detachable coenzymes are capable of separating themselves from the enzymes they help. Many enzymes, for example, split other molecules. The enzyme may bind the other molecule, then attract the coenzyme, which moves in to help complete the process. Other coenzymes are linked to an enzyme when the process begins and detach when it is completed, drawing atoms of the split molecule with them.

Vitamin C works as a detachable coenzyme, but it's more versatile than the B vitamins. First of all, vitamin C needs no extra equipment to become an enzyme helper; it works without changing its chemical identity. It also does a good many other jobs in the body in addition to working with enzymes. So think of vitamin C as the most independent of the water-soluble vitamins, a nutritional jack-of-all-trades. It participates in a wide range of reactions, then moves off again on its own.

grain (which is lost when grain is milled), and in 1926 they isolated it.

Only a few foods besides whole grains provide plenty of thiamin — organ meats like liver and kidneys, pork, beans, and nuts — and these are not basic to most American diets. The thiamin that *is* in food is fragile; it doesn't stand up to dry heat very well, seeps into cooking water, and can be lost in processing. There are also thiamin-destroying enzymes in certain foods (like raw fish), which will destroy the vitamin in the digestive tract.

As a result, most of us take a part of our thiamin in the same synthetic form TPN patients do. Even if we pass up B vitamin supplements, we find thiamin in such fortified foods as bread and breakfast cereals.

Thiamin travels through the bloodstream to every part of the body, with extra-heavy concentrations in the heart, liver, and kidneys. On the work site it joins the chemical crew involved in oxidizing carbohydrates — burning them for fuel — which is far from a simple operation. The step-by-step process involves several different enzymes, at least four of which need thiamin's help to function. Without thiamin, the process gets stuck at one step or another, and toxic levels of intermediate compounds build up in the cells.

Nutritionists assume that this toxic buildup causes the symptoms of thiamin deficiency, which are rarely seen in the United States these days. However, when they do occur, they can develop fairly quickly, for the body's thiamin reserves can be depleted in only a week.

RIBOFLAVIN

PROFILE

FUNCTION   Helps convert all bodily fuels to energy and maintain various tissues.

ADULT RDA   Men, 1.6 milligrams; women, 1.2 milligrams.

DEFICIENCY SYMPTOMS   Reddened mouth, sore tongue, cracks at corners of mouth, red eyes, light sensitivity and other vision problems, facial sores, and anemia in extreme cases.

RISK OF TOXICITY   Low.

TOXIC EFFECTS   None observed.

It is only in Third World countries that lack of riboflavin is common. People there don't eat much of the richest sources (liver, kidneys, and yeast) or the second-best sources (other meats, dairy products, and eggs). They may get some riboflavin in vegetables, fruits, beans, tubers, or grains, but these foods are relatively poor sources of the vitamin.

In the United States, however, severe riboflavin deficiency is rarely seen. Not only do we eat foods that are good natural sources of riboflavin but we get an average 25 percent of our needs from synthetically fortified bread and breakfast cereals.

While riboflavin stands up to heat much better than thiamin, it is highly sensitive to light. Back in the days when milk was delivered in clear glass bottles and often left out on sunlit doorsteps, more than half its riboflavin could be lost in just two hours. Even today, fluorescent lights in supermarkets may destroy some of the riboflavin and other vitamins in low-fat milk stored in clear containers, according to research at Cornell and Pennsylvania State universities.

In the body, riboflavin forms two major coenzymes, which team up with hydrogen-handling enzymes to take apart and put together carbohydrates, amino acids, and fats. They help release energy to cells, maintain the immune system, and form blood, nerve tissue, and collagen (the heavy-duty protein that reinforces cells).

Researchers can produce some extreme deficiency symptoms in laboratory animals, including cataracts, paralysis, debilitation, and death, but humans suffer nothing quite so severe. And even if you persisted in a no-riboflavin diet, it would take several months for the milder symptoms of human riboflavin deficiency to appear.

PANTOTHENIC ACID

P R O F I L E

FUNCTION   Helps break down and form fats; helps form cholesterol and several vital hormones.

SAFE AND ADEQUATE DAILY INTAKE FOR ADULTS   4–7 milligrams.

DEFICIENCY SYMPTOMS   (seen only when experimentally induced) Nausea, headaches, fatigue, numbness in hands and feet, muscle cramps; reduced antibody production; possible personality change, sleep disturbance, loss of coordination.

RISK OF TOXICITY   Low.

TOXIC EFFECTS   None observed.

It is hard to worry much about pantothenic acid. The very name, which means "from everywhere," lets us know how unlikely we are to be deprived of this vitamin, which is found in all animal and vegetable tissue. No human being has ever developed clear-cut pantothenic acid deficiency under normal conditions. Nevertheless, pantothenic acid is a heavyweight B vitamin. It forms the ubiquitous coenzyme A that nutritionists say "sits at the crossroads of metabolism" working on various steps in the breakdown and formation of energy-producing nutrients.

NIACIN

PROFILE

FUNCTION   Active in several coenzymes. The most important helps oxidize fats, carbohydrates, and amino acids in tissue cells to produce energy.

ADULT RDA   Men, 18 milligrams; women, 13 milligrams.

DEFICIENCY SYMPTOMS   *Moderate*: swollen tongue or changes in the tongue's surface. *Severe*: pellagra.

RISK OF TOXICITY   Moderate.

TOXIC EFFECTS   Irritated stomach lining, peptic ulcers, diabetes, loss of liver function, jaundice.

Along with thiamin, riboflavin, and pantothenic acid, niacin makes up coenzymes involved in the complex process of converting fuel to energy. It too works in all tissues. But unlike riboflavin and pantothenic acid, which pose little risk of deficiency, niacin can make its absence obvious and devastating. Lack of niacin is largely responsible for pellagra, which spread throughout the American South early in this century, creating a staggering public health crisis.

Pellagra first showed up in Europe almost a century and a half before the American outbreak. Indeed, the Italians gave the disease its name, from *pelle agra*, "rough or painful skin," for the raw, red rash that appears most often on the face, hands, or feet. Victims also suffer sore mouths and tongues and inflamed digestive tracts. Later symptoms include bloody diarrhea and anemia.

Pellagra's psychological symptoms can hit much earlier, however, and doctors once characterized the pellagra syndrome as "the three D's" — dermatitis, diarrhea, and dementia. Mental illness begins with irritability, anxiety, and depression but progresses to disorientation, hallucinations, and true delirium. In 1917, at the height of pellagra's march through the South, there were 200,000 reported cases and half the patients in mental institutions were believed to be pellagra victims.

When the U.S. Public Health Service assigned a task force to study the disease, researchers focused on an early clue: the puzzling link between pellagra and a largely corn-based diet. Physicians had long recognized the connection and suspected the culprit could be a corn-borne infection. But Joseph Goldberger, head of the Public Health Service team, proved that pellagra was caused by diet alone. He showed that liver, yeast, dairy products, and other good sources of B vitamins could prevent it. Soon after, the veteran vitamin hunters at the University of Wisconsin tracked down the pellagra-preventer—the nicotinic acid and nicotinamide which together are called niacin—and pellagra became a medical rarity by the end of World War II.

But the case wasn't closed. What was the corn connection? And why were certain foods more effective in preventing pellagra than their niacin content could explain?

The answer was uncovered in the University of Wisconsin labs when researchers found that rats on a nearly all-corn diet could be protected from pellagra not only by niacin but by the amino acid tryptophan as well. Rats, it appears, can convert tryptophan to the niacin they need, and so can people. The problem with corn is more than just its minimal niacin content. Corn also has particularly low levels of tryptophan and much higher levels of other amino acids. Pellagra turned out to need three conditions to develop: a minimal amount of dietary niacin, a low level of tryptophan, and relatively high levels of other amino acids (since these compete with tryptophan and render it less effective).

All this explains why niacin deficiency is so rare in the United States today. We can take care of our niacin needs by eating foods with enough of the vitamin itself or protein foods with an equivalent amount of tryptophan (provided they don't contain disproportionate amounts of other amino acids). Meat, fish, soybeans, peanuts, and yeast are all first-rate sources. As an extra safeguard, many foods are now fortified with synthetic niacin.

Even though most Americans don't need niacin supplements to fend off deficiency, many *are* now taking niacin as medication. Doctors have often prescribed the nicotinic acid form (which expands blood vessels, causing flushing) for cardiovascular problems. But there is no good evidence that the megadoses of niacin which many people now take to fight allergies or to boost athletic performance provide any benefits at all.

Sadly disappointing has been the use of niacin to treat schizophrenia. First popular in the 1950s, the practice seemed reasonable in light of the ability of niacin to counteract the psychosis of pellagra. But few careful studies have shown this vitamin to be an effective treatment for mental illness.

Whatever the therapeutic purpose, loading up on niacin has some substantial risks. While we can safely take on niacin in amounts up to 30 times our nutritional need, the likelihood of toxic effects starts to mount quite sharply at higher levels.

VITAMIN B₆ (PYRIDOXINE)

P R O F I L E

FUNCTION Involved as a coenzyme in at least 50 different enzyme reactions — the most important regulate nervous system activity. Also helps break down and form amino acids, convert amino acids to energy, release glucose from the liver, metabolize fatty acids, regenerate red blood cells, and produce antibodies.

ADULT RDA Men, 2.2 milligrams; women, 2.0 milligrams.

CANDIDATES FOR SUPPLEMENTS Dieters, pregnant or nursing mothers, adolescents, infants, and the aging.

DEFICIENCY SYMPTOMS *Moderate*: sores around mouth and eyes, smooth tongue. *Severe*: nausea, vomiting, dizziness, anemia, kidney stones, confusion, and extreme nervous disturbance (including convulsions).

RISK OF TOXICITY Moderately high.

TOXIC EFFECTS Numbness and tingling in hands and feet, difficulty walking, sharp pains in spine.

We have been learning a lot about vitamin B₆ recently. It may turn out to be helpful in ways we hadn't imagined. On the other hand, as the B's go, B₆ is a high-risk vitamin. And while many Americans don't get nearly enough of it, some are taking too much.

What can B₆ do for you? It may limit the severity of asthma attacks and relieve the symptoms of the carpal tunnel syndrome (basically, a painful pinched nerve in the wrist, which has put many office workers permanently out of action).

But there is little evidence that B₆ does much at all to relieve PMS (premenstrual syndrome), although many women swear by it. There is no physiological basis for the vitamin to have an effect on PMS, and no study has yet shown that it does (although these studies have been limited in number, and none was large-scale).

Even if some of the therapeutic benefits of B₆ are overstated, the risk of deficiency is very real. Of all 13 vitamins, B₆ and folacin (discussed later) are the ones we are most likely to lack. True, B₆ is found in pretty much the same foods as other B vitamins (whole grain cereals, potatoes, a number of vegetables, lean red meat, fish, and poultry). But the vitamin is extremely sensitive to air, heat, and light and often is lost in processing and cooking.

As a result, just about half of all Americans get substantially less vitamin B₆ than nutritionists recommend. And those who need it most are most likely to get less than they need. Prime candidates for deficiency are dieters, pregnant or nursing mothers, alcoholics, and the elderly.

There is probably a good deal more B_6 deficiency than we see. Borderline deficits cause few visible signs, although levels of antibodies, red blood cells, and certain hormones may fall. But there is no disguising a more serious lack. An early sign is a sore mouth and smooth tongue, similar to signs of niacin deficiency. That's no accident: B_6 helps convert amino acids to other substances, so it's involved in the transformation of tryptophan to niacin.

Severe B_6 deficiency, though, can cause nausea, anemia, and extreme nervous problems, including convulsions. These last symptoms reflect the major role of B_6 in maintaining nerve tissue and forming some of the neurotransmitters that allow nerve cells to communicate with each other. So much B_6 activity is concentrated in the brain that levels of the vitamin there are up to 50 times higher than levels in the bloodstream.

The neurological effects of B_6 deficiency can be the most devastating. In 1951 more than 300 infants in various parts of the United States began showing these disturbing symptoms, including convulsions. All these babies, it was soon learned, were being fed the same brand of canned formula. Although adequate amounts of B_6 were put into the cans, the vitamin was being destroyed when parents heated the cans to sterilize the formula.

More than 30 years later, some 3 million cans of infant formula were recalled by the Food and Drug Administration (FDA). The reason: suspicion that they contained far too little vitamin B_6. Investigators followed up reported cases of B_6 deficiency among babies being raised on this formula. The most serious cases involved permanent brain damage and symptoms similar to cerebral palsy.

Vitamin B_6 is hard to come by, since it is not regularly included in fortification formulas. Although three quarters of the B vitamins are lost when wheat is milled to make white flour, processors are quick to put many of them right back in. B_6, however, is one with which flour is not synthetically enriched.

Although there may be a good case for the moderate use of B_6 supplements, megadoses of the vitamin are a different story. A moderate dose of the vitamin protects the nervous system, but an overdose can actually hurt it.

There wasn't much cause to worry about B_6 toxicity until recently. It was considered safe even at 50 to 100 times the daily need. But when thousands of women turned to megadoses to cope with PMS, taking up to 400 times the daily recommended dose, evidence of nervous system damage started to appear. One of the first symptoms noted was a duck-like walk ("broad-based and stamping," it was called by the neurologist who traced it to B_6) accompanied by a loss of feeling in hands and feet. Other physicians have described the symptoms of B_6 toxicity as much like those of multiple sclerosis — though they are reversible — with numbness and tingling in the hands, difficulty in walking, and pains that victims describe as electric shocks shooting along the spine.

BIOTIN

PROFILE

FUNCTION   Helps convert glucose to energy and form fatty acids, proteins, and nucleic acids (the genetic material in cells).

SAFE AND ADEQUATE DAILY INTAKE FOR ADULTS   100–200 micrograms.

CANDIDATES FOR SUPPLEMENTS   Patients with intestinal disorders and genetically vulnerable infants.

DEFICIENCY SYMPTOMS   Rash, sore tongue, muscle pain, sleeplessness, nausea, loss of appetite, low-grade anemia.

RISK OF TOXICITY   Low.

TOXIC EFFECTS   None observed.

There is, or certainly should be, biotin in every TPN bag these days. But that was not always the case. Biotin is a vitamin doctors tended to ignore, since they hardly ever saw deficiency symptoms. So they were puzzled when certain TPN patients began displaying classic signs of B vitamin deficiency. Several had become severely depressed and lethargic or started losing hair before their physicians recognized the biotin deficiency, previously seen almost exclusively among infants with a genetic inability to transport biotin from the intestines to the blood.

For adults and even infants with normal digestive systems, biotin deficiency is just about unheard of. We get biotin from much the same foods that provide the other B's, and little is lost in the processing plant or in the kitchen. But what keeps most of us well supplied with biotin isn't diet so much as the bacteria in our intestines, which produce the vitamin. Much of our biotin need is fulfilled by our own bodies. So there's no danger of deficiency unless you put these microorganisms out of action for some reason, like treatment of an intestinal infection or prolonged use of antibiotics.

High doses of biotin have not proved toxic. But they haven't proved useful for anything either. Because hair loss among TPN patients was reversed once the vitamin was added to the bag, the notion that biotin might regenerate lost hair has been promoted by producers of biotin lotions. While these concoctions may have other values, they do not reverse baldness.

FOLACIN

P R O F I L E

FUNCTION   Helps produce nucleic acid, essential for rapid multiplication of cells; helps form hemoglobin.

ADULT RDA   400 micrograms.

CANDIDATES FOR SUPPLEMENTS   Pregnant women; patients with burns, blood loss, skin diseases, digestive disorders, cancer; users of certain medications, including sulfa drugs and oral contraceptives.

DEFICIENCY SYMPTOMS   Anemia, smooth and swollen tongue, diarrhea and other gastrointestinal problems.

RISK OF TOXICITY   Low.

TOXIC EFFECTS   None observed.

The doctors and nutritionists who first worked on total parenteral nutrition weren't about to leave folacin out of the bag, since lack of folacin causes the deficiency most likely to occur among hospital patients. The body doesn't keep much folacin on tap, but an extraordinary need for it develops rapidly whenever it's necessary to speed up cell production. Burns and blood loss create a demand, and so do cancer and diseases, like measles, that destroy skin tissues. To complicate matters, many therapeutic drugs block the effects of the vitamin (something we'll look at more closely in chapter 22).

Doctors have also worried about pregnant mothers getting enough of the vitamin (particularly if there's a chance they will give birth to twins or triplets). They have recognized, too, that folacin deficiencies are created by digestive problems and alcoholism (alcohol blocks folacin absorption chemically). But until 1962 doctors weren't aware that a folacin deficiency could result from poor diet alone.

That year a young Boston hematologist, Victor Herbert (named after his relative the celebrated composer), put himself on a folacin-free diet to prove it could cause a form of anemia unique to folacin deficiency. Herbert had learned that a patient being treated for both scurvy and this form of anemia ate nothing but hamburgers from a particular Boston chain, plus doughnuts and coffee. The burgers were cooked at a central location, kept on steam tables, then distributed to outlets throughout the city. By that time all the vitamin C and folacin (which is quite sensitive to heat) had been steamed out of them. That, Herbert thought, was the problem.

Herbert stuck with his own diet — and a bland, boring diet it was — for more than four months. He ate nothing fresh, nothing uncooked, lots of rice and potatoes, overdone chicken and hamburger, and sardines in soybean oil. He lost 26 pounds in the process, but he proved his point: he developed a mild case of the "right kind" of anemia.

This anemia results from the body's inability to produce new red blood cells in bone marrow. The number of older red cells decreases, and they carry fewer oxygen-transporting hemoglobin molecules. A lack of folacin brings this about because the folacin coenzymes are needed to produce nucleic acids (DNA and RNA), the genetic material of cells. And a nucleic acid shortage shows up first wherever the body needs to multiply cells rapidly, as it does in bone marrow.

Although it is possible to cut enough folacin out of your diet to develop a deficiency, it isn't easy. You would have to live on a marginal, monotonous diet with little that is fresh and much that is canned. There is more than enough folacin available not only in liver, yeast, and leafy vegetables but also in other green vegetables, dried beans, oranges, and whole wheat.

Folacin doesn't have much to offer in the way of toxic effects, even if you take truly heroic doses. Nevertheless, over-the-counter vitamin supplements are limited by federal regulations to no more than 400 micrograms. The restriction isn't prompted by fears of toxicity; it's designed to keep folacin intake well below the level at which it would mask symptoms of B_{12} deficiency.

VITAMIN B_{12} (COBALAMIN)

PROFILE

FUNCTION   Helps produce nucleic acid, form red blood cells, maintain nerve growth, and protect nerve cells.

ADULT RDA   3 micrograms.

CANDIDATES FOR SUPPLEMENTS   Strict vegetarians and persons genetically vulnerable to pernicious anemia.

DEFICIENCY SYMPTOMS   *Moderate*: fatigue, weakness, weight loss, back pains, sore tongue, tingling in hands and feet, apathy and other signs of emotional disturbance. *Severe*: poor immune response, paralysis, spinal cord degeneration, potentially fatal anemia.

RISK OF TOXICITY   Low.

TOXIC EFFECTS   None observed.

B_{12} and folacin are biochemically close cousins. Both work to produce nucleic acids so important for rapid multiplication of cells.

Although a lack of B_{12} causes an anemia that looks (in terms of the bloodstream) just like folacin deficiency anemia, its effects can be far more devastating, for vitamin B_{12} is also needed to keep nerves growing normally and to maintain the sheathing that protects them. So, in addition to anemia, a B_{12} deficiency can cause a creeping, potentially fatal paralysis that starts in the extremities and moves on to the spinal cord.

So treacherous is this deficiency that it has earned the name pernicious anemia. If it is misdiagnosed, folacin supplements will appear to solve the problem by returning the blood supply to normal, while the nervous system continues to degenerate.

An English physician first described pernicious anemia in 1849, but doctors could do nothing to stop it until 1926. In that year a Boston team found that plenty of liver — up to half a pound a day — would restore red blood cell production. Later, liver concentrates were produced to treat the disease. And in 1948, B_{12} (the last vitamin added to the list) was discovered by isolating a red pigment found in liver.

For most of us, developing a B_{12} deficiency by poor diet would be fairly difficult. We need only tiny amounts of the vitamin, about 3 *micro*grams per day. When you know that it takes 5 grams of sugar to fill a teaspoon, you can imagine how little three millionths of a gram amounts to. Furthermore, normally nourished adults store as much as 5– 10 milligrams (1,000 micrograms per milligram) in their livers, enough to last several years — longer than our stores of any other vitamin.

Nevertheless, some of us can still develop vitamin B_{12} deficiencies. Heading the list are strict vegetarians who spurn not only meat but also milk and eggs. Men and women who follow this regimen are called vegans (as opposed to lacto-ovo vegetarians, who include milk and eggs in their diets). Vegans are vulnerable because B_{12} comes only from animal sources (except for traces that growing plants pick up from the soil). Meat, seafood, eggs, and dairy products (other than butter) are particularly good sources. But there is no B_{12} in brewer's yeast (a fine source for other B vitamins) and none in grains, fruits, or vegetables.

Although American vegans should protect themselves with B_{12}- fortified soy milk or supplements, there is surprisingly little B_{12} deficiency found in traditionally vegetarian cultures of developing nations. The most obvious explanation is that B_{12} produced by microbes in the intestines of humans and animals passes into soil and water. This contamination then becomes the source of enough B_{12} to give even strict vegetarians just about all they need to avoid a deficiency.

More serious than dietary deficiency is lack of the protein (produced in the stomach) that transports B_{12} from the small intestine into the bloodstream. If the body doesn't produce this protein, which nutritionists call the intrinsic factor, for any reason (including a genetic condition that causes production to cease in midlife), then it can't get the B_{12} it needs. And lack of the intrinsic factor rather than any dietary deficiency is almost always the cause of pernicious anemia.

In these cases, B_{12} supplements must be injected, bypassing the digestive tract. This is the *only* time, however, when shots of B_{12} rather than pills are called for, even though B_{12} injections have become a fad treatment for a number of ills.

Because a B_{12} deficiency can produce the symptoms of certain neurological disorders, the vitamin is often prescribed when such symptoms appear. Doctors will also try hefty doses of B_{12} to remedy metabolic disorders (failure of the body to produce the substances it needs). The problem is that B_{12} can only correct these conditions when they have been caused by an absence of the vitamin. In all other instances, vitamin B_{12} won't do much good, but it isn't likely to do much damage either. There is so little evidence of toxicity that B_{12} tablets are often used as placebos.

VITAMIN C

PROFILE

FUNCTION   An antioxidant (see "What Is an Antioxidant?," p. 60). It promotes healing and fights infection, helps metabolize amino acids, is required for collagen synthesis, and increases iron absorption.

ADULT RDA   60 milligrams.

CANDIDATES FOR SUPPLEMENTS   Smokers; regular users of aspirin, oral contraceptives, tetracycline, and certain other drugs; patients recovering from infections, injury, or surgery.

DEFICIENCY SYMPTOMS   *Moderate*: restlessness, swollen or bleeding gums, superficial bruising, painful joints, loss of energy, and iron-deficiency anemia. *Severe*: scurvy.

RISK OF TOXICITY   Low.

TOXIC EFFECTS   Nausea and vomiting, diarrhea, kidney stones, loss of red blood cells, changes in bone marrow.

If Americans voted an award for what they believed was the Most Valuable Vitamin in their diets, vitamin C would win hands down. We spend more than $350 million a year on vitamin C supplements, even though no one really knows yet how this vitamin performs many of its functions in the body.

Foods rich in vitamin C will prevent and cure scurvy, of course; we knew that long before we knew the vitamin even existed. And C helps the body heal and resist infection, endure extreme temperatures, and handle toxic heavy metals. There is some reason to believe vitamin C also strengthens the body's defenses against cancer, although there is no good evidence that supplementation does much good once cancer has taken hold.

Most of us take vitamin C for a more mundane reason: to fight the sniffles. The fad was really started about 1970 by chemist Linus Pauling, twice a Nobel laureate (for chemistry in 1954, peace in 1962). Pauling recommended preventive doses that were high indeed—up to 10 grams per day, more than 150 times what nutritionists recommend. But more than 20 studies have failed to show any real benefit from those mega-doses.

The story of vitamin C is largely one of unfulfilled expectations. Although it has been taken to relieve symptoms of diabetes, arthritis, allergies, and stress, it doesn't seem to help any of these conditions. And there is little support for early hopes that C might reduce blood choles-terol levels and halt or reverse atherosclerosis ("hardening of the arter-ies," caused by fat deposits in artery walls).

But even if vitamin C is less miraculous than we would like to believe, it is still an amazingly versatile and potent substance. Before James Lind discovered in 1747 that oranges and lemons were able to cure

---

WHAT IS AN ANTIOXIDANT?

Many fans of vitamin supplementation attempt to load up on **antioxidants**. Vitamin C is one; so are vitamins A and E. But what are antioxidants, and why would we need them?

Oxidation—the chemical process by which we burn our fuel—is essential; it provides the body with usable energy. But during the process of oxidation, certain unstable molecules are created that contain oxygen in unique configu-rations. These molecules break down to form **free radicals**, highly reactive molecules that range through the body oxidizing and destroying tissue and creating new free radicals in the process. Such chain reactions, some research-ers theorize, may contribute to cancer and aging.

Think of free radicals as the body's pyromaniacs and antioxidants as its fire fighters. Though vitamin E is the most potent natural antioxidant, other vitamins also do their share. In membrane and muscle cells vitamin E protects fatty acids from free radicals' attacks. In the lungs, where a substantial amount of oxidation is always under way, vitamin A protects not only the mucous lining but also the red blood cells that pass through and pick up their loads of oxygen for delivery.

Until recently, nutritionists believed that vitamins provided just about all the body's protection from free radicals. Now, however, we know that uric acid (previously thought to be solely a waste product) is also a potent antioxidant.

But while these antioxidants are critical to normal body function, it's not clear that taking extra amounts of vitamins A, C, and E or synthetic antioxidants will retard the aging process or prevent cancer. High doses of antioxidants have not extended the life spans of laboratory animals.

scurvy, English ships were limited to voyages of less than three months, for scurvy took so great a toll of crews on longer trips. Lind's work made possible the exploratory voyages of Captain James Cook, who was careful to fill the hold of his ship with fresh fruits and vegetables whenever he made port. And it was Cook who discovered the "antiscorbutic" (scurvy-preventing) value of sauerkraut.

Despite Cook's good example, a later British explorer, the impetuous Captain Robert Scott, made the fatal mistake of ignoring the risk of scurvy. Scott and his companions died of the disease on a voyage back from the South Pole in 1912, the year after Norwegian researchers proved the need for what medical literature began calling the "scurvy vitamine" or "antiscorbutin."

Arresting scurvy is no mean feat, since this vicious disease attacks the body at a number of vital points. It starts with fatigue, roughening of the skin, and bleeding gums and progresses to painful joints, dry mouth, and hair loss. Finally, scurvy damages bone and muscle, including heart muscle. Wounds do not heal, teeth come loose, infections are common, and death can come suddenly, often as the result of massive internal bleeding.

While full-blown scurvy is rare these days, a condition known as latent scurvy occasionally shows up among infants fed on little more than heated milk. They become restless and irritable and suffer swollen gums and painful joints and legs.

Considering the massive assault scurvy mounts against the body, it seems almost unbelievable that the disease can be controlled and reversed in just five days by nothing more than daily doses of about 10 milligrams of vitamin C. That's only one sixth the amount recommended for healthy adults. Even in the best of times, we need much more vitamin C than we require of any other vitamin.

We humans are unusual in our need for C. Most animals have an enzyme that lets them make their own. But there are other exceptions: No primates can produce vitamin C, nor can guinea pigs, several species of salmon and trout, and some pretty odd birds, including a fruit-eating bat found in India and Turkey's red-vented bulbul.

Vitamin C operates quite differently from the other water-soluble vitamins (see "How Water-Soluble Vitamins Work," page 48). Although nutritionists have a good idea of where in the body vitamin C is active, they are not too certain just what it does there. But there is no question about several of the roles it plays. As an antioxidant, vitamin C protects easily oxidized vitamins and fatty acids from being destroyed by oxidation. It is involved in the production of collagen, the heavy-duty protein the body uses for repairs, which is why scurvy prevents wounds from healing. It also helps metabolize amino acids and aids the absorption of iron.

Plainly a busy little nutrient, vitamin C is a substance nutritionists believe we'd best have at levels about six times the minimum needed to prevent scurvy. Demand can increase sharply when the body is fighting infection (particularly when it runs a fever), and reserves of C are rapidly depleted by the healing process when the body has been damaged by injury or surgery.

Extra vitamin C is necessary if you are regularly using certain drugs — aspirin, oral contraceptives, or tetracycline — or if you are a smoker. But getting enough vitamin C can be difficult, since fruits and vegetables are pretty much the only natural sources. The fragile vitamin rarely survives processing or cooking; the C in milk, for instance, is lost during pasteurization. (Nevertheless, frozen vegetables and orange juice are first-rate sources, and both french fries and chips hang onto a good deal of their vitamin C.)

Given vitamin C's importance, it is easy to understand the popularity of supplements, even oversized ones, and nutritionists weren't too concerned when megadoses were first recommended. Since that time, however, the evidence of risk has been mounting.

DEPARTMENT OF FALSE HOPES: VITAMINS AND STRESS

When nutritionists say that stress increases the need for certain vitamins, they are not talking about the psychological stress brought on by career pressures, financial worries, or emotional problems. They mean physical stress, the extra demands on the body made by extreme temperatures, injury, or infection. That is when bodily reserves of stress-fighting vitamins can be depleted to help withstand cold, heal burns or wounds, or fight off infection. In times of severe physical stress, animal experiments show, the adrenal glands pump extra vitamin C into the bloodstream. There is more work for most of the B vitamins, too, particularly for folacin, a key player in the production of new blood cells and the maintenance of the immune system. The need for large doses of extra vitamins, however, has been shown to occur only with *extreme* physical stress — not anything as mundane as a bout with the flu or missing a night's sleep.

What can vitamins do to relieve psychological stress? The answer is, not much. But that hasn't stopped several vitamin manufacturers from advertising special "stress formulas" with megadoses of vitamin C and some B vitamins and implying that they will help you deal with the stresses of daily life.

This notion surfaced in 1952, when a National Academy of Sciences report recommended extra vitamins for people with several physical trauma, such as major surgery, severe burns, and bone fractures. One year later, pharmaceutical companies began producing "stress formulas" with levels of vitamin C and the B vitamins recommended by the Academy. Though the supplements were originally marketed to physicians, they eventually became popular over-the-counter items advertised with images of overworked executives — until, in 1986, one manufacturer agreed to change an ad campaign under pressure from the New York State Attorney General.

A daily 5–10 grams (5,000–10,000 milligrams) of vitamin C can cause nausea and vomiting. But, assuming you can keep it down, excess vitamin C will be excreted in feces and urine. By both routes, vitamin C makes trouble: it can cause diarrhea and even kidney stones.

It also interferes with certain medical tests of urine and feces. For patients on high doses of vitamin C, the standard test for blood in the stool (a sign of colon cancer) will come up negative whether blood is present or not. And megadoses of C make it impossible to test urine for the presence of glucose (an essential diagnostic tool for diabetics).

Patients with other medical problems also have special reasons to shun high amounts of vitamin C. If you need to take anticoagulants — drugs that reduce blood clotting — megadoses of C may deactivate them. If you have a genetic blood disease like sickle-cell anemia or thalassemia, too much vitamin C may make your vulnerable red cells self-destruct.

Even if you are relatively healthy, taking on more vitamin C than your body can comfortably handle will certainly affect your absorption of iron. While the vitamin normally *helps* you absorb iron, a megadose can backfire. Iron depends upon copper to become part of red blood cells. Several studies have shown that 1.5 grams (1,500 milligrams) of vitamin C per day, taken at mealtimes, can reduce the amount of copper in the blood. The net result: a diminished ability to make new red cells (a process we look at in chapter 7). There is also some reason to suspect that excess vitamin C may inhibit the body's use of vitamin B_{12}. Pregnant women have two special reasons not to megadose on C. First, animal studies have shown that sizable doses can cause spontaneous abortion. Second, pregnant megadosers can develop a vitamin C dependency that they pass on to their babies, who may develop scurvy unless they are given extra-high doses of C.

Although such dependency is rare, it can develop in anyone who keeps loading up on vitamin C over a considerable length of time. When it occurs, the healing vitamin becomes much like an addictive drug. The body responds to the constant oversupply of vitamin C by activating an enzyme whose sole purpose is to destroy the vitamin. Should the high-doser drop back to normal vitamin intake too quickly, without tapering off, the enzyme will keep on working. The former megadoser may then develop withdrawal symptoms, signs of vitamin C deficiency.

CHAPTER 5

The Fat-Soluble Vitamins: A, D, E, and K

T HE DISTINCTION MADE in 1916 between fat-soluble and water-soluble vitamins still holds today. Only we know now that there is a quartet of fat-soluble vitamins and that they work quite differently from the nine water-solubles (see "How Fat-Soluble Vitamins Work," below).

The fat-soluble vitamins (A, D, E, and K) are usually found in fatty foods: meat, fish, dairy products, and vegetable oils. But green and yellow vegetables are also sources of vitamins A and K. The fat-soluble vitamins travel in fats. They leave the digestive tract with fats, move through the body wrapped in fats, and are stored in fatty tissue. This makes them less

HOW FAT-SOLUBLE VITAMINS WORK

Unlike the B vitamins, which exist to help enzymes do their jobs, the fat-soluble vitamins are free agents. Like vitamin C, they operate independently in the body. But the exact way in which they work is less clear than it is for the water-soluble vitamins.

We do know that vitamin D is converted to a hormone, a substance that signals certain body cells to start a specific process or to halt it. In this form, vitamin D regulates the ability of intestinal cells to absorb calcium.

We also know precisely how beta-carotene, found in many vegetables, is converted into an active form of vitamin A and how vitamin A, in turn, is converted into chemicals that help form cell membranes, the retina of the eye, and the light-trapping compound responsible for vision. We know much less about how vitamin A and vitamin E work as antioxidants. And the mechanisms by which vitamin K participates in blood clotting and bone formation are at present the subject of intensive study.

fragile than their water-soluble counterparts; they're better able to survive the cooking pot and the processing plant.

It also makes them harder to get rid of, since they can't leave the body in urine. There are benefits to this relative immobility. The body can use fat-soluble vitamins over a longer period of time, and deficiencies develop more slowly. But there are penalties, too. Dangerous amounts can build up, and you are considerably more likely to get toxic levels of these vitamins than you are of the water-soluble ones.

VITAMIN A

PROFILE

FUNCTION Maintains vision; most important for night vision. *As an antioxidant, protects cells from free radicals.* Helps build bone and teeth, maintain skin, hair, gums, mucous membranes, nerve cell sheathing. Needed for reproduction.

ADULT RDA Men, 1,000 micrograms; women, 800 micrograms.

CANDIDATES FOR SUPPLEMENTS Children (particularly in low-income families and Third World countries).

DEFICIENCY SYMPTOMS Night blindness and more extreme vision problems; tooth decay, scaly skin or acne, diarrhea and other intestinal disorders; lowered resistance to infection, particularly in mucous linings of lungs, bladder, and other organs.

RISK OF TOXICITY High.

TOXIC EFFECTS Blurred vision, headaches, nausea, roughened skin, diarrhea, psychological disturbance (depression). *Extreme:* liver damage, bone loss.

Back at the time of Hippocrates, physicians were already prescribing vitamin A for patients who had trouble seeing at night. Of course, they didn't know they were prescribing a vitamin, but they did know that eating liver helped. By the start of the twentieth century, doctors hadn't learned much more, except that cod-liver oil had replaced liver as the remedy for night blindness in children.

In 1913 two research teams — one of which was later to describe "fat-soluble A" and "water-soluble B" — demonstrated a basic need for vitamin A. Experimenting with rats, they kept the animals on a purified diet free from all fats save lard. After the unfortunate first group of rats had all ceased to grow and eventually had died, a second group was fed on diets including cod-liver oil, butterfat, or egg yolk, now recognized as good sources of vitamin A. These rats thrived.

Today we know that vitamin A does not come from animal foods

alone. It can also be produced from beta-carotene and several other carotenoids, the pigments that give color to yellow and orange vegetables.
Nutritionists now generally measure vitamin A activity in Retinol
Equivalents (REs). One RE equals one microgram of retinol—the form of
vitamin A in animal products—or six micrograms of beta-carotene.

We also know more about its role, which goes far beyond maintaining good vision. Vitamin A promotes bone building; it helps break down
portions of bone that must be removed to allow further growth. It is one
of the nutrients necessary for healthy skin, teeth and gums, reproductive
glands, and nerve cell sheathing. A lack of vitamin A can reduce the
ability to resist infection and cause a sharp drop in the production of red
blood cells.

The vitamin also helps maintain the body's mucous membranes—
the importance of which is clear when you realize just how many mucous membranes we have. The lungs, stomach, and intestine are lined
with mucous membranes, and so are all the passageways that lead to
them. There are mucous linings, too, for the eyelids and sinuses, for the
bladder, and for the uterus and vagina.

In the eye retinol, the most common form of vitamin A, helps form
the pigment molecules of the retina, where light waves are trapped and
translated into nerve impulses. Night blindness results when there is not
enough retinol. Rarely seen in developed nations, the problem is still
common among children in Third World countries.

When vitamin A deficiency is chronic, the eyes become sensitive to
light and unable to produce tears. This disease, called xerophthalmia,
often leads to infection and ultimately to blindness. It strikes half a
million Southeast Asian children each year. Yet the means of prevention—carotene-rich mangoes, pumpkins, and dark green vegetables—
are often inexpensive and readily available.

There is little disease-level vitamin A deficiency in the United
States. Fortification has made milk a good and readily available source of
the vitamin, particularly for children. Even so, about one third of American youngsters get less vitamin A than the recommended dose.

Reasonably well-nourished adults can omit vitamin A from their
diets for quite a while without suffering any deficiency symptoms, since
most of us carry around more than a year's supply in our livers. But when
the vitamin A in storage runs out, severe deficiency effects can appear
quite rapidly.

Vitamin A deficiency can also be created by an imbalance of other
nutrients. If your diet is low in the mineral zinc (discussed in chapter 7),
the vitamin A in your liver may be unable to get to work. Zinc is needed
to take the vitamin out of storage. So is protein. But, curiously, the effects
of vitamin A deficiency are less severe when they are caused by a lack of
animal foods that provide both protein and vitamin A. Without the protein needed to transport the vitamin, the body is unable to tap its reserves

as readily and does not deplete them as rapidly.

But if protein is then suddenly supplied without adding more vitamin A, all the new protein carriers will empty the liver of vitamin A and bring on profound deficiency. This occurred in Brazil when UNICEF distributed skimmed milk along with vitamin A capsules to families there. Many parents gave the milk to their children and either took the capsules themselves or sold them. The result was an epidemic of childhood blindness.

Today, nutritionists have become as interested in the diseases vitamin A may help to cure as the diseases that result from its lack. There is evidence that vitamin A may be effective in arresting acne, psoriasis, and other skin disorders. And it may play a role in protecting us against cancer, since most cancer deaths result from tumors in the mucous linings that vitamin A helps maintain.

But taking extra vitamin A can be a high-risk practice. The fat-solubility of vitamin A, which lets us carry around a year's supply, also makes it difficult for us to rid ourselves of excessive amounts. So there is a danger that you can literally poison yourself if you take too much over a long period of time.

How much is too much? About ten times the generally recommended level of 1,000 micrograms (1 milligram) per day, continued for several years, will generally be too much. But some nutritionists warn that even five times the recommended level might create problems in only a matter of months.

One thing is clear: If you take very large doses — 20 milligrams or more — you will run into trouble faster. Arctic explorers learned this the hard way when they disregarded their guides' advice and added polar bear liver, loaded with vitamin A, to their rations. They became severely ill and suffered liver damage, although they subsequently recovered.

A number of children, given vitamin A at 100 times the recommended level by well-meaning but misguided parents, have experienced headaches and nausea. Their skin has dried and cracked. They have felt pain in their bones and sustained temporary liver and kidney damage.

The proper use of vitamin A presents a challenge. Supplements may help to prevent deficiency and conceivably to treat disease, but the risk of toxicity is very real. However, vitamin A's toxicity depends on its form. Only retinol and the other varieties found in animal foods are capable of doing much harm. Carotenoids, the vegetable sources of vitamin A, don't seem to be toxic even when extraordinarily large amounts are consumed. About the worst effect of overdoing carotenoids is picking up some of the color these vegetable pigments give to carrots and squashes and seeing your skin turn yellow. Partly because of their safety record, research on the use of vitamins to prevent cancer is focusing on these apparently benign compounds (see chapter 19).

VITAMIN D

PROFILE

FUNCTION Helps build bone and teeth and maintain levels of calcium and phosphorus in the blood; regulates many cellular functions, including cell division and metabolic activity.

ADULT RDA 5 micrograms.

CANDIDATES FOR SUPPLEMENTS The aging; infants who are not fed fortified milk or other fortified foods.

DEFICIENCY SYMPTOMS *Immediate*: muscle weakness, listlessness. *Prolonged*: tooth decay, deformed bones (rickets) and enlarged skull in children, softened bones (osteomalacia) or brittle bones (osteoporosis) in adults.

RISK OF TOXICITY Moderate.

TOXIC EFFECTS *Infants:* poor appetite, retarded growth, deformed bones. *Adults*: headaches, vomiting and diarrhea, weight loss, muscular weakness; also hypercalcemia, an excess of calcium in the blood that can form kidney stones and deposits in other organs.

Rickets, the disease of vitamin D deficiency, is a disease of civilization. At the start of the 1930s it was epidemic among urban American children, affecting one child in five. The disease prevented their bones from knitting properly, and as the children gained weight, the bones began to bend. The results were bowlegs, knock-knees, knobby joints, and other deformities that affected not only legs but arms, chests, and rib cages as well.

Rickets was actually an old story by then. In the crowded, smoky mill towns of nineteenth-century England, it was so common among children that it was known as the English disease. Before 1900, doctors realized that the lack of sunlight in these dismal cities was a cause of the disease and that exposure to sunlight could arrest and even reverse its symptoms.

But Dr. Edward Mellanby, a London physician, was convinced that there was more to rickets than sunlight. In 1918 he used puppies to demonstrate that rickets was caused by a dietary deficiency that could be remedied by cod-liver oil. Four years later, the University of Wisconsin team that first discovered there were both fat- and water-soluble vitamins showed that cod-liver oil prevented rickets even when all its vitamin A was removed. Thus, they proved the existence of a second fat-soluble vitamin, which they called the calcium-depositing vitamin, later known as vitamin D.

The nineteenth-century physicians who prescribed sunlight for rickets weren't wrong, though. Sunlight is indeed a source of vitamin D. Ultraviolet light turns an oily substance in the skin (a relative of cholesterol) into the same kind of vitamin D that occurs in food.

In the body, vitamin D is chemically modified and transformed into a hormone, one that controls blood levels of calcium and phosphorus to ensure that the right amounts are available for bone building. Without this hormone children's bones won't grow properly and cartilage will accumulate at the joints. But mature bones, and older bones in particular, need the right minerals too. Lacking them, these bones may become soft (osteomalacia) or porous and brittle (osteoporosis).

Getting enough *natural* vitamin D is difficult, since it is found in only a few foods, such as eggs, fatty fish, and liver. Neither cow's milk nor mother's milk contains all the vitamin D children need. But *synthetic* D is both plentiful and inexpensive. And it's the fortification of milk and other foods with this synthetic rather than greater exposure to sunlight that has made rickets rare in the United States today.

Since a number of foods are now fortified with vitamin D, and many parents believe in giving their children high-potency vitamin D supplements as "nutritional insurance," there is more than a little danger of overdose. Some infants are particularly sensitive to vitamin D, and too much can raise the level of calcium in their blood, blunt their appetite, and retard their growth. Among older people, excess calcium may form deposits in soft tissue.

VITAMIN E

PROFILE

FUNCTION   As an antioxidant, protects the body from free radicals. Helps form and protect red blood cells, muscles, and other tissue.

ADULT RDA   Men, 10 milligrams; women, 8 milligrams.

CANDIDATES FOR SUPPLEMENTS   Premature infants.

DEFICIENCY SYMPTOMS   None obvious in healthy adults or children, minimal effect on red blood cells. Possible muscle loss related to impaired digestion of fats; other symptoms occur in patients with liver disorders and premature infants.

RISK OF TOXICITY   Low.

TOXIC EFFECTS   Minimal; possible changes in hormonal activity plus risk of reduced white cell activity and blood clotting and of liver dysfunction.

When animal experiments with vitamin E began in 1922, it looked at first as though science was on to a true supervitamin. The newly discovered nutrient certainly worked wonders for rats: they just about couldn't reproduce without it. It promoted growth and maintained skeletal muscles. And, deprived of vitamin E, rats and other laboratory animals suffered fatal heart damage, liver damage, and brain damage.

For men and women, however, vitamin E proved considerably less of a panacea. Nevertheless, the myths persist, and exaggerated claims are still being made for the vitamin, even though there is much that vitamin E will *not* do for you. It will not restore potency or crank it up a notch or two. It will not enhance athletic performance or help you resist muscular dystrophy, cancer, heart attacks, or the hot flashes of menopause. It will not lower cholesterol levels in the blood or prevent premature signs of aging.

Although it is difficult to pinpoint specific therapeutic benefits of vitamin E, researchers have claimed that it can reduce benign breast cysts, intermittent claudication (an arterial blockage that causes pains in the calf muscles), and some symptoms of premenstrual syndrome (PMS). These benefits, as well as the protection from smoke and pollution it may give the lungs, are consistent with vitamin E's primary function. It is the most potent of the natural antioxidants, the fire fighters that suppress free radicals, the body's pyromaniacs.

Most of us get our vitamin E from vegetable oils — wheat-germ oil is one of the richest sources — and from beans, fruits, and vegetables. Liver, as you might suspect, is also a good source, but animal fats contain relatively little.

Although vitamin E supplements enjoy a brisk sale among the nutritionally wishful, there is little evidence of much need for them. Because the vitamin is in so many basic foods, deficiencies are rarely seen. Even where food is scarce, other deficiencies are likely to become evident long before there is a noticeable lack of vitamin E. In one six-year study, during which volunteers consumed minimal amounts of the vitamin, the worst symptom researchers could find after five years of vitamin E deprivation was some fragility in red blood cells. Men and women whose bodies do not absorb fat easily may have a somewhat greater response but nothing more serious than minor muscle loss.

By far the most common victims of vitamin E deficiency are premature infants, who are born with low levels of both vitamin E and iron. Their dual deficiency will generally show up as anemia, although edema (water retention) is also a clue. There is now evidence that supplementation with vitamin E may counteract free radicals generated by the use of iron supplements and may also help prevent retrolental fibroplasia, the eye disorder that can develop when premature infants are given oxygen.

The popular use of vitamin E megadoses has caused nutritionists to issue grave warnings about overdose, although evidence of vitamin E toxicity is minimal. Nevertheless, there are some indications that excessive amounts, say, 10 times the recommended levels, may disrupt hormonal activity, change levels of fat in the blood, keep white blood cells from doing their job, and interfere with blood clotting.

VITAMIN K

PROFILE

FUNCTION Helps blood to clot; promotes bone formation.

SAFE AND ADEQUATE INTAKE FOR ADULTS 70–140 micrograms.

CANDIDATES FOR SUPPLEMENTS Newborn infants; adults and children with low levels of intestinal bacteria (most often through use of antibiotics).

DEFICIENCY SYMPTOMS Impaired blood clotting and bone formation.

RISK OF TOXICITY Low.

TOXIC EFFECTS Loss of red blood cells, jaundice, risk of brain damage.

Vitamin K was discovered in Denmark and named, in Danish, "koagulation vitamin" because it helps make blood clot. Like most other fat-soluble vitamins, vitamin K works in the liver, where it is involved with about half a dozen proteins that help handle coagulation.

When doctors first started studying TPN, vitamin K got much attention, since TPN was originally used to give a nutritional boost to patients about to undergo surgery and to postsurgical patients whose digestive systems were temporarily out of action. In either case, the vitamin for coagulation was not one doctors were likely to ignore.

Although dietary sources of vitamin K are limited mostly to green leafy vegetables, cheese, and the inevitable liver, this poses little problem even for liver and vegetable haters. Vitamin K is manufactured in our bodies — but not *by* our bodies. Bacteria in our intestines do the job of producing vitamin K, and do it well enough for deficiency to occur only under abnormal conditions — when, for example, antibiotics given to combat intestinal infections reduce the bacterial population. Low levels of the vitamin, however, are often found in newborn infants before their intestinal bacteria have had a chance to develop, so some doctors routinely inject a starter dose.

Both natural forms of the vitamin — K_1, which is found in food, and K_2, produced in the intestine — are unlikely to do much harm. Neither has proved very toxic, even in exceedingly large amounts. But the synthetic, water-soluble forms of the vitamin *are* toxic. Excessive amounts will cause red blood cells to self-destruct and the liver to release bile pigment, which can damage the brain.

CHAPTER 6

Minerals:
The Big Seven

F OR A NUMBER OF years nutritionists had
known that the mineral chromium influ-
enced glucose levels in the blood. Experimental animals had developed
extraordinarily high levels when deprived of chromium. And rising glucose levels are cause for alarm, since they are a symptom of diabetes. But
no such direct relation had been observed in human beings until Judy
Taylor's blood glucose levels began to climb.

The first patient to undertake lifelong dependence on TPN, the
young Canadian mother had fared relatively well on her nightly bagful of
sterilized chemicals. From 1970 to 1977 total parenteral nutrition appeared to be providing every substance Judy Taylor's body required. But
when blood tests showed her glucose levels up in the diabetic range, Dr. K.
N. Jeejeebhoy, who had supervised her TPN regimen since it began, found
it hard to believe that his patient had suddenly contracted diabetes. When
diabetes starts in adulthood, it usually accompanies obesity, but Judy
Taylor was *losing* weight and had other disturbing symptoms as well.

Dr. Jeejeebhoy thought his patient might be suffering from a nutritional deficiency that hadn't been recognized yet. He considered chromium the most likely missing nutrient, since animal studies had already
demonstrated the mineral's impact on glucose levels. By adding chromium to the TPN formula, he brought Judy Taylor's blood glucose level
back down to a more normal range. Thus, he was able to demonstrate
that a deficiency did indeed exist.

Once Judy Taylor's deficiency had been discovered, chromium
moved onto the list of essential minerals. There are at last count 21 on
the list, including some that have thus far been shown to be essential
only for experimental animals. Nevertheless, most nutritionists believe

the list is far from complete. Two new minerals have been labeled essential since 1979, and researchers are pressing the case for the addition of several more.

Among the elements that make up our world and ourselves, the largest number are minerals. These are naturally occurring, inorganic substances found in the earth's crust and found in us too. There are 46 different elements in our bodies, and all must arrive via either the TPN bag or the digestive system (but not necessarily in food), for the body is incapable of producing any minerals of its own.

Although most minerals are present in truly minuscule amounts, we have a goodly supply of what are called the macrominerals — calcium, phosphorus, magnesium, sodium, potassium, chloride, and sulfur. Together, these big seven make up about 4 percent of our body weight. Macrominerals are the stuff of which bones are made. They are necessary to maintain both the amount of fluid in the body and its acid-alkaline balance, to transmit nerve impulses, to maintain cell membrane structure, and to work with enzymes.

The remaining 39 minerals in our bodies are called trace elements, for we have no more than traces of them. All of them combined barely fill a teaspoon, and they constitute just 1 percent of our mineral total.

There are 14 trace elements recognized at present as essential, and these operate in much the same way that vitamins do. Each has at least one specific role, and together they are involved in most of the body's major metabolic enterprises. They are necessary cofactors for some enzymes, key players in oxidation and reduction (allowing cells to convert fuel to energy), and heavily involved in distributing oxygen throughout the body.

Science was slow to realize how many trace elements are essential, although the need for iron was apparent early on. We have an immense amount of iron by trace element standards, more than 2 grams, and even the ancient Greeks recognized its importance. One of the oldest bits of pharmacological lore tells how Melampus, ship's surgeon to Jason and the Argonauts, laced wine with filings from their iron swords to help them sustain blood loss and boost their sexual potency. During the Middle Ages iron nails were embedded in apples and allowed to rust there to produce an iron supplement for children.

Other than iron, however, there was no trace element among the National Research Council's recommended dietary allowances (RDAs) until iodine was listed in 1968. Zinc was added in 1974. And six years later, six others appeared, not as RDAs but on a separate listing of "safe and adequate" amounts for nutrients that the council was less than certain were essential. Winning this qualified endorsement were copper, manganese, fluoride, chromium, selenium, and molybdenum.

Nutritionists can hardly be faulted for failing to recognize a need for elements they hadn't realized were in the body. Only in the past few decades has there been technology sensitive enough to detect the minute quantities of trace elements in body cells. To demonstrate deficiencies of these elements, it takes laboratory animals raised in dust-free environments on purified diets. Researchers must be sure that no trace elements enter the digestive tract in bits of dirt or other contaminants. It took such a supersanitary setting for Dr. Klaus Schwarz to show a dietary need for arsenic and to demonstrate the effects of selenium, chromium, and vanadium on growth.

Not all recent discoveries of mineral deficiencies, however, have been made in the laboratory. It was a large-scale experiment in the Chinese province of Keshan that revealed a dietary need for the trace element selenium. The experiment followed the outbreak of an epidemic that struck young boys and pregnant women with a heart muscle disorder unique to the area (called Keshan disease). The connection to selenium was made by a pathologist who found that the heart muscle of one young victim resembled descriptions he had read of a disease that attacks Australian sheep and is related to the low level of selenium in the soil where they graze.

The Chinese had discovered by this time that the soil of Keshan had little selenium to give to the grains grown there. They saw no cause for concern, however, since low selenium levels (though rare) had shown no signs of being dangerous to humans. Indeed, researchers in New Zealand, where the soil is equally selenium-poor, had looked for a connection between low blood selenium levels and disease and had found nothing. But with the Chinese pathologist's discovery, his government began a four-year study in which 36,000 children were given selenium supplements. Children receiving the selenium began to recover, most of their symptoms cleared up, and the death rate dropped abruptly. Chinese researchers reported, however, that the disease appeared to be caused by more than just a lack of selenium. Other minerals seemed to be involved, and they believed there was a connection to an overabundance of molybdenum in the soil of Keshan as well as to a shortage of selenium.

Mineral deficiencies often work this way. It is important to get not only *enough* of the minerals we need but a *balance* of minerals as well. And while adequate amounts of the essential minerals are vital, overloading is dangerous, because *all minerals are toxic at certain levels.*

THE MACROMINERALS

It is easiest to understand the big seven minerals in terms of the jobs they share. Calcium, phosphorus, and magnesium work together as bone builders; sodium, potassium, and chloride function as electrolytes — salts that dissolve in fluids to form the body's electrical system. Electrolytes maintain the body's fluid level, keep its acid-alkaline balance close to neutral, and are key players in transmitting nerve impulses and contracting muscles. Sulfur is a case of its own. It is present in certain amino acids and helps form lubricants for joints and substances involved in allergic inflammation.

The job descriptions of macrominerals do not, of course, break down quite as neatly as this. Just about all of them have extra duties. The bone builders — calcium, phosphorus, and magnesium — also pitch in as electrolytes, for example.

THE BONE BUILDERS

CALCIUM

P R O F I L E

FUNCTION Builds bone; essential to blood clotting and the structure of cell membranes. As an electrolyte, helps regulate fluid balance and transmit nerve impulses.

ADULT RDA 800 milligrams.

CANDIDATES FOR SUPPLEMENTS Growing children; most adults (both men and women).

DEFICIENCY SYMPTOMS Tingling sensations or stiffness in hands and feet, muscle pain, cramps, spasms, and even convulsions. Retarded growth and fragile, pliable, or deformed bones in children; osteoporosis in adults.

RISK OF TOXICITY Low.

TOXIC EFFECTS Loss of appetite, nausea and vomiting, constipation, weight loss, fever, muscular weakness.

There are close to 3 pounds of calcium in a healthy adult body, and 99 percent of it goes into bones and teeth. Although pregnant women and growing children clearly require more than average amounts of calcium, the need for this mineral is substantial among all adults, for the body is constantly involved in bone building, replacing the entire skeleton once every seven to ten years.

Calcium's stock has been booming these past few years, sparked by fears of osteoporosis, for it now appears that one out of five American women over 65 may have this disease. Osteoporosis ("porous bones") causes bones to deteriorate over time. Without preventive action a woman's bone mass can literally be reduced by half between the ages of 40 and 80. The end result is frequently spontaneous fracture of the hip or vertebrae.

The need for most women to increase their calcium intake to prevent osteoporosis is now evident. But men can have unmet calcium needs as well (and the increasing life expectancy of men may result in more male osteoporosis).

For reasons described in more detail in chapter 21, just getting enough calcium won't guarantee a lifetime of healthy bones. Skeletal strength depends on several factors: vitamin D (from sunlight or diet), hormones like estrogen, dietary phosphorus (you need some, but an excess *blocks* calcium), several trace elements, and exercise. Exercise actually increases the body's ability to retain calcium and helps prevent osteoporosis, while a sedentary lifestyle can directly weaken bone.

But no bone-building program can work if there's not enough calcium in the diet. And calcium is needed to prevent problems other than osteoporosis. There's now some evidence that calcium plays a role in maintaining moderate blood pressure levels, and it may even help prevent colon cancer.

The 1 percent of the body's calcium that does *not* go to bone building has lots of other chores to do. As an electrolyte, it helps to regulate the body's water balance, to transmit nerve impulses, and to maintain muscle tone. Calcium is essential to the blood-clotting process and to the control of several hormones and important enzymes. When the body does not have enough calcium in the bloodstream, it seeks it from the only available source: the bones. When there is more than enough in the blood, the body reverses the process and stores the excess in bone or excretes it in urine.

Most American adults are probably not getting all the calcium they need (800 milligrams per day for adults, 1,200 for adolescents). The daily requirement amounts to a quart of milk or a quarter pound of cheese. There are, to be sure, other dietary sources of calcium — vegetables, dried beans, nuts, eggs — but nothing equal to dairy products. If you are determined to get an adequate amount of calcium from vegetables alone, broccoli is a first-rate source. But you would need to eat 4.5 pounds per day.

Considering our relatively low intake of dairy products and the difficulty we have in absorbing calcium — we use only about one third of our dietary intake — there is a good case for calcium supplements.

Osteoporosis is not the only evidence of calcium deficiency. Indeed, it is just about the last to appear. Low blood calcium levels may cause tingling sensations or stiffness in hands and feet, muscle pains and cramps, and muscle spasms that can develop into convulsions.

In children, lack of calcium will stunt growth. When it does not affect bone size, it may affect bone strength: too little calcium will make bones either brittle and fragile or soft and pliable. And the bone deformities of rickets can be caused by lack of calcium as well as by lack of vitamin D or phosphorus.

In Third World countries, where calcium intake is substantially lower than it is in the United States (and nutritionists believe it is generally too low here), calcium deficiency is one reason children grow at much slower rates than American youngsters do. Still, calcium deficiency is less severe in many of these countries than we might imagine.

First among the mechanisms that compensate for low levels of dietary calcium is the body's response. Because relatively little calcium is consumed, proportionately more is absorbed. Greater exposure to sunlight in tropical and semitropical countries increases production of vitamin D, thus promoting more efficient use of calcium. There are also some unrecognized dietary sources. The eating of clay, a common practice in many parts of Asia, the Middle East, and South America, can provide calcium. But the addition of "stone powder" (calcium carbonate) to rice in Formosa is a more dependable source, as is the calcium hydroxide used in Mexico to soften corn before it is ground into cornmeal.

Calcium is not a particularly toxic mineral, and hypercalcemia (excessive calcium in the blood) is rarely caused by too much calcium in the diet. The body controls the rate of absorption from the intestines to prevent hypercalcemia. The disorder can, however, be caused by prolonged bed rest (during which the body reabsorbs calcium from the bones) or by malfunctioning kidneys, an overactive parathyroid gland (which produces the hormone that stimulates calcium reabsorption), or an excess of vitamin D. Calcium toxicity is marked by loss of appetite, nausea and vomiting, constipation, weight loss, fever, and weakened muscles. Elevated levels of calcium can also cause kidney stones and will interfere with sodium reabsorption, forcing the body to lose sodium and water.

PHOSPHORUS

PROFILE

FUNCTION Builds bone; helps maintain acid-alkaline balance; plays major roles in cell reproduction and the conversion of bodily fuels to energy.

ADULT RDA   800 milligrams.

DEFICIENCY SYMPTOMS   Loss of appetite, weakness and bone pain, plus demineralization of bone and loss of calcium. Prolonged deficiency will lead to bone softening, and extreme deficiency can cause seizures or stroke.

RISK OF TOXICITY Moderate.

TOXIC EFFECTS   Reduced levels of calcium in the blood and diminished bone-building capacity.

There is more phosphorus in the body than any other mineral save calcium, about 1.5 pounds of it, and 80 percent goes into bones and teeth. But phosphorus has lots of other chores to do as well. It is a major force in metabolism. Phosphorus-containing molecules are the fuel cells of the body. They store the energy generated by the burning of bodily fuels, and they can be tapped to provide power for all biological functions.

A number of enzymes and most of the B vitamins will go into action only if phosphorus is on the scene. It helps maintain the acid-alkaline balance, break down and transport fats and fatty acids, and convert carbohydrates into energy. Phosphorus is also an essential component of nucleic acid, so it is involved in cell reproduction and the synthesis of proteins.

A phosphorus deficiency is hard to develop by poor food choice alone, for phosphorus is widely available. It is present in dairy products, along with calcium, and also in meats, fish, grains, nuts, and beans. But deficiencies can be caused by several clinical conditions, including kidney and liver disorders, an inability to metabolize enough vitamin D, and persistent vomiting. The frequent use of antacids containing aluminum can produce phosphorus deficiency by blocking intestinal absorption of the mineral.

Symptoms of phosphorus deficiency include loss of appetite, weakness, and bone pain. Bone will begin to demineralize (as the body seeks to mobilize phosphorus for the bloodstream), and calcium is lost. Shortages of phosphorus in the blood will impede delivery of oxygen, damaging red blood cells and small, cell-like structures called platelets. A severe deficiency can cause seizures and coma, while a low level over an extended period of time will lead to osteomalacia (softening of the bones).

Excess phosphorus reduces the level of calcium in the blood and impedes bone building. Toxic levels can be reached not only through diet but by frequent use of laxatives and enemas that contain phosphorus. It is important to keep in mind that calcium levels fall as phosphorus levels rise, and a life-threatening loss of calcium is possible should the level of phosphorus rise high enough.

MAGNESIUM

PROFILE

FUNCTION   Builds bone, helps regulate heart function, activates enzyme systems, and is involved in the conversion of bodily fuels to energy.

ADULT RDA   Men, 350 milligrams; women, 300 milligrams.

DEFICIENCY SYMPTOMS   Muscle pain, tremors and spasms; vertigo and convulsions; altered heart rhythm, apathy, depression, delirium.

RISK OF TOXICITY   Low.

TOXIC EFFECTS   Depressed respiration and central nervous system function.

Most of us know magnesium best as the nasty-tasting stuff in milk of magnesia or as the magnesium sulfate in Epsom salts. But medical use of the mineral is now extending well beyond such nostalgic medicines and its long-acknowledged role as an anticonvulsant. There is solid evidence today that links a lack of magnesium to heart attacks, and at least one recent study found that injection of magnesium will give some heart attack victims complete relief from pain and prevent any further damage to heart muscle.

Less dramatic — but not to the patients involved — is the use of small doses of magnesium to keep the most common variety of kidney stones from forming. In a study of 149 patients with long histories of kidney stone problems, magnesium was able to reduce stone formation by better than 90 percent. Tests demonstrated that the magnesium was able to flush out excess calcium.

More than half of the magnesium in our bodies goes to bone building. But magnesium has some intensive electrolyte duties as well, including providing ions essential to normal heart function. It also activates a number of enzyme systems, and it is vital to the conversion of glucose, fats, and proteins to energy. Other chores of magnesium include triggering the release of the parathyroid hormone (which controls resorption of calcium from bone) and helping to balance out some of calcium's activities in the body.

Adults and adolescents need less than half as much magnesium as calcium, and younger children need only about a fifth as much. Sources of dietary magnesium include animal protein, vegetables, cereals, and milk. But some of the mineral becomes unavailable in processing, and only about one third of what enters the digestive tract makes it into the bloodstream. The evidence indicates that some Americans aren't getting all the magnesium they need. This is a matter of concern not only because magnesium has vital jobs to perform but also because low levels of magnesium are often matched by low levels of calcium and potassium, since these minerals are found in much the same foods. However, large amounts of calcium in the diet can interrupt absorption of magnesium, just as large amounts of magnesium can inhibit absorption of calcium.

Symptoms of magnesium deficiency develop slowly (since the body will take magnesium from bone to maintain adequate blood levels). When it occurs, it can be caused by diarrhea or steatorrhea (excessive fat in fecal matter), alcoholism, diabetes, kidney damage, or the use of diuretics as well as by poor diet. A liquid protein diet may lead to magnesium deficiency, and serious injury or extensive surgery will deplete body stores. Deficiency shows up as muscle pains and cramps, twitching, tremors and muscle spasms, vertigo and convulsions, all indicators of a lack of neuromuscular regulation and control. Dangerous changes in heart rhythm can result, and so can apathy, depression, and even delirium.

Magnesium's potency is also evident in its toxic effects. The elevated levels of the mineral that can result from kidney failure or an overdose of magnesium salts (an anticonvulsant) may be fatal, causing depression of both the respiratory and central nervous systems, followed by coma and death.

THE ELECTROLYTES

To function as electrolytes, macrominerals form salts that dissolve in fluid into electrically charged ions. The charges these ions carry allow them to maintain the balance of fluids in the body, to control acid-alkaline balance in these fluids, and to play vital roles in the transmission of nerve impulses and contraction of muscles (including the heart). Although all the big seven except sulfur serve as electrolytes, it is easiest to think in terms of an electrolyte group separate from the bone builders: sodium, potassium, and chloride.

To keep the fluid in cells at proper levels, positively and negatively charged electrolytes work together. By the laws of osmosis, the concentration of positive and negative ions must be the same inside the cell and in the blood plasma outside it. Water passes through the cell membrane by itself, but ions can't. So the cell controls the level of ions inside it, using proteins that latch onto ions and either draw them into the cell or carry them out through the membrane. When the concentration of ions is greater in the cell than in the blood, water flows into the cell; when it is greater in the blood, water flows out of the cell.

The body's acid-alkaline balance, determined by the concentration of hydrogen ions in its fluids, is kept carefully within a narrow, slightly alkaline range. If the level becomes too acid or too alkaline, you can't survive. Electrolytes do their bit to control the balance by picking up hydrogen ions from solutions that are too acidic and releasing them into solutions that are too alkaline.

While all electrolytes are involved in the transmission of nerve impulses, the major players are sodium and potassium. Their concentrations inside and outside the cell determine the nerve cell's electric potential and thus its impulse-transmitting capacity. The electrical charges of all the electrolytes — which you can think of as the body's own little batteries — make them indispensable to muscular activity too.

Since the body can neither produce electrolytes nor store them, regulating the supply is a delicate business that is left mostly to the kidneys. They make sure that no more of these minerals leave the body than are absorbed from the intestines. When intake is low or supplies are depleted, the kidneys will reabsorb as much as the body needs to maintain electrolyte balance.

SODIUM

P R O F I L E

FUNCTION   As an electrolyte, helps regulate blood pressure and is necessary for the transmission of nerve impulses; also involved in protein and carbohydrate metabolism.

SAFE AND ADEQUATE INTAKE FOR ADULTS   1,100–3,300 milligrams.

DEFICIENCY SYMPTOMS   *Moderate:* loss of appetite, thirst, vomiting, muscle cramps. *Extreme*: convulsions and coma.

RISK OF TOXICITY   Low.

TOXIC EFFECTS   Dehydration, elevated temperature, vomiting and diarrhea. Lethal doses will cause respiratory depression and circulatory failure.

Sodium chloride, or table salt (the form in which sodium is most often found), was probably the first of all food additives, used both to flavor and to preserve food. Today, sodium has gotten something of a bad name, because of the apparent connection between salt-heavy diets and high blood pressure (see chapter 18). But whatever the risks of excess may be, we can hardly get along without sodium. In addition to those functions it shares with other electrolytes — it provides most of the positively charged ions in the blood — sodium is involved in protein and carbohydrate metabolism.

There is sodium in almost everything we eat, sodium put there by nature and not by food processors. But extra salt is routinely added to canned and frozen vegetables, baked goods, breakfast cereals, and soft drinks, not to mention such salty goodies as corn chips, potato chips, nuts, and pretzels. And there is also the salt we add to food ourselves either in the kitchen or at the table. So a dietary deficiency in our culture is unlikely, except as the result of a self-prescribed sodium-free diet. And even that may not do the trick unless the dieter spurns meat, fish, and dairy products.

Deficiencies, however, can result from diarrhea or kidney disease, the use of diuretics, or heavy sweating. (But it needs to be truly heavy and prolonged; the kidneys can easily handle the sodium loss brought on by one or two sets of tennis on a muggy summer afternoon.) Signs of sodium deficiency include fatigue, loss of appetite and thirst, vomiting, and severe muscle cramps. Extreme sodium loss is life-threatening. It can cause convulsions, collapse of the circulatory system, coma, and death.

Excess sodium in the body, which will build up if you don't drink enough water in hot weather or if your kidneys aren't doing their job, will cause your temperature to rise and your skin to flush. Mucous membranes will become dry and sticky, and you will lose your thirst. True salt poisoning, however, is quite rare, which is all to the good, for it is extremely difficult to treat.

POTASSIUM

PROFILE

FUNCTION   Works with sodium to regulate blood pressure and transmit nerve impulses and with magnesium to regulate heart function; also involved in protein and carbohydrate metabolism.

SAFE AND ADEQUATE INTAKE FOR ADULTS   1,875–5,625 milligrams.

DEFICIENCY SYMPTOMS   Vomiting and diarrhea, loss of appetite, fatigue, apathy, and depression; irregular heartbeat, weakened pulse, falling blood pressure.

RISK OF TOXICITY   Moderate.

TOXIC EFFECTS   Weakened muscles, abnormal heart rhythm, kidney disorders.

Potassium provides most of the positively charged ions *inside* body cells to balance the sodium outside them. So potassium, like sodium, helps regulate blood pressure. Along with magnesium, it is essential to the proper functioning of heart muscle; and like many of its fellow electrolytes, it plays a role in the metabolism of proteins and carbohydrates.

Most healthy men and women get plenty of potassium in their diets, for the mineral is present in all foods except purified fats and sugar. Citrus fruits, bananas, and tomatoes are particularly rich sources, and potassium is readily absorbed from the digestive tract into the bloodstream. However, deficiencies may result from the use of diuretics, heavy sweating, frequent enemas, disorders of the intestinal tract, uncontrolled diabetes, or more rarely from a diet extremely low in calories. Injury and severe burns will cause potassium levels to fall, as will alcoholism and a rare kidney ailment that can be caused by using outdated tetracycline or by eating a large amount of licorice.

Symptoms of early deficiency include vomiting and diarrhea, while severe deficiencies will affect the heart, kidneys, and muscles. These effects will show up in a weakened pulse rate, irregular heartbeat, and falling blood pressure as well as loss of appetite, constipation, fatigue, apathy, and depression. If untreated, potassium deficiency can go on to cause paralysis and fatal heart damage.

Athletes need to be particularly wary of potassium depletion, and other men and women who exercise or do hard physical work in high temperatures should also watch for the signs. Weakness or weariness over an extended period of time may signal the need for more orange juice or bananas. Potassium supplements, however, should be used with caution, for the risks of toxicity are serious indeed. Excess potassium, most often the result of kidney disorders, causes weakened muscles and abnormal heart rhythm. The skin may lose its color and feel cold, while hands and feet will become numb or tingle.

CHLORIDE

PROFILE

FUNCTION Works with sodium and potassium in transmission of nerve impulses; helps blood cells transport carbon dioxide.

SAFE AND ADEQUATE INTAKE FOR ADULTS 1,700–5,100 milligrams.

DEFICIENCY SYMPTOMS Vomiting, diarrhea, sweating, increased alkalinity of body fluids.

RISK OF TOXICITY Low.

TOXIC EFFECTS Difficult to isolate, since they generally occur when there is an excess of sodium or potassium salts.

We get almost all the chloride we use from salt (sodium chloride). Our intake and the likelihood of deficiency are pretty much the same for chloride as for sodium (and the "safe and adequate" levels for both are similar). In the body, chloride ions have a special role in stabilizing the electrical potential of nerve cells and helping blood cells carry carbon dioxide to the lungs. These ions also do heavy duty as buffers, maintaining the acid-alkaline balance.

Chloride deficiency is rare, but it can occur with those conditions that can deplete other electrolytes (vomiting, diarrhea, sweating) or on a severely limited low-sodium diet. A chloride deficiency can make blood and body fluids more alkaline, with dangerous consequences. In 1978 insufficient chloride in one brand of infant formula made thousands of infants seriously ill.

But if a deficiency is dangerous, an excess of chloride is less threatening. Although its elemental gaseous form, chlorine, has been used as a poison gas, chloride itself is toxic only at extremely high levels.

CHAPTER 7

Microminerals: Iron and Other Trace Elements

A FEW YEARS AGO it seemed as though basketball star Bill Walton's career was over. Then under contract to the San Diego Clippers, he had not played regularly for several seasons. X rays of his twice-broken left foot showed a small fracture that stubbornly refused to heal. But they also revealed something else. The condition of the bone looked for all the world like osteoporosis, a disease generally attributed to a lack of calcium and most common among older women.

Yet it wasn't a shortage of calcium that had made Walton's bones so fragile. (Before his first foot injury he had broken several fingers and toes, a cheekbone, a wrist, a leg, and his nose.) Tested for trace elements, his blood showed an absolute zero level of manganese, and levels of zinc and copper at one third normal. What his blood had in abundance was calcium, because his body was dumping back into his bloodstream the calcium it couldn't use to make bone.

Walton's dietary preferences had been well publicized. A vegetarian, he ate plenty of brown rice and green vegetables, varying this diet with little more than one or two cups of milk a day and an occasional piece of fish. The result was levels of manganese and copper too low for his body to produce enough of the reinforcing materials (like the protein collagen) that must be present at bone-building sites before the body can lay down layers of calcium that will hold fast. His diet had also kept Walton's zinc level too low to promote normal healing.

Downing daily doses of supplementary minerals (in a salty concoction Walton called "tiger piss"), the athlete brought his copper and zinc levels up to normal. He also achieved a normal level of calcium in his blood, not the excess seen at first. And even though the level of manganese remained undetectable, his foot healed and he was back on the basketball court within six weeks.

Bill Walton's story makes two important points about trace elements. First, despite their low levels in the body, they are absolutely essential to the functioning of macrominerals like calcium. And, second, the *balance* of different trace elements — with each other and with the macrominerals — is as important as the levels themselves.

Balance is critical because minerals tend to get in each other's way much more frequently than vitamins do. If you take lots of zinc to beef up your immune system, you may well prevent your body from absorbing the copper it needs. And what happens if you're not getting enough copper? Well, one result is anemia, which is usually caused by a lack of iron, not copper. But your body can't use most of the iron it has on hand without the help it gets from copper.

One problem is that trace elements can't easily dissolve in the body's fluids. They become much more soluble, and more usable, when they're attached to molecules of sugars or amino acids. But when there is an excessive amount of any one mineral on hand, it can take over most of the available molecular carriers, making it harder for other minerals to get where they need to go. Essentially, an excess of mineral Y can lead to a functional deficiency of mineral Z, even though there may be plenty of Z in your diet.

For this reason, supplements of single trace elements are rarely prescribed; multimineral supplements are the rule. But to understand their diverse roles, it is important to look at the trace elements one at a time. These elements play four fundamental roles:

1. They are coenzymes for special enzymes, called metalloenzymes, that must link up with metal ions in order to function.

2. They help burn body fuels through chemical oxidation.

3. They help transport oxygen in red blood cells.

4. They form an integral part of the structure of proteins and nucleic acids.

IRON

PROFILE

FUNCTION Essential element in hemoglobin (which carries oxygen in red blood cells) and myoglobin (which does the same in muscle cells).

ADULT RDA Men, 10 milligrams; women, 18 milligrams.

CANDIDATES FOR SUPPLEMENTS All premenopausal women (pregnant women, in particular); infants, children ages 9–13.

DEFICIENCY SYMPTOMS *Marginal deficiency*: reduced physical and intellectual performance, impaired learning in children. *Anemia*: Chronic fatigue, lack of appetite, shortness of breath, cold extremities.

RISK OF TOXICITY   Low.

TOXIC EFFECTS   Liver damage; increased risk of infection; can be fatal.

A lack of adequate iron in the diet is the number one nutritional deficiency in the United States, and iron-deficiency anemia is second only to obesity as the nation's leading nutritional disorder. National surveys have shown that nearly 60 percent of the population isn't getting all the iron it needs, and nine out of ten women fall short of meeting the recommended daily allowance.

Iron is the the most abundant of the trace elements, and the body has — or should have — between one tenth and one fifth of an ounce of iron on hand. We need this much for a number of chores, the most important of which involves transporting and distributing oxygen.

Iron is the vital element in hemoglobin, the molecular container that picks up, transports, and releases oxygen through the bloodstream. Think of red blood cells as container ships filled with hemoglobin. In an adult man there are about 2 pounds of hemoglobin (aside from water, it's the major component of blood), and that's where nearly three quarters of the body's iron is to be found.

Myoglobin, which is much like hemoglobin in form — an essential bit of iron wrapped in protein — operates in muscles, where it shuttles oxygen from hemoglobin in the capillaries to tissue. At tissue cells, myoglobin passes on its oxygen to iron-bearing enzymes that are key players in the process by which cells burn fuel to produce energy. It is iron's roles as the body's chief oxygen handler and in the burning of bodily fuels that makes it the mineral that has concerned us most for the past few thousand years.

Although the body normally has a reserve supply of iron — a protein called ferritin provides storage bins in the liver, spleen, and bone marrow and protects cells from iron overload — reserves are limited. It doesn't take much loss for deficiency to develop, and the primary symptom is iron-deficiency anemia. Loss of hemoglobin diminishes the flow of oxygen through the bloodstream, reducing the ability of muscles and other tissues to generate energy. It causes chronic fatigue, pale skin and lips, cold hands and feet, shortness of breath, lack of appetite, and an all-around slowdown of the body's vital functions.

But does the generally low level of iron consumption in the United States mean there is an epidemic of anemia raging here? Clearly not, although there is far more iron deficiency about than doctors generally recognize. What is important for us to realize is how shortages of iron in

the blood can trouble us long before hemoglobin drops to clinically ane-
mic levels. As experience with schoolchildren, athletes, and others has
shown, you simply cannot feel as good or work as well when iron levels
are low as you can when they are high.

The body understands the value of iron and tries to hang on to all
that it has, recycling iron when it breaks down. Tiny amounts are lost in
hair, nails, sweat, and urine. To lose more, you must bleed, for that is how
most iron leaves the body. The 15–20 milligrams of iron that women lose
when they menstruate amounts to between one half and two thirds of
what is likely to be lost each month in other ways. And the need to
replace menstrual losses raises the iron requirements of women to about
twice that of men.

So how do we get the iron we need? If we eat lots of spinach, we will
become heartily sick of it before we come near getting all the iron we
should have. Green leafy vegetables just don't have enough iron. Using
the broccoli index, you will need to eat 8.5 pounds of broccoli (or more
than 3 pounds of spinach) to make up the recommended intake — and
your digestive tract is likely to expel that much fiber as rapidly as possible.

Meat (organ meats in particular), fish, and poultry are the best of all
possible sources, because they provide the best kind of iron — heme iron.
The body absorbs heme iron about three times as readily as it does the
iron in eggs, grains, and dried beans, and about six times as readily as the
iron in spinach.

But changing fashions in food, many of them based on priorities of
"the new nutrition," have altered the way we eat. Red meat now is
deemed unhealthy by many nutrition-minded young people, and organ
meats never were all that popular in this country. The new cuisine is
lighter, and low-calorie regimens are almost a way of life.

All in all, sources of sufficient iron are neither as common nor as
popular as they once were. True, iron fortification of flour, bread, and
breakfast cereals has increased our access to the mineral from these
sources. Yet fortified products provide most Americans with only about
one quarter of the iron they need.

The iron deficiency problem extends even to cookware. The heavy
iron skillets and pots that provided a rich source of dietary iron to generations of Americans have almost all been replaced by stainless steel. Not
that those old pots were an unmixed blessing; iron cookware occasionally raised iron intake close to toxic levels.

It is fear of toxicity that has prompted some nutritionists to raise
cautions about supplementation, even though iron deficiency is a clear
problem. Still, you would need to consume five to ten times the recommended allowance over an extended period of time to run much risk. And
your digestive tract, which doesn't absorb iron all that readily even in
times of need, is downright reluctant to accept more when body stores
are high. It will block a toxic dose under normal circumstances.

Nevertheless, iron overload does occur occasionally and usually involves damage to the liver plus infection (for bacteria thrive in iron-rich blood). Massive amounts of iron will cause death, and this has happened when small children have swallowed handfuls of iron sulfate pills. A genetic disorder can decrease the blocking action of the digestive tract, allowing the body to accumulate so much iron that the liver and spleen literally rust out. And iron overload can also occur through repeated blood transfusions or as a result of alcoholism.

Several years ago a Los Angeles pathologist, consulting with colleagues in Paris and New York, discovered that alcoholics in all three cities died from cirrhosis of the liver — but only the Los Angeles drinkers had livers heavily loaded with iron. The difference was less a matter of geography than taste and cost, for the alcoholics in Los Angeles favored muscatel wine, which is rich in both sugar and iron. The New York alcoholics preferred whiskey, with neither sugar nor iron, while those in Paris stuck with dry red wine, which has iron but no sugar. It was the combination of iron and sugar (which aids the absorption of iron) that caused the Angeleno alcoholics to build up heavy deposits of iron in their already damaged livers.

COPPER

PROFILE

FUNCTION   Releases iron from the liver; helps convert fats and carbohydrates to energy; helps build bone and maintain nerves and heart muscle.

SAFE AND ADEQUATE INTAKE FOR ADULTS   2–3 milligrams.

CANDIDATES FOR SUPPLEMENTS   Vegetarians and others whose diets contain little red meat.

DEFICIENCY SYMPTOMS   Anemia, cardiovascular aneurysms, and bone disorders (particularly in infants).

RISK OF TOXICITY   Moderate.

TOXIC EFFECTS   Psychological symptoms similar to schizophrenia.

You may be getting all the iron your body needs, but you still risk anemia if you lack an adequate amount of copper. Without enough copper, iron remains stored in the liver, and little goes to make hemoglobin. Other than premature infants, there are few victims of true copper deficiency (like Bill Walton's) in the United States. Still, Americans generally get less copper than they can put to good use, because the best sources — organ meats, shellfish, nuts, and dried beans — aren't all that popular or (except for shellfish) low in calories.

But lower than optimal levels of copper may do more than just reduce your energy and cut back your productivity, for copper is involved in a whole catalog of vital bodily processes. It plays a role in converting both fats and carbohydrates into energy. It is essential to building strong bones and connective tissue. More worrisome is the risk of damage to heart muscle and arteries. There's some evidence now that if you short-change yourself on copper, you raise the risk of heart disease.

Copper is necessary for normal neurological development, and lack of copper can cost you coordination through deterioration of nerve sheathing (which is produced by a copper-bearing enzyme). This is tragically evident in victims of Menkes' disease, a genetic disorder that prevents copper from reaching the central nervous system. Babies born with this disease will usually die before they are two years old. However, similar symptoms have been seen in South America, among children who do *not* have Menkes' disease but whose diets contain extraordinarily little copper. The American diet, while not exactly copper-rich these days, generally provides enough of the mineral to make severe deficiency so rare that it has been seen almost exclusively among early TPN patients on copperless formulas.

Excess copper is equally uncommon but quite toxic. We can see this in victims of another genetic disorder, Wilson's disease, which permits dangerous levels of copper to build up in the body. The results of this copper overload are psychological symptoms indistinguishable from schizophrenia, which clear up when levels of copper are brought down.

ZINC

PROFILE

FUNCTION   Promotes healing and growth; maintains immune function; wide range of metabolic activity.

ADULT RDA   15 milligrams.

CANDIDATES FOR SUPPLEMENTS   The elderly, dieters, alcoholics, pregnant women, infants, and victims of injury, burns, or infections.

DEFICIENCY SYMPTOMS   Loss of appetite and sense of smell; inflamed areas around the mouth, anus, or genitals, or on arms or legs. Apathy, depression, amnesia, or even paranoia. Mental or physical retardation in children will result from substantial, sustained deficiency.

RISK OF TOXICITY   Moderate.

TOXIC EFFECTS   Nausea, bloating, cramps, diarrhea, fever. At exceptionally high doses, bleeding and anemia.

Without enough copper, our bodies can't use their iron. With too much copper, they can't get the zinc they need. Copper and zinc compete to be absorbed from the digestive tract, and if you load up on one, you will tend to block out the other.

These days, with zinc supplements coming into vogue, it would seem that copper would lose out in the competition. But marginal zinc deficiencies seem at least as common as marginal copper deficiencies, and among aging Americans, dieters (both crash and chronic), and alcoholics, zinc deficiency occurs fairly frequently. In addition, there is a special need for zinc during pregnancy, infancy, certain illnesses, and recovery from injury or infection.

Zinc's present popularity is fairly earned. Although there is no reason to believe it will reduce psychological stress, as many supplement marketers imply, zinc does seem capable of giving the immune system a boost, and it plainly promotes the physical development of children (even prior to birth). Zinc is part of some 200 different enzymes that are involved in just about every aspect of metabolism — the synthesis of protein and nucleic acids, the conversion of bodily fuels to energy, the production of antibodies, and the maintenance of skin and bone.

Zinc's role in the formation of DNA and proteins gives the mineral extra importance when the body needs to multiply cells rapidly for healing or growth. According to a British study, low zinc levels in pregnant women appear to slow down fetal growth. In Iran a research team, headed by Dr. A. S. Prasad of Wayne State University, found dwarfism and retarded genital development among teenage boys could be overcome by zinc supplements.

The zinc deficiency in Iran was caused by a diet that included both clay (eaten in many parts of the world; discussed in chapter 8) and lots of unleavened whole grain bread. Nutritious as whole grain products may be — and they are good sources of zinc — they also contain a great deal of fiber, which can bind up trace minerals and move them down and out of the intestinal tract before they can be absorbed. The particular whole grains eaten by the Iranian teenagers also contained heavy concentrations of phytic acid, which disrupts absorption of zinc.

As to what zinc can do for your immune system, the evidence is piling up fast. Using no more than recommended amounts of zinc, researchers at the University of California, San Diego, were able to raise both levels of zinc and T cells (the immune system's attack force) in the blood of aging research subjects.

A study at the University of Colorado's medical school in Denver found that adolescents with less zinc than they needed in their bloodstreams lost not only a measure of immunity but a good deal of their appetite as well. Zinc, it appears, plays a substantial role in maintaining our senses of smell and taste. Lose these and appetite goes. Lose appetite and you eat less, further reducing the amount of zinc in your body and your immune response.

But while zinc supplements may boost appetite and immunity, they also pose some dangers. In early studies of zinc's impact on the immune responses of elderly people, megadoses produced substantial side effects. Although zinc was then considered one of the least toxic trace elements, it has recently been shown to cause nausea, bloating, cramps, diarrhea, and fever at doses well below 10 times recommended levels. More substantial overdoses can bring about bleeding and may eventually lead to anemia.

Zinc deficiency is not uncommon in the United States, but nutritionists can't tell for sure just how widespread it is. Although just about every food has some zinc in it, the best sources are animal foods and whole grains. Absorption from animal foods, however, is far better than from any vegetable source.

MANGANESE

PROFILE

FUNCTION   Works with copper and zinc to build bone. Wide range of metabolic functions. Maintains nerves and pancreas. Aids muscle function.

SAFE AND ADEQUATE INTAKE FOR ADULTS   2.5–5.0 milligrams.

CANDIDATES FOR SUPPLEMENTS   Vegetarians and others whose diets contain little red meat.

DEFICIENCY SYMPTOMS   Weak bones, osteoporosis.

RISK OF TOXICITY   Low.

TOXIC EFFECTS   Neurological disorders.

An industrious mineral, manganese works with a good many enzymes, rearranging carbohydrates, synthesizing fats, converting glucose to energy, forming nerve cells, maintaining the pancreas, and helping muscles to do their jobs. It also gets together with copper and zinc for bone-building purposes, and persons with poor bone metabolism may have low levels of all three minerals in their blood.

Now, though, there is new evidence that a lack of manganese may pose a special risk to bone. Following their experience with basketball star Bill Walton, who had virtually no manganese in his blood, researchers at the University of California, San Diego, began a series of experiments with manganese. Studies soon showed that rats fed a low-manganese diet developed porous bones. Then a study of 28 women — half with osteoporosis and half without — found the single greatest difference in their blood samples was their manganese levels. Women with osteoporosis had just *one quarter* the manganese of women without the disease.

Studies of college women now suggest that many may get significantly less manganese than the recommended amount. And if they take calcium supplements without adding extra manganese, the calcium may block enough manganese to drop blood levels of manganese even lower.

It's hard to get enough manganese from sources other than red meat, even though this mineral is present in most fruits, vegetables, and grains. Recent research by Dr. Constance Kies at the University of Nebraska has shown that manganese from nonanimal sources is rarely even half as absorbable as manganese from red meat and often much less absorbable than that.

Since it may eventually prove beneficial for some people to take manganese supplements, it is encouraging to note that manganese toxicity is rare. Still, it can occur if intake is great enough, and Chilean miners, who literally inhale manganese, have developed severe neurological disorders resembling Parkinson's disease.

IODINE

PROFILE

FUNCTION   Helps the thyroid to regulate basal metabolism.

ADULT RDA   150 milligrams.

CANDIDATES FOR SUPPLEMENTS   Persons who do not use iodized salt (particularly pregnant women and growing children).

DEFICIENCY SYMPTOMS   Goiter (enlarged thyroid gland) and cretinism among offspring of iodine-deficient mothers.

RISK OF TOXICITY   Low.

TOXIC EFFECTS   Disrupts thyroid function.

A single-purpose mineral as far as the body is concerned, iodine has but one job to do. It makes up part of the thyroid hormones that are the main regulators of basal metabolism, setting the rate at which basic bodily systems function. When adequate iodine is missing, the thyroid gland becomes enlarged, bulging out from the neck in a distinctive protuberance called a goiter.

The Chinese were treating goiters with seaweed and burnt sponges about 5,000 years ago. But although a Swiss doctor, J. R. Coindet, suggested iodine was the answer in 1820, the medical community didn't get around to testing his theory until 1917. The research then showed that both humans and animals were far less likely to develop goiters if they lived near the ocean, where the soil held more iodine and where seafood was eaten more frequently.

Other dietary factors also affect goiter risk. Early in this century goiter was common in inland areas of the United States (particularly through the Great Lakes Basin and the Northwest) — but not just because of low-iodine soil and little seafood. Diets in these inland areas of the country included large amounts of cauliflower, broccoli, and cabbage, and these related vegetables contain organic molecules that inhibit the thyroid's ability to take up iodine. Either too many of these inhibitors or too little iodine can cause goiter, but the risk is greatest when diets combine both factors.

After the iodine-goiter connection was established, many countries required table salt to be fortified with iodine. Although the United States didn't legislate such a requirement, iodized salt is widely available here. Today, goiters have pretty much disappeared wherever salt is iodized. But they still afflict some 200 million people throughout the world — and not only in Third World countries.

An excess of iodine appears able to disrupt thyroid function just as a deficiency can. Both clinical evidence and animal studies have shown that toxic levels of iodine will produce goiters.

FLUORIDE

PROFILE

FUNCTION Builds teeth and bones.

SAFE AND ADEQUATE INTAKE FOR ADULTS 1.5–4.0 milligrams.

CANDIDATES FOR SUPPLEMENTS Pregnant women, children, and victims of osteoporosis.

DEFICIENCY SYMPTOMS Dental cavities and weakened bones.

RISK OF TOXICITY Moderate.

TOXIC EFFECTS Tooth discoloration. At higher doses, bone spurs and possible deformities.

Fluoride is probably best known because of the controversy about its addition to public water supplies. Ever since 1950, when the U.S. Public Health Service endorsed a national program of controlled water fluoridation — fortifying local water supplies with fluoride at one part per million — the debate has raged over how much risk is involved.

By now, one thing is clear. Fluoridation has dramatically reduced tooth decay in this country. But then, no one ever questioned fluoride's ability to strengthen teeth and possibly bones as well.

What has been in question is whether we need as much fluoride as many of us are now getting. Just about every brand of toothpaste now comes fortified with fluoride, and more fluoride gets into our food through fluoridated water. Nevertheless, fluorosis — yellow or brown pits and patches on teeth — is seen only in areas where water contains naturally high concentrations of fluoride.

Where the water *is* naturally rich in fluoride, however, doctors picked up the first clues to fluoride's use in combating osteoporosis. Indeed, studies from Finland have shown that even at the recommended level for fortification — one part per million — fluoride can reduce the incidence of osteoporosis among postmenopausal women by 50 percent.

OTHER ESSENTIAL TRACE ELEMENTS

Chromium

It's not surprising that diabeteslike symptoms appear when chromium is missing, for one job this mineral does is to make body cells more sensitive to insulin. It is also involved in regulating the synthesis of fatty acids and cholesterol in the liver and the digestion of protein in the intestines. Deficiency symptoms include increased levels of fatty acids and cholesterol in the bloodstream, poor utilization of glucose, and possible degeneration of nerves.

Dietary chromium is most available in yeast, wine, meat, and beer. But there's a chance you can get a bit from stainless steel pots if you cook acid foods (like tomatoes or citrus fruit) that will release and absorb some of the chromium in the alloy.

Selenium

Like vitamin E, selenium is best known for destroying free radicals, as part of an enzyme that protects cell membrane in the liver, heart, kidneys, and lungs. Good sources include fish, whole grains (particularly wheat), and just about anything else grown in selenium-rich soil. Deficiency, which is almost nonexistent in the United States, shows up as heart disease (Keshan disease), but there is considerable speculation about links between selenium deficiency and such other diseases as atherosclerosis, hypertension, muscular dystrophy, cystic fibrosis, alcoholic cirrhosis, and cancer. The case for a cancer connection is a strong one (see chapter 19).

Although excessive selenium consumption is as rare as selenium deficiency in the United States, we got a good idea of how dangerous selenium can be before the 1930s, when it became clear that selenium-laden grass was toxic. Animals that grazed on it often were struck by the blind staggers: they became stiff and lame, paralyzed and blind, and ultimately died.

Molybdenum

It is difficult for healthy men and women eating any kind of varied diet to miss out on an adequate supply of molybdenum, for the mineral is present in many different foods. However, in 1981, a surgical patient on a TPN formula rich in sulfur-containing amino acids but lacking molybdenum developed rapid heartbeat and breathing, night blindness, headaches, mental disturbance, nausea, and vomiting. Adding molybdenum to his TPN bag relieved the symptoms, for his body was then able to produce the molybdenum-containing enzymes needed to deal with the amino acids he was getting.

For most of us, however, too much molybdenum is probably a greater danger than too little, for it will deprive our bodies of copper. In Keshan, too, researchers suggested that the outbreak of heart disease there was connected to an overabundance of molybdenum in the soil as well as to a shortage of selenium.

Cobalt

Only the cobalt in vitamin B_{12} is of nutritional use. But it must be absorbed as part of B_{12}. Cobalt supplements, therefore, are valueless and can be harmful. Overdoing cobalt may result in goiter as well as in overstimulation of bone marrow and a buildup of hemoglobin.

TRACE ELEMENTS YET TO BE PROVEN ESSENTIAL FOR HUMANS

These four trace elements — nickel, vanadium, silicon, and arsenic — are considered essential on the basis of animal experiments. Human need for them has yet to be demonstrated. However, we should bear in mind that these minerals are present in our bodies and quite likely to be doing whatever it is they do in animal bodies. All that remains to be proved is that we could not get along without them.

Chickens were the first to reveal a need for **nickel**; its absence changed the shape and color of their legs. Subsequently, other animals showed that they too had to have the enzymes that nickel is known to activate.

Deprived of **vanadium**, rats suffer arrested growth and skin disorders, loss of hair and muscle tone. But far more compelling, in terms of human needs, is the relatively recent discovery of this mineral's involvement in regulating sodium in body cells. This has raised the possibility of using vanadium clinically to control such conditions as edema and hypertension.

Silicon is an essential bone builder, at least for animals. But we too have silicon in our bones, and the heaviest concentrations are found where new bone is being formed. This would seem to indicate a role for silicon in the formation of connective tissue and bone mineralization.

There's little question about the toxicity of **arsenic** — that is what it is best known for. What Dr. Klaus Schwarz showed was that without arsenic the normal growth of rats slowed down, their coats grew rough, and their spleens became enlarged. Pigs and chickens too seem to need the deadly mineral. And the severity of arsenic deficiency is connected to levels of zinc and other minerals in the body.

PART III

ALL ABOUT EATING

CHAPTER 8

Getting Nutrients out of Food

F EW OF US MUST TAKE our nutrients straight, via the TPN bag, and not many others would opt for such a direct source of sustenance. In spite of inconvenience and risk we are content to resupply our bodies through the medium of food, because eating meets more than nutritional needs. It affords us the pleasures of taste and bodily contentment, enhances sociability and sexuality, and provides a basis for most of the ritual in our daily lives.

But what we eat is not simply a matter of what our bodies need. We don't leap out of bed in the morning and declare, "Hey, wow, let's get some glucose!" (even though our glucose reserves are likely to be bottoming out after a full night's sleep). Nor do we decide during the course of the day that what we'd really fancy for dinner is a mixed batch of amino acids garnished with an odd lot of micronutrients (pile on the B vitamins, calcium, and iron, but hold the selenium and zinc).

The specific hungers and cravings we have are for the likes of strawberries or tomatoes, rib eye steaks or poached salmon, for pizza, pasta or cold sesame noodles, ice cream or banana cream pie. These reflect nutritional needs — when they do at all — in only the most general ways. But they say a great deal more about our foodstyle (how, where, and when we eat), our heritage, upbringing, income, and state of mind. They also speak volumes about our culture. As individuals, we may have favorite foods, but the range of our choices is culturally determined.

WHAT IS FOOD?

Food is what society says it is. Although that definition is an expanding one in the United States and most other industrialized nations

99

today, it has traditionally served to limit individual choice. Every culture has certain plant or animal products that it recognizes as food and others that it does not.

This may be less a matter of societal sensibilities than of survival, for food is dangerous stuff. Plants protect themselves, sometimes at human expense. Most fruits and vegetables contain natural insecticides, and some have toxins potent enough to discourage animals (including people) from making a meal of them. Through trial and error, individual cultures developed catalogs of what was safe and sensible to eat and strong prohibitions against consuming what was not considered safe or sensible fare.

But cultural sanctions and restrictions have reflected more than just health and safety concerns. They are based on economic and ecological considerations as well.

Both the Muslim and the Jewish traditions, for example, bar pork from the list of edible foodstuffs, but not because of any early fears of trichinosis. For desert peoples, this prohibition was simply a sensible economic measure. Pigs, after all, must be fed on fruits and grains, which are hard to come by in arid regions and which humans also enjoy. Multi-stomached ruminants, however, like cows, sheep, and goats, can make do on the scratchy desert brush that humans are unable to digest. So a taboo against eating pork was a way of ensuring that Muslims and Jews made the most of the limited resources of the desert.

Access to a great variety of foodstuffs, a rich ethnic mixture, and sophisticated marketing techniques have made the list of culturally acceptable foods in the United States a lengthy one indeed. Even so, insects have yet to win a place on our edibles list. But a shortage of other available protein in many parts of Africa has made locusts and termites dietary staples there. For the same reason, nourishing stews of dog meat, which most Americans would find even harder to get down than insects, have been adding variety and protein to Far Eastern menus for centuries.

Cultural variations exist within nations as well as among nations. The eating of clay, for example — a practice known as pica or geophagy — is widespread in Asia, the Middle East, and parts of South America. But it is also practiced in some rural areas of the southern United States, where baked clay, flavored with salt and vinegar, is considered something of a delicacy. In Africa a variety of dirts, including sand, are culturally defined as food.

Anthropologists and nutritionists aren't at all sure why many clay eaters have adopted the practice, but dirt and clay could well supply missing minerals like calcium for some of these peoples (although it does not appear to serve any nutritional function at all in the American South). Clay can help relieve nausea and diarrhea. It allows Andean Indians to add wild potatoes — most of them highly toxic — to their food supply. The Indians claim a dip made from clay and a mustardlike herb will counter the potato's bitter taste (it appears to relieve the resulting gastrointestinal distress as well).

It would be wrong to assume that society always knows best. The folklore upon which cultural perceptions of food are based reflects centuries of experience and plenty of common sense. Nevertheless, it perpetuates attitudes and beliefs that may be dead wrong and even dangerous. Clay eating in Turkey, Egypt, and several other Middle Eastern countries causes a good deal of anemia, retardation, and delayed sexual maturity, for the nature of some clays found in these lands prevents proper absorption of iron and zinc. In parts of central Mexico, southeast Asia, and Africa, people who live near coastal or inland waters, including the Nile River, refuse to eat fish. Yet their diets often lack sufficient protein, a problem that fish would clearly relieve.

For centuries almost no one dared to eat tomatoes. Discovered by Spanish explorers in Mexico and Peru, the "love apple," as it was then called, was brought to Europe and became a popular ornamental plant there. Not until the start of the nineteenth century did tomatoes begin finding their way into salads and sauces. Before that time, they were generally considered poisonous (which is not quite as ridiculous as it may seem, for tomatoes belong to the deadly nightshade family).

INSTINCT AND APPETITE

Society clearly has a heavy hand in determining what we eat, but natural tastes and instincts also play a role. Humans with size, shape, and capacities pretty much like ours have been feeding themselves off what the earth provides for more than a million years. Only in the past 10,000 years, since agriculture began, have we even attempted to get our food supply under any kind of control.

Before then, we were hunter-gatherers, and our bodies evolved by adapting characteristics that would make us better hunter-gatherers, better able to live on the hunting-gathering diet, and better able to survive on such undependable sources of nutrients. That's one reason we find it so difficult to get our bodies to part with fat; evolution has given us stable fat stores as famine insurance.

We have a good idea of what our primordial hunting-gathering ancestors ate. Fossil remains of *their* primate forebears (dating back 8–10 million years) show that the teeth of early prehumans, who probably resembled the chimpanzees of today, had pits and scratches, indicating a diet made up mostly of fruit. Later prehumans, whose remains have been found in East Africa, at Olduvai Gorge and Koobi Fora, had become old hands at hunting and hacking up meat. Markings on large animal bones at these sites reveal a well-developed capacity to butcher animals and skin them.

In Paleolithic times, according to anthropologists at Emory University, Neanderthal and Cro-Magnon people were living on a diet that was one fifth to one half pure protein, with no grains or dairy products. Nevertheless, their meat had little more than one tenth the fat ours does, so there were fewer calories to the pound. Our Paleolithic ancestors may have had to forage extensively, but they managed to find a greater variety and consume a greater amount of vegetables than we do. Their vitamin intake (particularly of vitamin C) was generally much higher than ours. Despite a lack of dairy foods, they somehow managed to get considerably more calcium than we do, all of it from vegetable sources.

Still, the Neanderthal and Cro-Magnon lean-meat diet was probably far from ideal. It lacked grains or sugar; carbohydrates were hard to come by, and the low level of fat in the diet left only protein as the main source of calories. This meant that amino acids, which might otherwise go to build bodily protein and beef up muscles, had to be sacrificed for energy.

Faced with the same dietary problem today, the earth's surviving hunter-gatherers recognize the value of fat. They depend on the flesh of free-ranging herbivores, which contains only one seventh or one eighth the fat of domesticated animals. In lean times they may refuse to eat certain parts of the animals they kill — or even spurn whole animals — because the meat is so lean it would force their bodies to burn protein. For example, Australian Pitjandjara, who check the tails of slain kangaroos for signs of body fat, will abandon a carcass to rot rather than risk relying too heavily on lean meat.

In developed countries like the United States, of course, the problem is not getting too little fat but getting too much. Beef and other meat animals are routinely readied for slaughter by fattening them on grains, soybeans, fishmeal, and the like. Until recently, well-marbled cuts were the most popular — not because the extra calories were needed but because fatty foods simply taste better. Fats are the major carriers of flavor and aroma in food, which is a more likely reason for their popularity than any instinct inherited from our fat-starved ancestors.

What we have inherited from these hunter-gatherer forebears, however, are innate tastes for plenty of sweets and somewhat less salt, and for variety. Infants come into this world with a well-developed sweet tooth (as fetuses, they will consume amniotic fluid more rapidly if it has been sweetened with glucose). As strongly as they crave what's sweet, infants scorn what's bitter, and these preformed tastes are reasonable results of natural selection.

When humans were beginners at hunting and gathering, a preference for what was sweet and a reluctance to eat anything bitter were potent survival characteristics. By seeking the sweeter-tasting parts of plants, our ancestors treated themselves to the richest sources of energy. By avoiding what was bitter, they tended to pass up what was most likely to poison them.

Although infants are pretty indifferent to salt when they are born, they do begin showing a preference for moderately salted foods after about four months. A taste for salt appears to follow postnatal development of the nervous system. But instinct offers few clues as to why so many children subsequently acquire what amounts to a salt tolerance and crave the heavy doses that flavor most pretzels, chips, and other salty snack foods. At that level, a taste for salt seems to result from repeated exposure to larger and larger doses.

If the taste for salt is largely acquired, though, it may be possible to unlearn it, as many people prone to hypertension try to do. Studies at the Monell Chemical Senses Center in Philadelphia show that desired amounts of salt can be reduced by consistently and gradually decreasing the amounts in food. Research at the University of California, Davis, and the University of Minnesota have demonstrated taste changes within three months of sodium restriction.

The most valuable dietary instinct we have inherited is probably the innate desire for variety. And the instinct is still a strong one. At Johns Hopkins University's medical school in Baltimore, psychologist Barbara Rolls feeds volunteers different flavored test foods, checking their preferences and measuring their consumption. Her research reveals that we stop eating not when we are full but when we are bored. We will quit a monotonous menu much sooner than a varied one. Given nutritious foods to choose from, says Rolls, "people will, within a given meal, seek a healthy variety."

What's true of the individual is generally true of cultures. Even peoples with extremely restricted sources of food have been able to create diets of considerable variety. Among surviving hunter-gatherer cultures are the !Kung of southern Africa's Kalahari desert. (The ! represents a clicking sound in their language.) These Bushmen have few animals to hunt and so make do with little meat. What they consume are lots of mongongo, a nut the desert provides in abundance, plus more than a hundred different kinds of edible plants. While their diet is low in calories, it does provide all the nutritional essentials, and those !Kung who escape injury often live to a considerable age.

Humans are not unique in seeking dietary variety. So do animals. In fact, they do better than we do. Our taste for variety does not automatically lead us to the nutrients we need. But when laboratory rats pick and choose their food, they show an uncanny ability to select what serves their bodies best. Rats have been deprived of a specific amino acid and then offered a dozen different chemical solutions, identical in all ways save that the amino acid they lack is present in only one. The rats tend to pick the right solution. Not so the human subjects of Rolls's experiments.

Rolls had expected "that people would select their foods by their nutritional composition." "But," as she explains, "within a meal, we haven't seen this at all—the sensory effect predominates." People choose food by taste and not by nutritional content.

While Rolls's research hasn't proved that humans necessarily lack an instinctual sense of their nutritional needs, it does indicate that such an instinct doesn't automatically come into play under normal circumstances. About the only nutrient we invariably seem to self-regulate accurately is water (although, to slake our thirst we may choose to take our water in any number of forms — from milk and fruit juice to beer, wine, coffee, tea, colas, and other carbonated beverages).

According to Rolls, children seem more attuned than adults to what their bodies need. Left to make selections for themselves, they will generally pick out what's best for them as long as they are restricted to choosing among wholesome foods. In a famous study at Columbia University during the late 1920s and early 1930s, pediatrician Clara Davis showed how infants who had never tasted solid food before would choose a balanced diet on their own. Offered a dozen different foods at each meal (a total of 34 varieties over the course of the experiment), the babies soon established eating patterns that provided them, over time, with the nutrients they needed.

What the study did not reveal was the strength of this instinctive preference for a healthful variety, since all the foods offered the infants were natural, unseasoned, and unsweetened. So nutritionists generally put little faith in the innate ability of modern men and women to choose what's best for them, particularly in cultures like ours, where there are available so many tasty food choices with minimal nutrient density.

MORE CHOICE, WORSE CHOICES

Limited access to essential nutrients has tragic consequences for the peoples of many modern Third World nations. But in industrialized countries, nutritional problems are more likely to result from an expanding choice of foods than from a restricted one.

The !Kung Bushmen, limited by their environment to low-fat, low-calorie, nutrient-rich foods, show few signs of heart disease. This is true of many peoples whose diets contain relatively low levels of fat (we'll look at the reasons for this in chapter 17). The heavy carbohydrate diets of less affluent societies seem to pay off by preventing the diseases of civilization.

The great variety of human diets — the range of ways in which people meet their basic nutritional needs — has given scientists a natural experiment in the relation of diet to health. By comparing eating habits in different cultures, they've been able to measure the impact on health that results from an oversupply of specific nutrients, as well as from an undersupply.

Ancel Keys, professor emeritus at the University of Minnesota's School of Public Health (the man who developed K rations for American soldiers during World War II), began his pioneering study of diet and heart disease by looking at what Italians were eating at the start of the 1950s. He found that the cuisine of Naples then ran to more pasta, bread, vegetables, and fruit than the fare of northern Italy did. Southern Italians ate much less butter and nowhere near as much meat as their northern countrymen, and they dined on fish twice as often.

Keys then compared the health of police officers and fire fighters in the Sardinian port of Cagliari, where diets were close to Neapolitan, with the health of fellow public safety workers in Bologna, where dairy products were far more frequently used and the richest food in Italy was to be found. The difference, Keys discovered, "was like night and day." The Sardinians were in much better shape.

Equally effective in keeping down the risk of heart disease was the postwar Japanese diet, also low in fat though high in protein. While it featured little meat, it provided plenty of fish and soybean products like tofu and miso, along with vegetables, rice, and noodles. The drawback of the Japanese diet was its dependence on lots of salty, smoked, and pickled products, which raised risks of stroke and stomach cancer.

Foodstyle has changed dramatically in Japan during the past few decades. The good news is diminished consumption of salted, smoked, and pickled products, the need for which was reduced as refrigerators appeared in more Japanese homes. Today, just about every home has a refrigerator (only one in ten had one in 1960).

But one result of refrigeration has been to double the Japanese consumption of dairy products, and that's a mixed blessing. Although dairy products have given the Japanese needed calcium, they've also helped raise the level of fat in the Japanese diet. While the overall rise in fat intake hasn't yet reached levels that would increase the incidence of heart disease, it seems inevitable that this will occur. Japanese teenagers, who favor Western-style fried chicken and french fries, now come close to matching the heavy fat consumption of their American counterparts.

Affluence is not necessarily nutritionally beneficial. As nations become richer, food choice expands. Grains and beans give way to animal proteins, to more beef and butter, as they did in the United States over the past century and in Japan over the past few decades. Among individuals as well as nations, rising income seems to correlate with diets heavier in animal proteins. In Jamaica, wheat flour ranks as the primary source of protein for the poorest quarter of the population, among whom chicken ranks tenth and beef thirteenth. For the richest quarter of the Jamaican population, it is beef that ranks first as a protein source, with chicken second. Wheat flour is down in seventh place for the well-to-do.

KNOWING WHAT YOU NEED

If we cannot trust to instinct or taste to ensure that our diets include everything our bodies need, and if a greater range of food choices only gives us more opportunity to make unhealthful decisions, how can we be sure that what we eat supplies us with enough essential nutrients and not too many calories or too much fat? Clearly, we need guidelines and must learn how to use them.

This should be simple enough to do, since there is no shortage of nutritional guidance today. Bookstores and paperback racks are loaded with the latest dietary shortcuts to slimmer, trimmer bodies, greater energy reserves, more powerful immune systems, and any number of manifestations of fitness and health. The trouble is that many recent dietary plans — cashing in on rising nutritional awareness — are based less on research than on unproved theories. Most are fanciful and some are downright dangerous.

There is, however, a reasonable basis for determining adequate nutritional intake in the Recommended Dietary Allowances (RDAs) that the National Research Council of the National Academy of Sciences has issued every five years or so since 1943 (see Appendix Table A1). These include recommended amounts of nutrients for infants, children, and grown men and women of various ages.

To set these standards, committees of nutritionists have determined average requirements for protein, vitamins, and minerals and added about 30 percent, ensuring statistically that what the RDAs recommend is adequate for at least 97.5 percent of the population. For energy (or calories), the committees have given a range that covers the needs of almost all people (see Appendix Table A3).

From the RDAs, the Food and Drug Administration formulates its Recommended *Daily* Allowances, which give a single standard for each nutrient. They are meant to be adequate for anyone, of any age and either sex. (To avoid confusion with the Research Council's RDAs, these are usually called U.S. RDAs.)

It is the U.S. RDAs that provide the basis for reporting the nutritional content of packaged food products (see "How to Read a Label: Fake and Fortified Foods," page 107). Any food processor who fortifies a product or makes a specific nutritional claim for that product must list on the label the percentage of added or claimed micronutrients in each serving as well as the number of calories per serving and the amount of protein, carbohydrate, fat, and sodium.

A new set of RDAs was expected from the Research Council in 1985, and a Committee on Dietary Allowances had prepared recommendations to replace the 1980 set. But the 1985 edition never made it to the printer. A number of changes proposed by the committee, including reduced allowances for vitamins C and A, proved unacceptable to the Research Council's Food and Nutrition Board, whose job it is to review revisions of the RDAs. The dispute appears to have been based as much on fears of how the revised RDAs might be used as it was on any basic disagreement over what Americans now require in the way of nutrients. If the RDAs for certain nutrients were lowered (as the committee proposed), funding for such federal efforts as the food stamp and school lunch programs might be reduced.

The scientific and political debate and the delay in getting a new set of RDAs into print don't really affect most of us very much. Even in their 1980 version, the RDAs provide a sound basis for individual men and women to plan balanced diets. It is useful, however, to bear in mind that the RDAs were designed not for individual use but as nutritional standards for institutions (schools, hospitals, military installations).

Somewhat less useful are the Dietary Guidelines for Americans put out by the Department of Agriculture and the Department of Health and Human Services. These are no more than the title says; they are guidelines. What they provide is a sound approach to diet-making: encouraging us to consume a variety of foods and enough starch and fiber, suggest-

HOW TO READ A LABEL: FAKE AND FORTIFIED FOODS

The food tables in this chapter and in the Appendix can help you choose a diet that provides high nutrient value without excessive calories. But when you're buying processed foods, the nutritional content may not always be what you'd expect. Some foods are missing nutrients you might think they would have. Certain artificial cheese spreads, for example, may contain less calcium, zinc, vitamin A, and B vitamins than real cheese does. Food labels can tell you what is really in a processed food — if you know how to read them.

A "light" label tells you nothing specific about the calorie content of a food. But by FDA regulation a product marked "low-calorie" can have no more than 40 calories per serving. A "reduced-calorie" food must have one third fewer calories than the standard form of that food would.

Most products (except for condiments, canned vegetables, milk, margarine, and a few others) carry a list of ingredients. Ingredients are listed in order of their weight, from most to least. Although specific amounts of each are not given, the order in which the ingredients appear can tell you a lot — particularly if a product is adulterated with inexpensive fillers. In imitation cheese, for example, casein (a milk protein) is a main ingredient; in real cheese the first listed ingredient is cheese or milk. Processed meats may use soybean or vegetable protein as a meat substitute. And fruit juice is often diluted with water and sugar. (Sugar is added to food in many different forms: corn syrup and sweeteners, maple syrup, fructose, dextrose, sucrose, and honey.)

If a product carries any nutritional claims on the label, the FDA requires its manufacturer to add a more precise listing of nutritional information. Manufacturers may also include such a listing voluntarily — more than half of all packaged foods now carry it. The list typically includes calories and grams of fat, protein, and carbohydrate. (To translate these grams to calories, multiply fat grams by 9, protein and carbohydrate grams by 4.) Also usually listed are levels of sodium and certain micronutrients as percentages of the U.S. RDAs, in actual milligram amounts, or both.

ing we maintain appropriate weight, and urging us to avoid too much saturated fat, cholesterol, sugar, sodium, and alcohol.

THE SEARCH FOR VARIETY

As nutritional scientists have been telling us for years, variety is the key to sound nutrition. Not too long ago, schoolchildren and most other Americans were urged to seek a healthful dietary variety by eating several servings every day from each of the "basic four" food groups. From the milk group, where each serving provided as much calcium as a cup of milk or yogurt, children were expected to get three daily servings, adolescents four, and adults two. It was two servings per day for everyone from the meat group (each featuring 2 ounces of lean meat, fish, or poultry or the equivalent in eggs, cheese, beans, peas, nuts or peanut butter). Four servings per day was the ration for the fruit and vegetable group (at least one a first-rate source of vitamin C and another a top source of vitamin A). And four servings was also the daily grain group requirement (each consisting of a slice of whole grain or enriched bread, a cup of dry cereal, or half a cup of rice, pasta, grits, or cooked cereal).

All in all, the "basic four" formulation is still a reasonable way to organize a nutritionally balanced diet. But it has the shortcoming of all oversimplified diet formulas: it assumes that if just a few of the key nutrients are consciously covered, variety will attend to the rest. So it is possible to follow the "basic four" plan and still leave yourself short on nutrients like vitamin B_{12} and iodine.

The real problem with the "basic four" plan, however, is that not too many people eat basic four meals anymore. The lifestyle of Americans has changed significantly since the notion of four basic food groups was introduced, and foodstyle has changed with it. Fewer of us are now part of traditional families that eat two or three home-cooked meals each day. More of us depend upon fast foods and frozen dinners, regularly dine on Chinese, Japanese, Mexican, or Italian cuisines, or choose (for any of a number of reasons) to restrict calories or fats or the amount of red meat we eat.

To help ensure that—no matter what your foodstyle—you can track your access to all the essential nutrients, the tables on pages 113–116 provide an overview of nutrient content and density and a guide to the information you will find in the food tables in the Appendix. This is basic information for meeting your dietary needs from a variety of food sources. However, there are a few other points about the complicated business of getting nutrients out of food that you must also bear in mind.

First, consider just what is in food. There is water, our primary nutrient, which makes up better than half the weight of food. (Fruits and vegetables are 80 to 90 percent water.) Then, there are fats, proteins, carbohydrates, and the various vitamins and minerals.

But there is more in food than nutrients alone. There are non-nutritive substances that give food most of its color and flavor, as well as potentially toxic substances, small amounts of which are present in almost all natural foods. And there is also the "packing" of plant foods, the dietary fiber that our grandparents used to call roughage.

Fiber is defined as nondigestible complex carbohydrate and comes in two basic forms, soluble and insoluble. Bran, for example, is a prime source of cellulose, one of the insoluble fibers that move along the digestive tract collecting water and giving waste the bulk it needs to pass rapidly through the colon. (This kind of fiber can prevent constipation and quite possibly reduce the risk of colon cancer and diverticulosis as well). Soluble fibers, found in oats, barley, dried beans, and some fruits and vegetables, help control blood sugar levels and the amount of cholesterol that reaches the bloodstream. (See "The Different Kinds of Fiber," page 110.)

Finally, you should be aware that even average men and women are decidedly unaverage in a good many ways. Each of us has a unique set of nutritional needs, the result of heredity, lifestyle, foodstyle, age, sex, the demands we make on our bodies, and the demands we do not make on them. Subsequent chapters will deal with predictable variations from average dietary requirements; with special nutritional needs during pregnancy, infancy, adolescence, and later life; and with diet patterns that can lower the risk of disease.

BUILDING A BASELINE DIET

If you have been keeping a food diary and tracking your intake of nutrients (as described in chapter 2), you should know how close you come to getting an adequate daily ration of all the essentials. If you've skipped the chapter, passed up the food diary, or haven't finished compiling three days' worth of dietary input, then you may have little idea of what you're getting out of what you're eating.

Remember, the trick in eating nutritiously is to use the RDAs and other recommendations as a guide without turning them into a rigid diet plan. You want to ensure that the diet you naturally favor (for reasons of taste, convenience, or lifestyle) is giving you all you need in the way of essentials at a reasonable cost in calories. After all, you can only consume so many calories a day without picking up excess weight.

You also need to maintain a sensible balance of energy-providing nutrients. You can't overdo fats or take all your carbohydrates as simple sugars without chancing obesity and raising the risk of several major life-threatening diseases. So it's best to stick close to the kinds of dietary goals recommended by the American Heart Association and the National Cancer Institute:

- Meet at least 50 percent of your energy needs with carbohydrates but limit intake of refined sugars to only 10 percent.
- Take on no more than 35 percent of your calories in fats and only 10 percent in saturated fats (those high in saturated fatty acids). Cholesterol too should be limited, although not necessarily to the 250 milligrams per day the Heart Association suggests.
- Get about 15–20 percent of your calories from protein.
- And, within this balance, take all the vitamins and minerals you need.

THE DIFFERENT KINDS OF FIBER

Fiber is not a single or a simple thing, but the several different kinds of fiber all come from the cell walls of plants. They are all indigestible, and all but one are technically carbohydrates, made from chains of sugar molecules.

You can live without fibers. They are not essential nutrients. But you wouldn't live in much comfort, since fibers play a major role in keeping digestion running smoothly. They provide the bulk the intestines need to function well. They may also help prevent obesity, heart disease, and colon cancer. Different kinds of fiber do different jobs in the body; the fiber in oranges and green beans does things the fiber in bran does not.

Fibers come in two basic forms: those that are soluble in water and those that aren't.

The fibers known as **celluloses**, **hemicelluloses**, and **lignin** can't be dissolved in water. But they can *absorb* water, like molecular sponges. That means that they can swell up and add bulk, making it easier for the intestine to pass waste along. Breakfast cereals and whole grains are rich in insoluble fiber; so is bran, the classic remedy for constipation, which is derived from the outer coating of grains.

By keeping things moving in the intestine, insoluble fibers may also help prevent diverticulosis (a digestive disorder) and colon cancer. The theory is that potential carcinogens in the gut have less time to do damage if they're ushered out of the body more quickly. These fibers may also cut down on the body's absorption of fat by moving fat out of the intestine before it's fully digested.

The water-soluble fibers have a more subtle effect on fat metabolism. These fibers can bind chemically to bile acids, which the gallbladder produces out of cholesterol. As bile acids are removed from the body, the body compensates by producing more, taking cholesterol out of the bloodstream in the process. There are two main types of water-soluble fiber: **pectins**, found in apples, citrus fruits, and some vegetables, and **gums**, found in oatmeal and beans (and also used as thickeners in ice cream and salad dressing).

All the fibers can slow down the absorption of glucose into the bloodstream, since they are bound up with the digestible carbohydrates from which glucose is released. Pectin and gums can also slow sugar absorption from the intestine. Both effects may be beneficial for diabetics.

Fiber, like anything in the diet, can be taken in excess; it can lead to gas, bloating, and diarrhea. Some fibers can also block the absorption of trace elements (see "Food Interactions," page 198). Most Americans aren't at risk of

Also a goal, although harder to quantify, is a caloric intake that lets you maintain (or reach) an appropriate weight. The trick is to get the nutrients you need without tipping the caloric scales. It's a form of caloric economy that nutritionists describe as choosing nutrient-dense foods, those that have relatively high levels of specific nutrients for the calories they contain.

White rice, for example, is a fine source of carbohydrates. But if you're looking for proteins from the rice bowl, then you're paying 225

---

getting too much fiber, however, but rather of getting too little. The National Cancer Institute recommends 20–35 grams of fiber per day, but the average American gets only about 10 grams. (An apple and a slice of whole wheat bread each contain about 2 grams of fiber; a half cup of cooked broccoli has 3 grams.)

Because different fibers have different effects on the body, the safest course is to eat fair amounts of a variety of them in whole grain breads, bran and oat cereals, brown rice, legumes, and especially fresh fruits and vegetables. The table shows some of the best sources of soluble and insoluble fiber. It gives the number of grams of fiber per 100 grams of food (*not* per serving). Even though dry oat bran has more fiber per weight than apples, for example, that doesn't mean you'll get less fiber in an apple than in the bran you put on your cereal; the apple weighs much more. The numbers refer just to the type of fiber listed; for example, the "0.8 grams" next to cooked oats refers only to their water-soluble fiber content, not to the small amount of insoluble fiber they also contain.

Food Sources of Fiber

Food	Water-Soluble Fiber (grams per 100 grams of food)	Food	Water-Insoluble Fiber
dry oat bran	7.2	all-bran	24.9
dried white beans	1.7	wheat germ	15.0
dried split peas	1.6	shredded wheat	10.2
strawberries	0.8	barley	7.4
cooked rolled oats	0.8	asparagus	2.8
apples	0.7	Brussels sprouts	2.7
bananas	0.6	kale	2.3
grapefruit	0.5	green beans	2.3
oranges	0.4	carrots	1.9
		broccoli	1.7

Source: from James W. Anderson, M.D., *Plant Fiber in Foods* (Lexington, KY: HCF Diabetes Research Foundation, Inc., 1986).

calories for 4 grams of protein, while a lamb chop will give you five times as much protein for even fewer calories. You can get vitamin C from half an avocado, but it comes with 160 calories, while a cup of grapefruit juice has nine times as much vitamin C and only 95 calories. But your avocado has half again as much potassium as grapefruit juice, more than twice as much folacin, and 30 times as much vitamin A. Balancing caloric intake is pretty much like balancing your checkbook, figuring out what you're laying out in calories to meet basic needs and making sure there's a bit left over for some dietary indulgence.

When you look at your diet, it may be hard to tell just what it is you are getting in the way of nutrients. First of all, you don't always eat plain, unadorned foods. Roast beef often comes with gravy and salads with dressing. Then there are casseroles and quiche, fried rice, burritos, stew, pies and puddings, and many other multi-ingredient foods.

What's more, each ingredient may contain substantial amounts of several nutrients. Look at what's in a McDonald's Big Mac and how far it goes toward meeting the RDAs for a long list of essential nutrients (see "Nutrients in a McDonald's Big Mac," below).

There's far more to a Big Mac than the protein in the burger and the carbohydrates in the bun. There's all that calcium, thiamin, and niacin.

Nutrients in a McDonald's Big Mac

Nutrient	Percentage of RDA	
	Men	Women
Calories	21	28
Protein	46	59
Calcium	20	20
Iron	40	22
Zinc	31	31
Vitamin A	5	5
Thiamin	28	39
Niacin	36	50
Folacin	5	5
Vitamin C	3	3

Source: Jean Pennington and Helen Church, Food Values of Portions Commonly Used (New York: Harper and Row, 1985), p. 59. Calculations are for adults age 23–50.

On the other hand, there's too much saturated fat to make Big Macs a healthy everyday staple unless you cut back on saturates somewhere else in your diet. There isn't much vitamin C or A in a Big Mac either. But it's important to remember that we get a certain percentage of our nutrients from poor sources as well as from rich sources, and it all counts.

We can get a nutritional boost from fortified food products. Baby foods, flour cereals, and many other prepared foods are fortified with vitamins and minerals—from the familiar vitamin D in milk to the calcium now being added to orange juice and even soft drinks. Fortification can increase a food's nutrient density and make it easier to eat a nutritionally complete diet. Unless you are aware of how your foods are fortified, however, you may risk overloading on potentially toxic nutrients.

The tables on pages 113–116 are not meant to be a complete diet

Major Nutrients in Sample Foods

| Food | Amount | Calories (Kcal) | Percent of Calories as: | | |
			Protein	Fat	Carbohydrates
loin lamb chop, broiled	1	340	26	74	0
chicken with skin, roasted	3½ oz	239	47	53	0
shrimp, fried	3½ oz	225	37	45	18
pork and beans in tomato sauce	8 oz	255	17	14	69
cheddar cheese	1 oz	115	24	75	1
spaghetti	1 cup	216	14	3	83
white rice	⅔ cup	150	7	1	92
biscuit, homemade	1	103	9	42	49
broccoli, chopped	½ cup	25	36	9	55
avocado	½ medium	160	5	79	16
olive oil	1 tbsp	119	0	100	0
apple	1	80	1	5	94
dates	10	230	1	0	99
milk, whole	1 cup	150	21	49	30
root beer	12 oz	163	0	0	100

Sources: J.A.T. Pennington and H. N. Church, Food Values of Portions Commonly Used, 14th ed. (New York: Harper & Row, 1985). George Briggs and Doris Howes Calloway, Nutrition and Physical Fitness (New York: Holt, Rinehart and Winston, 1984), pp. A7–19.

guide. You'll find far more detailed information in the food tables in the Appendix. What the tables in this chapter will give you, however, is some notion of nutrient content and density in good sources and poor ones that can help you spot what you're likely to be missing and start to build a baseline diet that includes enough variety to remedy these deficiencies.

Vitamins and Minerals in Sample Foods

Nutrient and RDA–ESA[a] (Men/Women)	Food	Amount	Amount of Nutrient	Percent of RDA–ESA (Men/Women)	Calories
Vitamin A (1,000 RE/ 800 RE)[b]	beef liver, fried	3 oz	9,000 RE	900/1,125	185
	cantaloupe	½ small	510 RE	54/64	60
	broccoli	½ cup	170 RE	17/21	25
	mozzarella cheese (whole-milk)	1 oz	68 RE	7/9	80
	parsley, raw	1 tbsp	30 RE	3/4	2
Thiamin (1.4 mg/ 1.0 mg)	pork chop, broiled	1 medium	0.8 mg	57/80	300
	baked potato	1 large	0.2 mg	14/20	140
	white bread, enriched	1 slice	0.1 mg	7/10	65
	chicken breast, fried	½ breast	0.08 mg	6/8	220
	grapefruit	½	0.04 mg	3/4	39
Riboflavin (1.6 mg/ 1.2 mg)	Wendy's Double Hamburger	1	0.54 mg	34/45	670
	milk, whole	1 cup	0.40 mg	25/33	150
	chili con carne	1 cup	0.20 mg	13/17	340
	Brussels sprouts, frozen	1 cup	0.17 mg	11/14	63
	orange	1 medium	0.05 mg	3/4	60
Niacin (18 mg/ 13 mg)	salted peanuts	½ cup	19.6 mg	109/151	660
	tuna salad	1 cup	10.2 mg	57/78	340
	Cheerios	1 oz	5.0 mg	28/38	110
	roast beef	4½ oz	4.5 mg	25/35	570
	mushrooms, raw	1 cup	3.0 mg	17/23	20
Vitamin B₆ (2.2 mg/ 2.0 mg)	bran flakes	1 oz	0.5 mg	23/25	90
	lamb chops, lean	2 (4½ oz)	0.4 mg	18/20	240
	grape juice, bottled	1 cup	0.16 mg	7/8	155
	milk, skim	1 cup	0.1 mg	4.5/5	86
	cornmeal grits	1 cup	0.06 mg	2.7/3	145
Folacin (400 µg)	chick-peas	½ cup	125 µg	31	110
	asparagus spears, canned	½ cup	85 µg	21	16
	pineapple juice	1 cup	58 µg	15	140
	yogurt, low-fat	1 cup	25 µg	6	144
	bagel	1	13 µg	3	175

SHOULD YOU TAKE SUPPLEMENTS?

Even if you eat a fairly well-balanced diet, you may still want to take vitamin and mineral supplements—if only as nutritional insurance.

For some people, supplementation may be advisable or even necessary. People on low-calorie diets, or unbalanced diets (like a strict vege-

Nutrient and RDA–ESA[a] (Men/Women)	Food	Amount	Amount of Nutrient	Percent of RDA–ESA (Men/Women)	Calories
Vitamin B$_{12}$	liverwurst	1 oz	24.3 µg	810	95
(3 µg)	tuna, oil-packed	½ cup	2.2 µg	73	200
	milk, whole	1 cup	0.9 µg	30	150
	hamburger on bun	1 regular	0.8 µg	27	250
	egg, hard-boiled	1	0.6 µg	20	80
Vitamin C	orange juice	1 cup	125 mg	208	110
(60 mg)	broccoli	½ cup	50 mg	83	25
	baked potato	1 large	30 mg	50	140
	iceberg lettuce	⅙ head	5 mg	8	10
	milk, whole	1 cup	2 mg	3	150
Calcium	sardines, oil-packed	3 oz	370 mg	46	170
(800 mg)	milk, whole	1 cup	290 mg	36	150
	cottage cheese, small curd	1 cup	126 mg	16	217
	broccoli	1 cup	90 mg	11	50
	bran muffin	1	55 mg	7	110
Phosphorus	baked flounder	3½ oz	344 mg	43	202
(800 mg)	chick-peas	1 cup	212 mg	27	220
	vanilla ice cream	1 cup	134 mg	17	270
	grapefruit	1	20 mg	3	60
	popcorn	1 cup	20 mg	3	40
Iron	oysters	6	7.2 mg	72/40	60
(10 mg/	round steak, broiled	4½ oz	4.5 mg	45/25	330
18 mg)	bagel	1	1.6 mg	16/9	175
	lima beans	½ cup	1.2 mg	12/7	90
	broccoli	½ cup	0.7 mg	7/4	25
Zinc	round steak, broiled	4½ oz	7.5 mg	50	330
(15 mg)	cheddar cheese	3½ oz	3.1 mg	21	403
	roast turkey	3½ oz	3.0 mg	20	208
	2%-fat milk, fortified	1 cup	1.1 mg	7	137
	English muffin	1	0.4 mg	3	135
Potassium	dried peaches	½ cup	785 mg	14–42	190
(ESA 1,875–	banana	1 medium	450 mg	8–24	105
5,625 mg)	beets, canned	1 cup	290 mg	5–15	60
	tuna, water-packed	½ cup	275 mg	5–15	130

tarian regime), may not be able to get all the nutrients they need from food. Drinking and smoking can deplete nutrients, as can certain medications. And there are special requirements for people at different stages of life, from infancy through old age. Suggestions for supplementation are given in later chapters that deal with deficiencies, disease, and the special requirements of various ages and conditions of life.

If you need or choose to use a multinutrient supplement, here are a few basic guidelines:

- Choose a formula that's *balanced*, giving a full range of vitamins and minerals—don't overdo any single nutrient.
- As a general rule, use a formula that gives you roughly 100 percent of the U.S. RDAs for each nutrient other than calcium, phosphorus, and magnesium. The daily allowances of these macrominerals cannot and *should* not be taken in a single dose. Your formula may also include trace elements for which U.S. RDAs have not been established, and should contain at least 5 milligrams of manganese.
- You don't necessarily need to take supplements every day. Look at your food diary and figure out how good your ordinary diet is. You may find that taking a supplement once every two or three days gives you all the insurance you need.

Nutrient and RDA–ESA[a] (Men/Women)	Food	Amount	Amount of Nutrient	Percent of RDA–ESA (Men/Women)	Calories
	pumpernickel bread	1 slice	139 mg	2–7	82
Sodium (ESA 1,100– 3,300 mg)	pretzels	10 3-ring	480 mg	15–44	120
	peas, canned	½ cup	200 mg	6–17	75
	fig bars	4	180 mg	5–16	212
	club soda	12 oz	78 mg	2–7	0
	chicken drumstick	1	44 mg	1–4	120
Copper (ESA 2.0– 3.0 mg)	lobster meat	⅔ cup	1.6 mg	53–80	90
	avocado	1 medium	0.4 mg	13–20	320
	baked ham	3 oz	0.3 mg	10–15	250
	Wheaties	1 oz	0.13 mg	4–7	99
	potatoes, hash-brown, frozen	¾ cup	0.1 mg	3–5	72

Sources: J.A.T. Pennington and H.N. Church, *Food Values of Portions Commonly Used*, 14th ed. (New York: Harper & Row, 1985). George Briggs and Doris Howes Calloway, *Nutrition and Physical Fitness* (New York: Holt, Rinehart and Winston, 1984), pp. A7–19.
Note: mg = milligrams; μg = micrograms.
[a]RDA = Recommended Dietary Allowance; ESA = Estimated Safe and Adequate amount.
[b]RE = Retinol Equivalents (1 Retinol Equivalent = 1 μg retinol or 6 μg beta-carotene).

- Check the expiration date. Vitamins, like drugs, don't remain potent forever.
- Remember that a pill is no substitute for a healthy diet. But most of us seem to know this already. Studies have shown that people who use supplements tend to take *better* care of themselves in other ways (including eating a balanced diet) than those who don't take them. Apparently most of us use vitamin and mineral supplements as part of an overall approach to a healthy lifestyle. And in that context they can be useful and appropriate.

Bear in mind that the U.S. RDAs do not include all the nutrients people require. Neither do they provide levels high enough for certain people. Pregnant women, for example, need much more iron and extra measures of just about everything else as well. So a commercial multivitamin and mineral supplement may not give adequate nutritional insurance to everyone.

CHAPTER 9

Foodstyle

E ACH OF US HAS a distinct (but not necessarily unique) way of eating. This is foodstyle. It is an aspect of lifestyle embodying tastes and attitudes that reflect a broad range of influences — regional, ethnic, religious, educational — and eating patterns established in early childhood. How we eat is also determined by the importance we give to food and our expectations of diet as well as by where we eat, when we eat, and with whom we eat.

As for *what* we eat or how wisely we eat, foodstyle cuts both ways. Nutritional goals clearly shape foodstyle. But the reverse is often the case, and foodstyle is as likely to limit nutritional benefits as expand them.

When it comes to discovering how Americans now eat, one thing seems clear. We are no longer a nation of three- or more-member families, gathering around the table at least twice a day for nourishing home-cooked meals. It is doubtful that this was ever our society's prevalent mealtime scenario. And it is certainly not one upon which the nutrition of the nation is based today.

The cultural changes of the past two to three decades, the diminished role and altered structure of the family, the changing role of women, and the viability of other lifestyle alternatives have shifted the focus of society from the family to the individual. Nutrition too is now more usefully regarded from an individual perspective. As a result, individual foodstyle has become a major factor in determining our national nutritional status.

Foodstyle is not a fixed or static set of attitudes and practices. It evolves and changes through life, responding to different influences at different stages and reflecting the impact of fashions, the limitations of

118

income, and the role of a large, efficient, and a highly competitive food industry that depends heavily on advertising to influence public taste.

We start making our tastes known early on. Babies, once they have solid foods, are quick to act on their likes and dislikes, usually by rejection either passive or active (that's when the strained beets hit the floor). *Cookie* comes a close third to *mommy* and *daddy* as baby's first word. And the innate taste for sweets is soon followed by the development of other preferences that constitute the beginnings of a distinct foodstyle. Small children go through periods of extreme pickiness, unwilling to try new foods and often limiting diet to a few favorites — peanut butter, cheese, hamburger, or a particular brand of breakfast cereal.

Adolescents, while still nutritionally dependent on family food choices and eating patterns, engage in a good deal of free feeding and may get one fifth of their calories from "grazing," chronic, irregular snacking at home and away. Grazing isn't necessarily poor nutrition. Although most snacks that teenagers eat are relatively low in nutrient density, some (like certain "energy bars") are fortified with important nutrients. And some ordinary fast foods, especially pizza, are surprisingly well balanced nutritionally. On the other hand, snacks like chicken nuggets and fries can throw diets off, not only with excess calories but with surplus fat as well.

The foodstyle of adolescents is heavily influenced by peer pressure. If fitness is the local adolescent imperative, then the Burger King salad bar may get much of the afterschool trade. Concerns about appearance mount during adolescence, weight consciousness becomes common among girls, and the fear of blemished skin can trigger a cutback in chocolate and other high-fat snacks that may be nutritionally beneficial even if it is dermatologically of negligible value.

The foodstyle of college students reflects the interplay of institutional meals with the grazing patterns of adolescence, while young adults (living alone or together) adopt a wide variety of styles. Major influences on their diet include constraints of time and income, reluctance to cook, gourmet palates in the making, concerns about fitness, and the important social role of meals. This period — generally the first opportunity for full-time free feeding — is when the traditional three-meals-a-day pattern (which may have been pretty well bent before) is most likely to be broken and mealtimes shift to accommodate career demands or social goals.

For families with young children, regular mealtimes and early dinners are still pretty much the rule, but foodstyle now tends to reflect the absence of full-time homemakers in most American homes. Since single parents and working couples generally do not have the same time to invest in meal planning and preparation as stay-at-home parents do, they are likely to depend more on convenience foods and takeout meals. This can have a measurable impact on nutrition, not all of it negative. Surveys have found that children of mothers who hold jobs outside the home tend to eat less candy and fewer salty snacks than children of homemakers. On the other hand, families of working parents (according to research from Cornell University) tend to eat more fats and are more at risk of iron deficiency than families with a parent at home.

Foodstyles among the parents of young children and other adults moving toward their middle years reflect the competing attractions of fitness and "good living" (eating well, which generally means richly), plus time constraints and other pressures of career and family building. According to the National Center for Health Statistics, this age group appears to be picking up extra weight somewhat ahead of schedule. In the past, such a gain was generally associated with middle age. During 1980, the last census year, Americans aged 25–34 were about 6 pounds heavier than their counterparts of 1960.

The conflicting goals of fitness and "good living" also influence the foodstyle of middle years, during which income generally increases and children grow to semi-independence. Child-oriented meal patterns are abandoned, and fewer meals are eaten at home. During the move through middle age toward the later years, life stage changes (in activity levels and calorie needs) affect foodstyle, and so do social changes that have tended to diminish both family and community cohesiveness.

Among the aging, apathy is a primary determinant of foodstyle. The elderly lose interest in food, not simply because their appetites are reduced and they cannot taste food as well but also because of isolation, depression, and limited opportunities for the social benefits of mealtimes. As the aging become indifferent to regular meals and depend upon snacks for a substantial portion of their energy needs, they can develop serious nutritional deficits. Since their capacity to absorb nutrients is often compromised as well, they need all the nutritional assistance they can get for maximum performance of failing body systems.

In addition to life stage, changing food fashions also affect our foodstyles. And food fashions in the United States have created a conflict between eating for fitness and eating for pleasure, even though these goals no longer need to be mutually exclusive.

Eating primarily for fitness is often seen as not eating for much fun. It is sometimes perceived as embracing a kind of ascetic semivegetarianism — just about eliminating red meat, cutting fats to the minimum, and bulking up on complex carbohydrates (pasta, beans, and whole grains). On the other hand, there is an emerging American epicureanism, broadly reflected in the popularity of gourmet products like croissants, quiches of various kinds, and creamy (fat-packed) cheeses.

Today's gourmets, however, are developing other options. The light touch of French "nouvelle cuisine" has been picked up by a new breed of American chefs, whose meals are designed for fitness-conscious diners and feature regional specialties, imaginative use of uncommon American foodstuffs, and crisp flavorful vegetables. This "California cuisine" provides an alternative to traditional native notions of eating well, notions based on food preferences that can quite literally be described as "eating high on the hog."

There is more to food fashion than just the conflict between fitness and richness. Not to be overlooked is the role of kitchen technology. While the microwave oven isn't changing *what* we eat so much as how soon we eat it, the food processor provides a shortcut to all kinds of complicated recipes that were once not worth the effort. It has also loosed on the land a flood of new and sometimes bizarre soups, purees, and vegetables in less-than-immediately-recognizable forms.

The exotic, and increasingly the "authentic," have become fashionable, and both the variety and quality of foreign cuisines available to Americans have increased substantially during the past decade. Chinese food has long since ceased to mean bland hybrids like chow mein, even if the spicy specialties of Hunan and Szechuan are not yet available at full strength outside major metropolitan areas. Mexican food, also at varying degrees of authenticity and power, can be had just about everywhere — Mexican restaurants are proliferating faster than those of any other national cuisine — while our notions of Italian cooking (exclusive of pizza) have expanded well beyond the pasta and veal basics. As for Japanese food, it is moving rapidly inland from both coasts.

Income as a determinant of foodstyle pulls both ways. It is responsible for the enormous success of inexpensive fast-food restaurants. It is also credited by the U.S. Department of Agriculture with having more influence than nutritional concerns on the recent drop in beef consumption. Nevertheless, food remains one of the best bargains our economy has to offer. The percentage of disposable income Americans spend on food has dropped steadily — down to 15 percent in 1986 from 22 percent in 1945 — mostly because of technological advances and the sophistication of the U.S. food industry. Americans now spend a smaller fraction of their income on food than people of any other nation.

It is important to note that the low cost and generally high quality of food available throughout the United States is the result of technological advances in several areas. Increased agricultural efficiency is only part of the story. Sophisticated techniques for preservation and packaging can also be credited, as can the relatively rapid transport of foodstuffs. Food processing companies are able to extend shelf life and protect both nutrients and flavor not only with preservatives but also with such modern packing and packaging methods as vacuum pouches, high-temperature pasteurization, and the use of inert gases to prevent oxidation.

How is the food industry responding to current American foodstyles? Mostly by keeping up with them and sometimes by pushing them along. Americans have more food choices than ever before, and our giant supermarkets — it takes giants to handle the variety — have added products low in sodium or fats, free of preservatives or sugar, and high in fiber. Some markets offer the bulk foods (flour, beans, rice and other grains, dried fruits, and nuts) that once could be found only in health food stores. But new shelf space is also needed for more varieties of salty fried snack foods, butter-rich cookies, and sugared cereals.

Meat departments now carry low-fat chicken franks and new varieties of low-fat beef. To challenge the frozen fish sticks in the freezer row are full-scale fish departments. But the greatest changes are in the fresh produce sections, which now regularly offer more than 170 different items (nearly three times the number they carried in 1972). Pushed by competition from farmers' markets and roadside stands, the supermarkets have responded with greater selection and made popular such items as mangoes, kiwis, and alfalfa sprouts. Responsive to all aspects of changing foodstyle, many markets have added salad bars for the takeout trade (with enough nonsalad extras available to make up whole meals, if not nutritionally complete ones).

Market chains and manufacturers keep a sharp eye on changing tastes and trends, some of which are driven by nutritional concerns, some by taste. Campbell's twice tried to launch a line of low-sodium soups during the 1960s and 1970s before they were able to establish a market for them in the 1980s. But the company appears to have had no similar difficulty in winning acceptance for its most recent new line: Creamy Natural Soups, made with real butter and cream.

Nevertheless, the magic word in marketing over the past several years has been *light* or, as advertisers put it, *lite*. Equivalent pleasure for fewer calories has been a successful formula across the board, not only for frozen dinners and diet desserts but for everything from beer, bread, and snack foods to ketchup and mayonnaise. And nowhere is the less-is-more dictum more evident than in the burgeoning market for diet soft drinks.

"Lightness" can be achieved in different ways. It can, for example, be mostly a matter of packaging. Finn Crisp Lite crackers claim "only 20 calories per slice," while regular Finn Crisp crackers have just 19 calories.

Many "light" products, however, are genuinely low in calories. To create them, food manufacturers have developed a number of ingenious ways to remove fat from foods yet maintain high levels of important nutrients. The dairy industry, for example, has produced low-fat and no-fat milks, fortified with vitamins A and D and containing even more calcium than is found in whole milk. Even though vitamins A and D are fat-soluble, milk producers have kept them in low-fat milk by retaining the minimum amount of fat necessary to dissolve enough of these vitamins or by adding chemical cousins of these vitamins that are water-soluble but have the same biological effect.

Substituting a low-calorie ingredient for a high-calorie one is probably the major means of "lightening" foods. Tofu — iron-rich and protein-packed bean curd — can take the cream out of ice cream and any number of other rich desserts. More often, however, it is an artificial ingredient that is swapped for a natural one, with artificial sweeteners heading the list and imitation cream, butter, and eggs also helping shave off calories.

Substitute foods—not only margarine, artificial fruit juice, and nondairy creamers but also imitation meat, eggs, and cheese—have a substantial place of their own in the market these days. George Briggs, professor emeritus of nutrition at the University of California, Berkeley, warns that we may soon have a generation of children "who have never even tasted real orange juice or a pizza made with real cheese."

In general, substitutes are less expensive (although imitation eggs are not) and provide certain dietary advantages. But many have short-comings other than taste. For example, nondairy creamers, while choles-terol-free, have very high levels of saturated fatty acids and little, if any, calcium. Meat substitutes, which may be lower in saturates than real meat, are generally much higher in sodium and have substantially less usable iron and other trace elements. Briggs has found certain imitation cheeses to lack the amounts of calcium, zinc, vitamin A, and the B vitamins that real cheese has. Laboratory rats fed these substitutes failed to grow as well as rats on a real cheese diet.

MAKING THE MOST OF YOUR FOODSTYLE

Although headlines claim "Americans Eating Less Red Meat" or "Families Now Use More Fresh Vegetables," our actual eating habits are changing in more complex ways. The headlines reflect changes in *overall* food consumption patterns, not changes that are occurring in every American home. Many Americans have indeed cut back on beef and pork. On the other hand, others are buying more steaks, chops, and spareribs than ever before. The greater use of fresh fruits and vegetables, while widespread, is far from universal. It's clear from interview surveys, in which Americans are questioned about their food choices, that we are of many different minds about food (see "What We Eat Now," page 124).

But whatever your foodstyle, it is usually possible to meet most nutritional goals within its limits. It might be a bit difficult if you insist on taking all your meals at fast-food restaurants or restrict yourself to a limited number of favorite dishes. In general, however, you should be able to stay fairly close to a baseline diet that meets all your needs, even if your foodstyle leaves little room for leeway because of dietary restric-tions or other limitations.

It shouldn't be necessary to monitor your intake too closely either, not if you recognize the need for variety and moderation. They provide the best dietary insurance. If there's enough variety in your meals, and if you limit yourself to only occasional excesses, you're unlikely to do yourself much nutritional harm. But there are some specific ways in which you can realize the most nutritional benefit from your foodstyle.

COOKING AT HOME

Among the advantages of home cooking is how easy it makes controlling your diet. It also allows you to get the most — or the least — out of what you are cooking.

Many health-conscious cooks now make a special effort to use fresh

---

WHAT WE EAT NOW

Patterns of food consumption in the United States show no clear trends toward a "healthier" or "less healthy" diet. But our diets have been changing in some specific ways.

Red meat consumption is down, but not by much. During the 1970s annual consumption of all red meat (beef, pork, veal, lamb, and game) averaged 150 pounds per person. It has been averaging 144 pounds during the 1980s. Beef and veal have fallen sharply from favor — from close to 97 pounds per person in 1976 to just about 80 pounds in 1985.

But in spite of a drop in red meat purchases, total consumption of flesh foods (meat, fish, and poultry) were at record levels — 227 pounds per person in 1985, with new highs for fish and poultry. The popularity of **fish** (led by tuna, shrimp, and catfish) has been increasing slowly over the years, climbing from 12.9 pounds per person in 1955 to 14.5 pounds in 1985. Meanwhile, **poultry** has soared in favor, from 26.7 pounds per person in 1955 to 69.7 pounds in 1985.

Egg consumption has been steadily declining (from 361 per person in 1961 to 255 in 1985), and the consumption of **dairy products** has changed dramatically. We are consuming less than half as much whole milk as we did in 1955 and more than 10 times as much low-fat and skim milk. But this still leaves us 24 quarts per year below the 1955 average. Half as much butter is being sold as in 1955, but three times as much cheese (we're now up to over 22 pounds per person). However, the biggest dairy gainer other than low-fat milk has been yogurt, up from one third of a pound per person in 1965 to more than 3 pounds today.

Americans are, as a nation, eating more **fruits and vegetables** than we have in the past 25 years — 209.2 pounds of vegetables and 149.2 pounds of fruits per person in 1984, most of it fresh. Fruit juice consumption has increased by 50 percent since 1967 and is now about 7 gallons per person.

Potatoes (white and sweet), which had fallen from 220 pounds per person in 1910 to 71 pounds in 1981, have been coming back strong — up to 84 pounds per person in 1985. But a third of these potatoes are processed, most of them into frozen sliced, diced, or crinkle-cut fries and potato chips.

Sugar consumption is way down, from 108 pounds per person in 1973 to 63.4 pounds in 1985. But consumption of corn syrup sweeteners is way up; it has more than tripled since 1970. In 1984, *combined* consumption of sugar and corn syrup sweeteners hit an all-time high — an average of 150 pounds per person. Much of that corn syrup went into soft drinks, which we consumed at a record rate of about 45 gallons per person (three times the average of the 1950s). Although diet soft drinks increased in popularity, four out of every five sodas we drank were of the naturally sweetened variety, with about 160 calories in a 12-ounce can.

fruits and vegetables. They're rich in vitamins A and C and folic acid, enhance the flavor and appearance of a meal, and are high in fiber — which makes it easier to satisfy the appetite with a low caloric intake.

Clearly, you want the most vitamins out of your vegetables. This doesn't mean you need to eat them raw. In fact, there are substances in certain raw fruits and vegetables that you definitely don't want, like an enzyme in red cabbage, Brussels sprouts, blueberries, and blackberries that will wipe out thiamin unless it is destroyed by cooking.

Certain kinds of cooking, however, can also destroy vitamins, particularly vitamin C and riboflavin. The greater the heat and the longer the cooking time, the greater the loss will be. Microwave ovens seem to help keep vitamin loss to a minimum. And it's clearly better to stir-fry or steam than to boil. If you do boil, however, save the water (some water-soluble vitamins are still there) and use it as a base for soup.

Bear in mind, too, that even though cooking may destroy some vitamins, it generally makes food more digestible. In other words, it makes some nutrients, particularly carbohydrates and proteins, more accessible to the enzymes that break them down into smaller molecules which can be transported from the digestive tract to the bloodstream. Cooking is especially important for fruits and vegetables, which have stiff cellulose cell walls that enzymes can't easily penetrate. Heat and water cause these cells to burst open.

If you want to bring your fat intake under control, then watch the oils you cook with. Saturated fatty acid, the kinds found in butter, are essential for the flaky texture of pie crusts and other baked goods. But for ordinary cooking, replacing saturates with polyunsaturates in vegetable oils (like corn and safflower oil) or the monounsaturates in olive oil can help control blood cholesterol. Also, watch the total amount of oil you use; it's often possible to use less than recipes call for, particularly if you cook in a nonstick pan.

In recent years there has been some concern that heating polyunsaturated oils could produce free radicals (destructive molecules that may be linked to cancer). But that now appears to be a risk only when oil is heated to unusually high temperatures for unusually long periods of time and used more than once. And under those conditions, oil develops an unpleasant flavor that makes it unusable anyway.

Deep frying, however, does pose a chemical problem. Because polyunsaturates smoke at the temperatures needed for deep frying, saturates are required for this kind of cooking. And saturates increase the risk of atherosclerosis. Even the solid vegetable fats used for deep frying are heavily saturated. They're made from unusual vegetable oils, like coconut oil, that contain more saturated acids than animal fat. For these reasons, a diet that tilts heavily toward french fries, Southern fried chicken, and the like is not consistent with a concern about heart disease.

One way to save fat in cooking without losing much flavor is to trim all the exterior fat from meat and pour off what accumulates in the pan (it's already made its contribution to taste). Poultry is even easier to deal with, since most of the fat is in the abdomen and skin, where it can readily be cut away. A half a chicken breast fried with the skin has 9 grams of fat. Roasted without the skin, it has only 3 grams. And if it's carefully browned, skinless chicken will turn out pleasantly crisp but not dry.

If you're cooking red meat, the kind of meat you buy and the way you prepare it can also help lower your fat intake. (That is particularly significant, since 40–50 percent of the fatty acids in red meat are saturated, compared with about 30 percent in chicken fat.) Many supermarkets now offer beef from cattle especially bred for leanness.

But even meat from ordinary cattle can be quite lean, if you know how to shop for it. Beef comes in three grades — Good, Choice, and Prime — depending on the amount of fat in the cut. Prime has the most marbled fat; Good, the least. Good beef can be somewhat tough, but it cooks well when it's cooked slowly or thinly sliced. Choosing Good rather than Choice beef can reduce the amount of fat in a trimmed cut of meat by up to 30 percent. (Another way to reduce fat is by substituting ingredients in your favorite recipes. Turkey breast, for example, can replace veal, and ground turkey breast can replace ground beef.)

Not all fat control occurs in cooking; some takes place at the table. If you use oil in salad dressing, try varying the standard formula. Instead of one part vinegar to three parts oil, try one to one or two to three. Take the traditional advice to be "a miser with the vinegar and a spendthrift with the oil" and reverse it. And don't overdress your salads; one tablespoon of dressing per serving will do if you toss the salad well enough.

When it comes to butter, margarine, and sour cream, the nutritional facts may surprise you. Margarine actually has as many calories and as much fat as butter does. And if a stick of margarine is as firm as butter at room temperature, that means it's gone through a chemical process called hydrogenation, which essentially turns its polyunsaturated fatty acids into saturated ones.

But if margarine has more fat than most people suspect, sour cream has less. A dollop of sour cream on a baked potato contributes only one third as much fat as buttering the potato would. (And substituting yogurt for sour cream gives you even less fat and fewer calories.)

FROZEN FOODS AND DINNERS

Frozen fruits and vegetables are generally the nutritional equivalents of a supermarket's "fresh" produce, which has usually been harvested before it's ripe and has spent a week or so traveling to market. Frozen produce is not equal, however, to the fresh-from-the-garden variety. But meats don't appear to suffer much damage in freezing (although taste may be affected), and a fish that is frozen on board a factory ship is probably in better shape than the "fresh" one that spent last week at the bottom of the hold. So there's little trade-off of nutrition for convenience in using frozen foods.

When it comes to complete frozen meals, the quality seems to have improved considerably in recent years, with gourmet lines (which quadrupled in sales in 1985) leading the way. In general, the new gourmet frozen dinners have a fairly high nutrient density; they provide plenty of protein and controlled amounts of fat. Even the nondiet varieties limit calories, though some may be so low in calories as to leave an active adult hungry. Their biggest nutritional drawback, at least for people with hypertension, is that sodium levels tend to be high in proportion to calories.

EATING OUT

Eating more than one meal a day in restaurants raises the risk of throwing your diet off balance, increasing the chance of getting too many of your calories in proteins and fats and too few in carbohydrates. One way of balancing restaurant meals is by balancing restaurants and adding more Chinese, Japanese, or Indian meals. These cuisines traditionally use plenty of grains and vegetables, supplemented with meat or fish. Italian and Mexican restaurants can help your balancing act too, if you opt for a simple pasta and salad in the one and don't go too far beyond the beans and rice at the other.

Each kind of ethnic cuisine has its own benefits and potential drawbacks. With more exotic restaurants than ever now open in the United States, an awareness of these factors can be important to dietary planning.

Chinese Food

Long popular in the United States, Chinese food is very high in complex carbohydrates. A recent survey in Beijing showed that the average Chinese eats a diet that is 69 percent carbohydrates, 10 percent proteins, and only 21 percent fats. Although Chinese restaurants in America tend to use more meat and sauces then those in China, they still serve a relatively low-fat cuisine rich in vegetables. Stir-fried vegetables, cooked very quickly in a lightly oiled, very hot wok, also retain vitamins better than vegetables cooked the traditional American way. A drawback of Chinese cooking—at least for some victims of hypertension—is sodium, both in salty sauces (like oyster and black bean sauce) and in monosodium glutamate (MSG). Since certain people also may be allergic to MSG (see chapter 14), many Chinese restaurants will omit it on request.

Indian Food

This cuisine is rich in vegetables, legumes, and yogurt. But many Indian dishes are soaked in ghee (clarified butter) or coconut oil, one of the few vegetable oils that consists almost entirely of saturated fatty acids (86 percent). It's possible to avoid those fats by asking how each dish is cooked; some Indian restaurants will also use different kinds of cooking oils on request.

Japanese Food

Very low in fat, Japanese cooking is based on protein-rich soybean products (such as tofu), fish, vegetables, noodles, and rice. (This may well be the reason Japan has traditionally had a very low rate of heart disease.) The seaweed used in sushi and Japanese stews is high in calcium, magnesium, and iodine. But the traditional Japanese diet is high in salted, smoked, and pickled foods, which may be linked to the country's high incidence of stroke and stomach cancer.

Mexican Food

Growing quickly in popularity here, Mexican food varies greatly in nutritional composition. Some of the most popular dishes in American Mexican restaurants, like beef burritos with cheese and sour cream, are quite high in fat. But the rice, corn, and beans that are staples of the diet in Mexico have little fat and are nutrient-dense, although refried beans in the United States are often prepared with lard. Among the lowest-fat dishes available here are seviche (fish marinated in lime juice) and chicken tostadas. Although guacamole is high in fat, it contains mostly monounsaturated fatty acids, making it a relatively good source of fat for people concerned about atherosclerosis.

Italian Food

This cuisine — at least southern Italian — has been called one of the world's healthiest. It's based largely on pasta (which is rich in complex carbohydrates) and olive oil (78 percent monounsaturates) as well as on vegetables, fruit, and fish. But the dishes of northern Italy are much richer, with much more beef and veal, butter and cream. As epidemiological studies have shown, residents of northern cities suffer considerably more heart disease than those who live in the southern regions.

A growing number of American restaurants are learning foreign ways of cooking. One sign: They're catching on to stir-frying and other means of serving up crisp vegetables. But vegetables can still take a beating, particularly if they are cooked in batches and spend a good part of the day on the steam table, where their vitamins waste away.

The salad bar, too, can become a vitamin graveyard if the fixings are left out all day with minimal refrigeration. A slice of cucumber can lose one third of its vitamin C that way in just an hour.

The salad bar is not necessarily the place to save calories either. Researchers at Mississippi State University found that patrons of the student cafeteria who filled their trays at the salad bar selected a lunch with an average of 100 more calories than those who opted for a hot meal (with entrees like fried fish and spaghetti with meat sauce). The salad bar students (who chose meals with caloric values that ranged from 560 to 1,600) managed to outdo their schoolmates by loading up on extras — diced ham, egg, cheese, olives, croutons, and bacon bits — and using high-fat dressings.

If you are watching out for too much fat, then spare yourself the restaurant's house dressing and mix your own oil and vinegar. Beware of melted cheese — it's likely to appear on almost anything — and take your butter or margarine on the side (your coffee shop breakfast toast generally comes slathered with a mixture of margarine and oil). For a quick breakfast or midmorning snack, the answer is definitely not muffins. Today's soft half-pound variety has 500 calories, most of them in fat.

Fat is also the major problem with fast-food restaurants (although the sodium in their meals may also concern some hypertensive people). The average fast-food meal delivers about half its calories as fat. But that doesn't stop nearly 46 million Americans (one fifth of the population) from eating at least one meal a day at the more than 55,000 franchised fast-food outlets operating today.

Not only is there plenty of fat in most fast foods — 15 teaspoonfuls in a Wendy's Triple Cheeseburger, 10 in a McD.L.T., and 9 in a Burger King Chicken Filet Sandwich — but a substantial amount of that fat is saturated. Until 1986, it was close to 50 percent at McDonald's, Wendy's, Burger King, and most of the other majors, who did their frying in beef tallow (mixed with a little vegetable oil). McDonald's and Burger King have since switched to vegetable oil for everything but french fries, and Denny's makes much of frying in oil with only 18 percent saturated fatty acids. Howard Johnson's uses a vegetable oil lower in saturates than even Denny's to fry shrimp and clams. But it uses palm oil, more than half of which is made up of saturated fatty acids, to fry potatoes.

However, fear of frying needn't keep you away from fast-food restaurants, although it might be useful to find out how your favorite foods are made, and with what. McDonald's, Kentucky Fried Chicken, and others add bulk to their chicken nuggets by injecting ground chicken skin. That might put you off a bit. But a fat-heavy meal, even a few times a week, isn't going to throw your diet that far off.

In fact, you could lunch every day at a fast-food restaurant and still have a healthy diet, provided you select the foods you order with some care and balance them with your breakfasts and dinners. The main things missing from fast-food cuisine are the nutrients found in fresh fruits and vegetables, and calcium (unless you drink shakes or straight milk with your burgers). So even snacking on apples and yogurt can help balance a fast-food lunch.

Some fast foods also have a higher nutrient density than others.

Hamburgers lose much of their fat if they're grilled, yet retain protein and trace elements. Mexican fast food, served at chains like Taco Bell, is relatively high in complex carbohydrates and low in fat. And pizza, in general, has the highest nutrient density of the lot.

A pizza with sausage is a well-balanced meal in miniature: it has grains (in the crust), meat, vegetables (in the tomato sauce), and cheese (high in calcium). It's often only about 25 percent fat. And it has the additional advantage of being what most Americans, even finicky teen-agers, like to eat.

Paul Saltman has studied the use of pizza in California's school lunch program. An analysis of the pizza served there showed that it was a food of high nutrient density, just slightly low in six nutrients: iron, copper, zinc, manganese, folic acid, and vitamin B_6. With fortification, it was possible to produce a 4-inch-square pizza that by itself provided one third the RDA level of all those nutrients for which there is such a recommended allowance.

CHAPTER 10

All About Body Fat

IMAGINE THIS SCENARIO: You're offered two pills and told that one will make you fatter, and one will make you thinner. You won't have to work at it, and there will be no side effects (that's guaranteed). What's more, you can decide how much you want to change—a few pounds up or down, or a major overhaul. Which do you choose: to gain, to lose, or to stay the same?

Ask this question in a group and you'll find a striking uniformity in the responses. Almost everybody wants the reducing formula. A few say they'd pass it up, but virtually *no one* wants to get fatter.

We're so conditioned to think of thinness as good that the responses may not seem surprising. But many of the world's cultures consider our desire to be thin—particularly among women—something strange indeed.

Throughout most of the world plumpness, not thinness, is a key component of female attractiveness. In one anthropological study 81 percent of the 58 cultures surveyed equated plumpness with feminine beauty. Fat stores are critical to a woman's ability to bear healthy children. For that reason, women are biologically built to be fatter than men; girl babies are 10–15 percent fatter than boys, and the difference between the sexes increases visibly in adolescence.

Why, then, has our own culture reversed the standards of sexiness? One possibility is the realization that in our affluent society overnutrition is more of a health risk than undernutrition. Obesity does indeed bring with it certain health risks, and millions of Americans are fatter than is good for them.

But the roots of our cultural preference for thinness, especially among women, probably go deeper than health concerns. Doctors didn't really begin warning the public about the risks of excess weight until the 1950s, but the fashion for thinness began in the 1920s, the time of the flapper.

Sociologists have suggested that thinness has a symbolic meaning for American women, that it represents a casting off of the traditional, maternal female role. The 1920s, when thinness first came into style, also saw feminists make great strides. In the 1960s, when the present women's movement began in earnest, Twiggy ushered in the current era of fashionable semiemaciation.

For whatever reason, women much more than men now struggle mightily to be thin. And the struggle is particularly hard for them because they're fighting a biological pull to be plump. A recent government study found that half the women questioned were dieting at the time they were surveyed, while only one quarter of the men were.

The focus on fatness starts early. Roughly 80 percent of 10- and 11-year-old girls have already gone on diets, according to research from the University of California, San Francisco, and UCLA researchers have found dieting 8- and 9-year-olds. The early focus on dieting may be partly responsible for the current epidemic of eating disorders among young women (see chapter 25).

It's ironic that women should be more concerned with their weight than men, because the health risks of obesity are actually less severe for women. But our cultural imperatives are so strong, and so much a part of our consciousness, that we may not even be aware of why we wish to be thin. The task for anyone concerned about weight (in other words, most of us) is to sort out his or her goals. It comes down to four basic questions:

- What is the range of weight that would be healthy for me?
- What would I *like* to weigh?
- What weight can I realistically reach?
- And (usually) how do I reach a compromise among all of the above?

New research is making a strong case for setting realistic goals. It's showing that for many of us, a 32-inch waist and a size 8 body just aren't in the cards. The key is to be comfortable with your body, to shape it in a way that you like but not to try to shrink yourself beyond the bounds of genetics.

From a health perspective too there's reason to question the common notion that everyone has a single ideal weight for health. It seems, instead, that everyone has a *range* of weight that should be healthy for him or her. And the risk of going above that range is greater for some people than for others — it depends on your age, your genetic heritage, and how your excess weight is distributed.

If you do decide to try to lose weight, there now are strategies that can help increase your chances of success. Traditional approaches to weight loss — cutting calories and changing eating behavior — can be effective, particularly if you have only 10 or 20 pounds to lose. The battle may be easier, however, if you alter the composition of your diet — which may be a healthful change regardless of its effect on weight. But the primary problem of substantial weight loss is not reduction as much as maintaining lower weight, and for this, exercise appears to be the key factor.

To understand the dos and don'ts of weight control, you have to begin by understanding how the body regulates weight and the physiological reasons that dieting is so often ineffective.

DIETING, HUNGER, AND METABOLISM

Most of us talk about weight control as if it were simply a matter of willpower. If you're strong enough, the thinking goes, it should be a simple matter to eat less and lose weight.

On one level, weight loss *is* simple. If you take in fewer calories than your body needs to function, your body will burn its reserves, drawing on the calories in fat and muscle tissue to make up the deficit. The problem is that the body eventually rebels against this situation, and it often wins.

Every dieter soon hears that 95 percent of people who lose weight on diets will gain it back sooner or later. Since that depressing statistic comes from studies of people seeking help at weight-loss clinics, the odds may be better for people with a less serious problem who try to reduce on their own. Nevertheless, just about all the research on weight loss has consistently shown that most people who try to lose a substantial number of pounds by dieting alone are unsuccessful in the long run.

A dieter who hears this may assume that all those failures were just weak-willed and that he or she will be among the strong-minded few who succeed. But the problem is deeper than willpower. Fat tissue means more to our bodies than it means to our minds, and the body fights hard to keep it.

You think of fat as excess baggage you'd like to drop. But your body, programmed by millennia of evolution, sees fat as a vital storehouse of energy, a critical reserve that shouldn't be given up lightly. To the body, calories *do* count. In time of famine, a threat throughout our evolutionary history and still a real threat in many developing nations, calories make the difference between life and death.

When you go on the latest low-calorie wonder diet, you're thinking of a new wardrobe, but your body thinks, "Famine!" Food restriction is a signal to the body that times are hard, and it must batten down the caloric hatches.

Two things happen. First, you get hungry — truly, physiologically hungry. Many dieters think their hunger is just the product of a strong imagination and a weak will, a sentimental hankering for the foods they're missing, or a neurotic need for oral gratification. In fact, hunger is the body's cry for help, its signal that food is needed. (Although no one is sure exactly what triggers hunger and appetite, these responses are determined by physiological as well as psychological factors; see "What Makes You Feel Hungry or Full?," below.)

Second, as you diet, your basal metabolic rate starts to slow down. The metabolic rate is measured by the number of calories your body uses per day to take care of its basic physiological needs: breathing, heartbeat, body temperature, tissue repair, all the chemical reactions that keep you going. These functions, put together, burn up roughly two thirds of the calories you take in; much of the rest is spent in physical activity.

The caloric cost of metabolism is usually measured by how much oxygen you use in a given period of time. You need oxygen to burn the body's fuel, so there's a direct correlation between oxygen uptake and the number of calories your body is converting to energy.

As your metabolic rate gets lower, your body is able to get along on fewer calories, and your calorie-cutting diet becomes less effective. This is one reason that dieters hit a plateau and find, after a few weeks, that they're no longer losing weight as quickly, if at all. Another reason is that fluid loss caused by increased production of urine lasts only through the

WHAT MAKES YOU FEEL HUNGRY OR FULL?

In 1912 the great physiologist Walter Cannon thought he knew the answer. When your stomach is empty, he said, its muscular walls contract, and you feel hungry; when the stomach is full, you feel full. But later studies showed that stomach contractions have virtually nothing to do with a feeling of hunger.

In the 1950s researchers discovered that the brain's hypothalamus is sensitive to the amount of sugar in the blood and may respond to low levels by increasing the feeling of hunger. But this is not the whole story. Today, it has become clear that the mechanisms governing hunger are far too complex to be explained by any single hypothesis.

The hypothalamus clearly plays a key role, but other parts of the nervous system are involved as well. And more than a dozen different chemical signals (including level of blood sugar) are now thought by various researchers to play some part in the process. Rather than being controlled by a simple on-off switch, hunger and fullness result from something more like a tug-of-war. One set of forces pulls you to eat, another set pulls you to stop, and the balance at any given moment is what influences your behavior. This complicated system makes evolutionary sense. Hunger, after all, is critical to survival; and a highly redundant system, which we seem to have, gives the body many ways to maintain a healthy appetite.

Eating and digestion occur in stages, and different physiological signals affect your hunger at each step. Clearly, the smell of food, its appearance, even a clock that says it's lunchtime, all play a role in making you hungry early stages of most diets. The plateau problem can be especially severe for women, who have a lower metabolic rate than men to begin with (since they have less muscle tissue, and muscle tissue burns more calories than fatty tissue does).

It's not certain how long it takes for the body to turn down the metabolic fires, but a highly restrictive crash diet should dampen them within two weeks. With repeated dieting, however, metabolic compensation increases. The more diets you go on, it seems, the more quickly your body recognizes the game and lowers your metabolic rate. On each successive diet, you lose weight more slowly and regain it more quickly. Eventually, your metabolic rate may be slowed down permanently.

The phenomenon could help explain a puzzling fact. Many fat people claim that they don't eat unusually large amounts of food. While doctors were long skeptical of these claims (and many still are), they have been supported by studies on special metabolic wards and in other controlled settings. In one study at an English country estate, every morsel the 29 subjects ate was measured. They weren't allowed to leave without a chaperone, and their luggage was searched for hidden food. This study showed that many women really *were* maintaining their weight on as little as 1,500 calories per day and that the women with such low meta-

---

enough to eat in the first place. But there are internal hunger signals too. It has been suggested that endorphins — morphinelike brain chemicals involved in the responses to pain and pleasure — may boost hunger and that the hormone insulin affects the brain as an appetite stimulant.

There's also evidence that modest amounts of adrenaline and related substances can act on parts of the hypothalamus to promote hunger. But large amounts can cause an opposite response. This could explain why drugs like amphetamines, which mimic these natural substances, are able to blunt appetite.

What about that satisfied feeling nutritionists call satiety? Once you start a meal, what makes you stop? Not just a full stomach; if you ate until your stomach was distended, you'd overeat at every meal. But well before that point, some food reaches your small intestine, and the intestine itself seems to release signals to stop eating.

Small protein molecules (called peptides) produced in the intestine appear to be involved in suppressing hunger. One of these peptides, called cholecystokinin (CCK), seems to do this by stimulating the vagus nerve, which runs from the intestine to the brain. The bulk of the material in your stomach can also send a stop signal. In fact, several obesity treatments are designed to curtail eating by using such calorieless stomach fillers as fiber supplements.

All of these factors come into play within the time it takes to eat a good-sized meal. But there are long-term controls on hunger as well. It's almost certain, for example, that the state of your body's fat cells affects your overall hunger level — the background against which meal-to-meal variations are played out.

bolic rates were those who had been on the most diets. Other researchers report that women who are chronic dieters may reduce their caloric needs substantially below even the 1,500 level.

If you lose weight, regain weight, and diet again repeatedly, you may lower your caloric needs to the point where you can no longer diet yourself thin without depriving yourself of necessary nutrients. This yo-yo pattern of dieting may pose other health hazards as well. Because of the metabolic changes, there's a tendency to regain even more weight after a diet than you lost while you were on it. And repeated diets compound the problem. (You might start at 150 pounds, jump to 155 after your first diet, and be at 180 by the end of your fifth.) There's also evidence that yo-yo dieting can raise the risk of high blood pressure over time.

The obvious questions, of course, are: How does the body regulate itself? What exactly gives the signal to turn up hunger and turn down metabolism?

The physiological reasons are still not clear. Both hunger and metabolic rate are apparently controlled by several parts of the brain, including the hypothalamus, which also controls thirst, pleasure, sexual desire, and other drives. But no one really knows by what mechanism the brain learns you are taking in fewer calories in time to adjust hunger and metabolic rate so quickly.

In addition to short-term adaptations to dieting, the body also carries out a long-term fight to regain lost fat if the loss is substantial enough. At Rockefeller University in New York, researchers studied several members of Overeaters Anonymous who had successfully gone from more than 200 pounds to a normal weight. Once they've stabilized at their new low weight, these people are no longer actively dieting, that is, they're not reducing.

But many of these formerly fat people are substantially different from normal-weight people who have never been fat. Their metabolic rates are significantly lower, and they burn roughly 25 percent fewer calories per day. They have low white blood cell counts and low blood pressure, and the women no longer menstruate. What's more, they report chronic hunger, even obsessions about food.

According to the Rockefeller researchers, reducers who are able to lose such substantial amounts of weight may become in some ways similar to anorexics, who starve themselves to emaciation. Both groups seem to be living below a weight that's biologically natural for them and suffering physically and mentally as a result.

Studies like these suggest two things: First, that the body's rebellion against weight loss — at least significant weight loss of 50 or more pounds — is long-term. The pressure to regain stays on long after the diet is over. This is consistent with the observation that many dieters begin gaining their weight back even after they have maintained a slim shape for a year or more.

But second, the work suggests that individuals are somehow biologically programmed to carry different weights and that a "normal" weight may be abnormally low for a person structured to carry more fat. Although the concept is still under intensive study, many researchers now speak of a "setpoint" for body fatness — an amount of fat that each individual is biologically "set" to carry.

While it can be depressingly difficult to reduce below this setpoint, the theory holds a positive note. It may be difficult for some people to *gain* very much more than their setpoint weight. This has been demonstrated by experiments in which volunteers have attempted to put on pounds. As they get significantly above their customary weight, they lose their appetite, and their metabolic rates speed up — an apparent effort by their bodies to keep weight down to the volunteers' normal ranges.

According to the theory, a person's setpoint is largely determined by genes, but not entirely. Exercise, for example, may lower the setpoint, enabling the body to settle comfortably at a lower level of fatness. Dieting, on the other hand, doesn't appear to change the setpoint so much as to battle against it.

The concept of a setpoint for fatness is still theoretical, largely because no one has been able to describe the biological mechanisms that would make it work. In fact, the whole question of how weight is regulated remains unclear. But there's an increasing consensus that fatness *is* regulated — that the body cares how much fat tissue it carries — and that some bodies are biologically suited to carry more fat than others. In one of the most promising approaches to discovering how the system works, researchers have focused on the very cells that store the body's fat.

FAT CELLS AND FATE

Every one of us has billions of fat storage cells, though some of us have more than others. When we eat more calories than we burn, we add fat to our bodies, filling and expanding the individual cells. When we get thinner, these cells shrink. But there are limits to how far fat cells can be stretched or compressed.

Research on fat cells — much of it done at Rockefeller University under the direction of Dr. Jules Hirsch — suggests that the cells themselves somehow send chemical signals to the brain, saying "feed me" when they get too empty. Dieting may reduce fat cells below normal size. As long as the cells remain undersized, the signals persist. That could explain why dieters still suffer increased hunger and reduced metabolic rate months or years after they've lost weight.

The Rockefeller scientists and others are now trying to decipher the chemical signals by which fat cells tell the brain to refill them. The best guess comes from the chemistry of fat cells. Virtually all the fat in these cells is stored as triglycerides, the large molecules, described in chapter 3, that combine one molecule of glycerol with three fatty acids.

But fat cells aren't passive receptacles for fat; the triglycerides in them are constantly being broken down and reformed. When the body takes in more calories than it can use, fat cells form triglycerides to store the excess. When energy is needed, fat cells break down triglycerides and release their fatty acids into the bloodstream to be burned for fuel. One of the elusive chemical signals that triggers the brain to compensate when fat cells become too small may well be the concentration of fatty acids in the blood.

If it's difficult to shrink fat cells, it's even more difficult to make them go away. So the number of fat cells seems to determine a certain minimal amount of fat that your body is destined to carry. In fact, studies have shown that children and adults with an unusually large number of fat cells have a particularly hard time losing weight. The next question is, What determines the number of fat cells, and is there anything you can do about it?

A few years ago, it was widely believed that new fat cells could be formed through overeating, but only at certain critical periods of life, particularly infancy. Overfeeding infants would supposedly cause them to grow more fat cells and grow up into overweight, resentful children. That belief, however, was based largely on experiments with rats, which do develop excess fat cells if they're overfed in the first three weeks of life.

For humans the pattern may be quite different. But for a number of reasons, it's hard to determine exactly how or when we go about adding new fat cells. The technique of counting fat cells — taking a sample of adipose tissue with a needle and examining it under the microscope — makes it impossible to detect cells until they're filled with fat. If you study a volunteer over a period of time and see more fat cells appearing, you don't know for certain whether the cells are multiplying or whether cells that were shrunken and dormant have become full enough to be seen and counted.

Despite such uncertainties, there is some consensus about how human fat cells change through life. Although fat cells can be added at any point, it now appears that most infants don't add new ones in their first year; they just fill up those they're born with. But after early infancy the number of fat cells is most likely to increase during a child's second year and again during adolescence.

Fat accumulates more quickly in some children than in others, and the pattern of fat cell multiplication seems to be largely determined by genes. In obese infants who have a strong genetic propensity to gain weight, the number of fat cells can start increasing even during the first year and then increase rapidly. By the time they're a few years old, extremely obese children may have as many fat cells as an adult, and their fat cells may also be larger than normal. (Though early childhood weight gain does increase the risk of adult obesity, it does not predetermine it; see chapter 24.)

In adulthood, as in childhood, the luck of the genetic draw gives some of us a greater tendency to obesity than others. Genes may raise the risk of obesity by dictating a high number of fat cells, a low metabolic rate, or both. Whatever the genetic mechanism, the basic odds have been known for a long time. If one of your parents was obese, you have a 40 percent chance of becoming obese yourself; if both of your parents were, your risk is about 80 percent. (If both parents are lean, your risk is less than 10 percent.)

No one can say which is more at fault: parental genes or family patterns that encourage little physical activity and high caloric intake. But studies by psychiatrist Albert Stunkard and his colleagues suggest that obesity may be linked more closely to nature than to nurture. Their study of 540 Danish adults who had been adopted showed that the body type of the adoptee, whether very thin, very fat, or somewhere in between, was closely correlated with the body types of the *biological* parents. In contrast, the body types of the adoptive parents, who supplied the family environment but not the genes, bore no relation to the body types of the adopted children they raised. Similarly, a study of twins found through U.S. Army records showed that identical twins, who share identical genes, are much more alike in body size than fraternal twins, who are no closer genetically than ordinary siblings.

The exact nature of the genetic link is still being studied. There's some evidence that women with obese mothers have the highest genetic risk, while men with obese fathers have the lowest, although no one is sure why this should be so. It also seems that the genetic tendency to obesity may not be expressed until late in life: someone who's thin at 30 may become fat at 50. For this reason, Stunkard's advice to individuals with obese forebears can be summarized in two words: "eternal vigilance."

Genetics is not destiny, however. While our genes set limits on how thin or fat we can be, they leave us a certain range of freedom. Simple calorie cutting is not the best way to reach the lower end of that range, if that's your goal; and new diet fads, based on mysterious and "newly discovered" principles, probably won't help much either. But taking in fewer calories than you burn, particularly by changing the composition of your diet, and starting a regular exercise program may indeed help you lose weight, in a way that's natural and comfortable for your body.

The decision to lose or gain weight—or simply to stay where you are—has to begin with some kind of self-assessment. First, and most important, is your present weight endangering your health?

HOW HAZARDOUS IS FATNESS?

Everyone has seen those height-and-weight charts in magazines, on scales, in the doctor's office. They're supposed to tell you what your desirable weight is, based on your height and your frame size. The whole idea of desirable weight was developed by insurance companies, primarily the Metropolitan Life Insurance Company, because they wanted to know whether policyholders above a certain weight were at greater risk. In the 1950s, 26 companies joined in a huge study analyzing several million life insurance policies purchased in the two previous decades. They had a record of each policyholder's height and weight when the insurance was bought and the age at which the person had died. From this, they could calculate a weight for each height that seemed to be associated with the greatest life expectancy.

For each height, Metropolitan's statisticians, who analyzed the results of the full study, found mortality increasing at both ends of the weight range. Obese policyholders had high mortality rates and so did very thin ones. Weights in the middle range were associated with low mortality and greater longevity.

Metropolitan put those weights into its table of "desirable" weights for each height, published in 1959. But there were a few problems. First, they found that there was a wide range of weights — about 30 or 40 pounds for each height category — where weight seemed to pose no risk to health. It didn't seem right, though, that a 6-foot-tall man should be as healthy at 184 pounds as at 147 pounds. So Metropolitan decided that the lowest weights at each height were right for people with small frames, while the greatest weights were for large frames.

The problem here was that there was no scientific definition of frame size, and most people using the table tended to think of themselves as having a large frame if that would permit them a few extra pounds. When a new table was prepared from new data and published in 1983, it came with instructions for finding your frame size by measuring the width of your elbow. But that measurement wasn't actually done on the policyholders whose heights and weights the table is based on, so its relevance to weight and longevity is unclear.

Another problem with the construction of these tables was accuracy. People were weighed with clothes and shoes on, or were simply asked to report their weight — hardly a reliable measure. The accuracy of the tables became an issue when the 1983 version was released, because it showed that "desirable" weights had gone up since 1959 — as much as 10 percent for some heights. Since there's no biological reason for this to happen, the simplest explanation was that some unrecognized error in data collection had skewed the results.

Despite such criticisms of the Metropolitan Life tables, they still represent the largest studies of the relation between weight and life expectancy. So what can we conclude from them?

First, it's clear that extreme overweight is a health hazard. A study of morbidly obese men — those who weigh roughly twice what the insurance tables recommend — shows that the risk of death between ages 25 and 34 is eleven times greater than the risk for normal-weight men. But the riskiness of more moderate amounts of excess weight is less clear.

As a general rule, a National Institutes of Health committee has recommended that anything more than 20 percent above the midpoint of the medium-frame range should be considered dangerous (see chapter 2). But, as we'll see, an individual's actual risk may depend upon a number of factors.

Second, there's good evidence that being significantly *underweight* may shorten life expectancy. Several studies besides Metropolitan's have found this to be true, and a variety of explanations have been advanced, the most popular being that thin people are more likely to smoke. But several researchers have found life-shortening dangers of thinness independent of smoking.

And third, there's no reason to focus obsessively on a single weight as your ideal. The range of weights that would be reasonably healthy for you may be wide indeed.

But to really understand what weight is best for you, you have to go beyond the standard tables. You have to consider three factors the tables ignore: your age, fat distribution, and genetic heritage.

The Metropolitan Life tables treat age as if there were no reason for anyone to gain weight after 25. But experience tells us that most people *do* gain weight as they get older, and lab studies tell us that the metabolic rate falls 2–5 percent for every decade past age 30. Recently, some researchers have suggested that a little weight gain over the years may be both natural and healthy.

One of the chief proponents of this idea is Dr. Reubin Andres, clinical director of the Gerontology Research Center at the National Institute on Aging. Andres has looked at several different studies, including his own reanalysis of the life insurance data. Since these statistics include policyholders' ages, Andres recalculated the data to get desirable weights for different ages and heights. He constructed a new table, giving the same desirable weights for men and women (since that's what his analysis showed) and leaving out frame size (since it was never actually measured in the studies).

Andres's table (see "What's Your Best Weight?," page 143) has not been widely accepted, but it demonstrates how age may help determine the best weight for health. According to this analysis, the standard height-and-weight tables are just about right — for someone who's 40 years old. But to have the greatest life expectancy, a 60-year-old should weigh considerably more, and a 20-year-old considerably less.

Next comes the question of how your weight is distributed—how much muscle, how much fat, and where the fat sits on your body. While height-and-weight tables only give pounds, no researchers really suggest that weight itself is a hazard; it's fatness they're worried about. A 240-pound football player should certainly be healthier than the 240-pound fan who sits at home watching the game on TV. (Nonetheless, many professional football players were deemed unfit for service in World War

WHAT'S YOUR BEST WEIGHT?

Here are weights from the standard Metropolitan Life Insurance Company tables—both the 1959 and the 1983 versions—compared with the age-specific table constructed in 1985 by Dr. Reubin Andres. The frame size breakdowns used in the Metropolitan Life tables are not given here. Weights without clothing and heights without shoes are used.

Metropolitan Life Insurance Company
Desirable Weights in Pounds for Ages 25–59

Height	1959 Table		1983 Table	
	Men	Women	Men	Women
4'10"		91–119		100–131
4'11"		93–122		101–134
5'0"		96–125		103–137
5'1"	107–136	99–128	123–145	105–140
5'2"	110–139	102–131	125–148	108–144
5'3"	113–143	105–135	127–151	111–148
5'4"	116–147	108–139	129–155	114–152
5'5"	119–151	111–143	131–159	117–156
5'6"	123–156	115–147	133–163	120–160
5'7"	127–161	119–151	135–167	123–164
5'8"	131–165	123–155	137–171	126–167
5'9"	135–169	127–160	139–175	129–170
5'10"	139–174	131–165	141–179	132–173
5'11"	143–179	135–170	144–183	135–176
6'0"	147–184		147–187	
6'1"	151–189		150–192	
6'2"	155–194		153–197	
6'3"	159–199		157–202	
6'4"				

II because they were heavier than the standard charts allowed.)

What's more surprising, though, is that *where* your body stores fat is also important to health. Recent research in the United States and Sweden suggests that the body has two different kinds of fat stores, which are biologically and functionally separate. Fat on the hips is hardest to lose and is stored there for special purposes, primarily to provide energy during lactation and pregnancy. (Women store significantly more hip fat

Gerontology Research Center
Recommended Weights in Pounds for Both Sexes

Height	20–29 yr	30–39 yr	(by age) 40–49 yr	50–59 yr	60–69 yr
4'10"	84–111	92–119	99–127	107–135	115–142
4'11"	87–115	95–123	103–131	111–139	119–147
5'0"	90–119	98–127	106–135	114–143	123–152
5'1"	93–123	101–131	110–140	118–148	127–157
5'2"	96–127	105–136	113–144	122–153	131–163
5'3"	99–131	108–140	117–149	126–158	135–168
5'4"	102–135	112–145	121–154	130–163	140–173
5'5"	106–140	115–149	125–159	134–168	144–179
5'6"	109–144	119–154	129–164	138–174	148–184
5'7"	112–148	122–159	133–169	143–179	153–190
5'8"	116–153	126–163	137–174	147–184	158–196
5'9"	119–157	130–168	141–179	151–190	162–201
5'10"	122–162	134–173	145–184	156–195	167–207
5'11"	126–167	137–178	149–190	160–201	172–213
6'0"	129–171	141–183	153–195	165–207	177–219
6'1"	133–176	145–188	157–200	169–213	182–225
6'2"	137–181	149–194	162–206	174–219	187–232
6'3"	141–186	153–199	166–212	179–225	192–238
6'4"	144–191	157–205	171–218	184–231	197–244

Source: Adapted from Reubin Andres, Edwin L. Bierman, William R. Hazzard, eds., *Geriatric Medicine* (New York, McGraw-Hill, 1984), p. 317; and the 1959 Metropolitan Life Insurance Company's Height and Weight Tables.

than men.) Abdominal fat, however, is a more flexible stockpile and is more readily lost on a diet-and-exercise program.

Abdominal fat now seems to be significantly more dangerous than the fat on the hips. In other words, apple-shaped people are at greater risk than pears.

Researchers have found this by measuring the waists and hips of various subjects and correlating the waist-to-hip ratio with the risk of different diseases. (A high ratio means a big belly.) At the Medical College of Wisconsin in Milwaukee, Dr. Ahmed Kissebah has found that women with a waist-to-hip ratio greater than 0.85 ran three times the risk of diabetes as women whose waist-to-hip ratio was 0.75 or less. And in Sweden, Dr. Per Björntorp has shown that men with a ratio above the average 0.9 to 0.95 have a greater risk of coronary heart disease and stroke. In fact, fat distribution was a greater predictor of disease in these men than total body fat.

High-risk abdominal fat is easier fat to lose, because the abdomen seems to store it by expanding fat cells, which can also be shrunk (up to a point). But the hips store fat in a large number of smaller fat cells, which won't shrink much and can't be made to go away.

In the final analysis, the importance of losing body fat depends primarily on your own biology and your own heredity. Major life-threatening diseases are associated with overweight. But obesity is just one factor that contributes to illness. Nevertheless, weight plays a major role in adult-onset diabetes (see chapter 20) and is considered a risk factor for hypertension (see chapter 18), coronary heart disease (see chapter 17), and several forms of cancer (see chapter 19).

Current research, however, suggests that the risks caused by obesity can vary substantially from individual to individual. Though obesity is a hazard for many people, it doesn't uniformly raise the risk of cancer, diabetes, hypertension, and heart disease for everyone at all times.

There's another point to be made too. If you're really concerned with your health, it's important to manage your weight with a regimen that's healthy.

Certain weight-loss plans may raise the risk of the very diseases that weight loss is meant to prevent. Very-low-calorie diets — liquid protein, 300-calorie-per-day formulas, and the like — can raise the risk of heart attack (by disrupting the body's electrolyte balance or damaging heart muscle). No-carbohydrate diets, which go in and out of fashion, are often high in dietary fat and may thus raise blood cholesterol. Some over-the-counter diet pills have been linked to an increased risk of hypertension (as well as anxiety attacks and other psychological problems). And the yo-yo pattern of dieting may also raise blood pressure over the long haul.

The best approach to weight loss is none of these, but a more moderate, balanced method — a combination of a high-complex-carbohydrate, low-fat diet and the right kind of exercise. Such a regimen has two advantages. It gives you the best odds of actually reducing your body's fat stores, and it can work directly to prevent or treat the diseases linked to obesity.

Such a simple approach isn't always easy to follow. There are so many new diets, pills, and gimmicks every year that it's hard to believe none of them works better or more quickly than simply cutting down on fat. But, as we'll see in the next chapter, the arguments against weight-loss fads are clear. And, at the same time, the physiological benefits of a more moderate approach are turning out to be even greater than we had realized.

CHAPTER 11

Weight Control

A T SOME POINT in your life, you've probably bought a diet book. Maybe you've spent a few weeks avoiding carbohydrates and drinking eight glasses of water a day. Maybe you've lived on fruit, alternating grapefruit, watermelon, and pineapple. You may have tried a balanced diet that was just moderately low in calories. You may have given up food altogether for a powdered formula, or simply tried fasting.

Whatever you've tried, it probably worked—while you were on the diet. As every dieter knows, taking pounds off is much easier than keeping them off. The problem is that most diet plans focus on short-term weight *loss*, when what is needed is a program of lifetime weight *control*—what weight-loss experts generally refer to as "learning new eating and exercise habits."

The classic method of losing weight is to count calories—keeping a running tab of how many calories you're consuming and choosing what to eat on that basis. For this, you need some sense of your daily caloric needs. By using the food diary of chapter 2 and watching your scale, you can determine just what your intake is and whether it is making you lose weight or gain it. But actually counting calories on a daily basis is likely to be too obsessive an activity to maintain for long.

Another strategy is to learn behavioral tricks: eat slowly, chew your food thoroughly, put food on smaller plates to make portions look bigger. Many treatment programs for overweight people have been based on such strategies. However, several studies now suggest that the obese do not necessarily suffer from abnormal eating behavior (for example, they may not eat faster than thin people do). And long-term follow-up studies show that people who lose weight through behavior modification regain it as reliably as dieters do, although they tend to gain it back somewhat more slowly.

Still another approach, and a hazardous one, is to use amphetamines and related drugs to keep your weight down. But if you stop taking the drug after you've reached your desired weight, you'll regain more quickly than you would have if you'd lost weight by diet alone. And for most people, a lifetime commitment to this kind of drug therapy is more dangerous than remaining overweight (see "The Problem with Diet Pills," pages 148–149).

The riskiest weight-loss strategy of all is surgery. Various approaches have been tried, primarily intestinal bypass surgery, which creates a 6-foot detour in the small intestine, and stomach stapling, which reduces the size of the stomach so it can be filled up with less food. These drastic treatments, however, are not deemed appropriate for anyone whose level of obesity is less than life-threatening. (A newer and more limited procedure, called liposuction, or fat suctioning, is apparently safer, but can only trim fat from specific areas and will not significantly reduce overall body weight.)

Considering the alternatives, the best approach to long-term weight control for people who are no more than 40 percent overweight would seem to involve a three-way strategy.

First, you need to set realistic goals for yourself, using the guidelines in chapter 10. If your body is built to be comfortable at around 180 pounds, you may not be wise to try to get down to 140 pounds.

Second, you must burn enough calories through exercise. Unlike dieting, exercise is something you can do for the rest of your life. And, as we'll see later in this chapter, it has a range of effects that make it uniquely effective in weight control.

Finally, you may well be able to lower caloric intake with little sense of deprivation by maintaining a diet that is low in fats and high in complex carbohydrates.

The goal is to find a regimen that lets you eat well, feel pleasantly full, and maintain a weight you're happy with. For many people it's an attainable goal, but only if you go about it the right way. That means, first of all, being able to resist the lure of fad diets, even though all of them promise to make you svelte without pain.

QUICK-FIX DIETS

Popular diet books sell so well because they promise a new, slim body via a special no-pain, no-strain formula. But once you understand their strategies — and some basic nutritional realities — it's not that difficult to see where they fail.

Diet books commonly rely on anecdotal reports, not on scientific evidence. Authors will claim that tens, or hundreds, or thousands of people have lost weight by their methods. But unless a claim is backed by published research, there's little reason to pay attention to it.

Bear in mind, too, that even if claims of successful weight loss are true, they don't mean much. It's relatively easy to get people to lose weight, especially on a new program. The trick is to help them keep it off.

Many popular diets claim that an abundance of one kind of nutrient

DEPARTMENT OF FALSE HOPES: THE PROBLEM WITH DIET PILLS

Understandably, many people who are sick of dieting look for relief in pills. But although diet pills have been with us for decades, they are still largely ineffective, if not unsafe.

The first diet pills, of course, were amphetamines, widely prescribed for weight loss in the 1940s. They were considered so safe at one point that two thirds of patients treated for overweight were given them. The drugs were even prescribed to keep pregnant women from gaining too much weight. Since that time, however, the use of amphetamines and similar drugs has been sharply curtailed.

Despite their widespread use, amphetamines, which will reduce appetite while raising metabolic rates, proved to be of limited value in weight loss. An FDA review of the literature showed that amphetamines and other diet pills seem to help people lose only about 10 pounds. Moreover, when dieters stop taking them, their weight shoots back up, according to research at the University of Pennsylvania, and it shoots up *more quickly* than it does for dieters who lose weight without diet pills.

Most popular appetite suppressants now in use — like mazindol, phentermine, and diethylpropion — are chemically similar to amphetamine. Although these drugs may be safer than the amphetamines, they're hardly benign. Possible side effects, says the FDA, include nervousness, irritability, insomnia, blurred vision, dizziness, palpitations, hypertension, sweating, nausea, vomiting, and sometimes diarrhea or constipation.

One amphetamine-related drug — phenylpropanolamine, or PPA — is considered safe enough to be sold over the counter. It's now the major ingredient of nonprescription diet pills. But even PPA has been linked to a range of adverse effects, including anxiety, dizziness, and increased blood pressure, and is not recommended for use by people with hypertension, diabetes, or heart, thyroid, or kidney disease.

Not surprisingly, many drug researchers are now seeking a more effective and safer weight-loss pill, safe enough, perhaps, to take for a lifetime. But so far nothing seems to do the job. Many agents that help burn calories by raising the metabolic rate also pose a risk to the heart or other organs. (One of the first metabolic boosters, a chemical called dinitrophenol that was tested in the 1930s, led to weight loss but also caused cataracts.)

Meanwhile, there are plenty of over-the-counter diet aids for consumers to choose. The major categories, described here, are all generally safer than stimulants but not necessarily more effective.

or a shortage of another is the secret to their fat-burning potential. A few years ago, Paul LaChance, a professor of food science and nutrition at Rutgers University, analyzed 10 popular diets of that time. The lowest in protein — the infamous, eat-lots-of-fruit Beverly Hills Diet — provided only 6 percent of its calories as protein. On the other end of the scale, the eat-lots-of-protein Stillman Diet was 46 percent protein but only 5

Anesthetics

The active ingredient in diet candies and gum is benzocaine, a local anesthetic. Benzocaine is supposed to aid weight loss by numbing taste buds, but there is no solid evidence that this works.

Fillers

Several agents are intended to add bulk in the stomach and presumably leave less room for food. Most contain some type of fiber, like methylcellulose or a popular product called glucomannan (derived from the Japanese konjac root). There is evidence that these fibers can be of limited help, producing a feeling of fullness in dieters when taken in sufficiently large doses.

Water Pills

For many years, diuretics have been popular among dieters, like high school and college wrestlers, who want to lose weight quickly. But since the weight they take off is only water, it's regained almost immediately, and regular use of the drugs may pose a danger of heart damage.

Hormones

Thyroid hormone, still prescribed by some physicians, is one of the oldest weight-loss nostrums. Although it can speed up the metabolic rate, it is essentially useless in weight control, prompting the body to burn more calories of lean body mass than of fat. Moreover, the hormone has potentially dangerous neurological effects.

Recently, though, diet pill purveyors have marketed more sophisticated substances, like the intestinal peptide cholecystokinin (described in chapter 10) and the steroid hormone DHEA. Both were taken off the market by the FDA soon after they became popular — DHEA for safety reasons and cholecystokinin probably because it had no biological effect. While this hormone blunts appetite when injected into experimental animals, it appears inactive when taken orally.

Digestive Blockers

"Starch blockers," which surfaced in the early 1980s and which were banned by the FDA in 1982, are the major example of digestive blockers. Containing a protein derived from red kidney beans, the pills were supposed to interfere with an enzyme that digests starch in the body. But several studies showed that the blockers failed to disrupt starch digestion at all. Indeed, if they had, users would probably have suffered severe gas and diarrhea caused by a buildup of undigested starch in the large intestine.

percent carbohydrates. The Atkins Diet, based on eliminating carbohydrates, had a full 73 percent of its calories as fat, roughly twice as much fat as Americans normally eat.

Diets are designed to be odd, to distract dieters from the fact that diets are low in calories and make you feel hungry. (The ones LaChance studied, with the exception of the high-fat Atkins Diet, ranged from 737 to 1,316 calories per day.) Somehow, believing that some metabolic magic is taking place seems to ease the pain, at least temporarily.

But diets this low in calories also tend to be low in nutrients. LaChance found that most diets in his sample were below the U.S. RDA for B vitamins, calcium, iron, and trace elements. (The Beverly Hills Diet supplies no B_{12}, one third of the U.S. RDA for calcium, and one half of the U.S. RDA or less for at least five other essential nutrients.) As LaChance says, "No one will die as a result of these diets, but they could add up to health problems," particularly over a long period of time.

Of course, many diets aren't meant for long-term use. They're meant to take weight off in a week or two or three and to help you get thin fast. It's unlikely that any serious nutritional deficiency could develop that quickly. So what's wrong with a little semistarvation if it leads to fast weight loss?

There's plenty wrong. In addition to the metabolic slowdown that comes with quick weight loss (described in chapter 10), there's the question of the *kind* of weight you're losing. If the body is deprived of calories, it may burn either fat or the protein in muscle for fuel—muscle represents 30 percent of the calories stored in your body. Different approaches tend to promote one kind of weight loss or the other. If you severely restrict carbohydrates, your body will have to burn some of its protein to fuel the chemical cycles that carbohydrates normally drive.

The speed of weight loss, it turns out, is a direct indication of how much fat and muscle you're burning. It's a physiological law: *the faster you lose weight, the more water and muscle you are losing—and the less fat.*

The reason is simple. In the human body, as on the dinner table, fat is a more concentrated store of calories than lean tissue. So you have to deprive yourself of more calories over a longer period of time to burn a pound of fat than to burn a pound of muscle.

Let's say your daily caloric needs for metabolism and physical activity add up to 2,000 calories, and you go on a diet that only allows you 1,500. With this 500-calorie-per-day deficit, it would theoretically take you more than a week to burn a pound of body fat, which contains more than 4,000 calories. But if you burn only muscle—and, with it, excrete the water that's held in muscle tissue—you could lose a pound in about three days. Looking at it another way, fast weight loss, far from being a positive sign, is a signal that you're burning your lean tissue rather than the fat you really want to lose.

Even knowing all this, it can be difficult to resist new diet plans. The promises are enticing, the packages are slick, the rationales sound rational. It becomes easier to evaluate new diet fads, however, when you realize that very few of them are truly new; almost all are simply new variations of old and unfounded ideas. Old diets never die; they're just recycled. Here is a quick guide to some of the hardiest perennials — and to what's wrong with them.

Fasting

This approach, at least, has the virtue of simplicity: no recipes, no menus, no calories to count. But the benefits end there. Fasting more than a few days can lead to severe loss of muscle, fluids, electrolytes, and glycogen stores, as well as to nutritional deficiencies.

Modified Fasting: Very-Low-Calorie Formulas

If pure fasting is impractical, what about the next best thing — a formula that provides a minimum number of calories and all the essential nutrients? This is an approach that has in the past been linked to severe health problems. The basic notion comes from an experimental medical treatment, called the "protein-sparing modified fast" (PSMF), developed in the 1970s for the treatment of very obese patients.

The idea was to give patients the micronutrients they needed and all their calories in protein — just enough protein to prevent them from having to break down their own muscle for energy. Since that time, research has shown that an all-protein diet does not protect the *body's* protein stores as well as a mixture of proteins and carbohydrates.

Originally physicians gave their patients real food (tuna, chicken breast, and other lean meat), but many later switched to liquid protein formulas. Soon the formulas made the jump from the clinic to the drugstore, and several million Americans tried liquid protein diets. The fad came to a rapid end when five dozen deaths were reported among people using the diet formulas.

What went wrong? The early commercial liquid formulas were remarkably poorly designed. They were lacking in essential amino acids, vitamins, trace elements, and minerals (especially calcium and potassium). They created an imbalance of electrolytes, aggravated by the ketosis and uremia that result from very-low-carbohydrate diets.

Today's protein-sparing, very-low-calorie diets are based on powders rather than on liquid formulas and provide all the essential nutrients in 600 calories of protein and carbohydrate per day. These diets can be useful in a medically supervised, long-term regimen for serious cases of obesity. They may also help to get more modest reducing programs off to a safe, fast start.

Low-Carbohydrate Diets

In defiance of nutritional logic, low-carbohydrate diets have been the most popular of weight-loss plans for the last several decades. In fact, the fad began long before that, in mid-nineteenth-century England. The first published report of a weight-loss plan during the modern era was William Banting's *Letter on Corpulence Addressed to the Public*, an account of the low-carbohydrate diet the physician William Harvey had prescribed for him.

The diet makes no sense; carbohydrates contain only half as many calories, ounce for ounce, as fats do. Even sugar is a low source of calories in our diets. A pound of sugar contains no more calories than a pound of dry rice, flour, or cornmeal, and the teaspoonful of sugar in your morning coffee contains only 15.

But a side effect of low-carbohydrate diets makes them *seem* to work quickly. They have a pronounced diuretic effect: there is a rapid loss of body water, and hence of weight. The quick shift on the scale encourages the dieter to go on. But as soon as eating patterns revert to normal, so does water retention.

There is a more sinister rationale for low-carbohydrate diets. They increase the body's production of ketones (as described in chapter 3), which dietmongers claim reduces appetite. Indeed, individuals on fasts, who experience ketosis, often report a loss of interest in food. But there is no good evidence that what ketones affect is appetite. They may, in fact, simply produce nausea as well as hunger. (What's more, ketosis can pose a serious threat to health; see "Sugar Isn't Poisonous . . . But Lack of Sugar Is," in chapter 3.)

Low-carbohydrate diets have another clear drawback. If calories aren't coming from carbohydrates, they have to come from fats or proteins. Excess dietary fat poses some clear health risks. And excess protein, over a long period of time, may interfere with calcium metabolism and cause uremia, putting a strain on kidneys or triggering attacks of gout.

Food-Combining Diets

Many diet books, including some very popular recent ones, claim that the combination of foods within a meal can affect the way the nutrients in those foods are utilized. To some extent, as we'll see in chapter 13, this is certainly true; drinking orange juice at mealtimes, for example, will enhance iron absorption. But the popular diet books go way beyond such actual interactions, claiming that food combinations have major effects on the digestion of proteins, starches, and fats, not just on the absorption of micronutrients.

The typical recommendation of these diets is to separate different food groups by some stringent rules, ostensibly so that the foods will leave each other alone. *Fit for Life*, a recent diet best-seller, called for eating only fruit before noon and vegetables (with a little protein or starch) from noon until 8 p.m. The Beverly Hills Diet not only separated fruit from meat but separated fruit from fruit; you were supposed to eat only pineapple one day, only papaya the next, and so on.

There is no scientific evidence to support these diet plans, and their rationales make even less sense than those of most other diet books. A major claim of *Fit for Life* is that eating food in the wrong combinations will make it impossible for your body to digest a large portion of your dinner and that this will lead to weight gain. But the book doesn't explain how undigested food that doesn't get to your bloodstream and isn't converted to either energy or fat can increase weight for any longer than it takes to travel from one end of the digestive tract to the other.

A DIET FOR LIFE

Strange though many diet books are, the desire to believe them is understandable. There's universal appeal to the promise of being able to lose weight and keep it off without being hungry. Also, many dieters have come to believe that there *is* more to weight control than balancing calories. Their intuition is that some foods make it especially difficult to control their weight.

Recent research indicates that dieters may be right. It has been suggested that refined sugars may be uniquely fattening because they increase hunger by raising insulin levels. Fatty foods may promote weight gain, not only because they're concentrated sources of calories but because of their effects on appetite and metabolism. But foods that are high in complex carbohydrates — like fruits and vegetables, grains, legumes, pasta, and other starches — may provide an aid to effective weight control.

Any diet that promotes weight loss has to reduce caloric intake somehow. But a high-complex-carbohydrate, low-fat diet may make it possible to reduce calories with relatively little conscious effort. The fiber in complex-carbohydrate foods takes up space in the stomach without providing digestible calories. As a result, these foods seem to help people feel full before they've taken in as many calories as they would on another type of diet.

Several studies have now shown this effect. In one at Michigan State University, college students reduced their weight effectively by eating 12 slices of low-calorie, high-fiber bread per day, along with whatever else they wanted. Apparently the bread reduced their consumption of other foods.

At the University of Alabama, researchers on the Birmingham campus compared the caloric intake of volunteers when they ate high-complex-carbohydrate meals — with such foods as brown rice, broccoli, chicken, whole wheat rolls, and fresh fruit—and when they were fed more standard American fare. While they were always allowed to eat as much as they wanted, the volunteers were filled by 1,570 calories on high-complex-carbohydrate days but needed 3,000 calories when they ate more fats, sugar, and proteins.

It's possible, of course, to go overboard on barley and broccoli. Some recently popular diets, like the Pritikin regimen, are so high in carbohydrates and so low in proteins and fats that they are not only nutritionally unbalanced but also hard to follow, since they tend to be monotonous and relatively tasteless (lacking the fats that are the carriers of flavor). Although diets with too much fiber can lead to digestive problems, most Americans could easily eat more complex carbohydrates than they now do without risking these problems. More fiber would, in fact, probably improve their health. The key to balanced dietary change, however, is to consider what you may want to restrict in your diet as well as what you may want to add.

Research by Yale psychologist Judith Rodin offers some evidence that sugar may boost hunger and that restricting dietary sugar may be helpful in weight control. Her hypothesis is that insulin increases appetite, and eating sugar can lead to a rapid increase in insulin. In one experiment she showed that people given a sugar drink around breakfast time were hungrier, and ate more, when offered a smorgasbord at lunch. According to Rodin's hypothesis, however, substituting artificial sweeteners for sugar may not solve the problem. She believes the sweet taste of artificial flavorings may also trigger an insulin rise (as a conditioned response).

In general, the value of artificial sweeteners in weight control has probably been overrated. There is still no evidence that these sugar substitutes actually help people lose weight. Research suggests that diet foods and sodas are simply added to regular diets and do not replace high-calorie foods. One study of more than 78,000 older women—surveyed as part of a massive study by the American Cancer Society—showed that those who used sugar substitutes were *more* likely to gain weight over a one-year period than those who didn't.

Whatever else sugar does or doesn't do, it is our favorite flavoring for fat, and that may be the worst thing about it. Studies by Adam Drewnowski of the University of Michigan, using sugar in heavy, high-fat cream, have shown that the average person's taste for sweetened fat exceeds the taste for fatless sweets. So if you put sugar in your coffee, you may want to add more cream than you would otherwise; and it's the cream more than the sugar that will raise your body fat. Drewnowski has also shown that obese women have an even greater preference for fat than thin ones do.

Of course, fats aren't pure evil either. They're essential nutrients; we need them in our diets. But a surplus of dietary fat, more than a surplus of any other nutrient, is likely to contribute to obesity.

First, fats are concentrated sources of calories. A gram of fat has more than twice as many calories as a gram of protein or carbohydrate. What's more, fats make food more fun. They are the vehicles of flavor. Most of the molecules that give food its aroma and taste are dissolved in dietary fat. (That's why fried chicken is so "finger-lickin' good.")

There's also something about fat itself that makes us want to eat lots of it. This may well be a relic of our evolutionary past. Since our ancestors lived largely on fruits, vegetables, grains, and very lean meat (as described in chapter 8), the chance to indulge in dietary fat — when it came — was a rare opportunity to stock up on much-needed calories. Today, lab experiments have shown that the surest way to spark a rat's appetite is to feed it a high-fat diet; simply adding Crisco to its rat chow will do the trick. Such a diet will even cause the animal to form extra fat cells.

Finally, recent research suggests that your body uses more energy in the process of digestion when your diet is high in carbohydrates than it does when your diet is high in fats. This "diet-induced thermogenesis" burns a relatively small number of calories, however — no more than 10 percent of your daily caloric intake.

It's also easier for your body to store fats than to store carbohydrates. Dietary fat can be stored directly as body fat. But less than 1 percent of your body weight is made up of stored carbohydrate (primarily glycogen in the liver). All the rest must be turned into fat for storage, and that takes energy.

A high-complex-carbohydrate diet has one other advantage over other weight-loss regimens. It is likely to promote overall health rather than threaten it. As we'll see in later chapters, such a diet may be useful in preventing or treating heart disease, diabetes, and possibly cancer. But another essential aspect of disease prevention is exercise, which can help restore normal insulin activity in diabetics, bring down blood pressure, and reduce blood cholesterol levels. Increasingly, exercise is also being recognized as the key to effective weight control.

THE IMPORTANCE OF EXERCISE

Most of us believe that fatness comes from eating too much. The very word obese comes from roots that mean "overeat." But there's good evidence that obesity may just as easily be caused by inactivity.

Several studies have measured the activity levels of infants (gauged by pedometerlike devices on their arms and legs), teenagers' participation in summer-camp sports, and the daily walking habits of adults. Although the results aren't perfectly consistent, they strongly suggest that lean individuals tend to be more active than fat ones. One recent study has even shown that thin people tend to fidget more.

Government statistics also suggest that if Americans are getting fatter, inactivity may be largely to blame. One study showed that, between 1965 and 1977, Americans reduced their average caloric intake by about 10 percent, while other research has reported an average weight gain throughout most of this period. The only possible explanation is that Americans became less active, so although they ate less, they weighed more.

Whatever makes an individual overweight, exercise can usually play a major role in losing weight and an even more significant role in maintaining a lower weight. This is true even if the tendency to obesity is inherited. Researchers have done extensive studies of laboratory mice with genes that make them overweight under normal laboratory conditions. Recent work has shown that even these animals stay at a normal weight if they are allowed to exercise on a running wheel from the time they're weaned.

This is good news for anyone who wants to reduce, because exercise can be an attractive complement to dieting. A diet may offer immediate reinforcement when pounds are lost early on. But as the dieter continues, he or she becomes hungry and irritable and is likely to abandon the regimen. Exercise has just the opposite effects. It's hard to begin. But once a routine is established, it can offer powerfully reinforcing emotional rewards. (Psychologists have shown, for example, that an exercise program can help overcome mild depression or anxiety.)

The clear benefit of exercise for weight control is the calories it burns, more than even many exercisers realize. At first glance, the number of calories expended in running, bicycling, or whatever seems unimpressive. A mile of jogging, for example, burns only about 100 calories, roughly the number in a large apple.

But an active body also keeps burning extra calories even after it stops exercising. Exercise raises the metabolic rate and keeps it up. At the University of California, Davis, obesity researcher Judith S. Stern has studied obese people on a program of exercise and a 500-calorie-per-day diet. They would exercise just 30 minutes per day, but their metabolic rates were still elevated 12 hours later. Other research has shown a similar effect (although the duration varies from study to study). Moreover, exercise seems to counteract the drop in metabolic rate that almost invariably occurs soon after a diet begins. There's also evidence that fitness training raises diet-induced thermogenesis, the metabolic boost that follows eating.

If you exercise intensely enough, it's even possible to eat more than you did before and stay thin or become thinner. (Marathon runners in training can put away 5,000 or 6,000 thousand calories per day without gaining.) Rat studies show that even a high-fat diet won't overly fatten rodents that are well enough exercised (but it will make them heavier than exercising rats on a low-fat diet).

One big advantage of exercise, however, is not only that it burns calories but that it gets those calories from the kind of tissue you really want to shed — from fat — and not from muscle, which is among the first to go when you lose weight by diet alone.

With exercise, the body can burn fat exclusively and may actually build muscle at the same time. In another study by Judith S. Stern, overweight adolescent boys were put on a special summer weight-loss program. After seven weeks on a 1,200-calorie-per-day diet, with five hours of exercise per day, they had lost an average of 27 pounds each, virtually all of it fat.

Exercise can reduce fat without necessarily lowering weight. Since muscle weighs more than fat, you can become thinner without getting any lighter, as you lose fat and build muscle. For anyone trying to control body fat through exercise, it's a good idea not only to watch the scale but to check the mirror and to gauge progress occasionally with a tape measure, or simply by how your clothing fits.

But it's how exercise can help keep lost weight from returning that may be most critical. A researcher from the University of California, Berkeley, recently interviewed several hundred women patients of the Kaiser-Permanente Health Maintenance Organization. She found that those who were able to stay thin after dieting were those who exercised consistently — almost every day.

What kind of exercise is most effective? First, it's clear which approaches *don't* work. "Spot reducing" exercises, which are supposed to trim your belly, or thighs, or hips, simply don't help. They may tone muscles in an area, but they won't reduce the fat there. The overall distribution of fat on your body is determined genetically, and all you can expect exercise to do is to lower your *overall* fat stores — though you may lose the most fat from areas where you have the most to lose.

Aerobic exercises are the best kind for weight loss. These are exercises that elevate the heart rate over a sustained period of time. You can do them continuously, while breathing deeply. Jogging, cycling, swimming, cross-country skiing, and brisk walking are all aerobic (as long as you walk fast enough to break into a sweat). Rowing machines also provide aerobic benefits, even though they may raise blood pressure more than other forms of aerobic exercise. In any kind of aerobic training, the standard goal is to raise your heart rate to between 70 and 85 percent of maximum — the maximum is about 220 minus your age — for at least 20 minutes three times a week.

Most weight training, like stop-and-start, huff-and-puff workouts on Nautilus machines, is nonaerobic, or anaerobic. It mobilizes energy quickly but doesn't raise the heart rate for more than a short period of time and doesn't really raise the metabolic rate. So it's less effective for burning fat, though it can build muscle mass.

The kind of exercise you do, however, is probably less important than a commitment to do it and keep doing it. It's important to choose a form of exercise, or a combination of exercises, that is both enjoyable and accessible.

For weight loss, frequent exercise is also most effective, perhaps because it keeps metabolic rates high more continuously. One review of the literature showed that people who exercise four or five times a week lose weight three times faster than those who exercise only three times a week.

To be effective, exercise must be an integral part of a person's life-style — forever. When pounds are lost through exercise, and kept off by exercise, the body adjusts to a new "normal" weight range. But when exercise ceases, the body reverts to its old notion of what your normal weight should be. Judith Stern sees this rebound effect among rats that lose body fat by running on treadmills. When they're taken off the tread-mill, their body fat shoots up within a week, and they even make more fat cells. They may be the animal equivalent of college athletes who tend to put on more weight in later life than their nonathletic classmates.

To make exercise a lifelong practice, parents (especially if they have weight problems themselves) would do well to encourage physical activity in their children from an early age. Family patterns of activity, just as family eating habits, can set the stage for a lifetime.

Even cutting TV-viewing time can help. At Tufts University, pediatrician William Dietz has shown a direct correlation between excessive TV watching and obesity, presumably because kids who watch a lot of television are relatively inactive (and usually eat high-calorie snacks while they watch). In terms of behavior, the amount of time a child aged 6–11 spent viewing television was the single most powerful predictor of adolescent obesity in his studies.

Later in life, activity becomes especially important to weight control. Between ages 25 and 55, the average person gains 15–20 pounds. Even people who don't gain weight may gain body fat. But there's evidence that this gain results from inactivity as much as from any innate slowdown in metabolic rate. A study of Norwegian woodcutters, who stay very active well into their sixties, showed that they maintained low body fat on high-calorie diets and scarcely gained a pound for as long as they were working. Only when they retired did their weight finally begin to creep up.

That example is hard to follow, but it's instructional nonetheless. The advantages of an active life appear even greater than many American joggers may imagine.

CHAPTER 12

Exercise: Nutrition in Action

YOU CAN'T SEPARATE exercise from other aspects of nutrition. Clearly, the amount of energy you spend each day and how you spend it have a powerful overall impact on fitness and health. But activity levels also directly affect dietary needs and can enhance substantially the body's ability to make the most of its nutrients.

Exercise not only makes you feel better but also can get you to function better by making demands on body systems that increase their efficiency. The old notion (even some doctors once believed it) that the body will "wear out" if physically overtaxed turns out to be anything but true. Although excessive exercise can raise the risk of muscle and joint injury, few Americans come anywhere near the danger level, and most of us expend so little energy on activity that we deny our organs and body systems the opportunity to perform at full genetic potential. As a result, they can neither protect us from disease as effectively as they are able nor contribute as much to our enjoyment of life.

Even a moderate increase in physical activity can, for example, raise interest in sex. Listing another big advantage of exercise, Judith S. Stern, professor of nutrition and director of the Food Intake Laboratory at the University of California, Davis, adds, "It allows you to eat more." You can take in more food and get more pleasure (or less guilt) and more nutrients out of it.

Remember (from chapter 11) that exercise lets you eat more free (non-weight-adding) calories than you spend in activity. It isn't only the 100 extra calories you've earned by biking for 2 miles that you get to enjoy. They don't amount to all that much—a baking-powder biscuit (without butter) or half a bagel (without cream cheese). What really pays off is the fact that your body keeps burning calories after you've put your bike away. Exercise will raise your metabolic rate and keep it up long after your exercise period ends, particularly if you exercise daily or several times a week.

If you want to eat less and lose weight — rather than simply eat more without gaining — exercise provides a three-way benefit. First, there are the calories you expend by walking, jogging, biking, or whatever form of activity you choose. Then there are the additional calories your faster metabolism is burning up (and taking out of your body's fat depots). Finally, there are the calories your body is *not* hoarding — for unless exercise counteracts the process, your body will *lower* metabolic rate soon after a diet begins (protecting itself from frittering away calories that have suddenly become hard to come by).

Weight control, which can be influenced by exercise far more effectively than by diet alone, plays a significant role in reducing the risk of several life-threatening diseases. It is basic to the prevention and treatment of non-insulin-dependent diabetes (the form of the disease that strikes adults). Obesity is also a major risk factor for heart disease and hypertension and may increase risk of certain forms of cancer.

The exercises that are best for weight control, because they burn mostly fat for fuel and appear to have the greatest influence on metabolic rate as well, are aerobic exercises. These not only do the best job of weight reduction but also the best job of risk reduction for heart disease and hypertension. Aerobic exercises, such as walking, jogging, swimming, or biking, raise the heart rate and the body's need for oxygen over a sustained period of time. They do this by means of the demand they place on muscles, for it is the response of muscle cells — the way they use fuel and the kinds of fuels they use — that makes specific activities aerobic or not.

Although nutritionists talk about the body's energy needs in terms of carbohydrates, proteins, and fats, what cells actually use for power is a compound called adenosine triphosphate (ATP), which is created within the cells themselves. At any given moment, cells have no more than a tiny amount of ATP on hand (throughout the entire body there is rarely more than a total of 3 ounces). But this is enough for a strong fast burn, lasting no more than about 8 seconds, that can give you an intense burst of energy. Weight lifters must be able to make this kind of maximum effort, and so must track-and-field athletes who put the shot, throw the javelin, or run the 50- or 100-meter dashes. Other athletes often draw on ATP reserves as well, in football, baseball, tennis, volleyball, or golf.

If activity demands more than 8 seconds of intense energy, then muscle cells must produce more ATP. When the need is for high-speed production to power all-out efforts lasting a few minutes, then only glucose (stored in the muscle cells as glycogen) is used to make ATP, and the energy activates primarily "fast-twitch" muscle fibers, which contract rapidly. This anaerobic (or oxygenless) energy is what middle distance runners and swimmers count on, and long-distance runners turn to it for a final "kick." But anaerobic activity derives energy from only about 5 percent of the glucose used in the process. The remaining 95 percent is converted to lactic acid, and it is the buildup of lactic acid in muscles that causes them to tire and cramp.

Unlike your car's motor, which can't produce energy without oxygen, your muscles can. But they can do it only for a few minutes, and they do a much better job when oxygen is present. Not only does oxygen make it possible to get maximum energy value out of glucose but it also enables muscle cells to use fats and amino acids to produce ATP as well. Oxygen also cleans up the process. It releases only carbon dioxide and water, not lactic acid, as by-products in the conversion of glucose and fats. Aerobic energy (energy produced with oxygen) activates primarily "slow-twitch" muscle fibers, which take longer to contract than "fast-twitch" fibers, and it is these that are most needed for activities demanding more endurance than power.

The measure of aerobic fitness — the capacity that increases with aerobic exercise — is the amount of oxygen the body can use within a given length of time. It doesn't take much exercise to start raising this index, called maximum oxygen uptake, from the bottom-line (sedentary) level. Burning 400–500 calories per week — the equivalent of walking a brisk 4–5 miles (that's 50–60 blocks in most cities) — can be enough for an 8 percent boost.

But to continue increasing oxygen uptake, the demand for oxygen must keep rising, which is why aerobic exercise should be strenuous. The body isn't about to expand its oxygen-handling capacity without a demonstrated need to do so. This occurs when exercisers reach their aerobic fitness limits and exhaust their capacity to use oxygen. Muscles must then switch from aerobic energy to anaerobic. That's when exercisers feel a burning sensation in the muscles that means lactic acid is building up there.

Maximum benefits of aerobic exercise come with the training effect, and for this you've got to keep pushing yourself, raising your pulse rate to somewhere between 70 and 85 percent of maximum, and keeping it elevated for at least 20 to 30 minutes every other day. (Maximum pulse rate is generally 220 a minute minus your age, but it will drop as your physical condition improves.) Still, it's possible to achieve a training effect using little more than 1,000 calories per week — one and a half hours of jogging, swimming, or biking. When you're burning about 1,600 calories per week in aerobic exercise, gains in oxygen uptake start leveling off at about 25 percent above sedentary levels.

The training effect thickens and strengthens muscles, including the heart muscle. It lowers pulse rate. Blood pressure is likely to drop somewhat, and the number of red blood cells will increase, as the body becomes capable of taking in and using more oxygen. So it is not just by helping you avoid obesity that exercise lowers the risk of heart disease.

Stronger heart muscles, a slower pulse rate, reduced blood pressure, and an improved oxygen transport system all cut the risk of heart disease. What's more, exercise alters levels of fatty substances in the blood. It reduces the kind of cholesterol most likely to cause atherosclerosis and increases the kind that appears to help prevent it.

Exercise can help prevent and treat diabetes, not only by controlling weight but also by increasing the body's ability to use what insulin it has. The disease is caused both by relatively low levels of this hormone (which regulates distribution of glucose in the body) and by a diminished ability of body cells to respond to it. Through exercise, cells can actually regain some of the sensitivity to insulin that they had lost.

Preventing osteoporosis depends upon building up bone mass early in life and sustaining it after the bone-building years are past. Here the role of exercise is vital, for the body will not build bone it does not need. Although regular exercise will not make bones any bigger, it will make them stronger and heavier — more dense.

Sustained exercise helps preserve bone density. Immobility increases bone loss. When patients spend prolonged periods of time in bed, their bones tend to lose calcium, which the body withdraws for other uses and *does not bother to replace.* Anaerobic exercise, as well as aerobic exercise, can help reduce the risk of osteoporosis, and there are special benefits to activities that involve lifting or pushing and thus subject bones to some stress.

Psychological benefits, however, are most often achieved through aerobic exercise, which produces chemical changes in the body that affect production of certain neurotransmitters in the brain (the chemical messengers that carry signals to and from nerve cells). Exercise tends to increase production of those neurotransmitters that seem to be most useful in overcoming anxiety or depression. In addition, exercise provides a healthy release for anger or frustration and a means of building confidence. Self-image improves as body image changes, and awkward or overweight people gain pride in their new agility or shape.

HOW AND HOW MUCH

To provide permanent benefits, exercise cannot be a sometime thing. Just as there is a training effect, there is also a detraining effect. Dr. Stern cites the example of one athlete who had won several triathlons (the "iron man" type of competition that involves long-distance swimming, followed by a complete marathon, and ending with a 110-mile bicycle race). Although he had been in superb shape when preparing for the competition, there was, she says, "a fantastic rebound just seven to ten days after he stopped training." His metabolism changed, and the level of fats in his blood, which had been very low throughout training, escalated sharply once he had quit.

Metabolic rate, which increases to give exercise its multiplier effect in weight control, quickly reverts to the pre-exercise norm when regular exercise ends. And although exercise can control many aspects of aging, it can do so only if one remains active throughout life. For lifelong benefits, Stern maintains, "Exercise has to be a lifetime commitment."

To make exercise a habit, it should be as rewarding as possible, less like work and more like play. And it should be convenient. A study of one college faculty exercise program found the professors who stuck with it were those with offices closest to the gym.

Plainly, it's more fun to jog or bike along exciting new routes than to hit the same road or track every day. But few Americans have this option. On the other hand, they now have greater opportunities for exercise than ever before.

Health clubs add the rewards of sociability to exercise bikes and treadmills. Many of the clubs, as well as YMCAs, provide pools, racquetball, squash, basketball, and other sports. Along with a growing number of corporate fitness programs, the clubs and Y's offer exercise classes and often have exercise machines like the Nautilus. Although most of these machines are fine for building muscle (and bone too), they generally do not provide the aerobic stresses that raise metabolic rates and oxygen uptake. Dr. Stern's personal plan for sustaining the aerobic habit is to exercise on a stationary bicycle — the kind found in most health clubs — and to reward herself by reading fiction, reserved exclusively for this purpose, while she pedals.

The exercise habit should be started early, even before children begin school. As toddlers, they need help to develop motor skills and coordination and should be encouraged to take part in family athletic activities. The point is to set a pattern of physical activity strong enough to counteract the tendency toward sedentary television watching. "Kids who watch television more," Dr. Stern points out, "tend to be fatter than kids who watch television less."

During adolescence, athletic youngsters have more self-confidence and a better self-image than those who do not take part in sports. Exercise gives girls a means of controlling their weight and boys a chance to build muscle mass, while team sports provide opportunities for cooperation and for leadership. After college, however, time constraints and other demands interfere, and it becomes difficult to sustain high levels of physical activity. That's when a conscious effort to exercise must be made.

When the effort *is* made, exercise can provide some powerful reinforcement in both physical improvement and psychological rewards. But there are limits. The break-even point seems to come when you are expending about 3,500 calories of energy each week on intentional exercise and everyday activities (like walking and climbing stairs). Dr. Ralph S. Paffenbarger's long-term study of nearly 17,000 Harvard graduates (described in chapter 17) found that those alumni who burned a weekly 3,500 calories — equivalent to six hours of basketball or soccer, nearly 50 miles of biking, 10 miles of swimming, or 35 miles of walking — had reduced health risks as low as they could go.

Dr. Kenneth Cooper, the former Air Force physician who formulated a cardiovascular conditioning program for astronauts (and turned it into the best-selling book *Aerobics* in 1968), now runs a fitness clinic and research center in Dallas. He finds that injuries mount sharply when runners jog more than 25 miles a week (and burn somewhat fewer than 3,000 calories on their runs).

For women, the jogging limit may need to be lower. Those who exceed 20 miles a week can develop amenorrhea (they cease menstruating), because their body fat has dropped too low to sustain normal estrogen production. Low estrogen levels make it difficult for the body to retain calcium and cause bone to deteriorate. When this occurs, exercise is accelerating osteoporosis, not preventing it.

For weight control, a program of four or five 30-minute aerobic exercise sessions a week can be three times as effective (and take off three times as much weight) as a program of three sessions a week. But the injury rate triples when exercisers go beyond five sessions a week. It doubles when they extend sessions from 30 minutes to 45 minutes.

NUTRITIONAL NEEDS OF ATHLETES

The primary nutritional need of athletes is for sufficient calories to sustain high levels of activity. However, this need can vary enormously, depending not only on age, sex, and size but also on the physical demands of their sports. Male runners training for a marathon may consume 5,000–6,000 calories per day and still have difficulty maintaining their weight. On the other hand, female figure skaters get along on substantially less than half that amount. Nutritionist Ann C. Grandjean, associate director of the Swanson Center for Nutrition in Omaha, Nebraska, and chief nutrition consultant to the U.S. Olympic Committee, has studied the diets of professional athletes and amateurs competing at the national level. Her survey found figure skaters averaging only 1,800 calories per day, which was more than the 1,671 calories that junior gymnasts ate but nowhere near the more than 4,600 calories professional baseball players packed away.

Certain athletes — gymnasts and wrestlers, in particular — struggle to keep their weight down. As a result, their caloric intakes may be well below the levels needed to provide them with adequate amounts of essential nutrients. The Swanson Center study found wrestlers at the bottom of the male scale, averaging fewer than 2,000 calories per day.

Athletes have a greater need for certain nutrients than nonathletes. They need more protein, for example, not only to build muscle but also to supply the amino acids that provide some of the fuel supply for aerobic energy. Dr. Stern suggests that one and a half times the RDA for protein might be necessary, which would raise the requirement from about half a hamburger per day to three quarters of a hamburger. Among Olympic competitors and college athletes in the Swanson Center study, all had protein intakes that exceeded the RDA by far more than 50 percent, except for male wrestlers and female judo competitors.

In general, neither moderate exercise nor competitive athletics will raise the need for micronutrients more than 10 percent above RDA levels. However, research at Cornell University has found that very active women may increase their need for riboflavin substantially, perhaps even doubling it. Nevertheless, deficiency appears rare, and there seems to be no need for supplementation of riboflavin or any other vitamin. The greater caloric intake of most athletes will usually provide all the extra vitamins they need. Although it has been suggested that extra doses of certain vitamins, particularly vitamins C and E, might boost athletic performance, no research to date has shown this to be the case.

Athletes are generally able to sustain adequate levels of most minerals too, with the exceptions of iron and calcium. A 1982 study of middle- and long-distance runners found that nearly 30 percent of the men and more than 80 percent of the women had blood levels of iron low enough to put them at risk of deficiency. Recent studies of competitors in various other sports reported iron deficiency among men at 10 percent and among women as high as 25 percent.

The terms *sports anemia* and *runner's anemia* have been used to characterize what is either the athlete's greater need for iron or greater loss of iron. Increased need can result from a more active oxygen transport system, which requires iron to produce additional hemoglobin and myoglobin. Increased loss has been blamed on blood loss through the intestine, which has been found among competitive athletes. In either case, athletes or anyone who exercises strenuously should monitor iron levels and use supplements if necessary (see chapter 21).

Calcium levels are also likely to be below the RDA. A study of women skaters at the 1984 Olympics found that fewer than half were meeting the RDA. For all women athletes, but particularly for runners, dancers, and gymnasts, adequate calcium is vital. Low levels of body fat diminish both estrogen production and the body's responsiveness to the hormone. This compromises its calcium retrieval system and raises risk of osteoporosis. While even these weight-conscious athletes can get a substantial amount of calcium from low-fat and no-fat dairy products, they should turn to supplements for the balance if they are not getting all they need (see chapter 21).

Any athlete, male or female, who substantially limits calories to fight weight gain is probably not getting adequate amounts of all the essential vitamins and minerals and should take a multivitamin and mineral supplement. The Swanson Center study showed that 45 percent of college wrestlers surveyed were getting less than 70 percent of the RDA for vitamin A, and more than one third were getting less than 70 percent for niacin, calcium, and iron. A substantial number were short of thiamin and riboflavin as well. Among the female junior gymnasts, all had iron consumption below 70 percent of the RDA; 83 percent had calcium intake at least that low, and one third were that deficient in vitamin A and niacin.

The most common nutritional deficiency of athletes, however, is not one of the above. It is water. Athletes may sweat off 2 percent of their body weight during competition. If you weigh 150 pounds, that's 3 pounds of water (1.5 quarts). You can lose more, even a health-threatening 5 percent. But 2 percent is enough to impair performance.

If you are exercising in warm weather, you should drink a glass of cold water about 20 minutes before you start (cold water leaves the stomach rapidly) and try to replenish your water supply every 15 minutes while you exercise. This is critical in long endurance events, which is why cyclists (who strip away every spare ounce of equipment) still carry water along and why marathon runners hit a good many of the water stops along their 26-mile route. Fruit juices will not replenish your fluid supply as rapidly as plain water, but sports drinks will.

Thirst is not necessarily the best guide to this kind of water deprivation. When you have finished a strenuous workout, one glass of water may quench your thirst. But your body may still need three glasses more.

Although you can sweat off several quarts during prolonged competition, you do not need salt tablets to give your sodium levels a boost back to normal. Your body can't absorb salt unless it is dissolved in water. So salt tablets will also exacerbate dehydration — sometimes fatally — by drawing water from tissue into the stomach. Even after competition, there's no need for more salt than you're likely to sprinkle on your food. Just be sure to take in lots of water too.

SHARPENING THE COMPETITIVE EDGE

Most of what is known about upgrading athletic performance nutritionally applies primarily to endurance sports that keep you going for more than an hour and a half. These sports demand prolonged production of aerobic energy from the burning of glucose and fat. For muscles to do their best, and keep doing it for two hours or more, they must have a hefty amount of glycogen available to supply slow-release glucose that allows them to burn fat most efficiently.

Fat comes from both triglycerides and free fatty acids, and you are not likely to run short of it. But you may run out of glycogen, at which point your muscles will turn to the amino acids in their own protein for the glucose they need to keep going. This soon makes for trouble, because breaking down protein produces toxic ammonia waste. Eventually, it will put you at risk of ketosis (see chapter 3), but muscles become fatigued long before that point, and marathon runners "hit the wall" soon after they have depleted their muscle-stored glycogen.

For endurance athletes in training, high-carbohydrate diets, which keep glycogen levels topped off, should be the rule. But surveys of what competitive athletes actually eat have found few differences between their diets and the general public's. Among male athletes in the Swanson Center study, only wrestlers took in more than half their calories as carbohydrates.

To build up muscle stores of glycogen for competitive events like marathons and long-distance bicycle races, a strategy called carbohydrate loading was developed in Sweden during the 1960s and has since become common practice wherever serious endurance athletes compete. Carbohydrate loading begins with prolonged exercise that drains muscles of glycogen. This deprivation increases the muscles' ability to synthesize more glycogen (supercompensation, it's called). As originally devised, carbo-loading denied muscles the glucose they need to synthesize glycogen for two days after depletion. Athletes were fed an adequate number of calories but few of them (no more than 400) in carbohydrates. Meanwhile, training continued as usual. Then, training tapered off for two to three days and carbohydrates were packed away (more than 2,000 calories per day for men). This strategy, which amounts to force-feeding of muscles, can more than double their glycogen-storage capacity.

More recently, the carbohydrate-deprivation phase of the carbo-loading regimen was modified when it was discovered that athletes can consume half their calories as carbohydrates during phase two and still take advantage of supercompensation. Using a technique like this, researchers at the University of Iowa were able to triple glycogen levels in long-distance cyclists.

It is possible for a well-trained competitor to condense the carbo-loading process by exercising to the point of exhaustion two or three days before an event and then piling on the carbohydrates that evening. But, however it is done, carbo-loading should come at least two days before the event. Gorging on pasta, rice, and rye bread the day before — or worse, the night before — is more likely to dull the competitive edge than sharpen it. Finally, carbo-loading is not for most amateurs. It provides a real but slight advantage that is of value only to serious competitors, people for whom a 1 or 2 percent improvement in performance can provide the winning edge.

In addition to carbo-loading, a number of athletic coaches prescribe caffeine to boost the aerobic fuel supply. Caffeine can help muscles hoard their glycogen by mobilizing free fatty acids. As a result, muscles burn more fat and less glucose. The drawback of caffeine, however, is its diuretic action. It will draw water down to the urinary tract. So caffeine provides, at best, a trade-off of free fatty acids for water. Dr. Stern suggests passing up caffeine, saving the water, and counting on prerace excitement to stimulate enough increased adrenaline to get your free fatty acids mobilized.

DEPARTMENT OF FALSE HOPES: IN PURSUIT OF PEAK PERFORMANCE

Competitive athletes have shown a willingness to try all kinds of diets and supplements to enhance performance. But perhaps the most foolish practices are the means of weight control many young competitors use. College wrestlers, for example, will not only limit their diets so severely that they risk serious deficiencies but will also deprive themselves of water (even using diuretics, laxatives, saunas, and steambaths) to make a weight 7–8 pounds below normal for them. Gymnasts, dancers, and other young women athletes who practice abusive weight-control measures often develop food aversions that can lead to excessive and dangerously rapid weight loss. In one professional ballet company, the incidence of anorexia nervosa was found to be 1 in 20 (the incidence of this life-threatening eating disorder among teenage girls is 1 in 200).

Popular "peak performance" diets, although they may contain useful advice for the small number of professional athletes who need every competitive edge to succeed, often give inappropriate counsel for weekend amateurs. Very-high-carbohydrate diets (60–80 percent of calories) with exceedingly low levels of fat can be particularly harmful for women, who need sufficient body fat (to ensure adequate estrogen levels), as well as levels of micronutrients — such as calcium, iron, and other trace elements — that these diets are unlikely to provide.

When it comes to supplements, the list of useless products is seemingly endless. Bee pollen is more likely to trigger an allergic response than to improve athletic prowess. Ginseng root can prove toxic for anyone if taken in large enough quantities. For most athletes, protein supplements won't do much harm, but they won't do much good either. The average American diet already contains more than enough protein for the muscle-building even full-time athletes will require.

Research has shown that extra vitamin C or E will enhance performance not one bit, nor will vitamin B_6. Indeed, the notion that B_6 can help make your personal best even better is a dangerous one, for megadoses of the vitamin have recently been shown to cause neurological damage. The bottom line on all the substances touted as surefire shortcuts to a stronger serve and a longer "kick" is that just about all of them have been investigated and (except for caffeine) have been found to provide mostly a placebo effect.

CHAPTER 13

Down the Alimentary Canal

NUTRITION, IT SHOULD BE clear by now, is a complicated business. Its purpose is to provide the body with what it needs for metabolism. So nutrition is primarily involved in moving nutrients around and getting the right stuff to the right places.

It all starts with food and what we choose to eat and not to eat. But putting food in your mouth is not the same as putting nutrients into your body. Food must be broken down into nutrients, nutrients must be absorbed through the intestines, and waste must be excreted.

At every step, digestive problems can limit the way our bodies use nutrients, or limit the choices of foods we can comfortably or safely eat. Far from being an automatic process, digestion is a complex affair that works a little differently for each individual. The vagaries of digestion can profoundly affect our foodstyles. And food choices — including how we combine different foods to make up a meal — can affect the ways that nutrients in our food are absorbed (see "Food Interactions," pages 170–171).

Digestion, basically, is the process of getting substances from the outside of the body to the inside. Dr. Jerrold Olefsky of the University of California, San Diego, one of the country's leading diabetes experts, points out that "the stomach is not part of the body's interior." As he describes the digestive tract, it is "a long tube that is open at each end." In a sense, he explains, "its surface is part of the body's exterior," since nutrients must get out of the tube and into the bloodstream before they do us any good.

Let's take a look at what happens to food after we eat it — at each stop along the alimentary canal.

THE STOMACH

Leaving the mouth, food is shoved along the narrow foot-long esophagus by muscular contractions. When it reaches the stomach, food generally stays there for up to 30 minutes. A muscle at the end of the esophagus — the lower esophageal sphincter — keeps the contents of the stomach from backing up.

Food loses much of its identity in the stomach. This muscular bag kneads its contents into a semiliquid mass to which gastric juices are added. The enzyme pepsin goes to work on protein, while hydrochloric acid (for that's what "stomach acid" is) controls the level of bacteria and keeps the stomach environment acidic enough for pepsin to do its job.

From time to time, the stomach becomes overly acidic. The result is indigestion. And if the lower esophageal sphincter can't keep the acid

FOOD INTERACTIONS

One of the major influences on the absorption of nutrients is *other nutrients.* Foods interact, sometimes positively and sometimes negatively. Certain nutrients work together to enhance each other's absorption; others block one another.

There are four basic ways foods can interact. They can bind chemically to each other. They can impede or facilitate each other's transportation out of the intestine and into the blood. They can alter the activity of enzymes that transform nutrients into usable forms. And they can destroy each other. Here are some examples of how these interactions work.

Binding

When some nutrients link together chemically, they form compounds that the body's fluids are unable to dissolve. These insoluble complexes cannot be absorbed, and they pass out of the body in feces. Recent research has turned up some surprising examples. A substance in raw eggs binds with the vitamin biotin, making it inaccessible. Fiber and phytic acid, important components of many vegetables and grains, bind to calcium and trace elements, carrying them out of the body. The oxalic acid in spinach does the same thing, and if there is an excess of pectin (the soluble fiber in citrus fruits, apples, squash, and strawberries) in the intestine, some of it will bind with vitamin B_{12}. The tannins in red wine, tea, and sorghum and other cereals can bind iron and keep it out of the bloodstream.

But there are ways in which chemical binding can be helpful rather than harmful. Fiber can play a positive role by binding cholesterol and carrying it out in the feces, preventing it from accumulating in the arteries.

In addition, some nutrient molecules bind to minerals in a way that makes those minerals more soluble in blood and easier for the body to use. It becomes easier for calcium and trace elements to pass through the intestinal walls and into the bloodstream when sugars and amino acids bind to them. The complexes they form are far more soluble in body fluids than calcium or the trace out of the esophagus, there is also that burning sensation in the chest known as heartburn.

Heartburn is caused by stomach acid backing up into the esophagus. There are a number of reasons why the esophageal sphincter will allow this to happen. Abdominal pressure causes that muscle to relax, so overeating or being overweight increases the likelihood of heartburn. Tight clothing too may increase abdominal pressure enough to relax the muscle. Then there are hormonal changes that tend to let stomach acid escape into the esophagus, which is why pregnant women so often suffer heartburn.

A number of chemical relaxers affect the sphincter. Nicotine and alcohol are two, and others are found in fats, oil, chocolate, mints, and carbonated beverages. In addition, each of us has certain foods that are more likely than others to put us at risk of heartburn. For many of us that

elements are on their own. In a similar way, vitamin C helps the body absorb iron by binding it into a complex more soluble than iron alone.

This mechanism, though, causes some minerals to compete with each other in the body. An excess of calcium, for instance, will bind with so many of the available sugars and amino acids that fewer of these molecules are left to help put other minerals into a soluble, usable form. This is a danger of unbalanced supplementation: taking too much of one mineral decreases the availability of certain others.

Transportation

Fat-soluble vitamins — A, D, K, and E — need fat to carry them across the intestinal walls and into the blood. That's why people who have difficulty digesting fat can become vitamin-deficient. Even if they take supplements of fat-soluble vitamins, they aren't absorbing the fat that would let their bodies use those nutrients. People on very-low-fat diets may also be unable to absorb enough of these vitamins.

Enzyme Activity

Fiber, which is found in many of the same foods as digestible carbohydrates, can affect the way those carbohydrates enter the body. Fiber molecules can partly shield carbohydrates from the enzymes that break them down into glucose. As a result, high-fiber foods tend to release glucose into the bloodstream more slowly — a property that can make them very useful in a diabetic's diet (see chapter 20). There are other examples of enzyme interactions; for instance, chemicals in raw legumes, like peas, block an enzyme called trypsin that helps reduce protein to absorbable amino acids.

Destruction

Raw cabbage, fish, and oysters can literally destroy thiamin, rendering the vitamin inactive before it can enter the bloodstream. Alcohol too is a nutrient-killer and will put thiamin, folacin, vitamin B_{12}, vitamin D, and calcium out of action.

list includes onions, peppers, lettuce, and spicy Mexican or Chinese dishes.

To relieve the symptoms of heartburn, you often need only dilute the offending acid with water or send it back into the stomach with a few bites of food. Anything less acidic than the stomach's gastric juices will help relieve acidity, not only in the esophagus but in the stomach as well. That's why alkaline antacids are useful. What does not help is lying down after meals, since gravity contributes substantially to keeping stomach acid in its place.

Even if it stays where it belongs, though, stomach acid can cause trouble. Hyperacidity can cause irritation and pain in the stomach. The problem is often linked to stress. Tension or anxiety stimulates the hormone gastrin, which increases the flow of gastric juices. Grabbing quick meals and gobbling them down means food is chewed poorly and the stomach must work harder to break it all up. Alcohol will irritate the stomach lining, as will coffee (even the decaffeinated varieties) and a number of drugs, starting with aspirin but including medications for arthritis, asthma, and hypertension as well as a good many antibiotics.

Gastritis — inflammation of the stomach — can be countered by avoiding irritating foods and drugs and by neutralizing excess stomach acid. In general, liquid antacids are more effective than tablets, and most gastritis sufferers tend to undermedicate rather than overmedicate. Researchers at the University of Texas have found that persistent gastritis responds best to 2 tablespoonfuls of antacid taken one hour and again three hours after each meal, and at bedtime — a total of 14 tablespoonfuls per day. If this much antacid doesn't relieve your symptoms after a week, it's time to see your doctor.

Prolonged or chronic hyperacidity can cause ulcers, either in the stomach or in the duodenum, the pouch at the entrance to the small intestine, which is where food moves next on its travels. The symptoms of ulcers, other than the presence of blood in the feces, are not much different from those of gastritis and include severe and sustained pain. But rather than antacids doctors usually prescribe cimetidine, a drug that blocks histamine, which is the chemical that triggers release of stomach acid.

Long gone, and with no regrets, are the bland diets of yesteryear, which doctors once hoped would speed ulcer healing. Milk, cream, and other characterless comestibles were their mainstays, and anything highly seasoned was forbidden. Today, diet recommendations for ulcer patients generally include little more than a warning to stay away from alcohol, nicotine, coffee, aspirin, and arthritis drugs.

The heavy dairy diets of the past, it turns out, were more likely to aggravate ulcers than to help heal them, for both the protein and calcium in milk and milk products stimulate production of stomach acid. Researchers at the University of California, San Diego, tested milk against an assortment of other liquids, including coffee and soft drinks (regular and decaffeinated varieties of each) and beer, to discover which was most likely to stimulate production of stomach acid. Milk and beer tied for first place.

At the University of California, Irvine, College of Medicine, researchers have suggested that the growing preference of Americans for vegetable oils over animal fats may explain a recent decline in the number of stomach ulcer victims. Studies there show that the hormonelike compounds called prostaglandins, which the body produces from linoleic acid (a component of vegetable oil), may help prevent stomach ulcerations caused by aspirin, alcohol, bile, and other irritants.

THE SMALL INTESTINE

Passing through the duodenum, food moves into the small intestine. Along this 20-foot stretch of the digestive tract is where most food is broken down and most nutrients are absorbed into the bloodstream.

The small intestine is the vital digestive organ. You can live without a stomach or a large intestine and still process food for nourishment. But without a small intestine, the only way to supply your body the wherewithal for metabolism is through total parenteral nutrition.

Food components have to be broken down here into nutrient molecules small enough to be absorbed into the blood. The absorption is done by millions of tiny, fingerlike projections, called villi, that cover the small intestine's walls. No more than one twenty-fifth of an inch long, the villi are covered with even more minute projections called microvilli that can absorb glucose and amino acids. Each villus contains a blood vessel that carries these nutrients into the bloodstream.

There is considerable variety in how and where nutrients leave the digestive tract. By the time they reach the small intestine, carbohydrates have already been partly digested by enzymes in saliva. Other enzymes in the intestine continue the process until all carbohydrates have been reduced to simple sugars that can enter the bloodstream. Different sugars are handled in different ways: glucose is actively transported by the villi, while fructose follows the slower, passive route of diffusion through the intestinal wall. Not only is glucose the first to reach the bloodstream but it can be used immediately by the body's cells, while fructose must take a several-minute detour and travel to the liver for conversion to glucose before it is usable.

Protein breakdown is straightforward. Enzymes that originate in the pancreas, and others produced in the small intestine, work in the duodenum to divide proteins into their component amino acids. Those amino acids are then taken up by the villi.

What about fats? These are more complicated to break down than carbohydrates or proteins, and the process takes hours longer. First, fat slows down the movement of food out of the stomach; the more fat in a meal, the longer it takes to reach the small intestine. Then, when it does reach the intestine, fat must be broken down and readied for the blood-stream in several stages.

The appearance of fat in the intestine triggers release of enzymes from the pancreas. They break down triglycerides in stages (to di-glycerides, then to monoglycerides) until what's left are three fatty acids and a molecule of glycerol. Since these molecules aren't soluble in water, they can't pass into the villi directly.

The body's solution is bile, produced by the gallbladder. Salts in bile combine with fatty acids to form a soluble bubble that the villi can take up. Once inside the villi, glycerol and fatty acids link up again to form triglycerides, which are now packaged in new water-soluble complexes called lipoproteins, containing protein and cholesterol (described in de-tail in chapter 17).

The duct that carries bile from the gallbladder to the intestine is narrow. When gallstones (formed by cholesterol and other substances) block this passage, it can be excruciatingly painful. Until recently, doc-tors believed high-fat meals would make the gallbladder produce more bile and force gallstones into the duct. But it now appears that gallstones get stuck there at random, and there's no need for patients to shun dietary fat.

Most of the digestive enzymes do their work in the small intestine. But not all of us have every enzyme we need. Lack of an enzyme shows up as an intolerance for whatever food the missing enzyme is programmed to handle.

What's most important to know about food intolerance is that it is *not* an allergic reaction to food. Allergic reactions are immunological responses, while food intolerance is the body's *inability to digest* a spe-cific substance.

The most common example is lactose intolerance. It is caused by an absence of lactase, the enzyme that breaks down lactose, the sugar in milk. Lactose intolerance in adults is so common that it can hardly be considered a disorder or a malfunction at all. An estimated 70 percent of the world's adults lose some or most of their ability to produce lactase as they age. In the United States about 70 percent of black adults are lactose-intoler-ant to some degree, although only about 12 percent of white adults are.

Most lactose-intolerant adults are usually able to handle a modest amount of milk without much difficulty, for they still produce some lactase (between 5 and 10 percent of what they produced as infants). But anything more than 4–8 ounces of milk as part of a meal is likely to cause gut problems. Passing undigested from the small intestine into the colon, lactose absorbs water and causes bloating, cramps, and diarrhea. This undigested milk sugar is converted by bacteria into fatty acids and into gases that the colon must expel.

There are a number of solutions for lactose-intolerant men and women who want or need milk products. They can, for example, eat yogurt or similar dairy products, which are easier for them to digest than milk. The bacteria in yogurt, it seems, will produce lactase, although bacteria in some other fermented milk products (like buttermilk and sour cream) are not so obliging.

If you are lactose-intolerant, you can also take lactase tablets when you eat dairy foods or add lactase liquid or powder to your breakfast cereal, pudding, or hot chocolate. In addition, you can now buy low-lactose milk, cottage cheese, and ice creams in many parts of the country.

Many people have intolerances to foods other than milk. A lack of the sugar-digesting enzyme called invertase can make it impossible for you to digest sucrose. Failure of the pancreas to produce enough lipase, a fat-digesting enzyme, causes a form of sprue (an inability to digest fat) and a buildup of fat in the intestine.

Although the mechanisms of most food intolerances are fairly well understood, it is not at all clear how celiac disease works. This disorder affects about 80,000 Americans, who are unable to eat gluten, one of the major proteins in grain. The condition appears to be a true allergy in some cases, but not in all.

When victims of celiac disease eat gluten, the consequences are far more severe than cramps and gas, for the disease then destroys villi in the small intestine. As a result, children with celiac disease suffer general malnutrition and a number of specific deficiencies. They grow poorly, have little appetite, develop pot bellies, and suffer a persistent and unpleasant-smelling fatty diarrhea.

Although it takes time to undo the damage of malnutrition, celiac disease quickly comes under control once gluten is eliminated from the diet. This means giving up most baked goods and pasta and foods that are prepared from packaged mixes, thickened with flour, or that use malt or malt extract. What's left in the way of grains are corn, rice, and millet. Potatoes, however, can substitute for some grain products (gnocchi instead of linguini), and so can soybeans.

THE COLON

The last stop on the digestive journey is the colon, the main stretch of the large intestine, which not only temporarily stores undigested food but also provides access to the bloodstream for fluids and for many minerals. The large intestine is filled with bacteria (which are nourished by foods that we can only partially digest or can't digest at all). It is these bacteria that produce the gas we pass.

The colon thrives on work. But it is designed for heavy moving, not light housework. And it may have trouble expelling waste, causing constipation, when there is too little bulk or water to move it easily. If all it has to work with is a small pellet, the bowel may have to squeeze down to pencil size to move it along. Excessive contraction causes cramps and sometimes diarrhea — the common syndrome known as irritable colon. To prevent constipation, the colon generally needs only enough indigestible material — usually fiber — to bulk up waste matter so that it can be easily propelled.

Diarrhea can be more complex. It has three major causes. First, food poisoning can damage the cellular pumps that regulate water balance in the large intestine. A large amount of water then builds up within the digestive tract and cannot be reabsorbed by the colon. It must be expelled.

Second, water can be drawn into the intestine by the presence there of small molecules in solution. The driving force is osmosis, for water will move into the colon to dilute the solution there to the same concentration as the body's tissues. The buildup of lactose within intestinal fluids attracts water by this mechanism.

Finally, an excess of undigested fat in the intestine can literally grease it, causing diarrhea. That's what happens when sprue inhibits digestion of fats, and it's how mineral oil works as a laxative.

Problems of the colon are frequently caused by the small pouches, called diverticuli, that form along bowel walls. The formation of these pouches, a condition called diverticulosis, usually brings few if any symptoms, although some victims do experience alternating constipation and diarrhea, gas, and some pain in the lower left abdomen (where the last section of the colon is found). But when bits of waste material become trapped in the pouches and cause inflammation or infection, the painful result is diverticulitis. Victims feel cramping in the lower left abdomen, along with nausea and vomiting, and there may be fever and rectal bleeding as well.

Both the condition and the disorder are another example of greater food choice producing more dangerous food choices, for neither was common before 1900, and both are still rare in those countries where diets are low in meat products and heavy in whole grains and vegetables. In the United States, however, one third of the population over age 45 and two thirds over age 60 have diverticulosis. And each year, diverticulitis hospitalizes nearly 200,000 Americans.

Fiber has the main role in both preventing diverticulosis and controlling the condition once it develops. Lack of fiber is what causes diverticular pouches in the first place. When the colon must exert inordinate pressure to move waste matter along, because there is insufficient fiber to give it enough bulk, weak areas of the bowel will bulge under the strain. Often, these bulges remain after the colon relaxes, and they become the diverticular pouches.

Treatment for diverticulosis includes a high-fiber diet and mild laxatives. Generally patients gradually increase the fiber they consume, adding wheat bran and other whole grains plus foods that will carry lots of water as well as fiber to the colon (like apples, carrots, oranges, and lettuce). To be avoided, however, are food with pips and seeds that are likely to be trapped in the diverticular pouches. These include tomatoes and grapes, strawberries and raspberries.

Despite its prevalence, diverticulosis is probably not the most common lower-intestinal problem. That honor almost certainly belongs to the gas that causes flatulence, an annoyance that is virtually universal.

Let's get our gases straight. That bloated feeling in your stomach is not caused by beans or other "gassy" foods. It's caused by air that you swallow when you eat or that gets into your stomach in carbonated beverages, beer, and whipped foods. But the gas you pass, composed of hydrogen, methane, and carbon dioxide, is indeed caused by beans and a number of other foods that are digested by bacteria in the lower intestine.

It is the complex sugars in beans (called oligosaccharides) that are responsible for all the gas that bacteria make from them. We cannot metabolize these sugars, but they give bacteria no trouble at all. And beans are not the only foods that contain them. At least one survey found that onions, cooked cabbages, raw apples, and radishes beat out beans as causes of flatulence. Raisins and apple juice will double gas production, while bananas increase it by 50 percent.

Lactose intolerance is also a significant contributor to flatus. With no lactase in the upper intestine, lactose passes down to the colon, where bacteria do the job of digesting its simple sugars. What they actually do amounts to fermentation, and gas is what it produces.

Though passing gas has no medical consequences, it may have social ones. There are, however, no effective remedies other than diet. And if you are a bean fancier or impressed with the tremendous nutritional value of beans (as a source of fiber, protein, and slow-release glucose), then you might take the advice of Alfred Olson, a research chemist with the U.S. Department of Agriculture's Western Regional Research Center in Albany, California.

Olson's prescription for eliminating up to 90 percent of the gas-forming sugars in beans is first to rinse them and remove any foreign particles. Then — and this is the trick — pour boiling water over them and allow them to soak for at least four hours. Finally, toss out the water the beans have soaked in and cook them in fresh water. With the discarded soaking water will go most of the oligosaccharides along with small amounts of water-soluble vitamins.

CHAPTER 14

When Foods Hate You: Allergies and Sensitivities

P EOPLE HAVE ALL KINDS of negative responses to food — aversions, intolerances, and sensitivities. True food allergies, however, are rare and affect no more than 2 percent of the adult population. They are somewhat more common among children under three, probably affecting about 7 percent of them. What makes allergies different from other kinds of food sensitivities and aversions is the involvement of the immune system. Indeed, the trouble is caused by an overreaction of that system. It responds to food substances as though they were dangerous invaders.

The body does not wage quite the same kind of war against allergens (those harmless substances it mistakes for attackers) as it does against infection. Antibodies that fight bacteria actually latch onto the germs, ultimately destroying them. But allergen-fighting antibodies — called immunoglobulin E (IgE) — don't go one-on-one with their adversaries. Instead, they bombard them with chemical agents known as mediators, and these mediators interfere with normal bodily functions.

IgE-triggered mediators can cause anaphylaxis, a severe allergic reaction that causes swelling of the lips, tongue, face, or even the entire body. Victims of anaphylaxis become hoarse and have difficulty breathing. Extreme reactions can produce life-threatening anaphylactic shock.

Food allergies rarely cause such a severe reaction. When IgE-triggered mediators respond to food, they most often restrict their activities to the digestive tract. But they are capable of bringing on hives, rashes, runny noses, asthma attacks, and possibly arthritis and migraine headaches as well.

Considering the range of allergic reactions, it is possible to get carried away with the notion that food allergies might be to blame for whatever ails you. And a growing band of doctors who call themselves clinical ecologists encourage this kind of thinking. They claim that food allergies afflict more than half of all Americans and are responsible for everything from chronic fatigue and excess weight to anxiety and depression.

Clinical ecologists admit that the food allergies they are talking about are not conventional ones; they claim no evidence that IgE-mediated reactions lead to depression or overweight. Nevertheless, many maintain that the reactions they see *are* caused by the immune system, but in ways that do not involve IgE antibodies. Such claims are received skeptically by most immunologists.

Even without the contributions of clinical ecologists, popular understanding of what is and what is not a food allergy is far from clear. The problem is more semantic than clinical, for doctors as well as laymen tend to use loosely the terms that define various negative reactions to foods. There are, however, some generally accepted definitions.

While only IgE-mediated reactions are true food *allergies*, any reaction with a physiological cause is considered a food *intolerance*. (Both the milk allergy of infants and the lactose intolerance of adults fit the bill.) And any negative reaction to food can be considered a food *sensitivity*, even if the cause is psychological rather than physiological.

All kinds of food avoidance — from anorexia to the simple dislike of Brussels sprouts — may be blamed on food sensitivity, intolerance, or allergy by people who really know better. The victims of pseudo food allergies, however, do not know that their food sensitivities derive from emotional rather than physical conditions. Frequently their physicians may not be aware of this either, for psychosomatic reactions to food can trigger what appear to be full-scale allergic responses.

The tip-off is that a psychosomatic reaction will be triggered only when the alleged allergen is served in a recognizable form, not when it is disguised. At the National Jewish Center for Immunology and Respiratory Medicine in Denver, allergists are testing children between the ages of three months and 19 years with impressive histories of adverse food reactions. In this double-blind test (see "True and False Tests for Food Allergies," page 180), youngsters are given capsules containing various foods. Neither the child nor the person administering the capsule knows whether or not the capsule contains an extract of the food to which the child has had allergic responses. Reporting on the first 290 "allergic" youngsters tested, hospital allergists found only one third to be clearly allergic, while 60 percent showed no signs of true allergy at all.

Not long ago British researchers investigated the food sensitivity of patients diagnosed as having irritable bowel syndrome whose abdominal pain and diarrhea was unexplained by any other organic cause. Testing with elimination diets and double-blind challenges revealed that only 3 of 19 patients tested actually were hypersensitive to food. Psychiatric evaluation of 14 patients in this study found signs of significant psychiatric disturbance in 12.

It would neaten the results considerably if all 12 were among those patients whose irritable bowels could not be traced to food sensitivity. But this was not the case. Instead, all three of the hypersensitive patients also showed evidence of psychiatric disorders.

Emotional disturbance isn't necessarily the cause of a pseudo food allergy. It can be a simple conditioned response. A series of experiments at the Langley Porter Psychiatric Institute of the University of California, San Francisco, provides a fascinating clue to how such psychosomatic reactions may work.

In these experiments researchers sensitized guinea pigs to a protein called BSA so that exposure to the protein would produce an allergic reaction. By measuring blood levels of histamine — the chief mediator in allergic reactions — the researchers could determine the severity of the allergic response.

Next, the guinea pigs were conditioned to associate a specific but unrelated odor — a fishy or sulfurous smell — with BSA and with the allergic response. Within weeks, researchers were able to raise blood

---

TRUE AND FALSE TESTS FOR FOOD ALLERGIES

Testing for food allergies is both complicated and controversial. But there is at least one kind of test that allergists consider foolproof: the **challenge test**. A time-consuming process, the challenge test requires patients first to go on an elimination diet and drop all suspect foods.

After about three weeks of this restricted diet, patients are "challenged" by the reintroduction of the suspected allergens. To ensure that any reaction is truly allergic, the challenge is made using food capsules or disguising the food in some other manner. For research purposes, challenge tests are often double-blind, with neither researchers nor patients aware of what the capsules contain.

Simple **elimination tests** may also be used, which involve no more than cutting suspected allergens out of the diet. These may or may not involve subsequent reintroduction of suspect foods. And the **skin test**, which is a standard diagnostic procedure for nonfood allergies, can reveal dietary allergies as well. Using the skin test, or scratch test, allergists insert minute amounts of suspected allergens beneath the patient's skin and watch for a reaction (swelling or inflammation).

But there are, in addition, two testing procedures for food allergies, both employed by clinical ecologists, that mainstream allergists consider valueless. **Sublingual tests** involve placing the extract of a suspected food allergen under the patient's tongue and monitoring the reaction — a dangerous practice indeed for patients likely to have a severe allergic response. **Cytotoxic tests** combine patient blood samples with extracts of suspected allergens. An allergy is deemed to exist if the patient's white cells burst as a result. But immunologists point out that there is no relation between this test-tube reaction and the way a food may really affect a patient's cells in the body.

histamine levels without any BSA at all, simply by allowing the guinea pigs to smell the odor they had learned to associate with BSA.

There are several ways of testing for food allergies, but none is simple, straightforward, and foolproof. What's more, test results will not necessarily provide the basis for making decisions about your diet. After all, if you have what appears to be an allergic response to oysters, gherkins, or oregano, can you ignore your hives and itchy skin even if a test suggests that your mind and not your immune system is to blame? Of course not. Whatever the cause, the reactions are just as real and create just as much discomfort.

Both food diaries and elimination diets, however, offer practical ways of pinning down both true food allergies and pseudo food allergies, so you can be certain just which foods cause reactions and which do not. Diaries are easier to handle, but they demand scrupulous record-keeping and objectivity and make it difficult to discover allergens that appear as ingredients in many different kinds of food.

Elimination diets aren't much fun. They limit severely what you can eat, by eliminating all foods that are likely to provoke allergic reactions. This is a sizable list, and you must avoid everything on it for two to three weeks. At that point, you can begin trying foods that might possibly cause you trouble, adding a new one every three to seven days and discovering which, if any, provoke allergic responses.

A number of foods have been identified by researchers as most likely to cause immediate allergic reactions. These are eggs, milk and other dairy products, wheat, peanuts, soybeans, nuts, chicken, fish, and shellfish. Other foods have a reputation for rarely provoking reactions and are often on the starter list for elimination diets. Lamb and rice are the meat and cereal considered least allergenic, and peeled potatoes, carrots, lettuce, and pears are similarly well regarded.

Some nondietary factors can make allergic reactions to food more severe. Aspirin is one. Exercise is another. In several cases, people who experienced no symptoms while eating foods to which they were allergic have gone into anaphylactic shock when they exercised soon after completing the meal. The obvious lesson for allergic exercisers is to stay off the bike, jogging path, or tennis court for at least two hours after eating.

FOOD ALLERGIES AND CHILDREN

Children are more likely than adults to suffer true food allergies, and a recent study at Duke University indicates that rashes and eczema in children may often be caused by allergic reactions. Top allergens for the 33 subjects involved in the Duke study proved to be eggs and milk, followed closely by peanuts. Symptoms also were caused by wheat, rye, peas, beef, and fish.

Children who suffer rashes and itching as the result of food allergies are also likely to experience nausea, abdominal pain, diarrhea, nasal congestion, and wheezing. Elimination diets are generally recommended for allergic youngsters. But there's some good news for parents: children will usually outgrow their food allergies by the age of five. Adults, however, seem to be stuck with theirs.

FOOD ALLERGIES AND MIGRAINE HEADACHES

There is mounting evidence of some connection between food allergies and migraine headaches, although allergic reactions are clearly not the sole cause of migraines. They may not prove to be responsible for even a substantial number of these devastating headaches suffered by some 10–20 million Americans. Nevertheless, a growing body of research seems to show a food-migraine connection for some migraine victims.

A study of British children with frequent migraine headaches found that 93 percent became headache-free when put on an elimination diet. By then reintroducing suspected foods, researchers could discover which ones caused migraines, and their findings were confirmed by double-blind controlled tests. As supporting evidence, the study found that many different foods not only caused headaches but also produced abdominal pain, asthmatic attacks, and eczema.

More than 50 foods were on the study's "guilty" list, with cow's milk, eggs, chocolate, oranges, and wheat at the top. Cheese, tomatoes, and rye followed soon after. White wheat flour, however, was well down on the list and caused reactions in no more children than did lamb and rice, which are generally considered nonallergenic. Of special interest was the study's finding that children often crave the very foods that cause their migraines and eat large quantities when allowed to do so.

FOOD ALLERGIES AND ASTHMA

Some connection between allergies and asthma seems pretty clear, for eggs, fish, nuts, and chocolate all provoke asthmatic attacks in children who can be shown, by skin tests, to have allergic responses to these foods. Studies on British children have shown that many respond to cola drinks with asthmatic wheezing.

There is also a connection between dairy foods and asthma, for asthmatic patients appear to improve considerably on milk-free diets. It is far from certain that the reaction of asthmatics to dairy foods is caused by an immune response. Still, the evidence that dairy products can play a role in asthma is significant — strong enough for sensible asthmatics to check out their own reactions to milk and milk products.

Sulfites also appear to trigger asthmatic attacks. And sensitivity to these preservatives is so widespread that the FDA recently banned their use on fresh fruits and vegetables, including the tomatoes, lettuce, and other greens on restaurant salad bars. Sulfite sensitivity, which will cause coughing, wheezing, and shortness of breath in asthmatics, can provoke other allergylike symptoms in nonasthmatics, including abdominal pain, breathing problems, and even anaphylactic shock.

FOOD ALLERGIES AND ARTHRITIS

Since allergists began looking at a possible link between diet and rheumatoid arthritis, some investigators have come to believe that certain foods may trigger a delayed reaction, which takes anywhere from one to three days to show up as arthritic pain. But many rheumatologists are skeptical, and such delayed reactions would be hard to diagnose in any case.

However, rheumatoid arthritis *is* an autoimmune disease, an attack by an overactive immune system on the body's own tissue. So any true allergic reaction could make arthritis more severe by pushing the immune system into overdrive. If a food allergy is at fault, though, the solution will have to be a carefully tailored diet, not the simplistic diets of vinegar, grapefruit, and other foods that are the mainstay of "anti-arthritis" regimens.

OTHER FOOD REACTIONS

There are a number of substances in foods that can cause allergylike reactions without triggering true food allergies. This is hardly surprising, since histamine itself (the heavyweight IgE-triggered mediator) and various related bioamines are found in such foods as bananas, tomatoes, avocados, cheeses, chocolate, pineapples, sausages, and red wine. The histamine in wines, fermented cheeses, and sausages can cause hives, and so can histamine-releasing agents in strawberries and shellfish. Certain amines in cheese, chocolate, and citrus fruit can raise blood pressure and are believed to trigger migraines, while the "hot dog headache" is brought on by nitrate preservatives in hot dogs and other sausages.

There are other foods that by their very nature can be troublemakers in the gut. Prunes, soybeans, and onions may cause digestive tract problems that very much resemble the symptoms of food allergies.

Favism, endemic to North Africa and the Middle East, is a mild form of anemia caused by a reaction to the fava bean. A toxin found in the skin of the bean can destroy the red blood cells of genetically susceptible people.

Closer to home is the strange case of MSG sensitivity, or Chinese restaurant syndrome. The story began 20 years ago, when a doctor who suffered from numbness, weakness, and palpitations after a Chinese meal wrote to the *New England Journal of Medicine* about his experience. The letter was published, other sufferers came forward, and the flavor enhancer MSG (monosodium glutamate), a common ingredient in Chinese food, was soon found to be the culprit. Initial research showed that subjects given MSG could indeed develop a range of symptoms, including flushing, tingling, and headaches.

More recent double-blind studies suggest that many individuals who believe they are MSG-sensitive actually are not. Nevertheless, there is a reasonable physiological basis for MSG reactions, even if they are less common than we had thought. If MSG is consumed faster than the body can process it, it can be converted to GABA, a neurotransmitter. And MSG itself can directly affect nerve cells. So, either way, the chemical seems easily capable of causing neurological distress symptoms. However, the MSG reaction usually occurs when the MSG-flavored food is eaten on an empty stomach and can often be avoided if non-MSG-flavored foods are eaten first.

CHAPTER 15

Food and Mood

NOTIONS OF HOW FOOD influences mood have been around for 4,000 years or more (since the early Egyptians prescribed onions as a soporific and salt as an aphrodisiac). People have always claimed, "It must have been something I ate," to explain away bizarre behavior or perceptions. That's how Scrooge responds to Marley's ghost in Dickens's *A Christmas Carol*, insisting the fearsome spectre of his late partner is just a manifestation brought on by "an undigested bit of beef, a blot of mustard," or "a fragment of underdone potato."

Short of hallucinogens such as certain mushrooms, succulents, and the liver of the Pacific blowfish, however, food is unlikely to have such a dramatic impact on mood. Research to date shows diet capable of affecting mood and behavior only in subtle ways. When food does specifically affect mental state, it is usually by changing levels of the brain's neurotransmitters—chemicals that carry signals between nerve cells. The link between diet and brain chemistry has only recently been outlined, and it is still far from completely understood.

We know enough, however, to realize that much current folk wisdom about food and mood is way off base. There is little evidence that food allergies do much mood-changing, even though this is a fairly popular belief. Nor are there any studies to back up the notion, mysteriously widespread among health food advocates, social scientists, and even dietitians, that eating lots of sugar can trigger violent behavior. The celebrated "Twinkie defense," which helped convince jurors that the killer of San Francisco Mayor George Moscone was not fully responsible for his actions, was based on claims of such a sugar-violence connection. In fact, research shows that sugar is actually more likely to calm you down than to excite you.

Nevertheless, a drop in *blood* sugar can have a measurable impact on mental function. But blood sugar levels are determined more by overall nutritional status than by intake of dietary sugar or any other single nutrient. A sharp reduction in blood sugar level can cause irritability, sluggishness, and feelings of depression. So regular meals are important.

While we sleep, the blood sugar level is maintained at the low end of the normal scale by release of stored glucose from the liver. When we wake, it's time to boost the level at breakfast and build up reserves.

The blood sugar level starts to fall between two and a half and three hours after a meal, so you need to give it a boost. But it doesn't take much food to do that. Studies by the Medical Research Council in England show that a light 300-calorie meal is sufficient.

Loading up with a heavy lunch may leave you as logy as skipping the meal altogether. Researchers at the University of Sussex in England have found that a midday feast tends to accentuate the natural slump most of us hit in early afternoon. After hearty lunches (in the 1,000-plus calorie range), airplane pilots showed significant losses of visual perception and reaction time, equivalent to missing a night's sleep. Schoolchildren too suffered performance losses when overlunched; they found it harder to master new material. When you eat a large meal, the blood vessels supplying the stomach apparently dilate, drawing blood to the gut and away from the brain.

The impact of blood sugar level on mood is most evident in hypoglycemia, a severe, chronic form of low blood sugar that has been blamed for a host of problems, many of them psychological. But there's a world of difference between the effects of meal-to-meal variations in blood sugar and the effects of true chronic hypoglycemia, which is far more rare than most people realize.

HYPOGLYCEMIA

True hypoglycemia — a reduction in blood sugar caused by an excess of the glucose-regulating hormone insulin — will cause other symptoms (including headaches, weakness, and extreme hunger) as well as mood changes. Diabetics who depend upon an external source of insulin may suffer hypoglycemia when they eat less than they need to balance their insulin intake, or when they exercise too vigorously (see chapter 20). Their loss of blood sugar (sometimes called insulin shock) must quickly be countered by eating sugar or other foods that boost blood levels rapidly, or the victims are likely to pass out.

Hypoglycemia can also be caused by insulin-secreting tumors of the pancreas, severe liver dysfunction, high fevers, alcoholism, and certain hormone deficiencies. But these are just about the only ways true hypoglycemia occurs.

Nevertheless, it's become fashionable to blame fatigue, depression, and a host of other ills on chronically low blood sugar. It's hard to find anyone these days who doesn't have several friends or acquaintances afflicted by what they or their doctors maintain is hypoglycemia. Indeed, the number of alleged victims has risen well above the level at which experts believe this disorder could possibly be occurring.

Try telling self-diagnosed hypoglycemics how rare the disorder actually is, and they'll insist the experts are wrong. Hypoglycemia, they are likely to argue, is not only common but responsible for a substantial amount of mental illness and irrational behavior. And self-diagnosed sufferers are not alone in this conviction. Some social scientists contend that most juvenile delinquents and convicted criminals (as many as 90 percent) have chronically low blood sugar levels, even though the aggressiveness and violent behavior they attribute to hypoglycemia are not characteristic symptoms of the disorder.

The popularity of hypoglycemia derives, at least in part, from its lack of specific symptoms. The tremors, dizziness, or sweating caused by a *low* blood sugar level can just as easily accompany a *high* blood sugar level. They can result, for example, from acute anxiety, which triggers release of the hormone adrenaline from the adrenal gland and causes the blood sugar level to rise.

Most doctors now try to reassure patients that their dizziness or headaches, their sweating, shaking, or palpitations are not necessarily — nor probably — the results of hypoglycemia. Nevertheless, some doctors do diagnose the disorder in people who don't really have it. And the self-diagnosed may ignore their physicians altogether and put themselves on the regimen recommended for true hypoglycemics: a high-protein, low-carbohydrate, low-fat diet, with no sweets and frequent meals (six or more per day).

The most common test for hypoglycemia is the glucose tolerance test, also used to test the response to dietary sugar in diabetics. The test involves administration of a high glucose solution after an overnight fast. Blood samples are then drawn during the following five hours and checked for glucose content. In true hypoglycemia a heavy dose of glucose may cause the body to overproduce insulin; and that in turn can drive blood sugar even lower than it would normally be. But if the body can tolerate a large glucose dose well, then hypoglycemia is not a problem.

DIET AND BRAIN FUNCTION

Despite the popular obsession with sugar, much current research on food and mood is focused on another class of dietary components: amino acids. Several amino acids (as well as some other nutrients) are needed to make up the brain chemicals, called neurotransmitters, that govern all mental functions. But the relation between dietary levels of amino acids and brain levels of neurotransmitters is a complex one.

Neurotransmitters are manufactured and released by nerve cells as molecular signals that are passed along to other nerve cells, muscles, and glands. Neuroendocrinologist Richard Wurtman and his research team at the Massachusetts Institute of Technology (MIT) have spent almost two decades studying the way diet determines neurotransmitter levels in the brain.

Their research shows that the amount of the amino acid tryptophan reaching the brain pretty much dictates the rate at which nerve cells will manufacture the neurotransmitter serotonin. (Serotonin is a chemical messenger that encourages sleep, reduces sensitivity to pain, and decreases appetite.) The amino acid tyrosine determines levels of dopamine and norepinephrine, neurotransmitters involved in mood and the response to stress. In addition to these amino acids, choline, found in the bodily fat lecithin, sets the rate for production of the neurotransmitter acetylcholine, which seems to be involved in memory. (Victims of Alzheimer's disease, for example, have low acetylcholine levels in their brains.)

Simply eating foods that contain these nutrients, however, will not necessarily affect your neurotransmitters in the way you might expect. Initially, Wurtman and his colleagues fed rats on tryptophan-rich protein, expecting that this diet would bring an increase in serotonin. Instead, levels of both serotonin and tryptophan in the brain actually fell.

This seeming paradox was explained once the researchers understood that tryptophan must compete with five other amino acids for transportation from the bloodstream into the brain. Since most proteins contain less tryptophan than other amino acids, a high-protein meal creates more competition for transportation and less opportunity for tryptophan to reach its goal.

In fact, the foods that are most effective at getting tryptophan into the brain are those containing carbohydrates — even though they provide no tryptophan. But a high-carbohydrate meal raises the level of insulin, which moves most amino acids out of the bloodstream and into muscle tissue. When insulin is high, levels of all amino acids fall, except for tryptophan. As a result, tryptophan has little competition for transportation, and more of it moves from the bloodstream to nerve cells in the brain.

This means that when you eat a high-carbohydrate lunch — pasta and bread, for example — your brain serotonin levels will rise, and you're likely to be duller, sleepier, and less alert than if you ate a high-protein meal. On the other hand, if you're looking for a food to help you get to sleep at night, a snack that contains carbohydrates may be your best bet. That bedtime glass of milk is a good source of tryptophan, and it also has carbohydrates in lactose (milk sugar) that make it a pretty good sleeping potion.

A relatively high dose of straight tryptophan will probably do an even better job of fighting insomnia (a low dose doesn't tilt the odds enough in tryptophan's favor), but it may also prove a relatively high-risk soporific. Researchers have found tryptophan in doses of 1–4 grams to be a potent sleep inducer that doesn't interfere with memory or sleep stages or leave you fuzzy-headed in the morning. However, there is evidence from animal studies that regular use of tryptophan supplements may cause liver damage. This would seem to make further research necessary before tryptophan's use as a sleeping pill or a painkiller gets past the experimental stage.

While it is possible to boost serotonin production by taking on tryptophan via the high-carbohydrate route, no dietary strategies will provide enough tyrosine or choline to alter neurotransmitter levels very much. Nor are neuroscientists ready to recommend regular therapeutic use of high-dose tyrosine or choline, just as they will not recommend high doses of tryptophan. The feeling is that more laboratory and clinical work is needed.

Much of this work is well under way. Wurtman and his wife, Judith Wurtman, a research scientist at MIT, have focused on the possible role of serotonin in controlling eating disorders. Both tryptophan and tyrosine are being tested as antidepressants, and there has been some use of tyrosine to help drug abusers quit cocaine (which depletes levels of dopamine and norepinephrine in the brain). In addition, a number of researchers are now attempting to raise brain levels of acetylcholine with choline and related nutrients, an approach they hope will help control Alzheimer's and other diseases of aging.

Although tryptophan, tyrosine, and choline clearly play primary roles in the production of neurotransmitters, they are not the only nutrients involved in the process. Adequate supplies of vitamins C, B_6, and B_{12} are also needed to keep the brain's chemical messenger corps at full strength. Deficiencies of these vitamins have psychiatric consequences. However, attempts to treat psychiatric disorders with vitamin megadoses have been unsuccessful and may have put patients at risk of toxic effects. (See "Department of False Hopes: Vitamins for Schizophrenia?," page 190.)

HYPERACTIVITY

From 5 to 20 percent of American children, most of them boys, may be hyperactive. The diagnosis is a hard one to make, since symptoms of hyperactivity include a number of problem behaviors. In general, however, hyperactive (or hyperkinetic) youngsters tend to be overly active and often unruly, with short attention spans and a penchant for impulsive action.

In 1975 a California pediatric allergist, Dr. Ben F. Feingold, published *Why Your Child Is Hyperactive*, identifying diet as the villain. Feingold told parents precisely which foods hyperactive youngsters should avoid in order to control their behavior. His diet warned of dangers from food colorings and artificial flavorings, particularly those containing salicylates. He also banned natural sources of salicylates, from almonds and apricots to peppermint and Worcestershire sauce.

Thousands of parents tried the Feingold solution and believed that it worked for their children. But it was possible that these positive perceptions might reflect not the effect of the diet as much as changes in children's behavior or parental attitudes caused by a treatment that provided youngsters with lots of parental attention. To test the diet itself, the National Institutes of Health funded several large-scale double-blind studies. In these experiments neither children nor their parents knew whether or not the foods the kids ate contained artificial additives. Contrary to Feingold's claims, these chemicals did not prove capable of affecting hyperactivity.

More recently, excessive consumption of sugar has been suspected of being the primary cause of hyperactivity. But the relation between carbohydrate consumption and serotonin in the brain argues that sugar would be more likely to calm youngsters down than to overexcite them.

DEPARTMENT OF FALSE HOPES: VITAMINS FOR SCHIZOPHRENIA?

Unorthodox nutritional treatments tend to be most popular for diseases that have no standard effective therapy. Thus, there's a constant parade of nutritional nostrums for cancer (many of them originating in or relocating to areas, like Mexico, that are beyond the jurisdiction of the FDA). The same has been true for schizophrenia, perhaps the most devastating and puzzling of mental illnesses.

Megavitamin therapy for schizophrenia began in the 1950s and was initially based on a theory of schizophrenia that was later abandoned. At the time, some researchers believed that the neurotransmitter epinephrine could be transformed by a certain chemical reaction into a toxic compound that caused the hallucinations seen in some schizophrenics. Niacin in the form of nicotinic acid or nicotinamide — in doses tens or hundreds of times the RDA — was believed to interfere with that chemical reaction and bring schizophrenics back down to earth.

A decade later, the niacin treatment remained fairly popular, although still unproved, but both the rationale and the name had changed. In 1968, Linus Pauling, brilliant biochemist, Nobel laureate, and nutritional iconoclast, published a paper suggesting that even subtle deficiencies of certain vitamins could cause mental illness. According to Pauling, a vitamin intake that met the RDA and was perfectly adequate for most individuals might be insufficient for people with special genetic vulnerabilities. The solution to their resultant mental problems, he said, would be to provide "the optimum molecular environment

In fact, careful clinical tests have shown exactly that — and cleared sugar of the hyperactivity charge.

PREMENSTRUAL SYNDROME

Premenstrual syndrome (PMS) involves a number of symptoms: bloating, tender breasts, pelvic pain, constipation, a sense of weight gain, headaches, fatigue, insomnia, and a craving for sweet or salty foods. It can have a potent influence on mood as well, bringing on irritability and aggressiveness, anxiety or depression. Although doctors can't say for certain just what causes PMS, it's hard to imagine it resulting from anything other than hormonal changes that are part of the menstrual cycle.

To minimize the effects of PMS and its mood changes, a number of dietary strategies have been proposed and pursued. But nothing to date seems to work very well, and at least one dietary intervention has proved dangerous indeed.

Vitamin E has been tried as a PMS remedy. But there is no convincing evidence that it is of much help, and large doses of this fat-soluble vitamin are toxic.

Vitamin B_6 showed lots of potential in uncontrolled studies, with a

---

for the mind." Such an approach to psychiatry he termed "orthomolecular."

The proponents of the niacin treatment then came up with a new rationale that neatly fit under the orthomolecular rubric. Schizophrenia, they said, was a deficiency disease, caused by an undetected lack of niacin. They noted that pellagra — true, severe niacin deficiency — often brings with it a form of psychosis (see chapter 4). And they claimed further that the psychosis of pellagra is all but indistinguishable from schizophrenia — a claim that virtually all mainstream psychiatrists would dispute.

The problems with orthomolecular psychiatry have not all been theoretical. The niacin treatment itself has simply never been proved effective in carefully controlled studies. Although some early studies by the therapy's proponents did show positive results, other researchers have been unable to match their success. In addition, critics charge that orthomolecular psychiatrists keep changing their approach — adding other vitamins, hormones, drugs, even shock treatments — so that it's impossible to define precisely the therapy you're trying to evaluate. As one review of the research summarized it, "The real problem seems to be that the megavitamin proponents do poor science."

Orthomolecular psychiatry has turned up one intriguing lead: the possible role of other B vitamins in treating autism, the severe childhood withdrawal that is similar in some ways to adult schizophrenia. Several well-controlled studies in the 1970s suggested that large doses of B_6 might be helpful to a small group of autistic children, perhaps 10 percent of them. But without adequate replication of these findings — not to mention a good explanation of why B_6 would work — most psychiatrists remain skeptical of this treatment too.

great many women claiming it had given them substantial relief. In subsequent double-blind tests, however, women who received B$_6$ appeared to fare no better than women who did not. And there has been a growing number of reports of neurological damage resulting from megadose levels of B$_6$ to relieve PMS (see chapter 4).

Although PMS patients with low blood levels of magnesium appear to suffer fewer or less severe symptoms once their magnesium levels are up to normal, there is no evidence that magnesium can provide any relief for women who aren't deficient. Particularly dangerous is the notion of reducing calcium intake in order to increase magnesium absorption. This will cost bone mass and raise the risk of osteoporosis.

Restricting sodium is sometimes recommended as a means of cutting down water retention, bloating, and weight gain. But there is far less water retention involved in PMS than most women imagine. What occurs most often is that fluid shifts between blood vessels and compartments in the breasts and abdomen.

CHOCOLATE FOR LOVERS

Although there plainly are connections between food and mood, science is just groping its way toward understanding them. Meanwhile, the area of nutritional-emotional linkages offers an enormous number of opportunities for misunderstanding. Take, for example, the chocolate hypothesis that Michael Liebowitz, an assistant professor of psychiatry at Columbia University, reports in his book *The Chemistry of Love.*

Liebowitz knew that phenylethylamine (PEA) can play a significant role in emotional arousal; it's converted into the neurotransmitters epinephrine and norepinephrine. Realizing that chocolate is chock-full of PEA, he wondered if more than just sentiment was served by the traditional Valentine's Day box of candy. Could romance be advanced and depression averted simply by "pigging out" on chocolate?

The idea got plenty of press attention. But when Liebowitz tested it carefully, by having researchers at the National Institute of Mental Health stuff themselves on chocolate, he got none of the desired results. PEA levels in the brain were unaffected by the chocolate binge. The researchers reaped no emotional rewards. All they got were headaches.

CHAPTER 16 ═══════════════════════

Toxic Pleasures

A S MUCH AS OUR diets shape us, we shape our diets. Age, sex, size, lifestyle, and foodstyle all determine nutritional needs and food choices. Our eating habits do not exist independent of all our other habits, and whatever we ingest — foods and nonfoods alike — gets into the nutritional act.

Affecting both dietary needs and food interaction are a number of pleasure-providing but toxic substances that millions of Americans regularly consume. Chief among these are alcohol, caffeine, and nicotine. Clearly, these are not the only toxic pleasures that influence how we eat, what we eat, or whether we eat at all. Certain illicit drugs have a potent impact on foodstyle. Cocaine and amphetamines, for example, so diminish appetite that long-time users are usually malnourished. Nevertheless, it is alcohol, caffeine, and nicotine — the big three toxic pleasures — that most concern nutritionists.

ALCOHOL

Alcohol can be toxic, but moderate use of it isn't necessarily harmful. For most people, a reasonable amount of alcohol — up to about two drinks per day — can actually improve health and extend life. At this level, alcohol will reduce the risk of heart attack, mostly by helping keep arteries free of cholesterol buildup, and it won't raise blood pressure either.

But possible health benefits are not the reason most people drink, in spite of such traditional fictions as granny's "tonic" and the friendly practitioner's "medicinal brandy." Most people drink because alcohol relieves tensions and inhibitions, creates a sense of well-being, improves appetite, and enhances the pleasures of food. Although there has been some decline in alcohol consumption in recent years, nearly 115 million Americans over 18 still take a drink now and again, and the great majority keep their consumption within reasonable limits.

Nevertheless, there are now an estimated 10 million alcoholics in the United States. Most disturbing is the growing amount of alcoholism among younger adults and adolescents. By any measure — number of users, abusers, and fatalities, or costs of crime, violence, accidents, medical and psychiatric care, and lost productivity — alcohol has more impact on the United States than any other drug. Drunkenness is a messy but effective killer, responsible for 30–50 percent of all traffic fatalities, nearly half of all fatal falls, and between one half and two thirds of all homicides. And at high doses (well beyond two drinks per day) alcohol itself turns vicious, destroying the liver, weakening the heart, raising blood pressure, injuring the brain, and increasing the risk of cancer.

There is one other clear danger of drinking, which exists even at very low intake levels: the damage alcohol can do to a growing fetus. Abstinence is now the rule for pregnant women, because there is no way of knowing for sure just how much alcohol might threaten an unborn child. Although the extreme birth defects of fetal alcohol syndrome may be caused only by heavy drinking, a study of pregnant mothers in northern California has found that just one or two drinks per day during the first trimester will significantly increase the risk of retarded growth and mental development.

Anyone who has ever taken a drink knows how quickly it acts, for alcohol is absorbed rapidly from the stomach and small intestine. It enters the bloodstream just minutes after you've taken a sip. At least some of it does, for absorption depends on who's doing the drinking, what they're drinking (and eating), when they're drinking it, and how fast they're knocking it back.

The toxic impact of alcohol, intoxication, is measurable in terms of blood alcohol level, or BAL (see "How Blood Alcohol Rises," page 195). When your BAL reaches 0.05, which means there are five parts of alcohol to 10,000 parts of everything else in your blood (and the average drinker hits this level after only one or two drinks), alcohol is doing all the good things it can do for you. You feel relaxed, mildly euphoric, and not drunk. As BAL mounts, you start losing your grip on speech, balance, and emotions. With a BAL of 0.1 you are legally drunk, and at 0.2 you may pass out. When BAL hits 0.3, you can be close to comatose.

Size, sex, and age all influence the absorption of alcohol. The more weight you carry, the more water you have to dilute the alcohol in your bloodstream. Women, whose bodies contain proportionately less water and more fat than men's, need less alcohol to raise their blood level (hormonal changes just prior to menstruation will cause it to rise faster). As for older drinkers, they seem to tolerate proportionately less alcohol than younger drinkers do.

Although there is roughly the same amount of alcohol in a shot of whiskey (or other spirits) as there is in a glass of wine or a can of beer, they do not all have the same immediate impact on BAL. The more the alcohol is diluted, the more slowly it is absorbed. As a result, peak levels of alcohol in the blood may be lower when you are drinking beer, wine, or tall mixed drinks than when your tipple is straight whiskey or a minimally diluted martini.

Food will also slow down absorption. Maximum concentrations of alcohol in the blood may be only half as great when you drink after a meal as when you drink on an empty stomach. Fats in meat, cheese, and cocktail dips, for example, when eaten either before or while you are drinking, are particularly effective in retarding absorption.

No matter how slowly or rapidly alcohol is absorbed, your blood level will keep rising if you drink more, or drink it faster, than your liver

---

HOW BLOOD ALCOHOL RISES

The blood alcohol level (BAL) is a good indication of how drunk you're likely to become after a given number of drinks. This table shows how BAL increases (at various body weights) with the number of drinks consumed. One drink is equal to 1.25 ounces of 80-proof liquor, 12 ounces of beer, or 4 ounces of wine. Since alcohol leaves the bloodstream with time, subtract 0.01 of BAL for every 40 minutes of drinking.

Approximate Blood Alcohol Level (BAL)

No. of Drinks	Body Weight in Pounds							
	100	120	140	160	180	200	220	240
One	.04	.04	.03	.03	.02	.02	.02	.02
Two	.09	.07	.06	.06	.05	.04	.04	.04
Three	.13	.11	.09	.08	.07	.07	.06	.06
Four	.18	.15	.13	.11	.10	.09	.08	.07
Five	.22	.18	.16	.14	.12	.11	.10	.09
Six	.26	.22	.19	.17	.15	.13	.12	.11
Seven	.31	.26	.22	.19	.17	.15	.14	.13
Eight	.35	.29	.25	.22	.20	.18	.16	.15
Nine	.40	.33	.28	.25	.22	.20	.18	.17
Ten	.44	.37	.31	.28	.24	.22	.20	.18

Source: Mothers Against Drunk Driving.

can handle. Even a healthy liver can metabolize only about half an ounce of alcohol per hour, breaking it down into fuel that body cells can burn. When the liver is overloaded, alcohol is recirculated, and blood levels remain high.

Regular heavy drinking will cause alcohol metabolism to speed up and increase the drinker's tolerance so that it takes more alcohol to achieve the same effects. The liver, however, cannot sustain the punishing effects of alcoholism indefinitely. Over time, periodic inflammation destroys cells that are replaced by scar tissue. Thus, liver disease diminishes the ability of that organ to metabolize alcohol, and as a result, the tolerance of alcoholics is reduced. Less alcohol is required to relieve inhibitions, and alcoholics proceed more rapidly to intoxication.

High levels of alcohol consumption are clearly dangerous, not only to the liver but to the brain, the heart, and other organs. What is a high or unsafe level? More than 3 ounces of alcohol per day are likely to do damage even to otherwise healthy, well-nourished men or women. But 1.5 ounces per day appear to be physiologically safe for most drinkers. This is roughly equivalent to four 1-ounce jiggers of 80-proof whiskey, half a bottle (14 ounces) of wine, four 10-ounce glasses of regular (4.5 percent) beer, or four 12-ounce glasses of light (3.2 percent) beer.

Drinking these amounts, however, might make you tipsier than you care to be — at least on a daily basis. So it's fortunate that the health-promoting qualities of alcohol are available at significantly lower levels. Moderation is the key, and a number of large-scale studies have demonstrated that moderate drinkers live longer and healthier lives than either nondrinkers or immoderate drinkers.

In terms of specific benefits, research in the United States and Europe has found moderate drinkers with healthier hearts than nondrinkers. This beneficial aspect of alcohol was first documented by Dr. Arthur Klatsky of the Kaiser Permanente Hospital in Oakland, California. Using medical histories of 120,000 patients, Klatsky and his team discovered that those who averaged two drinks per day were 40 percent less likely to be hospitalized for heart attacks than were nondrinkers.

Although researchers aren't yet certain just what alcohol does to protect the heart, the most likely explanation comes from research at Stanford University, where two- and three-drink-per-day subjects were found to have particularly high levels of HDL cholesterol, the form of cholesterol that actually *protects* the body from coronary artery disease (see chapter 17). HDL-cholesterol levels rose in the blood when the subjects drank and fell when they did not. According to the Stanford team, the level of HDL is at present the best predictor of coronary heart disease. High levels mean low risk.

Klatsky's research showed the drinker's edge disappeared at between two and three drinks per day. Drinkers who averaged between three and five daily drinks had a 50 percent higher mortality rate than nondrinkers. When he looked at blood pressure, Klatsky found that at two drinks per day drinkers had blood pressure at least as low as abstainers. But pressure rose steadily at three drinks per day or more. At six drinks per day, risk of hypertension doubled among white patients and increased by 50 percent among black patients.

There is a strong link between alcoholism and nutrition, although diet is clearly not responsible for alcohol dependency. Alcoholism seems most influenced by cultural conditioning, the ways in which youngsters see alcohol used and perceived by adults (as either a normal part of life or as a separate kind of behavior). There is now, however, some evidence of genetic predisposition as well — at least for a certain portion of the alcoholic population.

But what makes alcoholism a nutritional concern is the substantial risk of dietary deficiency to which alcoholics are exposed. Indeed, although the toxic impact of alcohol itself is responsible for the most devastating results of alcohol abuse, the effects of nutritional deficiencies are usually the first to appear.

While a modest amount of alcohol will increase appetite (it stimulates the flow of stomach acids), heavy drinking diminishes the desire for food. As a result, some alcoholics get as much as half their calories from alcohol alone. Although this helps to meet their energy needs, it generally leaves them substantially short of daily requirements for most other nutrients.

Alcoholics often suffer deficiencies of B vitamins and trace elements and can develop some highly uncommon deficiency diseases — even overt scurvy and pellagra. Alcohol seems to depress the general ability of the small intestine to absorb nutrients. And alcoholics, after all, are taking many of their calories from a source whose nutrient density is close to zero.

There is some iron and a negligible amount of vitamins in wine, plus some residual carbohydrates in heavier beers. But this is about it for nonalcoholic nutrients, at least in industrialized societies where alcoholic beverages are generally filtered, clarified, or distilled. In nonindustrialized societies, however, alcoholic drinks can contribute a good deal more to dietary needs. Unclarified and unstrained beers and wines contain rich residues and lots of yeast, a source of proteins and B vitamins.

In the United States the most widespread nutritional drawback of heavy alcohol use is excessive weight. Alcohol is high in calories; an ounce of alcohol has substantially more calories than an ounce of carbohydrate, though not quite as many as an ounce of fat. Most drinkers take their alcohol in addition to food, not instead of it, so their drinks add calories on top of their regular intake. And populations that tend to drink mostly with meals have a propensity for portliness. True alcoholics, however, who lose their appetites, are more likely to risk emaciation than obesity.

CAFFEINE

Researchers keep looking for evidence that caffeine poses a health hazard, because it *seems* that caffeine should be bad for us. But the studies so far show only limited negative effects. And the most frightening suspicion — that caffeine raises the risk of cancer — now appears to be groundless. So for the present, at least, there seems to be no good reason why healthy adults can't drink a few cups of coffee a day, or slightly more tea, soft drinks, chocolate milk, or cocoa (see "Caffeine in Common Foods and Drinks," below).

Caffeine is a fairly potent stimulant. For nonusers, just the amount in two cups of coffee will affect both blood pressure and heart rate. Respiration will accelerate, adrenaline levels will rise, and urine production will increase. Functioning as both a vasoconstrictor and a vasodilator, caffeine will cause blood vessels in the brain to constrict and those about the heart to expand. Regular users, however, develop a tolerance to caffeine and rarely experience more than a brief boost in their metabolic rates. The price of tolerance, of course, is withdrawal symptoms, and confirmed coffee drinkers can suffer relatively severe headaches when they quit caffeine cold.

As for toxicity, 5–10 grams of caffeine can be fatal. But that would

---

Caffeine in Common Foods and Drinks

Food/Drink	Caffeine (mg)
Drip-brewed coffee (5 fl oz)	130
Instant coffee (5 fl oz)	60
Decaffeinated coffee (5 fl oz)	3
Tea, brewed 1 minute (5 fl oz)	28
Tea, brewed 5 minutes (5 fl oz)	46
Cola and "pepper" sodas (12 fl oz)	38
Baking chocolate (1 oz)	35
Milk chocolate candy (1 oz)	6
Hot cocoa (6 fl oz)	5

Source: Specified data from "Caffeine Content of Selected Foods and Drugs" from *Food Values of Portions Commonly Used* by Jean A.T. Pennington and Helen Nichols Church. Copyright © 1980, 1985 by Helen Nichols Church and by Jean A.T. Pennington. Reprinted by permission of Harper & Row, Publishers, Inc.
Note: Figures are averages for these products.

mean drinking between 75 and 100 cups of coffee in a single day. And caffeine poisoning was just about unheard of until 1980, when fake amphetamine capsules (containing as much as half a gram of caffeine) appeared on the market. These look-alike drugs were implicated in more than a dozen deaths during 1980 and 1981.

The worst and the best of common caffeine effects—"coffee nerves" and the quick pickup—result from the drug's ability to stimulate the nervous system. The process wasn't fully understood until 1981, when a research team at the Johns Hopkins University School of Medicine explained the mechanism. They found that caffeine is similar in molecular structure to adenosine, a natural tranquilizing agent that can reduce the activity of brain cells by making them less sensitive to neurotransmitters. By blocking the effects of adenosine, caffeine prevents brain cells from getting the natural tranquilizer's slow-down signals.

Even though it clearly works against what the body believes is best (adenosine levels rise to calm you down when you're under stress), caffeine isn't too much of a villain. It can, for example, increase the effectiveness of aspirin, acetaminophen (the active ingredient in Tylenol), and other analgesics.

But we shouldn't get carried away with the notion of how benign caffeine may be. It causes caffeinism, a chronic low level of toxicity that can make you nervous and irritable, give you insomnia, and cause your heart to palpitate. It doesn't do ulcers much good either (since it stimulates the flow of stomach acid).

Since it can cross the placenta, caffeine poses a special threat during pregnancy. Because animal studies have shown caffeine capable of causing birth defects, the U.S. Food and Drug Administration advises pregnant women to use caffeine with caution. Danger appears greatest during the first trimester, when just one cup of very strong coffee per day can nearly double the chance of spontaneous abortion.

With its impact on metabolism, the nervous system, and the heart, caffeine is naturally suspect as a heart disease risk-raiser. And here the evidence is mixed. A number of long-term studies, including the prestigious Framingham Heart Study (which has been under way since 1948), have produced no evidence that moderate use of caffeine can cause heart attacks.

But recent research has come up with different findings. Cardiologist Thomas Pearson studied more than 1,100 male graduates of the Johns Hopkins medical school. After taking into account all the other risk factors (smoking, hypertension, cholesterol, age) among the victims of coronary disease in the group, Pearson found that those graduates who drank more than five cups of coffee per day were two and a half times more likely to develop heart disease than those who shunned coffee.

Making it easier to believe in a caffeine-coronary disease connection is recent evidence of a link between coffee and cholesterol. Although no such link showed up in earlier studies, those were conducted when Americans drank a weaker, percolated brew. Today, more than half the nation's coffee drinkers use drip brew, and three U.S. studies have seen a tie-in to higher cholesterol levels. In one study, just two cups per day seemed to increase serum cholesterol for men, while in another, four cups per day raised levels for women, even when they were on low-fat diets.

This cholesterol connection may stem from a major role of caffeine in the body: it helps certain enzymes take body fat out of storage and move it into the bloodstream. When you need to burn fat for energy, this may be beneficial, which is why some endurance athletes use caffeine (as described in chapter 12). But if you're not burning a lot of fat, your body has no special reason to mobilize fat stores, and doing so could be harmful.

Caffeine has other effects on nutrition as well. It saps calcium by interfering with the process of reabsorption in the kidneys. What's more, only by adding half a cup of milk to their coffee can adults replace the loss. As for adolescents, who get their caffeine in the soda they drink instead of milk, lost calcium is even less likely to be replaced.

Coffee will cost you iron too. But it's not the caffeine that's to blame. It's a group of organic compounds called polyphenols that bind iron in the digestive tract and keep it from being absorbed. If you drink coffee with your meals or right afterward, you risk reducing iron absorption by almost 40 percent. Drinking coffee an hour before you eat (which is not all that popular, however) seems to have little effect on absorption.

Substituting tea for coffee at mealtime does not help. Tannin, another polyphenol, which is found in tea, also interferes with iron absorption. Although tea itself is rich in manganese and zinc, tannin also keeps these minerals out of the bloodstream. If, however, you take milk in your tea, the casein in milk (its principal protein) binds the tannin and liberates all the minerals.

NICOTINE

Unlike alcohol or caffeine, nicotine appears to be unsafe at any level and beneficial at none. Nicotine and other smoke-borne substances can do serious damage in the lungs, and nicotine in the bloodstream has dramatic effects on body tissues, releasing adrenaline that raises heart rate and blood pressure. In the brain it acts as a neurotransmitter and can make you either more alert or more relaxed, depending upon whether levels of the drug are high or low.

Smoking creates some specific nutritional needs. Heavy smokers require extra vitamin C. Their bodies deplete vitamin C reserves as much as 50 percent faster than the bodies of nonsmokers do. And smoking appears to affect diet in other ways as well.

Although plenty of overweight people use cigarettes, smoking seems to limit weight gain. Research has shown that the average weight of regular smokers is 5–8 pounds less than the average weight of non-smokers. But limited weight gain is an advantage smokers lose when they quit, for most quitters gain about 8 pounds.

Although there is no hard evidence that shows just why smoking affects body weight, there are several possibilities, all of which may be partly true. There are indications that smoking increases the body's metabolic rate, so more calories are burned. (Given nicotine's role as a stimulant, this makes sense.) Some research suggests that because of the metabolic slowdown, former smokers gain weight when they quit, even if they eat no more than before.

There are also findings suggesting that smoking curbs appetite, perhaps by limiting the taste for sweets. When laboratory rats were dosed with nicotine at a government research center in Bethesda, Maryland, they ate less sweet food and gained less weight than their undrugged cagemates. Human smokers at the same center, given their choice of sweet, salty, and bland foods, chose a mix that was less sweet than the one nonsmokers chose.

Weight control, however, is hardly an argument for smoking, considering all the hazards involved. Nor does nicotine have any other benefits to offer as a trade-off for its toxicity. Although moderation provides sensible safeguards for the use of alcohol and coffee, there is simply no level of reasonable risk when it comes to nicotine.

PART IV

DIET AND DISEASE

CHAPTER 17

Preventing
Heart Disease

ALTHOUGH HEART DISEASE remains the major cause of death in the United States, it now is less threatening to Americans than it was two decades ago. The death rate from cardiovascular disease declined by 36 percent between 1963 and 1983, and the United States, which had the world's second highest rate in 1969, is now in eighth place.

To put this progress into perspective, we must realize that heart disease wasn't even among the nation's top 10 killers in 1900, when infectious diseases still led the list. But modern medicine has been whittling away at the total U.S. death rate ever since. As a result, says Dr. David Kritchevsky, professor of biochemistry at the University of Pennsylvania and associate director of Philadelphia's Wistar Institute (the nation's oldest independent biological research center), "We have a lot of heart disease now because we don't have other things to die from."

Much of the reduction in cardiovascular mortality is credited to improved medical care — not only the development of coronary care units but also the increased use of cardiopulmonary resuscitation (CPR) procedures and better drugs for the control of coronary artery disease and hypertension. Yet most of this reduction — as much as 60 percent — is attributed to better control of those aspects of health, diet, and behavior that tend to increase risk. Researchers have identified more than 200 such risk factors, but there is little argument that the major ones are smoking, high levels of cholesterol in the blood, high blood pressure, obesity, diabetes, and lack of exercise.

The declining number of smokers, particularly among that portion of the population most vulnerable to heart disease — men aged 35–64 (more than one third of whom now suffer fatal heart attacks) — is believed to have pared down the heart disease death rate considerably. But most heart disease experts also believe that dietary changes have had a substantial impact.

Most of the major factors that raise the risk of heart disease — high levels of blood cholesterol, high blood pressure, and obesity — can be modified by diet. Adult-onset diabetes, as well, can be controlled by food choice and eating habits (as described in chapter 20). Some kind of dietary modification will probably be helpful for anyone with significant heart disease risk.

But the importance of dietary changes and the optimal dietary strategy will vary from individual to individual. People with a low risk of heart disease — reflected, for example, in a low level of cholesterol in the blood — may have little reason to worry about their diets. Since the causes of heart disease are so diverse, the kind of dietary change that is most helpful for one person may be of no use at all for another.

All heart disease threatens the ability of the heart to function properly. In order to pump oxygen and nutrients through the bloodstream to every part of the body, the myocardium (the muscle in the heart wall) contracts about 100,000 times a day. The most common form of heart disease, which causes heart attacks and which doctors call ischemic, damages the myocardium. Ischemic heart disease is caused by a malfunction in the coronary arteries (so named because they encircle the heart like a crown) that supply the myocardium with blood. A failure of these arteries destroys part of the heart muscle by cutting off its supply of blood and oxygen. The result is myocardial infarction (injury to the myocardium), which reduces the muscle's ability to contract.

Two conditions are generally to blame for this damage: atherosclerosis and hypertension. These disorders work both together and separately, for atherosclerosis is one of the factors that contribute to hypertension (and both conditions are affected by obesity). However, hypertension (discussed in chapter 18) involves a number of separate physiological changes and threatens the heart in ways that do not involve depriving it of oxygen. So let's consider for now only atherosclerosis, which is responsible for blocking or narrowing arteries leading into and through the heart and is considered the chief villain in coronary heart disease.

ATHEROSCLEROSIS

Atherosclerosis, or hardening of the arteries, occurs throughout life and throughout the body. But it is most life-threatening when it affects the coronary arteries. The process, which is much the same wherever it occurs, involves the formation of plaque (deposits of fatty material and other debris) on artery walls.

Although researchers have developed a number of theories to explain it, scientists are not yet certain just how the formation of plaque actually starts. It may, for example, involve action by free radicals (unstable oxygen molecules) that damage the thin layer of cells lining the artery. To repair the leak in this lining, the body may form what amounts to a lumpy patch. In any event, the result is a lump or protrusion on the artery wall where all kinds of matter can collect. Plaque also forms at junctures in the arteries, even when no injury has scarred the arterial wall.

What seems to collect first and continues to pile up is cholesterol, a fatty compound in foods that is also produced by the body itself. (It is found in all body cells and is essential to the formation of certain hormones, liver bile, and that form of vitamin D produced in the skin by exposure to sunlight.) Along with cholesterol, plaque also contains a sizable number of blood particles called platelets. These become trapped in plaque because they are sticky (it is the clumping together of platelets that causes blood to clot). Collagen and other materials also accumulate there. Calcium can harden the deposits, forming rough edges where still more debris collects.

Over time, plaque will narrow the artery. Eventually, it may seal it, cutting off the flow of blood and the oxygen it carries to the heart. This can occur when an artery already narrowed by atherosclerosis is blocked by a blood clot, which may consist of clumped platelets that have broken free from a plaque deposit somewhere farther up the bloodstream. Sometimes it is a hemorrhage in tissue below the plaque that creates the obstruction by forcing plaque out from the artery wall.

Although cholesterol is not the sole ingredient in arterial plaque, it is certainly the most important, for the rate at which plaque develops depends primarily upon how much cholesterol piles up there. To some extent this is determined by the amount of cholesterol in the blood, which is why high levels of cholesterol constitute a significant risk factor.

To better gauge the risk of heart disease, it helps to know not only how much cholesterol is in your bloodstream but what form of transportation it is using. Since fats are plainly not water-soluble, they need some form of protection to travel in blood. Protein provides that protection in fat-carrying compounds called lipoproteins.

It's easy to understand how lipoproteins work by thinking of them as globs of fat wrapped in protective protein, something like M&Ms (with fat instead of chocolate inside and protein as the candy coating). The chemistry of lipoproteins is actually far more complex, however, and several different kinds of fat-transporting vehicles are formed, varying in size, composition, function, and density. They consist almost exclusively of protein, cholesterol, and triglycerides (which are how the body's fatty acids are assembled for storage and transportation). But only two lipoproteins are involved in the formation of plaque: low-density lipoproteins (LDLs) and high-density lipoproteins (HDLs).

LDLs, the body's major cholesterol carriers, are very fragile vehicles that transport cholesterol to cells. HDLs are far more sturdy, and they generally remove more cholesterol from cells than they deposit there (they transport it back to the liver, where all bodily fats are processed). Partly because of the relatively small amount of protein they contain, LDLs are not only less dense than HDLs but extremely vulnerable as well. When they come racing through the arteries — particularly when they hit the turbulent areas where plaque has built up or where arteries divide — LDLs can crash and strew cholesterol along the walls, which is how accretions of plaque are usually enlarged.

The proportion of LDLs to HDLs in the bloodstream now appears to affect development of atherosclerosis more directly than the overall amount of serum (blood) cholesterol. Indeed, LDL is often referred to as "bad cholesterol" and HDL as "good cholesterol." Generally, about two thirds of the cholesterol in the bloodstream is carried by LDLs. But the more of it that is found in HDLs, the lower the risk of heart disease. Women, for example, usually have higher levels of HDL than men, and nonsmokers have higher levels than smokers. Exercise correlates with high HDL levels, and so does moderate use of alcohol (about two drinks per day), while obesity correlates with low levels.

Most often, it is the total cholesterol level that physicians measure, although a growing number now check both total cholesterol and the amount in HDLs. The result is expressed as a ratio: total milligrams of cholesterol (per 100 milliliters of blood) over HDL cholesterol. (A reading of 200/50 would be normal for a young adult, but it is not necessarily risk-free.) Even without an HDL count, total cholesterol levels are significant, and there is no longer any question that risk of heart disease increases as levels rise above the 200–220-milligram range.

The medical community has recently become increasingly aware of the relation between serum cholesterol levels and heart disease. In the long-term Framingham Heart Study, men with an average serum cholesterol level of 260 milligrams have had a heart attack rate three times greater than men with an average cholesterol level below 195 milligrams. Data from the federal Multiple Risk Factor Intervention Trial show that men with serum cholesterol levels in the top 10 percent (263 milligrams or higher) run four times the average risk of heart disease. This study, which involved 350,000 men aged 35–57, also found correspondingly greater risk of heart disease for those with serum cholesterol levels in the top 25 percent (above 238 milligrams).

Researchers at the University of Southern California School of Medicine have been able to show that reducing high serum cholesterol levels, by means of drugs and diet, can actually shrink atherosclerotic deposits. But these positive results were achieved by relatively few subjects in the small study group.

Doctors have generally not been overly sanguine about the possibility of reducing risk by lowering serum cholesterol levels, since half of all patients with high cholesterol levels do *not* die from heart disease, and half of all heart disease victims do *not* have high serum cholesterol. As late as 1984 a survey by the National Heart, Lung, and Blood Institute (NHLBI) found that fewer than 40 percent of the physicians queried believed reducing blood cholesterol levels would have a "large impact" on controlling coronary heart disease.

During that same year, however, the NHLBI also released the results of its Lipid Research Clinics Coronary Primary Prevention Trial (CPPT), a study that significantly changed physicians' thinking about cholesterol. For more than seven years the trial recorded the effects of diet and drugs on middle-aged men with high levels of serum cholesterol (above 265 milligrams) who had shown no signs of heart disease when the trial began. Divided into two groups, the 3,806 subjects in the study *all* followed diets designed to lower cholesterol. But 1,907 were also given the cholesterol-lowering drug cholestyramine while the other 1,899 received placebos.

The trial did more than re-establish that high cholesterol levels *raise* risk. It demonstrated, for the first time, that lowering cholesterol levels can *lower* risk. Indeed, the CPPT showed the payoff was a 2 percent reduction in the incidence of coronary heart disease for every 1 percent reduction in serum cholesterol. But it was the drug-taking subjects who derived the greatest benefits. During the time the trial lasted they reduced serum cholesterol an average of 15 percent. They also had fewer heart attacks — and fewer deaths from heart attack — than the non-drug-taking group, whose serum cholesterol reduction averaged somewhat less than 5 percent.

While these results did indeed show that risk could be reduced, they did not provide much evidence that dietary intervention unassisted by drugs was very useful in bringing serum cholesterol down to lower risk levels. (Furthermore, the minimal reduction in cholesterol achieved by trial subjects on diet alone may have resulted from their weight loss, not from the composition of their low-cholesterol and fat-restricting diet.) Nevertheless, trial results were taken to demonstrate the effectiveness of cholesterol reduction as therapy and of diet as the therapeutic agent.

The news media picked up quickly on this. It was widely reported that severely limiting dietary cholesterol (found mainly in eggs, dairy products, and organ meats) and reducing consumption of all fats, particularly saturated fats, would lower serum cholesterol levels and reduce risk of heart disease. The *Time* magazine cover for its cholesterol story showed the face of the newly convicted health thief — a plate of eggs with yolks for eyes and a bacon-strip mouth. A National Institutes of Health (NIH) panel (called a consensus conference), which was convened to discuss the CPPT findings, went on to recommend a low-fat and minimum-cholesterol diet to the nation. They prescribed it for all Americans over the age of two, even though the CPPT sample had included only middle-aged men, all of whom had had high serum levels to start with. The CPPT said nothing about the effects of a low-cholesterol diet on anyone with low-to-normal serum cholesterol levels. Nor was much other research available on the benefits of lowering cholesterol among women, children, or the elderly.

THE CHOLESTEROL PUZZLE

The promotion of low-cholesterol, fat-restricting diets by public health officials reflects the difficulty of translating complicated nutritional findings into dietary advice. There is no disputing a connection between what we eat and the level of serum cholesterol in our bloodstream. But it is far from simple and direct. Nor is there evidence that the recommended dietary changes (while they might well provide other health benefits) can by themselves reduce the risk of heart disease for most Americans to any measurable degree.

Although concern about the connection between diet and heart disease has peaked in recent years, researchers began epidemiological studies of the relation soon after World War II. Dr. Ancel Keys of the University of Minnesota, who had earlier noted the health consequences of dietary differences between southern and northern Italians, put together a study of 16 population groups in seven different countries. This celebrated project looked at the impact of various risk factors on men aged 40–59; among its findings was a significant association of saturated-fat intake, serum cholesterol levels, and heart disease rates.

Such connections between diet and heart disease turned up regularly in studies that compared different populations. What was missing was clinical evidence of a cause-and-effect relation, which was what researchers had been trying to find in animal studies since the early part of this century. That's when Russian scientists first discovered that feeding cholesterol to animals would raise serum cholesterol levels high enough to produce atherosclerosis. Since that time researchers have worked with just about every kind of animal and bird, from chimpanzees to quail. Natural herbivores, like rabbits, have proved particularly susceptible to diet-induced atherosclerosis, while carnivores (whose regular fare includes cholesterol) are predictably least susceptible. But this research has come up with almost as many questions as answers.

Raising serum cholesterol isn't a simple matter of adding dietary cholesterol. Total fat intake also counts, and the more saturated fatty acids a food contains, the more it will raise cholesterol in the bloodstream. Protein will raise serum cholesterol levels in rabbits — even defatted protein — and turkey protein is twice as cholesterolemic (capable of raising cholesterol levels) as pork protein. As for vegetable protein, wheat gluten turns out to be twice as cholesterolemic as protein from soybeans. All of which, according to Dr. Kritchevsky, proves that "everything in the diet counts."

Dietary experiments with human subjects, usually in institutional settings, have found that serum cholesterol levels can be altered by the kinds and amounts of fats the subjects are fed. But the responses of patients to these diets vary substantially. The same diet that causes the cholesterol levels of some subjects to shoot up may have no effect on the cholesterol levels of others.

What seems clear is that there are great differences in the ways our bodies deal with cholesterol. However, it is a substance we produce in some quantity — about 800–1,000 milligrams a day (which is equivalent, since only about 55 percent of dietary cholesterol is absorbed, to 1,600–2,000 milligrams taken in food) — and it makes up about 0.2 percent of our body weight.

When we have a surplus of cholesterol, our bodies can respond in several different ways: by cutting back cholesterol production in the liver, by converting excess cholesterol to bile and dumping it out through the intestines, or by circulating the excess in the bloodstream and storing it in cells. At Rockefeller University, studies of adult men have found that two thirds of them showed no unusual fluctuations in serum cholesterol when their intake of dietary cholesterol was increased from 250 to 800 milligrams per day. For one third of the subjects, however, this increased intake caused serum cholesterol levels to rise more than 10 percent. In a similar experiment, which increased the amount of saturated fats in their diets, more than one third of the subjects responded with a rise in serum cholesterol greater than 10 percent.

Heredity plainly plays a significant role in determining our cholesterol-handling capacity. Science has been aware of this since 1939, when the genetic origins of familial hypercholesterolemia were discovered. In its severe form this disease produces levels of LDL in the bloodstream six times higher than normal. It causes heart attacks that strike children as young as two years old and almost inevitably occur before victims of the disease reach age 20.

Recently, the work of Michael S. Brown and Joseph L. Goldstein (for which they won the Nobel Prize for Medicine in 1985) has shown how levels of circulating LDLs are controlled by LDL receptors, particularly in the liver, where they regulate removal of LDL from the bloodstream. The University of Texas researchers found the genetic defect responsible for familial hypercholesterolemia allows victims of the more common form of the disease to synthesize only half the normal number of receptors, and prevents victims of the more severe form from synthesizing any functional receptors at all. Brown and Goldstein believe that much atherosclerosis in the general population may result both from more subtle genetic factors, including abnormalities in hormone production, and from dietary influences that also limit production of LDL receptors.

In addition to the physiological influences on cholesterol levels,

there are psychological influences as well. Stress, for example, raises serum cholesterol. The first clues to this phenomenon came from cardiolo-
gists Ray Rosenman of the Stanford Research Institute and Meyer Friedman of Mount Zion Medical Center in San Francisco (the team that first
used the term *Type A* to describe hard-driving, aggressive personalities
prone to heart attacks). While studying a group of tax accountants, they
noted that cholesterol levels, which had averaged 212 milligrams throughout the year, rose to about 230 as the April 15 tax deadline drew near.

In animal studies stress-induced increases in cholesterol levels
have been demonstrated in monkeys by relocating alpha males (the alpha
is the boss of the cage, and generally has lower cholesterol levels than his
cagemates). Several alpha males placed together react to the loss of status
and unstable social situation with stress and become more susceptible to
cholesterol-raising diets.

Like blood pressure, blood cholesterol levels can rise quickly under
stress. What pushes them up is the body's sympathetic nervous system.
Responding to stress, it signals for the production of more adrenaline and
cortisol. Both these hormones mobilize energy reserves to deal with
whatever crisis has set off the alarm by releasing stored glucose and fat
into the bloodstream. They also release cholesterol, and cortisol may
even trigger increased cholesterol production by the liver.

RESPONDING TO HIGH SERUM CHOLESTEROL

Because cholesterol levels are such a significant indicator of risk, it
makes sense to have them checked periodically. This is particularly
important if there is a history of coronary heart disease in your family. If
close relatives (grandparents, parents, or siblings) suffered heart attacks
early in life, it is unlikely that you are among that portion of the population enjoying a measure of genetic protection from heart disease (and for
whom high cholesterol levels represent substantially less risk). If the
genetic odds are against you, then annual cholesterol testing should probably be started during adolescence.

Bear in mind that your cholesterol level varies over time. It changes
during the course of the day and during the course of the year. For reasons
no one understands, cholesterol levels tend to peak during January and
February (except for tax accountants, whose annual high point comes
somewhat later). In a five-year Pentagon study the 177 officers who took
part had cholesterol levels that fluctuated as much as 100 percent, although some officers had levels that remained absolutely unchanged.
Unless you realize that cholesterol levels fluctuate and one high reading
may not necessarily mean all that much, you are likely to bring to your
next test enough anxiety to produce a stress-inflated second reading.

There is, according to the NIH consensus conference, moderate risk
of heart disease at relatively common cholesterol levels. Remember, this

is the group that recommended a cholesterol-reducing diet for every American over the age of two, so their assessment of risk is a most conservative one. During your twenties, the conference concluded, anything over 200 milligrams indicates moderate risk, as does anything over 220 during your thirties. At 40 plus, they found moderate risk starting at 240 milligrams and high risk at 260 milligrams. High risk for younger people, they maintained, begins with levels as low as 185 milligrams during childhood and adolescence, 220 milligrams between ages 20 and 29, and 240 milligrams between ages 30 and 39.

If your serum cholesterol approaches risk level, there are several ways you can go about lowering it. Not every strategy may pay off for you. Genetics plays a major role. But high cholesterol levels, particularly if they are accompanied by low HDL levels, may well indicate that something is amiss in the way you are eating or living. If you smoke, now is a good time to quit (while this won't have much effect on total cholesterol levels, it may well give your HDLs a boost). Unless you are well within the normal weight range for your age and height, you should also make the loss of surplus poundage a major dietary goal. Obesity raises serum cholesterol in some people, and studies have continually demonstrated the cholesterol-lowering effect of weight loss.

When it comes to diet, you should at least stay within the guidelines that the American Heart Association (AHA) recommends for the general population. The AHA recommendations issued in the summer of 1986 set limits for cholesterol, saturated fats, total fats, protein, sodium, and alcohol. They restrict daily consumption of dietary cholesterol to 100 milligrams for every 1,000 calories, with a top limit of 300 milligrams (slightly more cholesterol than there is in a single egg or four quarter-pound hamburgers). The Association recommends taking less than 10 percent of your calories in saturated fats, and AHA officials point out that this is the key cholesterol-lowering aspect of reducing overall fat consumption. Americans now are getting about 7 percent of their calories from polyunsaturated fats and roughly 16 percent from monounsaturates (see "Fats and Oils," below), but at present we consume 14 percent of our calories in saturates. Only the saturates, says the AHA, have any direct negative impact on cholesterol levels, and the overall fat-limiting recommendation is intended to reduce total calories and thereby help control weight.

Protein, says the AHA, should make up 15 percent of all calories, and carbohydrates should make up 55 percent. As for weight, AHA officials believe Americans should meet the standards of the 1959 Metropolitan Life Insurance Company tables, and not the heavier 1983 standards (see chapter 10). The recommendation for alcohol — no more than two drinks a day — recognizes the possible benefits of moderate consumption while setting a limit that will not raise the risk of hypertension. The limit on sodium to no more than 1,000 milligrams (about half a teaspoon of salt) per 1,000 calories — with a 3,000-milligram ceiling — is also aimed at hypertension rather than atherosclerosis.

To meet its recommendations, the AHA suggests avoiding any milk product with more than 1 percent fat (which can make it difficult to get sufficient calcium). Cream, of course, is out, along with evaporated milk, butter, certain cheeses, and nondairy cream substitutes. Vegetable oils (but not palm or coconut oil) are okay, and so are mayonnaise and nuts (other than coconuts). Solid shortenings and chocolate are out. Meats to be avoided include corned beef, pastrami, spareribs, and duck, while just about all fruits and vegetables are fine (with such obvious exceptions as avocados).

FATS AND OILS

The American Heart Association recommendations (which are designed not to *lower* cholesterol levels but to keep them from rising) are based on the notion that the most potent nutritional influences on serum cholesterol are the amounts of dietary cholesterol and saturated fats we consume. As far as anyone knows, this seems to be the case. But other aspects of nutrition also affect cholesterol levels, and the role of fats is far too complex to be dismissed as simply "saturated bad, unsaturated not so bad."

Let's take a closer look at the fats we find in food. There is cholesterol, which is chemically quite different from other fats, and found only in foods of animal origin (meat, fish, milk, eggs). Then there are the saturated and unsaturated fatty acids in triglycerides (described in detail in "The Different Kinds of Fat," page 39). It is important to realize that all fatty acids are made up of linked carbon atoms, which form a chain. A pair of hydrogen atoms is usually attached to each segment of the chain, one on each side. In saturated fats, *all* the carbon atoms are flanked by hydrogens. In unsaturated fats, some of the hydrogen atoms are missing. Monounsaturates lack one pair, while polyunsaturates lack several pairs.

The differences in their chemical composition make for other differences among fatty acids. A saturated fatty acid forms a straight line, unlike an unsaturated fatty acid, which can bend (since the missing hydrogen atoms create what amounts to a hinge). Saturated acids can therefore be packed together more tightly in cells. They also have higher melting points, which is why hydrogenation (the addition of missing hydrogen) makes unsaturated vegetable oils in margarine and shortening solid even at room temperature.

Animal foods generally have, in addition to cholesterol, more saturated fatty acids than other foods. But they have unsaturated fatty acids as well. What's more, there are plenty of saturated fatty acids in nonanimal foods like beans, nuts, grains, and vegetable oils (see "Fatty Acids and Cholesterol in Sample Foods," pages 216–217). Coconut oil, for example, is the *most* saturated fat available, and palm oil comes a close second.

Recent evidence indicates that unsaturated fats play a more active role in lowering serum cholesterol than nutritionists had previously realized. In addition, the kind of unsaturated fats you eat can influence the kind of cholesterol you reduce. Research by Dr. Scott M. Grundy at the University of Texas Health Science Center at Dallas, and Dr. Fred H. Mattson of the University of California, San Diego, has shown that replacing saturated fats with either monounsaturated or polyunsaturated fats will lower total cholesterol levels to the same degree. But while the polyunsaturates will indiscriminately reduce both HDLs and LDLs, the monounsaturates will focus on the LDLs, leaving the HDLs intact. In other words, monounsaturates tend to knock out the "bad cholesterol" and spare the "good cholesterol."

Olive oil, which is high in monounsaturates (as is peanut oil), may make a better substitute for bacon fat or lard than corn or safflower oil, which have far more polyunsaturated fat than monounsaturated. The low incidence of heart disease in southern Italy and throughout most of Greece could well reflect the LDL-reducing capacity of olive oil, which is a dietary mainstay in these areas.

The extraordinarily low incidence of heart disease among another population group, one dependent upon protein and fats for most of its nutritional needs, provided the clue to a family of polyunsaturates with exceptional cholesterol-reducing powers. Although the Eskimos of Greenland can put away a pound of seal or whale meat in a day, plus supplementary blubber, some fish, and precious few vegetables, they have a death rate from heart disease of just 3.5 percent and an average life span of more than 60 years. Danish researchers have found that the Eskimos' blood contained not only low levels of cholesterol but low levels of *all fats*. The secret ingredient in the Eskimo diet turns out to be fish oil.

Several studies have produced additional evidence of the risk-reducing capacity of a diet rich in fish and the ability of fish oils to lower high cholesterol and triglyceride levels. These include one from the Netherlands, where researchers followed the fish-eating patterns of middle-aged men for 20 years (starting well before Danish scientists had discovered what fish oil seemed to be doing for the Greenland Eskimos).

Since the fat in fish must be fluid (otherwise it will freeze in cold water), fish oil is polyunsaturated. But it also contains a group of fatty acids, designated omega-3, chief among which are eicosapentaenoic acid (EPA) and docosahexaeonic acid (DHA), with characteristics quite different from the omega-6 fatty acids (like linoleic acid) in seed and vegetable oils. Not only are they two to five times more effective in reducing serum cholesterol but they also help protect arteries from plaque in other ways. The omega-3 fatty acids, and EPA in particular, produce substances that make blood platelets less sticky, less likely to clump together and form clots. There is a drawback to this aspect of EPA, for Greenland Eskimos tend to bruise easily and their cuts and scrapes will bleed longer than usual.

Omega-3 fatty acids are most abundant in cold, deep-water, ocean fish like salmon, mackerel, tuna, sable fish, and sardines, and such fresh-water fish as rainbow trout. Just two servings of these fish each week will generally provide enough omega-3 fatty acid for an anticoagulant effect, but a truly enormous intake of fish oil is required to lower serum cholesterol levels. Few people, other than Eskimos, are able to pack this much fish oil into their diets, and nutritionists are wary of the fish-oil supplements that have become a fast-moving item in health food stores. It takes a great many pills—15–20 a day (at considerable cost in cash and calo-

Fatty Acids and Cholesterol in Sample Foods

Food	Total Grams of Fat	Fatty Acids (grams)			Calories
		Saturated	Mono-unsaturated	Poly-unsaturated	
olive oil (4 tbsp)	56	7.6	41.2	4.8	500
vegetable shortening (4 tbsp)	52	13.2	23.2	13.6	460
avocado (1 medium)	30	4.5	19.4	3.5	305
filberts (1 oz)	18	1.3	13.9	1.7	180
beef sirloin (3 oz)	15	6.4	6.9	0.6	240
croissant	12	3.5	6.7	1.4	235
Cheddar cheese (1 oz)	9	6.0	2.7	0.3	115
milk, whole (1 cup)	8	5.1	2.4	0.3	150
flounder (3.5 oz)	8	3.2	1.5	0.5	202
milk, 2% fat (1 cup)	5	2.9	1.4	0.2	140

Source: Susan E. Gebhardt and Ruth H. Matthews, *Nutritive Value of Foods* (United States Department of Agriculture, 1981).

ries)—to get the cholesterol-lowering effects the studies have shown.

In addition, the long-term effects of omega-3 fatty acids are not known, and their anticlotting action is potentially as much a danger as a benefit at these levels. So the best nutritional bet would be just to replace some of the fat you are currently consuming in beef, pork, or even vegetable oils with some extra servings of fish each week.

As a final word about fats, it's important to realize that science still does not know everything that is to be known about how diet affects serum cholesterol. When the three major ongoing studies of heart disease (the Framingham Study and two similar large-scale studies in Hawaii and Puerto Rico) looked at subjects who had suffered heart attacks as compared with those who had not, they found three significant differences,

Food	Total Grams of Fat	Cholesterol (milligrams)	Calories
quiche lorraine, 8-inch (⅛ quiche)	48	285	600
egg, large	6	274	80
Custard pie (⅙ pie)	17	169	330
loin lamb chop (2.8 oz)	16	78	235
chicken breast, half, without skin (3 oz)	3	73	142
baked salmon (3 oz)	5	60	140
cheese pizza (1 slice)	9	56	290
butter, salted (1 tbsp)	11	31	100
cottage cheese, small curd (1 cup)	9	31	215
half-and-half (1 tbsp)	2	6	20

none of which was related to cholesterol consumption or fat consumption. The heart attack victims all ate fewer carbohydrates and fewer complex carbohydrates and drank less alcohol (although drinking above moderate levels would tend to raise risk rather than lower it). As Dr. Kritchevsky notes, fat is only part of the picture. "There's something else going on," he maintains.

OTHER DIETARY STRATEGIES

Serum cholesterol levels respond to dietary changes other than reduced consumption of cholesterol and saturated fats. Adding fiber to your diet can help bring serum cholesterol down, and Dr. James Anderson, professor of medicine and nutrition at the University of Kentucky, has found that the addition of half a cup of dry oat bran to the typical (high-fat) American diet can lower cholesterol levels substantially in a relatively short period of time. In addition, the bran appears to draw LDLs out of the bloodstream while sparing HDLs. Other sources of soluble fiber, like pinto and navy beans, do almost as good a job. Oatmeal, when combined with a low-fat diet, seems as effective as bran, and barley has also shown cholesterol-lowering potential (although only in animal studies).

There is evidence that garlic—in more than normal dietary quantities (even for garlic lovers)—can reduce serum cholesterol, and researchers have found in it the precursor of a substance that, like EPA, inhibits blood clotting. Onions, too, may help. According to Dr. Victor Gurewich, professor of medicine at Tufts University and chairman of the vascular laboratory at St. Elizabeth's Hospital in Boston, the juice of a single white or yellow onion taken daily can raise levels of HDL in the blood of otherwise healthy patients by 30 percent. Copper deficiency may raise serum cholesterol levels (as it has in animal studies), and there are indications that therapeutic doses of niacin may work as effectively as prescription cholesterol-lowering drugs.

The benefits of alcohol have been well documented (see chapter 16). Researchers at the Kaiser Permanente Hospital in Oakland were first to reveal that people who average two drinks per day stand a 40 percent better chance of avoiding hospitalization for heart attacks than nondrinkers. Subsequent studies at Stanford University found subjects who downed two to three drinks per day had particularly high levels of HDL, which fell when they stopped drinking. The drinker's advantage, however, starts to diminish when consumption rises above three drinks per day. At three to five drinks per day, cardiovascular mortality is 50 percent higher for drinkers than for nondrinkers.

THE ROLE OF EXERCISE

The clearest possible proof that exercise can dramatically reduce not only cardiovascular mortality but overall mortality as well appeared in the spring of 1986, when the results of a long-term study of nearly 17,000 male Harvard graduates was published. Dr. Ralph S. Paffenbarger and his associates at both the Stanford University School of Medicine and Harvard's School of Public Health were able to show that moderate exercise is the key to longevity. Burning up at least 2,000 calories per week lowered mortality rates for men in the study by one quarter to one third. The researchers counted not only planned exercise like jogging, which uses about 500 calories per hour, but also "background exercise" like walking to work (100 calories per mile) or climbing stairs (4 calories per flight). Heart attacks among those who burned more than 2,000 calories were reduced by more than one third.

To produce data for the study, Dr. Paffenbarger and his team recruited subjects during the mid-1960s from among alumni then aged 35–74 and tracked their health and lifestyles until 1978. At that time, 1,413 had died, 45 percent from heart disease. Analyzing their findings, the team found that a sedentary lifestyle (spending fewer than 2,000 calories on exercise) was less of a risk than high blood pressure. But it was more dangerous than obesity, smoking, or a family history of heart disease. Moreover, exercise could cut the high risk of high blood pressure in half and reduce the risk of smoking by one third. It was even able to reduce the risk of genetic predisposition.

Results of the Harvard study paralleled Dr. Paffenbarger's earlier findings from a substantially different sample of male subjects: San Francisco longshoremen. Using data collected by California's Bureau of Chronic Diseases on smoking, obesity, and the incidence of diabetes among these dock workers, he added an analysis of their work assignments to estimate the energy they'd spent on the job. It turned out to be more than 8,500 calories per week (about the same energy it takes to run three marathons). What their high-calorie expenditures had bought for these longshoremen was approximately half as many heart attacks as less active men.

To lower risk of heart disease, muscle-building activities like weight lifting and straining at the Nautilus are far less effective than aerobic exercises like running, swimming, cycling, tennis, or basketball. It's sustained exercise, including walking, that builds up the body's capacity to take in and use oxygen. As coronary heart disease destroys heart muscle tissue by cutting off oxygen, supplying additional oxygen to this tissue will improve heart muscle function. Over time, aerobic exercise improves muscle tone and increases muscle mass, so the heart becomes stronger and better able to withstand stress. As a bonus, aerobic exercise at the 2,000-calorie-per-week level will also raise HDL levels and lower LDL levels. (Moderate aerobic exercise, in fact, has the same effect on HDL and LDL levels as moderate use of alcohol.)

The San Francisco longshoremen Dr. Paffenbarger studied in 1969 were burning up far more calories than many of the Harvard alumni were likely to burn. But the later study showed few additional health benefits accrued when more than 3,500 calories per week were spent on exercise. At this point, the risk of death was reduced a full 50 percent. Beyond it, mortality rates did not decrease further, possibly (as the authors suggest) because of the risks of injury involved in vigorous activities.

Dr. Paffenbarger's research is far from the first to produce evidence of how exercise can lower the risk of heart disease. He points to the work of Bernardino Ramazzini, who discovered in 1700 that tailors didn't live as long as men who did more active work.

Among more recent evidence was a fascinating finding by NHLBI researchers who followed more than 16,000 subjects of the three large-scale heart studies (the Framingham Heart Study, the Honolulu Heart Study, and the Puerto Rico Heart Health Program) for up to six years. Within this group of subjects, none of whom had shown evidence of heart disease at the start of this period, men with higher caloric intake (or greater intake per kilogram of body weight) were *less* likely to develop coronary heart disease than men whose caloric intake was lower. Men of higher weight, however, were *more* likely to develop heart disease than men of lower weight. Calories, it appeared, didn't count, but body weight did. To explain this seeming anomaly, the authors suggested that lean men with a high caloric intake might experience "the benefit of greater physical activity."

THE BOTTOM LINE: ESSENTIALS OF PREVENTION

Although the level of cholesterol in the blood constitutes a major risk factor for coronary artery disease, it is not the only one, nor is it the only one that can be modified by changes in diet and behavior. Smoking, obesity, and inactivity are all independent risk factors—and all modifiable—as is high blood pressure (see chapter 18). Smoking significantly raises risk of heart attack. So does body weight 20 percent above ideal. But exercise and other activities that burn at least 2,000 calories per week can reduce risk by one third.

When it comes to cholesterol, danger of atherosclerosis rises with overall blood levels and a high ratio of LDL to HDL cholesterol. Excess weight and a sedentary lifestyle tend to boost cholesterol levels, and overall fat intake influences both weight and cholesterol levels. Annual testing to determine levels of serum cholesterol (and HDL/LDL ratios) is a prudent practice, particularly if there is any genetic vulnerability to heart disease. Even moderately high levels can increase danger and should be lowered by weight loss, exercise, and reduced fat intake.

Although consumption of saturated fatty acids (found most often in meat and dairy products) appears to have the greatest influence on serum cholesterol levels, wholesale replacements of saturates with polyunsaturates (in seed and vegetable oils) can raise the risk of cancer (see chapter 19). So a balance of saturates and unsaturates, including the monoun-saturates (like the fatty acids in olive oil), seems a safer bet.

Fish and fish oils (omega-3 fatty acids), although extremely unsatu-rated, nevertheless provide specific risk-reducing benefits. They may help lower serum cholesterol levels and can diminish the clotting capac-ity of blood platelets (making them less likely to form the plaque that causes atherosclerosis).

CHAPTER 18

Controlling Hypertension

HYPERTENSION, WHICH IS what doctors call high blood pressure, threatens life and health in several ways. It raises the risk of heart attack, and it can bring on congestive heart failure by making heart muscle work so hard that the muscle essentially wears out and can no longer pump blood efficiently. It causes stroke by depriving brain regions of blood. This occurs when hypertension subjects the brain's fragile blood vessels to such high pressure that they rupture or when it causes clotting, which blocks the blood flow. Chronic high blood pressure can also damage the kidneys (which filter the blood) and ultimately cause them to fail.

For all these reasons — plus the fact that it gives no early warning symptoms — high blood pressure has been called the "silent killer." Over the past several decades, doctors and their national organizations have consistently urged Americans to monitor their blood pressure and, if it is high, to seek medical help in lowering it.

Although everyone agrees that hypertension is dangerous, there has been less agreement on precisely what should be done about it. In recent years doctors have debated every aspect of high blood pressure treatment, and a range of dietary treatments — weight loss, salt restriction, calcium and potassium supplementation — have each had their champions. In short, no one fully understands what causes high blood pressure or which nutritional therapies can best lower it.

There's no difficulty, however, in determining blood pressure levels. They are as easily quantified as body temperature and measured in millimeters of mercury. The millimeter standard was established in the days when a cuff strapped around the arm would transmit the pressure of pumping blood to a column of mercury, and a doctor or nurse would read the height of the column in millimeters. Today, a simple pressure gauge on the cuff supplies the reading.

A reading such as 140/90 reflects two kinds of pressure. The first and higher number, called *systolic* pressure, is the pressure exerted by the heart when it contracts to pump blood. The second number, the *diastolic*, reflects the pressure in the arteries when the heart rests between beats.

It is a simple matter, therefore, to detect the presence of hypertension but far more difficult to discover its origins. Like fever, high blood pressure is not a disease so much as a sign of some imbalance within the body, an imbalance that may be caused by many different factors.

Whether it is normal or elevated, blood pressure, the force of fluid against the artery walls, is determined by several variables. One is heart rate. In general, the more rapidly the heart pumps, the higher the pressure will be. Second is the total volume of blood, which increases when the body retains fluid. Pressure goes up when there is more blood to pump. Finally, blood pressure reflects the size of the arteries; the narrower the arteries, the higher the pressure.

Day-to-day changes in any of these factors can bring about transient (and harmless) increases in blood pressure. During physical activity, the heart pumps more rapidly and blood pressure rises. It also rises when one experiences stress and the body releases hormones that tighten artery walls. This response is part of the "fight or flight" reaction and may well have evolved as a means of limiting blood loss during physical combat.

Normally, however, the body strives to maintain blood pressure within a moderate range. A great number of physiological systems are involved in that task. The kidneys influence blood pressure primarily by controlling the fluid balance of the body. Prostaglandins, hormonelike substances derived from fatty acids, seem to lower blood pressure by dilating the arteries. The central nervous system can directly signal the artery walls to dilate or contract. And a recently discovered hormone produced by the heart, called atrial natriuretic factor (ANF), helps govern blood pressure by regulating blood volume.

Unfortunately, none of these systems is infallible, and if any of them goes seriously awry, chronic hypertension can result. Should that occur, certain dietary changes may help bring blood pressure back to normal. When damaged kidneys retain too much fluid in the body, for example, a low-salt diet may be able to restore a normal fluid balance.

But dietary strategies seem more effective for *treating* hypertension than preventing it. Although a low-salt diet may help some hypertensives lower blood pressure, it provides only marginal benefits at best for people with normal blood pressure. Nor are large amounts of salt likely to raise normal blood pressure. Because a damaged kidney is unable to handle salt very well, it doesn't follow that lots of salt will damage kidneys or lead to hypertension.

Since hypertension can have so many different causes, people with equally high blood pressure may be helped by very different diets. Some will be helped by weight loss, some by salt restriction, others by calcium supplements. While no one is sure what accounts for these individual differences, they presumably reflect differences in the underlying problems that keep blood pressure high in the first place.

There is now no good evidence that Americans with normal blood pressure should change their diets out of fear of developing hypertension. What everyone *should* do is to check blood pressure regularly — at the doctor's office, at home, or both — and watch for signs of trouble. People with a family history of hypertension should be especially watchful, as should men (who are more prone to hypertension than women), particularly black men (who have a greater risk of hypertension than white men of the same age and weight).

When is blood pressure too high? Until the start of the 1980s, the generally accepted cutoff point for high blood pressure was 140/90. The estimated 25 million Americans with diastolic pressure between 90 and 94 were not then considered to have true hypertension but a borderline condition that might or might not need treatment.

Subsequently, however, the National Institutes of Health redefined hypertension and physicians have become much more aggressive in diagnosing and treating the condition. Now anyone with a diastolic pressure over 90 is considered at definite risk, and anyone with pressure between 85 and 89 is thought to need careful monitoring. By these standards, an estimated 60 million Americans are now hypertensive, with a diastolic pressure of 90 or more.

For roughly half of these hypertensives, however, doctors are more likely to prescribe dietary changes than drugs. At the same time physicians were becoming more aware of the risks of mild hypertension, they were also coming to realize that drugs used to treat the condition pose risks of their own. Possible side effects include gout, fatigue, and impotence, which explains why roughly half the people for whom these drugs are prescribed don't always use them. The medications can also increase the levels of fat in the blood. Even more disturbing, results of a government study released in 1982 reported that certain antihypertensive drugs — thiazide diuretics, which block the reabsorption of sodium — might actually increase the risk of a fatal heart attack for patients with abnormal heart rhythms (since these drugs also block reabsorption of other electrolytes).

As a result, doctors now attempt to reduce high blood pressure with minimal use of drugs. Even for patients with relatively severe hypertension, lifestyle changes can make it possible to lower dosages, use fewer drugs, or eliminate drugs altogether once blood pressure has stabilized.

Unfortunately, there is still no simple test to determine which dietary treatment is best for any individual hypertensive patient. Simple trial-and-error is how many physicians now seek the right approach—trying a diet for several weeks or months and seeing whether or not blood pressure goes down.

WEIGHT REDUCTION

On one dietary principle there is virtually universal agreement. Weight loss can reliably lower blood pressure for patients who are overweight, as up to 60 percent of all hypertensives are. Obesity seems to raise blood pressure both by increasing blood volume and requiring the heart to pump harder. But researchers have recently found evidence that hypertension associated with obesity may be different—and somewhat less dangerous—than hypertension related to other causes. Overweight men with high blood pressure have a somewhat lower rate of heart disease or stroke than thin men with equally high blood pressure.

Overweight hypertensives have another advantage too, for there is ample evidence that losing weight can reduce blood pressure more reliably than any other lifestyle change. And the overweight needn't drop all the way down to the optimum "desirable" weight to realize significant benefits. Even losing 7 pounds can reduce systolic pressure by about 7 millimeters and diastolic pressure by 4 millimeters—a clinically significant change. Losing 25–30 pounds can have a much more substantial effect, lowering systolic pressure by more than 20 millimeters and diastolic by 10–15 millimeters.

A recent Australian study showed that weight loss of about 15 pounds may be at least as effective as the common antihypertensive drug metoprolol in lowering blood pressure. And while the drug has an adverse effect on blood fats—it lowers the ratio of HDL to total cholesterol—weight loss actually improved this ratio.

Why does blood pressure fall as weight goes down? Part of the explanation may lie in the metabolic changes that come with dieting (described in chapter 10). As part of the general metabolic slowdown caused by caloric restriction, the body produces less noradrenaline, a hormone related to the stress hormone adrenaline that is involved in a number of metabolic functions and affects heart rate. A drop in noradrenaline means the heart will pump more slowly and blood pressure will usually drop.

At one time it was believed that weight-loss diets lowered blood pressure because dieters consumed less salt. But the best evidence now suggests that weight loss and salt restriction have independent effects on blood pressure. A study at the University of Mississippi showed that many overweight hypertensives could cut their need for medication by losing weight, even if they didn't reduce their salt intake. Conversely, many normal-weight hypertensives in this study were able to stabilize blood pressure by cutting down on salt, but without losing weight.

SALT RESTRICTION

The FDA, the AMA, and other organizations have proclaimed that Americans eat too much salt and have suggested that this excess is a major contributor to hypertension. But although we indisputably eat more salt than we need — the human body only requires about one tenth of the average American intake — there's little evidence that the excess is really bad for most of us.

Several recent surveys have shown that wide variations in salt intake have little effect on blood pressure in the general population. In one study of Connecticut adults, those with salt intake in the top 10 percent had virtually the same blood pressure on average as those in the bottom 10 percent. Similar studies in Arizona, Massachusetts, and Michigan have failed to find a general link between salt intake and blood pressure. (When populations in different countries are compared, however, those with a high sodium intake, like Japan's, have been shown to suffer far more hypertension than those whose diets contain less salt. But there are so many other cultural, genetic, and dietary differences between such populations that factors other than sodium could well explain the different incidence of hypertension.)

The only people with a pressing reason to be concerned about salt intake are those who already have high blood pressure. For them there are two relevant questions: Is my hypertension the kind that will respond to salt restriction at all? and How severely must I cut back on salt to lower blood pressure significantly?

Physicians aren't worried about salt itself but about the sodium it contains. Every molecule of common table salt is made up of one atom of sodium and one of chloride. In theory, your blood pressure becomes chronically high when your kidneys malfunction and don't excrete enough sodium. When the concentration of sodium in the blood is too high, osmotic pressure pulls fluid out of tissues to dilute the blood. As a result, blood volume goes up, and so does blood pressure.

The low-sodium diet, a possible remedy for this physiological problem, first attracted attention in the 1940s. That's when Walter Kempner, a Durham, North Carolina, physician, devised a salt-free diet for patients with severe hypertension. Initially, Kempner's renowned rice diet consisted only of rice, fruit, and fruit juice. Sugar and vitamin tablets were added later.

Although Kempner's plan worked for many patients, it didn't prove the general benefit of cutting down on salt. For one thing, patients on the plan also lost weight — so much that the rice diet became more famous for weight loss than for hypertension control. Nevertheless, the Kempner diet did reduce sodium intake to remarkably low levels, a total of about 150 milligrams per day.

There are about 2,000 milligrams of sodium in a single teaspoonful of salt, and the average American takes in around 5,000 milligrams per day. Many physicians now advise hypertensive patients to cut back only to 2,000 milligrams per day, more than 10 times the amount in Kempner's diet.

Although the rice diet's rock-bottom level of sodium can reduce hypertension in some patients, it's virtually impossible to maintain a sodium intake this low except in a special treatment setting. And there is no clear evidence that more moderate salt restriction is capable of lowering blood pressure.

A number of recent studies have attempted to show that more modest restriction works. In 13 different studies published between 1973 and 1985, only three found that patients who went from an average sodium intake of 3,600 milligrams per day down to about 1,800 milligrams experienced any significant reduction in blood pressure, and there was no correlation between the drop in blood pressure and the level of sodium restriction.

This kind of research is complicated, however, by the fact that many hypertensives simply will not respond to a low-salt diet, no matter how severe. Several groups of medical researchers — at the University of Alabama, the Veterans Administration Hospital in San Antonio, Texas, and elsewhere — have experimented with very-low-sodium diets for hypertensive patients in a hospital setting. They have found that 250 milligrams of sodium per day can indeed bring blood pressure to normal within a few days (before weight has been lost). But even this extreme sodium restriction works for only about one half of the hypertensive patients tested; the rest are unaffected.

Many hypertension experts are now trying to find ways of predicting in advance who will respond to a low-sodium diet and who will not. In theory, those hypertensives most sensitive to sodium should be those whose high blood pressure is caused by a kidney malfunction. And some investigators now believe salt sensitivity is correlated with high blood levels of renin, an enzyme produced by the kidneys.

Normally, the kidneys put out renin only when blood pressure is too low. Once it's released, the enzyme produces a hormone that constricts the walls of the arteries, steps up the heart rate, and triggers the production of yet another hormone, aldosterone, that makes the kidneys retain more salt, thus increasing blood volume. As soon as all these changes have brought blood pressure back to normal, the kidney responds by shutting down renin production. But if kidneys malfunction, they may keep secreting renin even when it's not needed. Result: chronic hypertension.

Some hypertensives do have higher renin levels than others, and hypertension specialist John Laragh of New York Hospital–Cornell Medical Center has recommended testing blood levels of renin to predict sensitivity to salt. But other researchers point out that blood tests for renin are expensive, inconvenient, and inaccurate if they're done outside a hospital. So at this point the best approach for someone with hypertension may be simply to try a low-sodium diet under a doctor's supervision and see how blood pressure is affected after a few weeks or months.

Even if moderate cutbacks in sodium don't lower blood pressure, they may make it easier to manage the drug therapy prescribed for hypertension. People on low-salt diets, like those who lose weight, are likely to need lower doses of antihypertension medication.

For hypertensives who want to reduce blood pressure entirely without drugs — and whose physicians approve — reducing sodium intake to 1,000 milligrams per day may be more effective than the more liberal restriction generally prescribed. But a true low-salt diet requires more than a light touch with the saltshaker. Only about one third or less of the salt we eat is added in cooking or at the table. Another third occurs naturally in food, and the rest is added by food industry processors.

Canned, preserved, and other prepared foods are major sources of sodium, and it's easy to discover how much they contain. The FDA now requires that the sodium content of all fortified foods and all products making nutritional claims be listed on the container. In addition, the federal agency has defined the various terms that can be used on food labels: *low-sodium* (140 milligrams of sodium or less per serving); *very-low-sodium* (35 milligrams or less); *sodium-free* (less than 5 milligrams); and *reduced-sodium* (if the usual sodium level for that food has been cut by at least 75 percent).

Cookbooks now offer tips for cooking without salt and include palatable low-sodium recipes. Lemon juice is a good salt substitute. In a taste test at the University of California, Berkeley, volunteers said that lemon-spiked, low-salt tomato juice tasted just as salty as regular juice. No-sodium spices — ginger, peppers, fresh herbs, curry, and mustard powder — can also help. So can garlic, onions, vinegar, and Worcestershire sauce (which has some sodium but not much).

Research offers convincing evidence that people do indeed adjust their tastes to a low-sodium diet. They don't continue to miss salt, although it may take two months or so to make the adjustment. At bottom, however, salt restriction is a difficult dietary strategy and useful only for certain hypertensives.

CALCIUM AND OTHER NUTRIENTS

Disillusionment with low-sodium diets — and intriguing data from new studies — have led to some new approaches in the dietary treatment of hypertension. Researchers are now studying whether adding certain nutrients to the diet rather than reducing calories or sodium can help lower blood pressure. Calcium supplementation is the route most actively being investigated.

The focus on calcium really began in 1984, when a research team at the Oregon Health Sciences University published an analysis of a government survey on the dietary intake of Americans. They looked at data on more than 10,000 people to see how the intake of 17 different nutrients related to blood pressure and found no evidence that excess sodium was linked to hypertension. If anything, people with high blood pressure seemed to have a somewhat lower salt intake than the average. But the researchers did find that "lower calcium intake was the most consistent factor in hypertensive individuals." On average, people with high blood pressure took in less calcium than the RDA.

Although this study was criticized on statistical grounds, several other population surveys have shown a similar pattern. A National Institutes of Health study, for example, has demonstrated that milk consumption is linked to the risk of high blood pressure among Puerto Rican men. Those who drink no milk have twice as much hypertension as those who drink more than a quart a day.

If a calcium deficiency can raise blood pressure, calcium supplementation might lower it. The Oregon group, led by David McCarron, gave 1 gram of calcium per day to people with mild hypertension. After eight weeks, their systolic blood pressure fell about 4 millimeters and diastolic fell about 2 millimeters. Similar results have now been reported by other researchers.

Although the average change was small, clinically significant changes were achieved in some individuals. As with dietary sodium, there seem to be marked individual differences in the way blood pressure responds to dietary calcium. Some hypertensives may not respond to calcium supplementation at all, while others can improve dramatically. In the Oregon study, for example, 22 of the 48 subjects (44 percent) had systolic blood pressure drops of 10 millimeters or more.

There is unfortunately no way to know who will be most sensitive to calcium in the diet, largely because no one really knows why calcium intake should affect blood pressure in the first place. Among the mechanisms that have been suggested is a blood-pressure-raising signal by the parathyroid hormone. This hormone, which is released when blood calcium levels are low, moves more of the mineral into the blood (as described in chapter 21) and may boost blood pressure as well. Calcium may also be linked to the activity of renin, the kidney enzyme that helps regulate blood pressure and sodium retention. Or blood levels of calcium may directly affect the artery walls and cause them to dilate or constrict.

In addition to calcium, the Oregon study also found potassium prominent among nutrients that hypertensives are likely to lack. Several researchers have since demonstrated that potassium supplementation can also bring about moderate blood pressure reductions in some hypertensives.

The possible role of other nutrients in blood pressure is also being explored. There's growing evidence that a diet rich in polyunsaturated fatty acids may lower the risk of hypertension as well as of atherosclerosis. Animal experiments also show that a magnesium deficiency can raise blood pressure, but the explanation for this effect, and its relevance to human beings, is far from clear.

OTHER LIFESTYLE CHANGES

Although research on hypertension has focused largely on weight control and diet, other lifestyle factors are being studied as well. They offer several approaches to control of blood pressure without drugs or with minimal dependence on medications.

Exercise, not surprisingly, can play a positive role, partly because it helps reduce weight. A 10-year study of several hundred Chicago men who exercised three times a week showed that both weight and blood pressure dropped with activity.

Other research suggests that aerobic exercise can lower blood pressure independently of its effect on weight, perhaps by lowering blood levels of stress hormones related to adrenaline. In one recent Australian study of 13 subjects with mild hypertension, 45 minutes of aerobic exercise a day lowered systolic pressure by 16 millimeters on average and diastolic by 11 millimeters, even though the patients' weight remained the same. The authors pointed out that these changes are greater than those generally seen with dietary treatments for hypertension; only weight loss gives comparable results. Exercising three times a week, the Australians showed, lowered systolic pressure by 11 millimeters and diastolic by 9 millimeters.

Exercise programs for hypertensives clearly require a doctor's input to minimize risk of stroke. Strength-training routines — isometrics, wrestling, weight lifting — and even intensive aerobic exercise like use of a rowing machine can give blood pressure a short but intense boost and are high-risk, low-gain activities for hypertensives.

Psychological stress clearly contributes to hypertension. There's some evidence that it may affect kidney function, causing salt and fluid retention in susceptible people. Various psychological approaches, from biofeedback to meditation, may be helpful. But because these treatments are difficult to standardize, it's hard to say exactly how effective they are, and for whom.

The toxic pleasures can also affect blood pressure. Caffeine may make you jittery if you're not used to it, but people who drink coffee regularly develop a tolerance to it and their blood pressure doesn't seem to suffer. Hypertension is linked to heavy drinking (more than three drinks per day) but not to moderate imbibing.

While researchers speculate that smoking may lead to hypertension, the case is unproved. Nevertheless, cigarette smoking *does* raise risk of both stroke and heart attack, regardless of its effect on blood pressure.

THE BOTTOM LINE: ESSENTIALS OF
PREVENTION AND TREATMENT

For prevention, weight control is the best bet. There is a strong connection between obesity and hypertension, so keeping your weight below the danger level for your height (see "Are you Overweight or Underweight?," pages 16–17) will reduce risk of high blood pressure.

Restricted use of alcohol will also reduce risk, for the incidence of hypertension increases sharply among drinkers who consume more than three drinks per day. Other dietary strategies, however, including sodium restriction, are not likely to reduce risk to any significant degree. But stress management may lower it, for stress hormones like adrenaline tend to constrict blood vessels and thus raise blood pressure.

Treatment of hypertension varies with the origin of the condition, and dietary interventions that can lower blood pressure for some hypertensives will not necessarily lower it for others. Specific strategies include the following:

- Weight loss, which will lower blood pressure more reliably than any other means (but works only for hypertension resulting from obesity), can result in significant reduction with the loss of relatively few pounds.
- Sodium restriction, if appropriate, can reduce hypertension, although the degree of restriction required may be more severe than can be sustained outside a hospital or other treatment setting.
- Dietary supplements of calcium and potassium have been shown to reduce high blood pressure for some hypertensives, and the effects of other nutrients are now being studied.
- Exercise can lower blood pressure, both by facilitating weight loss and by improving the overall performance of the cardiovascular system. Australian studies have demonstrated that aerobic exercise can reduce blood pressure even when it does not lower weight.

CHAPTER 19

Can Diet Prevent Cancer?

THE NUTRITIONAL IMPACT on heart disease and hypertension has been recognized since at least the 1950s, but the 1980s is the decade of diet and cancer. Only in recent years have we heard so much about cancer-fighting nutrients, from common calcium and fiber to exotic selenium and beta-carotene. Simultaneously, new studies have warned us that excess calories or fat can increase cancer risk.

These developments have led millions of Americans to re-examine their diets or to seek out supplements. Yet although research has provided plenty of clues to the diet-cancer connection, the exact nature of the relation remains unclear.

Animal experiments have shown that certain chemicals, including some found in food, can turn normal cells into cancerous ones. Some nutrients seem to enhance tumor growth after cells have become malignant. Others, however, seem to check the development of cancer and help to keep experimental animals healthy.

But lab animals aren't human beings, and human cancer patterns are extremely difficult to study. To examine heart disease, researchers can feed volunteers special diets, track their blood pressure or blood cholesterol, and learn fairly quickly whether the dietary change has altered the risk of heart attack. But you can't predict the risk of cancer with a simple blood test. There's no way to tell who will get the disease until they actually get it. What's more, cancer can develop slowly. It may take 20 or 30 years before it becomes detectable. To learn much of anything, researchers must follow their subjects for a decade or more and see which dietary factors promote or prevent the disease.

To make matters worse, cancer is not a single disease. Breast cancer, lung cancer, colon cancer, and more than a hundred other types all differ — in their biochemistry, their victims, and their susceptibility to treatment. All they have in common is a pattern of uncontrolled cell growth that ultimately destroys healthy tissue. But they have decidedly different causes and seem to be affected in different ways by various dietary factors.

For all these reasons, our nutritional knowledge about cancer is still far from complete. But the pressure to apply that knowledge is great. Cancer strikes one American in four at some point in life and is responsible for about 20 percent of all deaths in this country. Even though the incidence of some forms of cancer has been dropping, the overall incidence of the disease has been increasing slowly but steadily since 1950.

How much can dietary changes help prevent cancer? The best estimate, based on an analysis of the other known causes of the disease, is that roughly one third of current cancer deaths might be prevented by changes in diet. That is slightly more than the number of cancer deaths that doctors contend is now caused by cigarette smoking.

For the kinds of cancer most prevalent in America — lung, colon, and breast cancer — researchers have begun to identify dietary factors that may increase or decrease risk. Such understanding has come largely from basic research into the ways various environmental factors, including compounds in food, can turn normal cells into cancer cells.

HOW GOOD CELLS GO BAD

The uncontrolled cell growth of cancer begins with a genetic mutation: a change in a cell's DNA, the nucleic acid that carries the body's genetic program. According to one current theory, each of our cells contains a handful of genes that normally lie dormant. But if activated, they can make the cell multiply wildly. In some forms of cancer, viral infections will change DNA and trigger cancerous growth. Radiation can damage DNA, which is why ultraviolet rays, like those in sunlight, produce skin cancer. Chemical agents can also put the cell's genes awry. The common denominator is that cancer always begins with a change in DNA.

Chemicals that produce cancer (called carcinogens) have been recognized since the nineteenth century. They range from soot, which then caused cancer of the scrotum among chimney sweeps, to asbestos, which was discovered to cause lung cancer in our century. Several drugs too have been recognized as carcinogenic. The very drugs used to treat cancer are so toxic that they can cause secondary cancers years later. But the single greatest cancer-causing agent, in terms of the number of deaths for which it may be responsible, remains tobacco.

Chemicals in food have also proved carcinogenic. Aflatoxin, a mold that grows on contaminated peanuts, is highly toxic and directly linked to liver tumors that are common in parts of Africa where peanuts are a dietary staple. (American peanuts are carefully screened to be sure they're aflatoxin-free.) Recently, researchers have found that a staple food of southern China, a preparation of salted, partly rotted fish, is linked to a type of nose cancer endemic there.

But such direct connections of specific foods to specific human cancers are rare. Most diet-cancer connections are far more subtle and complex. For one thing, the process of mutation — the derailment of DNA that sets the cancerous process in motion — is only the beginning of the chain of events that results in cancer. Some dietary factors don't actually mutate cells but seem to give cells that have *already* mutated a better chance to grow into tumors.

One model of cancer growth holds that there are two kinds of carcinogenic chemicals: initiators and promoters. The initiators cause the initial mutation; the promoters act on a mutant cell to make it grow. Tobacco is so potently carcinogenic largely because it contains both initiators and promoters. In a charcoal-broiled hamburger, the toxic compounds formed on the charred outside of the burger seem to be initiators, while the fat in the hamburger may be a promoter.

There is another factor to consider in gauging the effects of various foods on cancer risk and that is individual genetic heritage. Some cancers, like the eye tumor called retinoblastoma, are totally heritable, the result of an inborn genetic flaw. Much more commonly inherited is a *tendency* to develop certain kinds of cancer, a predisposition that will be manifested only under certain environmental or dietary conditions.

Although the genetic influence on cancer is less pronounced than the genetic influence on heart disease or diabetes, the most common forms of cancer in the United States can all involve genetic vulnerability. Having a mother or sister with breast cancer significantly increases a woman's own risk of the disease. One form of colon cancer develops from precancerous polyps, which often run in families. (When President Reagan developed colon cancer, his brother had contracted a virtually identical disease at almost the same time.) And there's recent evidence that having a parent or sibling with lung cancer may mean that your risk is three to four times the norm. In each of these cases, if a near relative develops cancer at an unusually early age, it is evidence of increased genetic risk.

WHAT CAUSES CANCER?

Because the development of cancer is a complex, multistage process, there is no simple way to tell whether a given nutrient will raise risk. But several kinds of research now enable scientists to estimate the effects of different foodstuffs.

First is a test that determines whether or not a chemical (from food or any other source) can cause mutations in DNA. Chemicals that can do this are called mutagens, and while they won't necessarily cause cancer in animals or people, there is evidence that they might.

The simplest, least expensive, and most sensitive and accurate test for mutagenesis uses bacteria (salmonella bacteria, to be exact). This procedure was developed in the 1960s by Bruce Ames, now chairman of the department of biochemistry at the University of California, Berkeley. The Ames test measures the way various chemicals affect bacterial growth by mutating the bacteria's DNA.

The test has been used on thousands of synthetic chemicals as a quick, inexpensive way to see if they're likely to be carcinogenic. It has now been applied by Ames and others to measure levels of mutagens in different foodstuffs. The results show that mushrooms, peanut butter, black pepper, burnt toast, charbroiled hamburger, and alfalfa sprouts, among other foods, contain high levels of natural mutagens. Celery contains psoralen derivatives, chemicals that become potent mutagens when activated by light, and bruised celery has 100 times more of these psoralen derivatives than undamaged celery does.

"Of all the compounds that attack DNA, my guess is that 99 percent occur naturally, many of them in the common foods we eat," says Ames. "Every meal you eat is full of mutagens and carcinogens." Plants don't produce these chemicals to cause trouble for the people who eat them but to keep the insects that prey on them at bay. These toxic chemicals are natural pesticides, so plants that can synthesize them have an evolutionary advantage.

Many cancer researchers, including Ames, now believe that the total impact of these natural mutagens is far greater than that caused by the additives or preservatives we might get in our diets. Take nitrites, for example, the preservatives that have made millions of Americans wary of hot dogs and bologna. Nitrites are converted in the stomach into compounds called nitrosamines, which are mutagenic and carcinogenic. But most of the nitrites in your body come not from processed food but from the action of your own saliva. Bacteria in the mouth make nitrite out of nitrates, chemicals found in many vegetables, including beets, lettuce, spinach, and radishes. By comparison, the amount of nitrite you get in preserved meats is small.

Even though many common chemicals can mutate bacteria in the Ames test, this does *not* mean that "everything causes cancer." The test shows only that these chemicals are mutagens when they're extracted from food, concentrated, and put in a culture of bacteria. The same chemicals may have effects on animals or people that are very different from those on salmonella bacteria.

Mutagens may also be far less hazardous when they come packaged in a whole food. Ames notes that most fruits and vegetables containing mutagens also contain antioxidants, chemicals that can *lower* the risk of cancer.

Although they are more costly and cumbersome than the Ames test, animal experiments give a truer measure of whether a chemical or food is carcinogenic. Mutagens are not always carcinogens; a chemical can damage DNA without necessarily leading to cancer. Animal tests help separate the more hazardous mutagens from the less hazardous ones. In addition, they make it possible to study the effects of whole foods and specific diets, not just isolated chemicals.

But animal studies aren't perfect either. Results are influenced by dosage, the length of time an animal is exposed, the total composition of the diet, the kind of animal used in the experiment, and other factors that researchers may be unable to pin down.

Although researchers cannot feed potential carcinogens to human subjects, they can study cancer rates among people with different diets and lifestyles. By comparing groups living in different parts of the world, epidemiologists have gotten some valuable clues to factors that affect human cancer.

Epidemiological studies of large population groups have found some of the clearest links between lifestyle and cancer, like the connection between smoking and lung cancer and the link between alcoholism and gastrointestinal cancer. They have also helped show how dietary factors can affect cancer risk. But the data from these studies are often hard to interpret.

The problem is that groups of people usually differ in many different ways besides their diets. Seventh Day Adventists generally have less breast and colon cancer than other Americans. Since roughly half the members of this religious group are vegetarians and many others eat meat sparingly, it would be tempting to conclude that a diet low in meat offers them protection from cancer. But Mormons, who have a cancer risk about as low as the Adventists', eat plenty of meat. When you look at these groups together, it seems that diet may have less to do with their resistance to cancer than with another factor: both religions forbid smoking and drinking. Both groups are also close-knit communities of the like-minded, within which there is the kind of security and clear-cut evidence of status that minimizes stress.

An ongoing puzzle is why the inhabitants of rich countries generally develop different kinds of cancer from the world's have-nots. Cancers of the prostate, breast, colon, and endometrium (the lining of the uterus) seem to be tumors of affluence. In contrast, there are the cancers of poverty: liver, cervix, esophagus, and stomach. A number of hypotheses have been offered to explain these patterns. Cancers of the rich, for example, may be linked to dietary fat, while stomach cancer may stem from a lack of refrigeration in poor countries. But none has been proved. No one really has a clue, either, as to why American colon cancer rates should be low in the Southeast and high in the Northeast and Midwest, with the highest incidence occurring in the state of Connecticut.

The three major methods of carcinogen hunting each have their shortcomings. But taken together, these different approaches are starting to provide a basis for some plausible theories about the causes of cancer.

The best hypotheses are backed up by several different kinds of studies. Epidemiological studies have revealed, for example, that smokers who eat substantial amounts of certain vegetables have a reduced risk of lung cancer. Chemical analysis shows these vegetables contain compounds that can block the effect of mutagens, while some animal studies demonstrate that feeding these protective compounds may slow down the growth of tumors. In this instance, the data are converging to highlight the important role antioxidants play in protecting us from carcinogens, including some carcinogens produced within the body itself.

FREE RADICALS, ANTIOXIDANTS, AND CANCER

Among the most potent and prevalent of mutagens are free radicals, the highly reactive, "pyromaniac" compounds that can harm cells throughout the body (see "What Is an Antioxidant?," page 60). Whatever they touch, they oxidize, and one of their most destructive actions is to damage DNA, producing mutations that can eventually lead to cancer.

Free radicals are formed by many of the chemical reactions of metabolism, particularly those involving the trace elements. The role of iron and copper in free-radical production can be seen among victims of certain genetic disorders that allow deposits of these minerals to build up in the liver and spleen. Since iron and copper trigger free-radical chain reactions in these organs, the victims of storage diseases have a higher-than-average risk of spleen and liver cancer.

Polyunsaturated fatty acids are a major dietary source of free radicals. These fatty acids react with oxygen fairly readily; that's what causes fats to go rancid. But it is only unsaturated fatty acids, not saturated ones, that are able to react directly with oxygen to form free radicals, and polyunsaturates do so more easily than monounsaturates.

For this reason, polyunsaturates seem to increase the risk of cancer, at least in experimental animals. When groups of rats are exposed to a chemical carcinogen and then put on different high-fat diets, the rats consuming the most unsaturated acids will develop more breast cancer than the rats consuming fewer unsaturates.

The body is not helpless in the face of free radicals. It produces several antioxidant enzymes that can trap free radicals chemically and prevent them from injuring body tissue. In addition, several nutrients are natural antioxidants. And so are certain synthetic preservatives added to foods to extend shelf life. High levels of these substances in the diet may help prevent cancer.

One trace element, selenium, has generated a considerable amount of attention as an antioxidant in recent years. New Zealand, a country with unusually low levels of selenium in the soil, also has a high rate of breast and colon cancer. And studies have shown that the mineral can slow the growth of virus-induced breast cancers in experimental animals. But there's little evidence to justify use of selenium supplements, even experimentally. Most people get plenty of selenium in seafoods, wheat germ, and whole grains, and the toxic dose of selenium is so low (compared with the effective dose) that supplements could pose a real danger.

A much safer antioxidant is vitamin C. In addition to blocking free radicals, vitamin C can also interfere with the conversion of nitrites to carcinogenic nitrosamines.

But most of the research on dietary antioxidants and cancer has focused on vitamins A and E and a host of compounds related to them. These natural antioxidants are produced in plants, including edible ones, that need to protect themselves from the oxygen they produce during photosynthesis.

Many of the fruits and vegetables we eat are complex chemical storehouses and contain a range of different antioxidants. This chemical complexity poses a puzzle for cancer researchers. There is good epidemiological evidence that a diet rich in certain fruits and vegetables can lower the risk of some kinds of cancer. But it is not yet clear whether antioxidants in these foods or other compounds make them most cancer-protective. And if it is the antioxidants, then researchers must discover which ones are most potent.

Much work has focused on the carotenoids — biologically active pigments, chemically related to vitamin A — that give orange, yellow, and green vegetables their color. Squash, especially winter squash, can contain up to 500 or more natural carotenoids. About 50 of those 500 chemicals are converted in the body to vitamin A; the rest, though chemically similar to the vitamin, are not converted.

Researchers don't yet know which carotenoids are most cancer-protective. Many of the compounds that are *not* converted to vitamin A are stronger antioxidants than those that are, and may thus provide more benefit in cancer prevention.

The bulk of research on the carotenoids, however, has focused on beta-carotene, a major source of vitamin A. Japanese studies in the late 1970s showed that heavy smokers were less likely to develop lung cancer if they had eaten a diet high in foods that contain beta-carotene. Although these foods also contain other carotenoids, beta-carotene was the compound chemists were most familiar with, and the one on which further research has focused.

In studies now under way, researchers are looking for linkage between lower rates of cancer and blood levels of beta-carotene, vitamin A itself, vitamin E, and selenium. In one recently reported Johns Hopkins study, more than 25,000 Maryland residents had their blood sampled in 1974 and were then followed over the next decade to see who developed lung cancer and who did not. Study subjects with low blood levels of beta-carotene turned out to have four times the average rate of a certain type of lung cancer (squamous-cell carcinoma). Those with low levels of vitamin E had two and a half times the normal rate of lung cancer in general.

Beta-carotene is so often given as an experimental supplement because, unlike vitamin A, high levels are nontoxic. In a Harvard Medical School study, 22,000 physicians are taking either placebos or beta-carotene (50 milligrams every other day), and will do so for years, in order to show whether those who take beta-carotene are less prone to cancer.

Other researchers are testing the effects of various antioxidants, including beta-carotene, on groups especially susceptible to lung cancer, like heavy smokers and people who have worked with asbestos. But, as Charles Hennekens, director of the Harvard study of beta-carotene, points out: "Even if beta-carotene were effective in reducing deaths from lung cancer by as much as 50 percent, lifelong smokers would still have a risk 10 to 15 times greater than nonsmokers — rather than 20 to 30 times greater, as they do now."

At this point, there's more evidence that high-carotenoid foods are able to prevent cancer than that any specific nutrient in these foods can lower risk. So eating foods with a variety of carotenoids is a more prudent course than supplementation.

Winter squash is especially rich in carotenoids; a cooked half cup has the equivalent of 140 percent of the adult RDA for vitamin A. Other especially good sources are pumpkins, sweet potatoes, cantaloupes, apricots, papayas, and carrots, all brightly colored by the beneficial pigments. Carotenoids are also found in peaches, mangoes, tomatoes, red peppers, romaine lettuce, and spinach.

These pigments reach high levels in many of the cruciferous vegetables (so called because they have four-petaled flowers that form a crucifer, or cross). The crucifera — which include broccoli, Brussels sprouts, cabbage, cauliflower, turnip greens, kale, and bok choy — and red peppers also contain more vitamin C per calorie than any other food except citrus fruit.

Unique to crucifera are indoles, isothiocyanates, and related chemicals that stimulate the liver enzymes responsible for inactivating toxic chemicals. Although the theory is yet to be proved, some researchers believe these chemicals may help the body to inactivate carcinogens more quickly.

FIBER

Despite their other differences, vegetables have one nutritional factor in common — their high fiber content. And for the last two decades researchers have studied the possibility that dietary fiber may lower risk of colon cancer.

The current interest in fiber stems from the 1960s, when British physicians in Uganda noted that colon cancer was rare there. Other gastrointestinal disorders (diverticulosis, hemorrhoids, and constipation) were also less common in Africa than in the West. While there were several dietary differences between Africa and Britain — the British, for example, eat more animal fat — the surgeon Denis Burkitt focused on fiber as a possible explanation for the Africans' healthier digestive tracts. Burkitt found that the Africans ate much more fiber than Westerners, an aspect of diet reflected in daily stool bulk three times as great.

Although the idea has won popular acceptance (and makes physiological sense), the link between fiber and cancer protection is still not proved. Since groups that eat high-fiber diets also tend to eat relatively little fat, it's hard to tell whether reduced incidence of colon cancer is due to more fiber, less fat, or both.

Some studies have failed to find any protective effect of fiber at all. Recent South African research revealed that although the different racial groups in the country ate very similar amounts of fiber, blacks have virtually no colon cancer, Indians have little, and whites have a great deal.

If fiber does protect against colon cancer, it's insoluble fibers that do the job, not the soluble fibers that seem to lower risk of heart disease (see "The Different Kinds of Fiber," pages 110–111). Vegetables and bran are common sources of insoluble fiber. (South Africans get much of theirs from corn, West Africans from millet, and East Africans from cassava.)

Insoluble fiber, a bulking agent, makes the stools larger and softer and dilutes substances in the feces that could have a mutagenic effect on cells of the intestinal wall. One potential mutagen is bile acid, which fiber tends to bind and remove from the colon.

In addition to whatever specific protection fiber provides, there are general benefits to a high-fiber diet. If you are eating lots of high-fiber foods, you'll have a relatively low intake of fat and calories. High-fiber foods not only allow you to quell hunger with fewer calories, they can actually decrease the absorption of calories by pushing food through the intestine more quickly.

These benefits of high fiber consumption can be important in cancer prevention, for there is substantial evidence that lowering fat and caloric intake tends to lower cancer risk. The reasons are still not clear. But much current research is designed to discover whether it is excess fat, excess calories, or only a combination of the two that promotes cancer.

FATS AND CALORIES

Epidemiology doesn't offer much help in sorting out the fat-versus-calories conundrum. It is often noted, for example, that breast and colon cancer occur frequently among groups that eat lots of fat. But these groups tend to be affluent, which means they also have a high caloric intake.

Clinical studies don't resolve the confusion. A recent British study compared 50 patients with colon cancer and 50 people without the disease. The cancer patients ate a diet with 14 percent more fat but also ate 16 percent more calories. Was it the fat or the calories that made them cancer-prone?

In practical terms, the answer may not make a great deal of difference. Since fat is the most concentrated source of calories, cutting down on fat will automatically lower the number of calories you take in, and conversely, any good calorie-cutting program must curb fat intake. But understanding which dietary factor is more important could tell researchers something about how cancer develops and improve future efforts at prevention.

Until fairly recently, animal studies focused on the hypothesis that fat itself promoted tumor growth. In fact, a high-fat diet does seem to increase mammary and colon cancer in rats. In these experiments the cancer is initially triggered by a chemical carcinogen, a virus, or some other agent that damages DNA. The fat in the diet then seems to make it easier for mutant cells to grow into tumors, although the mechanism of cancer promotion is not clear.

One possibility is that the calories in fat simply promote the growth of cancerous cells as well as healthy cells. If this is so, then a low-calorie diet could lower the risk of cancer and possibly prolong life. In fact, animal studies dating from the early part of the twentieth century have suggested that caloric restriction might make mice more resistant to tumor growth.

The current experimental approach is to design special animal diets that are low in calories but that have the same amount of fiber, protein, and micronutrients as ordinary diets do. Researchers can then manipulate the amount of fat and carbohydrate to measure effects of fat restriction and caloric restriction separately.

At the Wistar Institute in Philadelphia, David Kritchevsky has found evidence that cutting calories can reduce tumor growth in animals, no matter what percentage of those calories come from fat. In one set of experiments Kritchevsky and his colleagues gave rats chemicals that induce either colon tumors or mammary tumors. Restricting calories by 40 percent while severely reducing fat intake virtually halted tumor growth. Even a 10 percent cutback in calories — closer to a realistic dietary change — cut the average weight of tumors by half.

Kritchevsky then attempted to measure the separate effects of fat and calories as follows: One group of rats was allowed to eat as much as they wanted of a diet that was 20 percent fat, while a second group was fed a diet with the same amount of fat but with 25 percent fewer calories. Since the second group got as much fat with fewer calories, they actually had a higher *percentage* of fat in their diet. Nevertheless, they had many fewer tumors, and the tumors they developed were smaller. It seems, Kritchevsky observes, as if caloric restriction had starved the tumors and slowed their growth.

Michael Pariza, director of the Food Research Institute at the University of Wisconsin, has performed similar experiments with similar results. He finds that both fat and calories promote tumor growth but that calories seem to be more important. In Pariza's experiments, three quarters of rats on a high-fat/high-calorie diet developed tumors. When the diet was high in calories but low in fat, the tumor rate dropped to 45 percent. But when rats went on a low-calorie diet — even one with a relatively high fat content — only 7 percent developed cancer. So both fats and calories are important, but calories may be *more* important.

Whether cancer is related to fat intake, caloric intake, or both, you would expect to see a correlation between cancer and obesity. And there is evidence of such a relation. Much of it comes from a 12-year American Cancer Society study that found an increased incidence of uterine, stomach, colon, and breast cancer among overweight Americans.

The risk is clearest, however, for people who are at least 40 percent over the standard of the height-weight tables — in other words, the seriously obese. There's also some evidence that underweight people may have a higher-than-average cancer risk (as discussed in chapter 10).

It appears possible that obesity has a different effect on different kinds of cancer. Women, for example, do not have a significantly higher risk of breast cancer unless they are 40 percent overweight, but the risk of uterine cancer rises at only 20 percent overweight. For men, being even 10 percent overweight increases the risk of prostate cancer.

Whatever the connection between body weight and other cancers, there are plausible physiological explanations for obesity to raise the risk of breast and uterine cancer. Fat tissue is an endocrine organ. It is involved in the production of the sex hormone estrogen and is the major source of that hormone for women past menopause. Obese women tend to have higher estrogen levels in the blood than thin ones. And estrogen, in excess, seems to be carcinogenic.

OTHER FACTORS

Several other dietary and lifestyle factors may also be related to cancer risk. The case against smoked, pickled, and other salt-cured food, for example, is now persuasive. Cancers of the stomach and esophagus, which are fairly rare in the United States, are far more common in countries where large amounts of these foods are consumed, particularly in China, Japan, and Iceland. Japan has the highest rate of stomach cancer in the world — this form of cancer causes more deaths per capita than the total of stomach, breast, and colon cancer combined causes in the United States. Studies of Japanese who migrate to the United States and change their diets show that their risk of stomach cancer drops (but their risk of colon cancer rises).

Although cured and pickled foods do not figure prominently in the American diet, charcoal-broiled meat does. Picnickers have worried for years about the "burnt stuff" on their hamburgers, which contains mutagens. But overall, most of us eat too little smoked or charred meat in a lifetime to worry about.

Alcohol in excess, however, is a much more serious carcinogen and is responsible for a significant number of cancer deaths. Immoderate use of alcohol, particularly combined with cigarette smoking, is clearly associated with cancer of the upper gastrointestinal tract. If alcoholics develop cirrhosis, they may also be prone to liver cancer. But when it comes to another toxic pleasure, coffee, drinkers can relax; early reports associating coffee with pancreatic cancer have not held up.

On the positive side, there's some evidence that calcium and vitamin D may offer protection against colon cancer. A survey of 2,000 middle-aged men, analyzed by Cedric Garland at the University of California, San Diego, School of Medicine, has shown that men who drink milk have a lower risk of colon cancer than men who don't. Among people with family histories of colon cancer, calcium supplementation may reverse a dangerous pattern of cell growth in the lining of the colon, a pattern that often precedes cancer.

Exercise too may have a role in cancer prevention. One California study found that men whose jobs required heavy manual labor had significantly less colon cancer than more sedentary workers. Other recent studies, in New York State and Washington State, have had similar results. There's also some evidence that women who have been athletic since college run a lower-than-average risk of breast or uterine cancer, perhaps because exercise affects their fat stores.

IS THERE AN ANTI-CANCER DIET?

During the last few years various groups have tried to put these diverse findings together. They've asked whether it's possible, with our present knowledge, to devise a diet that gives us the best chance of preventing cancer.

The National Academy of Sciences made the first attempt and convened a Committee on Diet, Nutrition, and Cancer that began meeting in 1980. When the committee issued its report two years later, it concluded, "Unfortunately, it is not yet possible to make firm scientific pronouncements about the association between diet and cancer." But the committee did believe evidence supported these interim recommendations for the public:

- Reduce total fat intake to 30 percent of total calories.
- Include fruits, vegetables, and whole grain cereals in the diet, with special attention to cruciferous vegetables and others rich in carotenoids.
- Minimize consumption of smoked, salt-cured, and pickled foods.
- If you drink, do so in moderation.

The Academy's advice was much like similar recommendations of the American Heart Association and the American Diabetes Association. It was soon endorsed by the American Cancer Society with a few additions, notably, the injunction to avoid obesity.

But the notion of an anticancer diet became more controversial as other groups issued more specific recommendations. Take the case of fiber. The National Academy of Sciences committee found "no conclusive evidence" that dietary fiber could reduce the risk of cancer, and the American Cancer Society's "professional education" booklet acknowledges, "Agreement on fiber's role in cancer prevention is not universal."

Nevertheless, the federal goverment's National Cancer Institute (NCI) has been considerably more aggressive in promoting fiber for cancer prevention. NCI now recommends that Americans double their intake of fiber from about 10 grams (the current average) to 20 grams. More, they suggest, might be even better, since "populations that consume approximately 20–35 grams of dietary fiber have a lower rate of cancers of the colon and rectum."

Food and Drug Administration officials were taken aback by this advice when it appeared on a cereal box with NCI endorsement. Here was a food being advertised for medicinal purposes. The FDA pointed out that studies on fiber and cancer hadn't even used the specific fiber found in this product.

Many cancer researchers are cautious about recommending any significant change in diet, even one as seemingly innocuous as doubling the intake of fiber. There's new evidence from animal experiments that certain fibers may actually *promote* cancer under certain circumstances. There is also the troubling epidemiological finding that groups of people with very high fiber intake have a high rate of stomach cancer, although their risk of colon cancer is low.

None of this means that Americans who start eating more fruits, vegetables, or grains are endangering their health. Far from it. Our average intake of fiber is so low that we're far from the dangers of excess.

But the fiber controversy underscores the importance of striving for balance rather than focusing on large amounts of any single dietary component. Special fiber supplements are probably neither necessary nor useful in cancer prevention. By the same token, supplements of vitamin A or selenium are as likely to prove toxic as to lower risk of cancer.

THE BOTTOM LINE: ESSENTIALS OF PREVENTION

The National Academy of Sciences guidelines offer a sensible guide to risk reduction.

• Reducing fat consumption should limit not only saturated fatty

---

DEPARTMENT OF FALSE HOPES: CAN DIET CURE CANCER?

The notion that a good diet can help prevent cancer is very different from the idea that nutrition can *cure* the disease. Nevertheless, a variety of nutritional cancer treatments have been proposed. Thus far none has demonstrated any real ability to halt or reverse cancer.

Vitamin C, for example, may well help prevent cancer by blocking free-radical activity. But that doesn't mean it will help people who already have cancer, as Linus Pauling and the Scottish physician Ewan Cameron proposed in the 1970s.

To put that idea to the test, researchers at the Mayo Clinic gave 10 grams of vitamin C per day to 51 patients with advanced, untreatable cancer. One year later, 49 percent were still alive, compared to 47 percent of a control group who took placebos. No significant difference.

Many cancer patients these days are also drawn to the macrobiotic diet, a Japanese-inspired, largely vegetarian regimen. Since macrobiotics represents a philosophy as well as a nutritional strategy, it's hard to define, but for most Americans who follow it, the diet includes mostly whole grains, vegetables (including seaweed), nuts, oils, and soy products. Some followers eat more liberally, adding fish and seafood; others are even more stringent. But all macrobiotic dieters shun meat, eggs, and dairy products.

The composition of the diet — at least in its more liberal forms — is not too far removed from the low-fat, high-fiber regimen that many researchers believe may help prevent cancer. But there is no good evidence that such a diet is helpful in cancer treatment. Yet that's what proponents of the macrobiotic diet maintain. To support their claim, they point to celebrities, TV stars, even a physician, who have gone on the macrobiotic diet and watched their cancer go into remission.

What such case histories don't tell you is that a number of other cancer patients have also gone on the macrobiotic diet and died. A recent review of macrobiotics in the *Journal of Clinical Oncology* summed it up this way:

> It is impossible to evaluate the safety and adequacy of the macrobiotic diet in cancer treatment because relevant scientific data are lacking. . . . Reports of miraculous cures of a small number of patients are included in much of the macrobiotic literature; however, definitive data to establish the diagnosis of cancer as well as follow-up clinical data are lacking. In addition, many of these patients have received conventional medical therapy concurrently.

In other words, in the absence of well-controlled studies, the macrobiotic cure must be considered closer to magic than to medicine.

acids (which raise risk of atherosclerosis) but also cut back intake of polyunsaturates, a major dietary source of free radicals.

- Plenty of fruits, vegetables, and whole grains will reduce intake of fat and calories, both associated with increased risk of cancer.
- Foods rich in carotene — brightly colored fruits and vegetables — contain potent antioxidants, while cruciferous vegetables (like cabbage and Brussels sprouts) are not only rich in carotene but have lots of vitamin C, which also fights free radicals.
- Restricting use of alcohol to moderate levels (two to three drinks per day) allows you the benefits of alcohol (including a reduced risk of heart disease) without the increased risk of cancer associated with heavy drinking.
- Limiting consumption of smoked, salt-cured, and pickled foods to low-risk levels should pose no problem for most Americans. Our diets contain only a limited amount of these foods. Even our intake of charcoal-broiled meats is generally less than will raise risk of cancer.

Other dietary strategies that may be of use:

- Increased consumption of fiber, specifically, insoluble fiber (found in vegetables and bran), which provides bulk for feces and may reduce the impact of potential mutagens in the colon. Although fiber has not been proved beneficial, increased intake seems a prudent dietary option. If nothing else, it will lower intake of fat and calories while providing other health benefits as well.
- Weight control, by means of diet and exercise, should reduce risk. Various degrees of obesity appear to increase risk for different forms of cancer. However, there is evidence that a significantly low body weight can also raise cancer risks.

CHAPTER 20

Diabetes and Diet

W E'VE BEEN LEARNING a lot about diabetes in recent years. And even though we're still not sure of what causes it, how to prevent it, or how to cure it, we're at least learning what's *not* true about the disease.

We can now say with certainty that eating refined sugar (or any other kind of sugar) will not by itself bring on diabetes. And although obesity usually goes along with diabetes, it alone won't cause the disease either. In fact, the cause is probably more genetic than dietary, which explains why diabetes is so difficult to prevent.

Some of our new knowledge flatly contradicts what doctors have long told diabetics to do and to eat. For example, demanding physical exercise, even competitive sports, will benefit rather than overtax young diabetics. And ice cream (sweetened with real sugar) turns out to be safer than potatoes for them to eat.

The good news is that we now know how to help diabetics control the disease without radically changing either their lifestyles or their diets. But the bad news about diabetes is that more than 11 million Americans have the disease, and only about half of them know it.

Diabetes disrupts the process by which the body's cells take up glucose and convert it to energy. No one is quite sure what makes this process suddenly start to go awry. Once it's under way, though, diabetes either deprives the body of the glucose-regulating hormone, insulin, or makes it more difficult for cells to respond to this hormone.

The most severe form of the disease, now called insulin-dependent diabetes (and known in the past either as juvenile-onset or as Type I), usually strikes young children or adolescents who are genetically vulnerable. Often it is one of several viral infections that triggers onset of the disease, causing the immune system to attack and destroy insulin-producing cells in the pancreas. Insulin-dependent diabetes rarely goes undiagnosed for long, because its symptoms are hard to ignore: frequent urination, extreme thirst and hunger, rapid weight loss, weakness, fatigue, irritability, nausea, and vomiting.

These symptoms give us just a clue to what happens when the body is deprived of insulin. The hormone plays a unique role in keeping blood glucose at normal levels (between 70 and 150 milligrams per 100 milliliters of blood). When levels exceed 80 milligrams in a healthy individual, the pancreas will release insulin into the bloodstream. The hormone then tells muscle cells to take on more glucose for energy, and fat cells to convert glucose to fat and stash it away.

Without sufficient insulin on the scene, cells will not take on enough glucose, no matter how much is floating around in the blood. For its energy needs, the body must then turn to fat and protein. To supply the brain and central nervous system, it will start producing ketones, the "mock glucose" it makes from fatty acids (as described in chapter 3). Over time, excess ketones accumulate in the bloodstream and eventually reach toxic levels. In severe cases of diabetes, rising levels of glucose and ketones in the blood can lead to coma and death unless an external source of insulin is provided.

Diabetes causes the body to lose vast amounts of glucose in urine (which is why symptoms include both weight loss and hunger). Glucose that stays on in the bloodstream often binds chemically to hemoglobin and to proteins in the capillaries and the retina of the eye. As a result, protein structure is altered in a way that can lead to blindness, heart and kidney disease, infections of the feet, and gangrene.

Each year, some 300,000 Americans die as a result of diabetes or its complications, and 5,000 victims lose their sight. Diabetes is responsible for nearly half of all leg and foot amputations not caused by injuries and for close to a quarter of all new dialysis patients (about one diabetes sufferer in ten develops kidney disease).

Insulin-dependent diabetes, as its name implies, is treated with insulin. Since the body can no longer produce the hormone, it must be supplied from the outside, most often by self-administered injection. Recently, however, diabetics have been able to use an implanted pump that automatically delivers insulin to the bloodstream. (And new forms of delivery, by pills or nasal sprays, are being developed.)

In addition to insulin, diet and exercise are part of any treatment plan. These days, insulin dosage is tailored to individual diets. In the past, it worked the other way around: the doctor set insulin dosage and then prescribed a rigid diet to match it.

There are about 1 million insulin-dependent diabetics in the United States today. But more than 10 million people have non-insulin-dependent diabetes, the form of the disease that used to be called adult-onset or

Type II. This form generally strikes overweight men and women past 40 with some history of diabetes in their families. And often it can go undiagnosed for years.

What causes non-insulin-dependent diabetes is not the destruction of insulin-producing cells in the pancreas but the inability of body cells to make proper use of the hormone (see "Diabetes and Weight," pages 250-251). This type of diabetes can usually be controlled by diet and exercise alone, although insulin may occasionally be required as well.

Symptoms include blurred vision or any vision change; numbness or tingling sensation in legs, feet, or fingers; drowsiness; itching skin or frequent skin infections; and cuts or bruises that are slow to heal.

If you're troubled by any of these symptoms, particularly if you're overweight or have a family history of diabetes, a visit to the doctor may be in order. Medical tests can tell whether you're developing diabetes by checking urine for the presence of glucose and ketones and measuring blood levels of glucose. The earlier diabetes is diagnosed, the better the chances for successful treatment.

DIABETIC REACTIONS

In even the best-controlled cases of diabetes, glucose and insulin will occasionally get out of balance, creating problems that must be dealt with at once.

Hyperglycemia

A high blood level of glucose, hyperglycemia, occurs when diabetes goes untreated or when diabetics eat too much or take too little insulin. It can also be brought on by illness or emotional stress. Thirst and nausea as well as high sugar levels in blood or urine are symptoms that should be brought to a doctor's attention.

Hypoglycemia

Often called insulin shock, hypoglycemia is a sudden drop in blood sugar that can strike insulin users when they eat too little, delay a meal, or exercise more vigorously than usual. If low levels of blood glucose aren't countered quickly with sugar or some other food that can raise these levels rapidly, the victim is likely to lose consciousness.

Warning signs include extreme hunger, weakness, nervousness, pallor, headaches, and a cold, clammy feeling. Since many nondiabetics display these symptoms from time to time, large numbers of people are convinced that they have chronic hypoglycemia. But only a few actually do (see "Hypoglycemia" section in chapter 15).

Ketoacidosis

This is diabetic coma. It occurs when insulin and glucose are so out of balance that the body can't use much glucose and starts producing ketones from fat. Unless the condition is detected (through blood or urine tests) and corrected, the buildup of ketones can reach toxic levels and the victim will lose consciousness. Warning signs include dry mouth, great thirst, pungent bad breath, abdominal pain, and occasionally vomiting.

DIABETES AND WEIGHT

There is a close link between obesity and non-insulin-dependent diabetes, the form that hits middle-aged men and women. A full 80 to 90 percent of non-insulin-dependent diabetics are significantly overweight (weighing more than 20 percent above ideal). The connection is so strong that some researchers even speak of the condition as "diabesity."

But does this mean that getting fat *causes* diabetes? Not necessarily. Non-insulin-dependent diabetes appears to be almost totally genetic in origin. The evidence comes largely from studies of identical twins who have been separated at birth. By studying these twins, who have identical genes but grow up in different environments, it is possible to measure genetic influences. Virtually 100 percent of diabetics in these studies have twins who are also diabetic. But similar studies of insulin-dependent diabetics find only 50 percent with twins who share the disease.

The very genes responsible for diabetes may also be to blame for obesity. Although clearly a negative influence on health today, this genetic inheritance may once have been beneficial.

Even with a strong genetic pull toward diabetes, the disease usually won't develop unless and until the person at risk becomes overweight. Then excess fat actually seems to make the body's cells less sensitive to insulin.

Here's how it works. Normally, when the body is taking on carbohydrates, the pancreas pumps out insulin. The hormone travels to fat and muscle cells, each cell containing thousands of insulin receptors, which are special chemicals designed to respond to the hormone. These receptors pick up the insulin signal and tell the cells how much glucose to accept for immediate energy needs or for storage.

When the body is storing too much fat, the number of insulin receptors declines, and cells become less sensitive to the hormone's effects. This phenomenon, called insulin resistance, develops to some extent in all obese people. But if there is a genetic predisposition to diabetes, the situation can get out of hand. When cells fail to respond to insulin signals, glucose levels in the blood keep rising. This prompts the pancreas to pump out even more insulin, and the receptors become even more indifferent. Thus, the body's complex glucose-regulating system starts to break down and hyperglycemia develops.

Even if you have a family history of diabetes, non-insulin-dependent diabetes is reversible if caught in time. This makes early diagnosis vital. The sooner you begin to deal with the condition once hyperglycemia has developed, the greater chance you have of reversing it. Some oral drugs may be helpful; they can enhance the cell's insulin sensitivity, although they cannot boost insulin production.

But you can also deal with diabetes by losing weight — not on the best-selling shape-changing regimen of the moment, but with your doctor's help and with the suggestions in chapter 11. The important point — and a surprising one — is that you don't have to lose *much* weight to bring your glucose-regulating system almost all the way back to normal. If you're 40 or 50 pounds overweight, you may only need to shed 15 or 20 pounds to get the system functioning pretty well. You needn't go from fat to slim, just from overweight to somewhat less overweight.

The hardest part is not taking off the necessary weight but keeping it off. Should you regain lost weight, losing it again will be less beneficial. If you have ignored diabetes for several years, then chronic hyperglycemia may have done too much damage to cell tissue for weight loss to put it right. And when the disease has progressed to the point that substantial amounts of glucose are leaving the body in urine, the pounds you shed as a result are unlikely to do much good.

Exercise clearly has a role in weight control, for diabetics as well as anyone who's trying to reduce. But it can do more than merely keep surplus poundage off and burn up excess glucose in the blood.

Exercise can boost insulin sensitivity directly by making insulin receptors on the surface of cells more available. It may also increase the number of these receptors and their ability to bind with insulin.

DIABETES AND DIET

Before insulin was available, about the only way doctors could control diabetes was to keep carbohydrate consumption so low that little glucose was able to build up in the bloodstream. The tradition of carbohydrate restriction continued long after insulin was being widely used. It continued, in fact, until almost the end of the 1970s. By that time, however, a number of researchers were experimenting with high-carbohydrate, high-fiber diets.

One clue to the value of such diets for diabetics came from developing nations, where rates of both diabetes and heart disease were mounting as traditional diets, heavy on whole grains and cereals, gave way to diets rich in animal fats. Research showed blood sugar levels were much lower after high-fiber meals than after low-fiber meals. Yet fiber was noticeably absent from the carbohydrate-limiting diets that doctors had been insisting diabetics should follow.

There is little argument today about the virtues of either carbohydrates or fiber in diabetic diets, for doctors now recognize that the dietary goal for diabetics is not low levels of glucose so much as relatively *even* levels, with no abrupt increases that overburden limited glucose-regulating capacity. Putting together the new diets, doctors have assumed that foods high in fiber and complex carbohydrates—like whole grains, legumes (beans, lentils, and the like), vegetables, and fruit—would release glucose slowly into the blood.

As studies of the new diets are completed, evidence suggests that they do indeed increase insulin sensitivity as well as encourage weight loss. The University of Kentucky's James Anderson, who has been a pioneer in the development of the new diabetic diets, points out that the fiber in these diets can also help prevent atherosclerosis. A common condition among diabetics, this may well have been caused, at least in part, by carbohydrate-restricting diets of the past that were heavy on fats.

Today's diabetic diets generally provide for at least half of total energy needs in carbohydrates, most of it in complex carbohydrates. Diabetics no longer need to live sugar-free, but simple sugars generally make up only a small part of their diets. Fats are now limited to no more than 30 percent of energy needs, with only 10 percent in saturated fats and a very low level of cholesterol (no more than 100 milligrams per 1,000 calories). As for fiber, the recommmended level is now at least 30 grams per day.

What nutritionists find fascinating about today's diabetic diets is how close they come to what the Dietary Guidelines for Americans recommend and to the kinds of dietary changes the National Cancer Institute and the American Heart Association are encouraging. High-carbohydrate, high-fiber diets recommended for diabetics may also give the rest of us a good shot at preventing cancer and heart disease.

THE GLYCEMIC INDEX

A basic premise of the first high-carbohydrate, high-fiber diets was that complex carbohydrates are better sources of slow-release glucose than simple sugars are. The reasoning was that the digestive system would take longer to break down the chains of several thousand glucose molecules that make up complex carbohydrates. It also made sense that high-fiber foods would provide slow-release glucose, since fibers are bound up with starch molecules, and slow down the enzymes that digest starches. And quite often, that is just the case—but not always.

A new way of measuring foods (not only carbohydrates) in terms of glucose release time has produced some surprising findings. Ice cream, it turns out, hits the bloodstream with glucose more gradually than potatoes do. Why this is true, nobody is sure, not even the researchers who developed what is called the glycemic index, a ranking of how quickly different foods raise blood glucose. It might be the temperature of the ice cream, or the fat content, or the fact that it was sweetened with fructose rather than sucrose.

Sucrose — table sugar — is made up of a combination of fructose and glucose, and the glucose is quickly released into the blood. But pure fructose, the kind of sugar found in fruit and now used as a commercial sweetener, enters the bloodstream more slowly. The reason is biochemical: while glucose is actively pumped across the intestine, fructose just leaks across. Fructose also doesn't affect the body's cells until it's converted to glucose in the liver, a process that also takes time.

To establish the glycemic index, diabetes researchers Jerrold Olefsky and Phyllis Crapo at the University of California, San Diego, School of Medicine, David Jenkins at the University of Toronto, and others, have been testing the blood of volunteers to discover how various foods affect glucose levels. Foods are rated by the degree of change, with the lowest rating going to those that raise glucose the least (see "The Glycemic Index," below).

Results have provided more surprises than just the slow release of glucose from ice cream. Parsnips, for example, have a rating almost as high as glucose itself. Legumes, however, have proved their slow-release value by the new standard, with soybeans and lentils receiving close to bottom line ratings. Recent findings by glycemic indexers have given much more positive (low) ratings to whole grain breads than to white

---

THE GLYCEMIC INDEX

Here are the glycemic index levels for a variety of different foods. The higher the number, the more quickly glucose gets into the bloodstream. White bread is now used as a standard of comparison; therefore, its glycemic index is set at 100.

Glycemic Index

glucose	138	white rice (parboiled)	83
baked potato	135	rye bread (sourdough)	83
cornflakes	119	boiled potato	81
instant potatoes	116	buckwheat	74
lima beans	115	all-bran cereal	73
Weetabix cereal	109	white spaghetti	66
whole wheat bread	100	whole wheat spaghetti	61
white bread	100	whole grain rye bread	58
shredded wheat	97	kidney beans	54
brown rice	96	ice cream	52
Rye Crisps	95	whole milk	49
raisins	93	chick-peas	49
sucrose	86	red lentils	43
oatmeal	85	grapefruit	36

Source: From David J.A. Jenkins et al., "The Glycaemic Response to Carbohydrate Foods," The Lancet, No. 8399 (Boston: Little, Brown, 1984), pp. 388–391.

bread or even conventional whole wheat breads.

Processing and cooking methods can alter the ratings dramatically. For example, parboiled rice releases glucose much more slowly than regular boiled rice. By breaking down carbohydrates before digestive enzymes get a crack at them, processes like flaking and puffing cut glucose release time, and "instant" anything is likely to rush glucose to the bloodstream faster than slower-cooked forms of the same food.

What the glycemic index does is force doctors to take a second look at the rules of carbohydrate exchange basic to diabetic diets. These are the tables that tell diabetics what foods may be switched for what other foods. But with the glycemic index as a guide, diabetics may be able to measure their own responses to various foods and work out the trade-offs for their own individualized diets. As scientists and doctors come to understand more about how different foods affect blood glucose, they can start to make life even more normal and pleasurable for people with diabetes.

THE BOTTOM LINE: ESSENTIALS OF PREVENTION AND TREATMENT

For insulin-dependent (juvenile-onset) diabetes, no preventive measures are possible. Although this form of the disease is somewhat less heritable than non-insulin-dependent (adult-onset) diabetes, it is still strongly influenced by genetics, and there appears to be no way of averting the infections that seem to trigger onset. Treatment invariably includes supplementary insulin and careful balancing of insulin intake with consumption of carbohydrates (both simple and complex).

For non-insulin-dependent diabetes, weight control is the sole preventive measure (although this may be difficult to achieve, for an inherited vulnerability to the disease is usually accompanied by a similar vulnerability to obesity). Early diagnosis is vital, so blood glucose levels should be checked periodically if there is a family history of diabetes. Weight control is the primary means of treatment as well as prevention (see chapter 11). Even modest weight loss can reverse the course of the disease. Supplementary insulin is rarely required, for the condition can most often be managed by dietary means alone. High-fiber, high-complex-carbohydrate diets are the rule, and diet management may be aided by use of the glycemic index to help ensure that blood glucose levels remain stable.

CHAPTER 21

Deficiency Diseases of Today: Anemia and Osteoporosis

R EMEMBER WHAT MAKES a nutrient essential: the body must have it to survive. To miss out on any one essential nutrient will lead eventually to disease or dysfunction and ultimately to death. In some cases, the lack of a particular nutrient causes a specific and unique set of symptoms, and it is these disorders that we call deficiency diseases.

Medical science has been dealing with deficiency diseases for centuries, long before anyone had a clue to what caused them. Although doctors realized fairly early on that citrus fruits could prevent scurvy, they struggled for centuries to understand how to protect patients from rickets, pellagra, or pernicious anemia. Today, the nutritional causes of these diseases and such other classic deficiency diseases as beriberi and goiter are no longer a mystery. Nevertheless, we have not been able to eliminate them all.

Rickets remains a public health problem even in Britain, for milk there is not routinely fortified with vitamin D. More than 200 million people today have the bulging thyroid gland of goiter, the characteristic symptom of iodine deficiency, and a good many of them are in industrialized countries. Nor is pellagra an affliction of the past, for it is still prevalent in several countries where corn provides a major part of daily energy needs.

DEFICIENCIES AND DISEASES OF TODAY

For people living in the United States, however, yesterday's "diseases of ignorance" now pose little threat. Nor are we at risk of the "diseases of want" that ravage populations in famine-stricken Third

World lands.

But there are modern deficiencies and deficiency diseases, like iron-deficiency anemia and osteoporosis, from which our medical science, industrialized society, and sophisticated economy do not protect us. An abundant food supply and a hefty per capita income don't prevent us from shortchanging ourselves on several of the nutrients our bodies most need: iron, zinc, and calcium, vitamins A, B_6, and C, thiamin, and riboflavin.

Low levels of these do not necessarily bring on specific deficiency diseases. For example, a lack of vitamin B_6 can lead to a number of conditions, including anemia, kidney stones, and convulsions. But there is no specific, distinctive, and unique set of symptoms associated with B_6 deficiency — nothing you could really call a B_6-deficiency disease.

What's more, deficiencies can affect health and behavior even when they're not severe enough to cause clinical symptoms. Few Americans are likely to be so short on B_6 that they go into convulsions, but many may suffer in more subtle ways.

Think of deficiencies as progressing through four stages. First, there is simply the reduction of bodily levels of a nutrient, often measurable in blood, tissues, or bone. At this point, the shortage may have no effect at all on fitness or health.

But at the second stage it does have such an effect, for the deficiency now influences one bodily function or another. It may reduce production of red blood cells or collagen, lower activity of enzymes, lower hormone levels, or slow down the conversion of bodily fuels to energy. Still, second-stage effects are far from dramatic and generally go unnoticed.

At stage three, however, deficiencies can begin to do real damage. Because so many nutrients are involved in sustaining growth or maintaining the immune system, third-stage deficiencies often become apparent when they impede growth or reduce immunity. They can also make themselves evident by diminishing the body's ability to deal with stress — injury, infection, exhaustion, or extreme temperatures. Finally, at stage four, deficiencies reach the level of true disease. And from there further deprivation becomes life-threatening.

A good number of children in the United States have third-stage zinc deficiencies, enough to keep them from reaching their full growth potential. These youngsters generally have fairly peculiar eating habits and little appetite. However, loss of appetite is more likely to be the *result* of low zinc levels in the blood than the cause (see chapter 7), and it will come back to normal when zinc levels rise.

While it would certainly be helpful to pick up on zinc deficiencies in children before they reached the growth-arresting stage, moderate deficiencies of the mineral are hard to detect. Present tests can effectively measure only fairly extreme deficiencies of zinc. Indeed, testing for most nutritional deficiencies is still a fairly complicated, costly, and far from precise practice (see "Department of False Hopes: Testing for Deficiencies," pages 258–259).

For iron, however, considerably more sensitive tests are available. A shortage of iron can be detected at any stage. And it is often found, for lack of adequate iron is today's most common nutritional deficiency.

IRON DEFICIENCY

At the start of 1983, Alberto Salazar was a marathon champion and one of the fastest long-distance runners in the world. That March he ran in Phoenix, Arizona, expecting to break his own 10,000-meter world record. He didn't. He finished eighth. When the race was over, he told a national television audience how he hadn't slept well in over a year, was listless and irritable, and could barely keep up with the demands of his training schedule.

What had slowed Salazar down was today's most common dietary deficiency. He wasn't getting enough iron. Once he did, he was back on track, running well enough to make the 1984 U.S. Olympic team.

Although runners and other competitive athletes do have a somewhat greater need for iron than more sedentary types, Salazar's problem appeared to be purely of dietary origin. He was going through heavy training on a largely vegetarian, low-meat diet. What makes Salazar's experience so interesting is the devastating impact the deficiency had on his performance, even though it had not reached disease level.

About half a billion people in the world now suffer from iron deficiency, and the great majority of them are in worse shape than Salazar was, for their deficiencies have progressed to iron-deficiency anemia. This, the most widespread of modern deficiency diseases, is prevalent in both industrialized and developing nations. Its victims are most often infants, adolescents in early puberty, and women between the ages of 15 and 50.

In the United States, iron-deficiency anemia is far from rare. By conservative estimates, 15 percent of American women, infants, and adolescents, and 5 percent of American men are overtly iron deficient. This means that they meet the clinical criteria for iron-deficiency anemia.

Iron equals energy. It is essential for the enzymes of respiration and oxidation, the mechanisms that allow us to burn fuel. And it is iron that shuttles oxygen through the bloodstream to individual cells, so that muscles and organs get all they need to produce energy. Healthy men usually carry around about 4 grams of iron, healthy women about 2.5 grams. Most of it is in hemoglobin, the protein-and-iron oxygen carrier that fills red blood cells and gives blood its color.

There are literally billions of red blood cells in the body (about 5 million in each cubic millimeter of blood), and the turnover is substantial. The body continually replaces red blood cells, generating a full set of new ones about three times a year. Replacement cells are produced in bone marrow, and damaged or defective cells are salvaged in the spleen. There, just about every bit of iron is saved and recycled, for the body parts with iron grudgingly, giving up little in sweat and urine, less in hair and nails.

Since the body is unable to manufacture iron for itself, every milligram that is lost must be replaced. If it is not — and if the body's reserves are exhausted — then production of hemoglobin starts to decline. It is the drop in hemoglobin that causes anemia, for soon there is not enough hemoglobin to equip new red cells properly. Lacking adequate hemoglobin, the new cells are neither as red nor as large as normal, and they are unable to move as much oxygen, so less oxygen reaches muscles and organs. The result is loss of energy and appetite, weakness and fatigue, shortness of breath and a rapid heartbeat. Physical and intellectual productivity declines and bodily functions slow down.

All anemias lower the hemoglobin content of the blood, so the symptoms of iron-deficiency anemia are no different from the symptoms of other anemias. If you are feeling weak and lethargic, it may not be iron

---

DEPARTMENT OF FALSE HOPES: TESTING FOR DEFICIENCIES

Despite the widespread concern about nutrient deficiencies, there is still no simple way to detect them (although keeping a food diary can let you know if you are likely to be at risk). In principle, blood levels of every essential vitamin and mineral can now be measured accurately, when there's a clinical reason to do so. But many tests are expensive and involve the use of elaborate technology. All require blood samples and can generally be done only in clinical laboratories at a doctor's request. The much-touted shortcuts to nutrient measurement are all but useless when it comes to determining an individual's nutrient needs.

Even measuring iron — the most abundant trace element in the body, and the one we are most likely to lack — requires four different tests for an accurate diagnosis of deficiency. The cheapest and fastest measures circulating hemoglobin. But even if hemoglobin is low, that only establishes anemia, not necessarily iron deficiency as the cause (see "The Different Anemias," page 260). The next diagnostic step is to measure the actual amount of iron in blood serum. Then comes a test of iron-binding capacity, measuring blood levels of transferrin, the protein that binds iron and takes it from the intestine into the bloodstream and the cells. Finally, to get a full picture of iron status, it's necessary to measure the amount of ferritin (the protein package in which iron is stored) circulating in the blood.

Sometimes blood levels of a nutrient, however they're measured, are virtually irrelevant to the question of deficiency. Measuring the amount of calcium in the blood, for example, will tell you nothing about whether the bones have

you are lacking, but folacin, riboflavin, B$_6$ or even B$_{12}$ (see "The Different Anemias," page 260).

You're unlikely to have any kind of clinically definable anemia at all unless your symptoms are truly severe, in which case you'd best let your doctor make the diagnosis. But low energy can signal a developing deficiency.

Before an iron deficiency gets started, however, the body must use up its stock of stored iron in the liver, spleen, and bone marrow. When this occurs, blood levels of ferritin (stored iron, packed in protein) begin to fall. Next, the amount of ready-to-use iron in the blood (in protein carriers called transferrin) falls below the normal range as well. At this point, an iron deficiency exists, although it may not be severe enough to cause anemia. But should iron loss continue, the disease would develop in several weeks.

Long before anemia develops, the body starts paying penalties for not replacing lost iron. To compensate for the reduced capacity of its oxygen transportation system, it makes greater demands on other systems. The heart, for example, must pump harder to move red cells

---

enough. The body usually regulates its blood calcium levels very precisely; if you're not getting enough of the mineral, the deficiency will show up in your bones, which will surrender their calcium to the blood.

Offering a cheap and simple shortcut to detecting deficiencies are entrepreneurs who promise they can do it just by analyzing a lock of your hair. But although hair analysis does have some legitimate use — primarily in studies of large populations, where the numbers involved make up for the inaccuracy of the method — it cannot give an accurate picture of individual nutritional status. To begin with, hair grows slowly, so it doesn't directly reflect your status at any one time — just over a period of time. And although it may tell you something about your mineral levels, there are no vitamins in hair (except at the root).

The methods used to analyze hair are insensitive and often inaccurate, particularly when analysis is performed in commercial laboratories. In a survey reported in the *Journal of the American Medical Association*, hair samples from two healthy 17-year-old girls were sent to 13 different laboratories. Each sent back a very different analysis of hair from the same girl; mineral levels reported by some were 10 times higher than those found by others.

The labs also sent back computer-generated reports warning these girls that they might suffer from hypoglycemia, goiter, headaches, or a "critical tendency" toward emotional problems. Not surprisingly, half the laboratories prescribed nutritional supplements — as many as 46 doses a day.

Hair analysis laboratories claim they can detect not only deficiencies but toxic levels of some minerals as well. But here another kind of inaccuracy enters the picture. Hair is easily contaminated by the environment. So any number of factors — using a certain shampoo or hair dye, combing your hair with an aluminum comb, walking around Los Angeles during a smog alert — can add minerals to your hair that will trigger a toxicity warning.

through the bloodstream more rapidly. As a result the body is less able to handle stress and responds more slowly and less efficiently to heat or cold, injury, or infection.

Easier to measure is the decline in performance. You simply cannot work as well when there is any appreciable drop in hemoglobin. Indeed, there is a linear relation between hemoglobin and productivity: if hemoglobin is reduced by 10 percent, not only heavy labor but any kind of physical activity will decrease proportionately. If hemoglobin is increased, the amount of work or exercise you can do will increase a like

THE DIFFERENT ANEMIAS

Ultimately, all anemias do the same thing — they reduce the amount of hemoglobin in red blood cells, primarily by blocking the production of this complex molecule in various ways.

The hemoglobin molecule is made up of four large proteins bound together. Within each protein sits a heme group — a ring-shaped molecule containing a single iron atom — and each iron atom can carry a single molecule of oxygen.

Iron deficiency is the most common cause of anemia. The reason is simple: iron atoms are the essential elements of the heme groups.

Copper deficiency also causes anemia, because copper is necessary to move iron atoms into heme groups.

Vitamin B$_{12}$ and folic acid are required for the synthesis of nucleic acids (DNA and RNA), which in turn guide the synthesis of proteins. Since large amounts of hemoglobin are constantly being produced (in order to meet the demands of red cell replacement), deficiencies of these vitamins are often first evidenced by the falloff of hemoglobin production.

Starvation and protein deficiency drain the body of the amino acids necessary to make the proteins of hemoglobin.

Vitamin C plays a vital role in transporting iron from the digestive tract into the bloodstream; thus, scurvy can cause anemia. **Vitamin B$_6$, riboflavin,** and **vitamin D** help govern other essential parts of hemoglobin synthesis, and their absence can cause anemia.

Genetic abnormalities can lead to faulty hemoglobin structure, compromising its oxygen-carrying capacity. For example, **favism**, a genetic vulnerability to a toxin in the fava bean, blocks an enzyme that keeps hemoglobin's iron chemically active.

Sickle-cell anemia results from a single mutation in the gene that produces two of the four proteins in hemoglobin. It changes the hemoglobin molecule so that it bends the entire red cell into a sickle shape, which clogs the capillaries. The genetic disease called **beta-thalassemia** limits production of hemoglobin proteins to a single form (there are normally two forms of these proteins). As a result, hemoglobin function is severely reduced.

Finally, environmental toxins can lead to anemia in several different ways. **Lead** interferes with production of heme; **nickel** and **zinc** can keep iron from being incorporated into the heme group. And **radiation** and **organic solvents** (like benzene) damage the bone marrow, where red cells originate.

amount.

Bicycle racers know this, which is why "blood doping" became such a common practice in the sport. To increase energy and endurance by raising the hemoglobin in their blood, bikers would inject their own (or a compatible donor's) red cells just before a race.

Intellectual activity also falls off when an iron deficiency exists, even if it's not at the level of anemia. Schoolchildren will not learn as much or as rapidly as they should. The problem may be caused not only by lowered hemoglobin but also by lack of iron to resupply neurotransmitters in the brain. Studies of schoolchildren have shown that iron supplements will improve the academic performance of iron-deficient youngsters.

For a deficiency to exist, the body must lose iron that it does not replace or need extra iron that it does not get. Since the body voluntarily surrenders so little, the only substantial amounts of iron to leave do so in blood. The 15–20 milligrams of iron that women lose when they menstruate amounts to between one half and two thirds of what is likely to be lost each month in other ways. This makes it necessary for women who menstruate to replace twice as much iron as men.

Women generally need about 1.5 milligrams of iron per day, which is supplied by about 18 milligrams in the diet (only one tenth of the iron in our food or in supplements is actually absorbed). But when a woman becomes pregnant, her iron needs can increase by more than 300 percent (see chapter 23).

Children of mothers who get enough iron during pregnancy generally come into the world with almost all the iron they will need until they double their birth weight. After that point, they must increase supplies for their rapidly growing bodies. Mother's milk will meet these needs until babies start on iron-fortified cereal when they are three to six months old. But when infants aren't breast-fed, they need an iron-fortified formula, for cow's milk alone will not give them the iron their bodies require.

How then did small children survive before the era of fortified baby foods? Mostly, they did it by scrambling around in the dirt and picking up there whatever it was they needed in the way of iron and other trace elements. They picked up a good many diseases and infections as well. So, on balance, sanitation plus fortification is probably a better answer.

Older children, eating a normally nutritious diet, generally have no special need for extra iron. But iron demand rises in early puberty, and with it rises the risk of iron deficiency. The period of accelerated growth that most children experience between ages 9 and 13 requires an increase in the body's iron supply. This is true for both boys and girls. The iron needs of boys, however, will decline in later adolescence, while the needs of girls will remain high after the onset of menstruation.

Americans in general, both men and women, rarely get all the iron they can effectively use. Nearly 60 percent of the population lives on diets that fall short of recommended levels.

Red meat (organ meats like liver, in particular), fish, and poultry are the best sources of iron. They provide heme iron, which the body absorbs about three times more readily than any other form and about six times more readily than the iron in such good vegetable sources as spinach and other green leafy vegetables. Indeed, you can wreck your digestive system trying to get all the iron you need from vegetables alone. But you can add a good deal to your diet with no increase in calories simply by cooking in old-fashioned cast-iron pots.

Certain foods aid the absorption of iron, while others inhibit it. Vitamin C is a big help. But that doesn't mean you must serve your roast with orange juice. You can do as well with mustard or collard greens, kale or even broccoli (which is not an adequate sole source for iron but is great for vitamin C). Meat is not only a first-rate source of iron itself but it will also aid absorption of iron from less satisfactory sources. Sugars will enhance absorption, but whole grains are likely to reduce it, because of both the fiber and phytic acid they contain. The tannins in tea will also inhibit iron absorption and, to a lesser extent, so will coffee.

It is probably unrealistic to expect most women or adolescents to make the dietary changes that will give them the added iron they need, and it is difficult for pregnant women, no matter how willing they may be to alter their diets, to meet their daily iron requirements without supplements. Extra iron, in the form of ferrous sulfate, should probably be the rule for pregnant women, women on diets, and children aged 9–13.

But with iron, as with other trace elements, unbalanced supplementation of one mineral can block the absorption of others. You may supplement with iron alone, as long as you don't do it at mealtimes, when a heavy dose of iron is likely to inhibit absorption of zinc (and this could cause serious problems for pregnant women). If you want to take your supplement at mealtimes, then choose a balanced multimineral formula that will provide extra zinc as well as extra iron.

Since iron deficiencies are so common, even among groups not considered at high risk, there is a good case to be made for the fortification of additional foods. At present, white flour, bread, and breakfast cereals are all fortified with extra iron, and they provide most Americans with about one quarter of their daily iron needs. What else might we fortify? Well, experiments in Latin America have shown that milk is a good fortifiable food (not only for iron but for copper and manganese as well), and in the Scandinavian countries, sausage and other preserved meats are now being fortified.

Would additional fortification place those of us who eat nourishing and iron-rich meals at risk of iron overload? This might be a serious question if the body did not protect itself from iron's toxicity (as described in chapter 7). Reluctant as the body is to give up iron, it is just as reluctant to accept more than it needs. Iron absorption pretty much matches iron loss. Except for women near the end of pregnancy and individuals with a genetic susceptibility to iron overload, absorption generally will not exceed 3.5 milligrams per day, even when iron reserves are exhausted. And most often the body will accept far less.

OSTEOPOROSIS

Like iron-deficiency anemia, osteoporosis is not newly arrived on the scene. But both diseases have stuck with us, while others were overcome, and they are today the most prevalent deficiency diseases in countries like the United States — modern, industrial countries where food supplies are abundant and adequate medical care is generally available to the entire population.

Osteoporosis ("porous bones") is the result of progressive deterioration of bone over time. For many victims, bones can be so weakened that they will literally crack under the strain of the weight they carry. The disease now afflicts between 15 and 20 million Americans and is responsible for more than a million fractured wrists, hips, and spines every year.

Generally, osteoporosis strikes the porous bone found in the spinal column and at the ends of the long bones in arms and legs; it can strike suddenly, often with no warning discomfort. The spinal column may begin to collapse, and some older women suffer a series of small fractures that can reduce their height by as much as 2 inches in only a matter of weeks. Deformities like "widow's hump" develop as the spine gives way. Hip fractures too are common, usually at the joint that links hip to pelvis. And when it is the hip that gives way, resulting complications can prove fatal as often as 30 percent of the time.

To understand the disease, it's important to realize that bones are not inert. They are living tissue, and the body is constantly rebuilding and replacing them (see the section on calcium in chapter 6). In addition, the body uses bones to store extra calcium, much as it uses the liver and spleen to store extra iron. When calcium levels in the blood drop so low that there may not be enough to do the mineral's other important jobs — regulating fluid levels, transmitting nerve impulses, powering muscle contractions — then the body draws on the calcium reserves in bone.

During the growth years and well into adulthood, bone will normally build up rapidly enough to exceed any resorption (withdrawal of calcium from bone) that might occur. Bones not only become larger but also heavier and denser. But by age 35 most adults have about as much bone mass as they ever will. This is the point at which resorption catches up with replacement. And from here on, bones lose density, becoming progressively lighter and weaker.

Men, who have about 30 percent more bone mass than women, develop osteoporosis later in life than women do. Even then, the disease seldom strikes them as severely, because their bodies remain more capable of limiting calcium loss than the bodies of women do. Women suffer the sudden loss of estrogen that accompanies menopause. A falling level of estrogen accelerates bone loss, because the hormone is so intimately involved in the complicated system the body uses to regulate levels of calcium in the blood.

Osteoporosis, however, is not exclusively a disease of age. A number of young women — far from menopausal — are stricken each year. Almost invariably, they are long-distance runners, gymnasts, dancers, or anorexic women who carry dieting to the point of emaciation. What these women have in common is very little body fat, irregular menstruation, and low levels of estrogen.

Heredity clearly has a significant influence on the development of osteoporosis. Black women, for example, have greater bone density than white women, for reasons that have nothing to do with either diet or exercise. Thus, even though the bones of white women and black women deteriorate at pretty much the same rate, black women are stricken by osteoporosis far less often and usually later in life. Most vulnerable to the disease are small-boned, fair-skinned women of northern European descent.

Osteoporosis is plainly a disease of calcium deficiency. But dietary calcium, even in extraordinary doses, is not enough either to prevent the disease or to cure it. The body not only must get enough calcium, it must be able to retain it and use it to strengthen bones as well. To do this, the body must also have estrogen, exercise, and certain other nutrients (vitamin D, copper, zinc, and manganese).

To reduce risk of osteoporosis, it's best to begin early, by building up bone mass during the bone-building years and sustaining it with enough calcium, other nutrients, and exercise. You're not going to make bones bigger between ages 20 and 35, but you can make them stronger, increasing density by about 10 percent. After age 35, however, the goal is to keep calcium loss to the irreducible minimum. But whatever strategy is appropriate for you — building, strengthening, or preserving bone — it starts with calcium.

Calcium

The RDA for calcium — 1,200 milligrams for adolescents, 800 milligrams for adults — is generally all you need. Extra calcium isn't likely to provide any extra protection, except for older men and women who have already experienced considerable bone loss. For them, the adolescent RDA of 1,200 milligrams is a more prudent daily allowance than the adult level of 800.

However, the three cups of milk or 4 ounces of cheese it takes to get an adult's 800 milligrams is a lot more milk or cheese than most people may want in a day (even if it's skim or low-fat milk). But other dietary sources (with the exception of fish like salmon and sardines, canned with bones intact) aren't likely to provide more than a fraction of daily calcium needs.

It's hard for adolescents to meet the calcium RDA, and harder for adults, who tend to ignore many dairy products or actively to avoid them, because they are watching calories or are lactose-intolerant. For whatever reasons, most adult Americans are only getting about half enough dietary calcium, and they aren't necessarily absorbing all they should of this.

Fiber blocks absorption of calcium, particularly fiber with phytic acid (you'll find it in wheat bran, nuts, seeds, and beans). Oxalic acid, though not as potent, will also reduce absorption (it's in spinach, chocolate, rhubarb, and almonds). These interactions are significant for people on high-cereal diets, whose calcium intake is generally low.

Then there are drugs that interfere with calcium absorption, including antacids containing aluminum or magnesium. Magnesium competes with calcium for transportation out of the small intestine and into the bloodstream. As long as there is a balanced amount of both minerals (half as much magnesium as calcium) in the digestive tract, an adequate amount of both will get through. But an excessive amount of one will inhibit transport of the other. So calcium carbonate antacids are a better bet when it comes to preventing osteoporosis, for they are a good source of supplemental calcium. However, prolonged use of the antibiotics erythromycin and tetracycline will interfere with calcium uptake, and so will use of certain laxatives and diuretics.

If you drink more than moderately, alcohol will block calcium uptake. And while caffeine doesn't interfere with absorption, the diuretic effect of more than five cups of coffee a day will cause you to lose too much in the urine. Too much salt in your diet will have the same effect. When the kidneys have to dump excess sodium, they are unable to reclaim the calcium the body may need.

All things considered, most women are not going to get as much calcium as they need unless they use supplements. Calcium carbonate provides calcium in its most usable form, and supplements are best taken in several small doses throughout the day rather than in one giant dose. Although calcium supplements raise the risk of kidney stones, the increased danger is minimal if you are getting enough water or other fluids and have no genetic vulnerability.

You'd be wise to be wary of the bone meal (pulverized animal bones) and dolomite pills that many health-food stores carry, for both may contain lead and other toxic metals in addition to calcium. Not long ago the FDA found concentrations of lead in a 40-brand sampling of bone meal running as high as 13 parts per million.

The food industry hasn't ignored the nation's new calcium

consciousness. Any number of products are now being fortified with calcium — flour, breakfast cereal, bread, and even dairy foods like milk, yogurt, and milk powder. There's a calcium-fortified diet cola now being test marketed for the calorie-conscious, and even orange juice with as much calcium, glass for glass, as milk.

Taking calcium supplements at mealtimes, however, can cause problems. Calcium itself then becomes the big bad blocking agent and can deprive you of zinc, copper, iron, and magnesium. So it's best to take your calcium supplements between meals, with a bit of milk or yogurt to boost absorption, and to reserve calcium-fortified foods for snacks.

Estrogen

What makes estrogen essential to the prevention of osteoporosis is its key role in regulating blood levels of calcium. Estrogen is a major player in two processes that limit calcium loss. The first occurs when blood levels of calcium fall, and it causes the body to retrieve escaping calcium and increase calcium uptake. The second occurs when blood levels are too high, and it causes the body to stash away some of the excess calcium in bone.

When blood calcium levels drop, the body converts a placid form of vitamin D, called calcidiol, into the aggressive hormone calcitriol. It is estrogen that stimulates this conversion. Calcitriol then helps halt the release of calcium in urine and boosts absorption of calcium in the intestine.

When blood levels of calcium are too high, the second process begins. Now estrogen stimulates production of the hormone calcitonin, which raises the rate at which the body stores calcium in bone.

This complex system starts to deteriorate when estrogen levels fall. Low estrogen means low calcitriol, so the body is less able to prevent calcium loss and must draw more calcium from bone. Low estrogen means low calcitonin as well, so the body can replace less of the calcium it resorbs. As a result, bone loss increases rapidly after menopause. Most women start losing at a rate of about 1.5 percent a year.

Because loss of estrogen is primarily responsible for the devastating effect of osteoporosis on so many older women, the most direct means of countering the disease at this point is by replacing the missing hormone. And replacing missing estrogen — as long as calcium intake is high and none of the other necessary nutrients are lacking — can retard bone loss, even if it is begun well after menopause. A University of Southern California study indicates that the use of replacement estrogen can reduce osteoporosis-related fatalities by more than 40 percent.

There was some initial reluctance to prescribe estrogen, however, after early studies suggested that replacement estrogen could raise the risk of cancer. But most doctors believe the forms of estrogen now available are safe. Estrogen is at present given at only 10 percent of the original strength and balanced with a second hormone, progesterone. New techniques are also being developed and tested to further reduce the danger. Estrogen patches, for example, release the hormone directly to the bloodstream. By avoiding the liver (the route estrogen pills must take), the patches can use much lower doses to raise blood levels.

The treatment of the future is likely to involve not only estrogen but a form of the vitamin D hormone calcitriol as well. Since the kidneys become less able to produce this hormone as the body ages, replacing estrogen is not always enough to get the calcium-regulating system operating efficiently again. Studies at the Mayo Clinic have shown that use of hormonal D not only increases the body's ability to preserve and absorb calcium but does it particularly well *after* the first 10 years of menopause.

Other Nutrients

The importance of vitamin D should be evident. Not only is the vital calcium-regulating agent calcitriol a vitamin D hormone but the vitamin itself regulates transport of calcium from the digestive tract to the bloodstream. Furthermore, calcium isn't likely to do a very effective job of building bone or strengthening it if there isn't an adequate amount of vitamin D at the construction site.

If you're getting all the calcium you need from fortified milk, then you have no need to worry about running short of vitamin D. But if you're not drinking much milk, sunlight is a good source. (It acts on fatty deposits in the skin to produce vitamin D_3, an inactive form that's ultimately turned into calcitriol.) For pale, fast-burning skin, just five minutes of summer midday sun on the face, hands, and arms three times a week is enough. Get these short doses before you put on sunscreen or sunblock; and if your skin is darker, stay in the sun a little longer. *No* amount of exposure to winter sun in most northern states will produce much vitamin D, no matter how sensitive your skin. However, there are full-spectrum fluorescent lights that can trigger release of the vitamin.

For some people, however, vitamin D supplements may well be needed, particularly older men and women who drink little milk and spend little time in the sunlight. A Boston hospital study has found that 80-year-olds generally get between one third and one half the amount of vitamin D_3 that 20-year-olds get.

Although deficiencies of bone-building macrominerals other than calcium are rare, a shortage of necessary trace elements is not uncommon. Remember, what caused basketball star Bill Walton to suffer frequent fractures was a condition much like osteoporosis, and it was caused by insufficient blood levels of manganese, copper, and zinc. You will find these minerals in milk (along with calcium and vitamin D), but meat and fish are generally richer sources.

There is a role for fluoride in the treatment of osteoporosis, for it has caused bone thickening among older residents in areas where the water is naturally rich in this mineral. So the use of fluoridated water (at one part per million) can help prevent the disease. Side effects make use of more potent fluoride supplements a relatively high-risk intervention. Nevertheless, British studies have shown that (when taken with adequate amounts of calcium) they can reduce the incidence of bone fractures among women already stricken by osteoporosis.

Exercise

Exercise will build bone as well as muscle. The kidneys, which regulate how much calcium is recirculated and how much is released in urine, become reluctant to let calcium go when you are active, and the body responds to exercise by increasing bone density. A University of North Carolina study of 500 women (ages 25–70) showed that those who exercised twice a week had denser bones than those who exercised once a week, and the latter had denser bones than those who never exercised at all.

The reverse is also true. Lack of exercise will reduce bone density. This can be seen in the calcium loss of the sedentary elderly or of patients who require extended bed rest. Astronauts working in gravityless space also lose bone mass. Among Soviet astronauts, who have experienced weightlessness for much longer periods than Americans, bone loss has proved irreversible. Astronauts on the Gemini flights lost a significant amount of bone minerals in just five days of weightlessness. The crew of Gemini VII, however, who performed isotonic exercises during that flight, lost less than others.

While exercise is important to bone strength, not all exercises are equal. The best aid in preventing osteoporosis is weight-bearing exercise, the kind that forces the body to work against gravity. In addition to the general effect of exercise on calcium retention, weight-bearing exercise has specific effects on bones. Stress a bone by putting weight on it and it gets stronger, and bones that are most stressed become strongest. Tennis players, for example, have stronger bones in their playing arms than in their nonplaying arms. And overweight women probably reduce the risk of osteoporosis because they stress their bones more.

Although swimming is generally good exercise, it's not the best for bone building, since it buffers the body against gravity's pull. But simple walking can be highly effective.

THE BOTTOM LINE: ESSENTIALS OF PREVENTION AND TREATMENT

To avoid iron deficiency, your diet should include enough red meat — one-quarter pound per day — or the equivalent (half as much liver or twice as much chicken or fish). Vegetables alone cannot provide all the iron you are likely to need. But supplements will do the job if your foodstyle restricts natural sources.

To prevent osteoporosis and limit its consequences requires adequate amounts of calcium — RDA levels for adolescents (1,200 milligrams per day) and most adults (800 milligrams per day). For older men and women, however, the adolescent RDA is probably prudent. If you cannot or choose not to get your calcium from dietary sources (primarily dairy products), then calcium carbonate supplements should be taken.

Also needed are recommended levels of vitamin D, manganese, copper, and zinc. The use of fluoridated water will promote greater bone density. But without exercise bones can neither increase density nor sustain it. For women past menopause, dietary strategies and exercise are unlikely to prove effective in limiting bone loss without replacement estrogen therapy.

CHAPTER 22

Eating When Ill

D IET HAS A PROFOUND effect on health, and there are connections, both clear-cut and less obvious, between diet and a great many disorders. But what role does diet play when illness is *not* the result of nutrition?

Until quite recently, medical science had few answers to this question. There was, of course, the cultural imperative (stronger in some cultures than in others) to ply the ailing with chicken soup. But, beyond this, little conventional wisdom existed, save for the grandmotherly injunction to "starve a fever and feed a cold."

Grandma, it turns out, was on to a good thing, and doctors are just getting around to figuring out what it is. She wasn't denying the feverish any food they wanted, because illness lowers appetite. It now appears that loss of appetite is how the body signals its reluctance to accept nutrition when it is involved in controlling an acute infection.

Since fever speeds up metabolism, burns calories and proteins, and depletes vitamins and minerals, you might think that the body should be signaling frantically to be resupplied. But the body, an infinitely resourceful organism, is up to something far more clever than we may realize. It can starve the invaders — bacteria, in particular — by denying them the vitamins and minerals they need to survive. Not only does the body reduce appetite but it also withdraws iron, zinc, and other nutrients from the bloodstream and stashes them away, usually in the liver.

Before this phenomenon was understood, doctors who noticed rapidly falling blood levels of vitamin A often prescribed supplements. But vitamin A had not left the body. It was merely hiding until the infection subsided. When it did and the fever fell, vitamin A came out of hiding. In a number of cases, where heavy supplementation had been prescribed, patients survived the infection only to suffer vitamin A toxicity.

Normal well-nourished adults aged 18–45 can deal with the nutritional depletion that a serious infection may cause. But after five days or a weight loss of 5 percent it's time to overrule appetite. A vitamin and mineral supplement may be all that's necessary at this point, but doctors or dietitians may also recommend special milklike fortified formulas designed specifically for people whose nutritional needs exceed their appetites. Growing children also may need protein supplements during a prolonged illness.

When the fever breaks, it's time to load up and replace those missing nutrients, starting with water. An essential nutrient, it's the most important one lost during fever. For patients who are "sitting up and taking nourishment," both doctors and nutritionists recommend plenty of fruit juices — citrus juices, in particular — since these are loaded with some of the vitamins and with the potassium that must be replaced. Other recommendations for the sickroom menu include grapes and other juicy fruits, milk shakes, whole grain breads, and broth.

The combination of poor appetite and the unappealing nature of

---

CAN NUTRIENTS FIGHT A COLD?

A common response to a cold these days is to take vitamin C — by the gram. Now some people are trying zinc tablets, too, while others rely on traditional staples, from chicken soup to spicy foods. But can any of these home remedies really help?

Vitamin C got its biggest boost in 1970, when Linus Pauling published *Vitamin C and the Common Cold.* When he and his wife took megadoses of vitamin C, he wrote, they became aware of "an increased feeling of well-being, and, especially, a striking decrease in the number of colds and their severity." Pauling recommended preventive doses of up to 10 grams (10,000 milligrams) per day, more than 150 times the RDA.

By now, more than 20 experimental tests have shown that these doses do virtually nothing to reduce the number of colds people get. There is some evidence, however, that taking vitamin C during a cold may help reduce its severity, but a single 60-milligram dose (the RDA) is just as effective as a much higher one. In other words, people who are low in vitamin C might take a supplement for the sniffles; others probably needn't bother.

For zinc, the story is much the same. A mild zinc deficiency may impair the immune system and make it harder to fight a cold. But that doesn't mean supplementary doses above the RDA will help normally healthy people recover from colds more quickly.

Some folk wisdom on feeding a cold, however, may actually be on the mark. Hot, spicy foods like chili peppers, horseradish, pepper, garlic, and Tabasco sauce stimulate the flow of mucus and may help relieve symptoms of asthma, bronchitis, sinusitis, and colds. And a steaming hot bowl of chicken soup could have the same effect.

most hospital food produces a dangerous situation for patients. It is estimated that nationwide between 30 and 50 percent of patients hospitalized two weeks or more may be malnourished. A study at the University of Alabama Medical Center in Birmingham found malnourished patients three times more likely than normally nourished patients to die during their hospital stay. It also found that three out of four patients entering the hospital with no signs of malnourishment were likely to leave in worse nutritional shape than they were when they entered.

The Alabama study, published in 1974, sparked a flurry of hospital surveys. They found as many as one quarter of hospital patients so undernourished that it affected their metabolism, and one out of ten were malnourished to such an extent that it dramatically reduced the effectiveness of their treatment. As a result of these and other findings, a growing number of hospitals are now organizing nutritional support teams to oversee patient nutrition.

DIET AND SURGERY

Surgeons were worrying about undernourished patients long before the recent studies of hospital malnutrition. Indeed, early work on total parenteral nutrition (TPN) focused on ways to build up malnourished patients so they could meet the demands of surgery. Clearly, it's best if patients can build themselves up — but not too much. You should enter the hospital for surgery at close to your ideal body weight. Overweight patients have a thick layer of fat that hinders surgery, while underweight patients lack the energy reserves needed to fight infection and promote healing.

Most important, before a hospital stay, is stocking your body with an adequate supply of the vitamins, minerals, and protein it will need to repair tissue and replace blood after surgery. It's worth risking an extra calorie or two to make sure your presurgery diet provides these, for average weight loss after a major operation runs between 10 and 15 percent of total body weight, the result of both trauma and lack of appetite.

The vitamins that have a direct impact on recovery include vitamins A, C, K, and all the B's. Vitamins A and C promote healing, K gets blood to clot more quickly, while riboflavin, niacin, and B_{12} protect against infection by maintaining tissue. Vitamin B_6 and thiamin help form antibodies, and folacin is needed both by the immune system and to build red blood cells. As for minerals, iron is essential for replacing red blood cells, copper is needed to help iron do its job, and zinc beefs up the immune system and helps replace tissue.

FOOD AND DRUGS

Food doesn't interfere all that much with the absorption of most common prescription drugs from the digestive tract into the blood-stream. Major exceptions are tetracycline and other broad-spectrum anti-biotics. Calcium, iron, and zinc will interfere with absorption of these drugs. That means no milk or meat within a half hour before taking the drugs or for two hours after.

Once they're in the bloodstream, however, nutrients and drugs in-teract in many different ways. Riboflavin, for example, seems to lose out to certain psychoactive drugs that have similar chemical structures. These drugs can block receptor sites for riboflavin, those molecules on cell membranes that are designed to react with this B vitamin. The anti-psychotic drug chlorpromazine and the tricylcic antidepressants imip-ramine and amitriptyline are all able to displace riboflavin, and patients taking these drugs should probably take riboflavin supplements as well.

But the most serious problems occur in the liver, for it's the liver's job to detoxify alien substances — drugs as well as contaminants, poi-sons, and other chemicals — and convert them into forms that are easier for the kidneys to dispose of. When liver function is sluggish, drugs travel around in the bloodstream for longer periods of time. If the liver is busy dealing with an overload of alcohol or has been weakened by years of alcohol abuse, then it takes its time getting around to processing any drugs in the system. As a result, drug effects are more potent and last longer.

Recently, research at Rockefeller University in New York has shown that certain substances in food can speed up liver function and rush drugs out of the system before they do their jobs. These substances include protein, chemicals called indoles (found in cabbage, Brussels sprouts, and other cruciferous vegetables), and the hydrocarbons on char-coal-broiled meats. Researchers tested the effects of these substances on three different drugs, theophylline (an asthma medication) and phen-acetin and antipyrine (both fever-reducing drugs that are now off the market but still used in animal experiments). However, it is likely that other drugs too are affected by the same food substances.

THE BOTTOM LINE: BASIC CONCERNS

For a cold or sniffles, megadosing on vitamin C or zinc will not help, but a precautionary supplement at RDA levels will ensure that no mar-ginal deficiencies slow down recovery.

For a fever, don't overrule your appetite and eat more than you feel like eating. Your body may be trying to starve out the invader. So go along up to a point, being certain, however, to get sufficient water or other liquids. After five days or a weight loss of 5 percent, it's time to intervene with a vitamin-mineral supplement or whatever else your doctor recom-mends.

For surgery, substantial bodily reserves are needed. It takes energy to fight infections and promote healing, and weight loss after a major operation (from trauma and loss of appetite) runs an average 10–15 percent of body weight. Most important are substantial reserves of the protein, vitamins, and minerals (notably vitamins A, K, C, all the B's, iron, copper, and zinc) you will need to recover, repair tissue, and replace blood.

PART V

NUTRITIONAL NEEDS THROUGH LIFE

CHAPTER 23

The Pregnancy Diet

GENERALLY, BIGGER IS BETTER — that's the bottom line for babies. It's birth weight that determines what kind of start your infant gets in life, or whether he or she gets any start at all. Although being oversized (above 9 pounds) can increase the dangers of delivery and the chances of lifelong obesity, it is being undersized (below 5.5 pounds) that creates the greatest risks of infancy. Bigger babies stand a better chance of survival than smaller ones. They are less likely to suffer birth defects and more likely to enjoy good health.

Infant mortality is higher in the United States than it is in a good many other industrialized nations — 16 of them do a better job than we do of keeping their newborn children alive. But high mortality rates are found almost exclusively among populations that have a substantial number of underweight infants. Throughout most of the United States infant mortality rates are as low as they are in the Scandinavian countries and Holland, which rank lowest in the world. But in poor inner-city neighborhoods and rural communities, they can be as high as they are in parts of the Third World.

The reason is not just poor access to medical care but poor nutrition. A recent federal study of the government's WIC (Women, Infants and Children) program provided a dramatic example of the impact that diet has on birth weight, and that birth weight has on survival. Among the 3 million participants in the program (which improves diets by providing selected foods to pregnant women, infants, and children) fetal deaths fell by one third and premature births by as much as 25 percent.

Nutritionists have ample evidence of how important a proper diet is to low infant mortality and good infant health, but they have less evidence of how well diet can help prevent premature births. While some studies appear to confirm a connection between maternal nourishment and prematurity, others have found no significant linkage.

What no one questions is the relation between maternal nourishment and infant weight. Obstetricians were well aware of this even at the turn of the century. But in those days they intentionally undernourished mothers in order to keep their infants small. Maternal mortality was then a greater threat than infant mortality, and large babies increased the risk of delivery, so doctors tried to restrict the growth of the fetus.

Today, when the goal is bigger babies, obstetricians encourage bigger mothers as well. How much bigger? Figure a 20 percent increase in weight during pregnancy (which for most women means an additional 25–30 pounds) if you are at your ideal body weight when you become pregnant. If you are underweight at the time of conception, you'll need to put on even more extra pounds. If you are substantially overweight, your infant won't suffer if you gain somewhat less. But even if you start pregnancy at 20 percent over the ideal, you should still count on adding another 15 pounds.

Clearly, pregnancy is no time to go on a diet. In fact, a woman who's planning to conceive would do well to reach optimal weight and nutritional status before becoming pregnant.

Both the weight at which a woman enters pregnancy and the weight she gains during it are important. The mother is the source of all the bodily materials that are needed both for the unborn child and for the elaborate system that sustains the fetus until birth. To a great extent, the well-being of her infant depends upon how nutritionally well supplied her body is when she enters pregnancy.

But — and doctors have only come to realize this in recent years — unborn children cannot make do on their mothers' bodily stores alone. As Dr. Myron Winick, professor of pediatrics and director of the Institute of Human Nutrition at Columbia University, puts it, "The fetus is not the perfect parasite."

The body, let's remember, is a most resourceful organism and a conservative one. It isn't about to put itself at risk for the sake of the fetus. This became clear during World War II, when food supplies to western Holland were cut off, and the caloric level of diets there dropped sharply. Pregnant women, who had been well nourished before the food supply was restricted, nevertheless bore children below average weight.

The body isn't necessarily ignoring the well-being of the fetus when it puts the mother's needs first. It is employing what amounts to biological foresight and recognizing that the fetus, when born, will need mother's milk to survive. By allocating more calories to the mother than to the fetus, the body not only allows her to retain the fat she will need to produce milk but also restricts her infant's size, for a smaller child puts less demand on a nursing mother.

The period of her pregnancy during which a woman puts on her extra pounds is almost as important as how many she adds. She should start out slowly, gaining less weight during the first trimester than during the second, and adding most during the third. Those final three months, when both the fetus and placenta are growing fastest, are when nutritional deficiencies have their greatest impact on infant size.

Where do all these extra pounds go? When a pregnant woman gains 24 pounds, 6–8 go to the baby, 1 to the placenta, and 1.5 to amniotic fluid. The breasts gain 3 pounds and the uterus 2.5. The remaining 8 pounds are found in stored fat and protein, retained water, and an increased blood supply.

Blood supply increases by as much as 40 percent during pregnancy, but not every organ of the body gets the full benefit of this additional flow. Priority goes to the key players in the reproductive process: the uterus, the placenta, and the ovaries. Moving all this extra blood around requires a mother's heart to work harder. Moving her own extra weight around takes more effort too. So pregnancy demands an increase in energy for the mother as well as for the growing fetus and fetal support system.

There is an absolute need for additional calories during pregnancy if the fetus is to develop normally. But the need for other nutrients is less absolute, at least as far as fetal development is concerned. If the mother's body has stashed away enough fats, proteins, vitamins, and minerals — iron, in particular — then it is possible to meet all fetal needs save for calories by tapping these maternal reserves.

If, however, the mother's store of these other nutrients is limited, then the fetus will deplete them without drawing enough to meet its own needs. This leaves both the mother and child in poor nutritional shape. And in those parts of the Third World where diets contain sufficient calories but are low in nutrient density, a woman's health can be imperiled by the repeated depletion that results from bearing several children.

Clearly, no reasonable mother with access to an adequate diet chooses to deplete her own bodily resources to nourish her unborn child. The aim throughout pregnancy is the optimal health of both participants, and this requires more than additional calories alone. For mothers to complete pregnancy successfully — not only by bearing a healthy child of sufficient weight (5.5 pounds or more) but by retaining their own nutrient reserves and sustaining them through breast-feeding — they must have a greater supply of several nutrients than most mothers are likely to get through diet alone. Research has pointed out a need to supplement some of these, and a woman may want to start supplementation even before conception (see "A Guide to Supplements During Pregnancy," pages 284–285).

Some researchers have suggested that women naturally develop a taste for the nutrients they need most during pregnancy. They propose, for example, that pica—the practice of eating clay, common among pregnant women in many Third World countries and also in the American South—may help meet an increased need for calcium.

The other view of cravings, however, is that they are shaped more by psychology than by physiology. One theory holds that women learn to hate the foods they happen to consume just before an attack of morning sickness and love the foods they chance to eat when morning sickness is abating. (Presumably they associate those foods with relief from nausea.) Some psychologists have found that women actually have no more food cravings during pregnancy than during other parts of their lives, but pregnancy gives them license to indulge themselves.

In any case, there's no good evidence that a woman's tastes will lead her to eat the foods she needs most for a healthy pregnancy. A pregnant woman's wisest course is to be fully aware of the nutritional necessities of pregnancy and to meet them consciously.

SPECIAL NUTRITIONAL NEEDS

Although nutritionists underline requirements for those nutrients that will prevent the most likely deficiencies, it's important to realize that the need for *all* nutrients increases during pregnancy and remains at pretty much the same level as long as mothers nurse their infants. Even marginal deficiencies during pregnancy can have health consequences for children, so mothers need to get all the nutritional benefit they can out of the extra calories they are adding on at this time. Nutrient density is an important consideration in the pregnancy diet.

Because of new tissue needs—for the uterus as well as the fetus and placenta—additional protein is required. Few women have much trouble picking up the recommended extra 30 grams, which brings their daily allowance up to about 75 grams. This amounts to less than 4 ounces of meat or fish and is well within the range of what most women in the United States eat whether they are pregnant or not. Even vegetarians—at least those who eat milk and eggs—should have no problem meeting pregnancy's protein needs.

Among the micronutrients, there are five that pregnant women should pay particular attention to—calcium, iron, zinc, folacin, and vitamin B_6—because shortages can cause special problems or because the additional amounts needed during pregnancy are substantially greater than the extra amounts of other micronutrients.

Calcium

Lack of calcium can plague mothers long after pregnancy ends. Most young women in the United States today are not getting enough of the calcium they need—800 milligrams a day, the amount available in a quart of milk or yogurt or a half pound of cottage cheese—to protect themselves from osteoporosis later in life (see chapter 21). During pregnancy the fetus must have calcium to build bones and will draw as much as it can from what is stored in the mother's bones. Doctors used to believe that pregnancy invariably cost mothers some of their stored calcium and reduced their bone mass. As the saying went, "For every child a tooth." What they did not realize is that women can *gain* calcium during pregnancy, because pregnancy doubles their ability to absorb the mineral.

To take advantage of the opportunity pregnancy gives them to build bone mass, women must increase their daily intake of calcium by 50 percent, raising it to about 1,200 milligrams (1.2 grams). While it is possible to get this much calcium from diet alone, most pregnant women will be neither willing nor able to do so. And there is no reason why they cannot supplement their diets with calcium carbonate (an inexpensive and readily absorbed source of nondietary calcium).

Iron

Like calcium, iron is rarely in oversupply. Most women are not getting as much as they need even before pregnancy begins (see chapter 21). During pregnancy, iron requirements increase three- to fourfold. A woman needs to produce healthy red blood cells for herself and her unborn child. Her blood supply is increasing, and the fetus is not only forming red cells of its own but also laying down an iron reserve.

A woman requires roughly a full gram of iron during the course of her pregnancy: 300 milligrams for the fetus and placenta, 500 milligrams for her own blood supply, and the rest to replace ongoing losses (through skin and the gastrointestinal tract). Should she leave herself short of iron, then she would be unable to rapidly replace red cells lost during delivery, and her milk (should she nurse) would lack adequate iron for her child. The infant, however, would pay a higher price. Starting life with an oxygen supply system without sufficient hemoglobin, and dependent on iron-poor mother's milk for nourishment, he or she would probably soon develop infant anemia.

To help mothers take on all the iron they need, the body, which normally severely limits the amount of iron it will absorb, relaxes this restriction during pregnancy. Nevertheless, much more iron is consumed than absorbed. At best, about one quarter of the iron in animal foods is absorbed and substantially less of the iron in vegetable foods. So women need between 48 and 78 milligrams per day of dietary iron for all nine months. Considering how difficult it is to meet even the basic RDA for iron, except from diets rich in red meat, fish, and poultry, iron supplements are clearly needed during pregnancy.

Zinc

Nutritionists have been learning lately just how important an adequate maternal supply of zinc is to normal growth of the fetus. Recent animal studies have shown, for example, that a shortage of zinc during the second and third trimesters will damage the immune system of fetal mice (and this damage is passed along for three generations).

If women could get all the iron they needed during pregnancy from their diets, then they would be sure to get enough zinc as well, for zinc is found in the same foods as iron. In contrast, they might expect to short-change themselves on zinc if they depend too heavily on iron supplements. However, since the zinc requirement during pregnancy is only 20 milligrams — just five milligrams above the prepregnancy level — there is rarely any reason to look to supplements to be sure of getting enough.

Folacin and Vitamin B₆

Like calcium and iron, maternal folacin reserves are likely to be low when pregnancy begins, for most women fail to get all they need of this vital B vitamin before conception. According to government analysis of eating patterns in the United States, a shortage of folacin is our most common vitamin deficiency. But B_6 deficiency comes second and is a special risk for women, who generally have a lower caloric intake than men.

Lack of adequate folacin during pregnancy can result in anemia, particularly during the final trimester, when the fetus is drawing heavily on maternal reserves. In serious cases, the mother's heart, liver, and spleen may become enlarged, and her red blood cells so depleted that the life of the fetus is threatened.

Even a marginal deficiency of maternal folacin can have tragic consequences for certain infants. About five babies in every 10,000 in the United States are born with the "neural tube defect," the failure of the spinal canal to close properly during the first month of fetal life. This causes a condition called spina bifida, which is the result of genetic predisposition rather than nutrition. Nevertheless, there is solid evidence that high folacin levels can help prevent the defect.

One British study proved the case dramatically. The infants of women who took no supplements were compared with the infants of women who were given folacin supplements at one or two times the RDA. Within a year, the benefits of folacin in preventing the neural tube defect became obvious — so obvious, in fact, that Britain's Medical Research Council decided to stop the experiment and give folacin to *all* pregnant women. The need for folacin during pregnancy is profound — at 800 micrograms per day, it is twice the prepregnancy requirement. Since normal folacin intake is generally low, it isn't reasonable to expect women to meet the demands of pregnancy only through dietary sources (organ meats, green leafy vegetables, and certain fruits). Here again, supplements are called for, and most obstetricians routinely prescribe a daily multivitamin tablet containing all the B vitamins.

Such a supplement will also supply all the B_6 a woman needs for proper development of the fetus. In all experimental animals, including monkeys, even marginal deficiencies of the B vitamins, including B$_6$, raise the risk of birth defects, particularly those affecting the central nervous system.

EXERCISE

Exercise can be an important component of overall fitness during this period. One study of female athletes who stayed in training through the first three or four months, and then tapered off, found that they experienced a lower than average number of complications during pregnancy.

Unfortunately, exercise will not, as many women have been told, shorten labor. It can, however, help reduce the number and severity of backaches and varicose veins, relieve constipation, and avoid "postpartum belly." Exercise during pregnancy can help restore the body's muscle tone and shape afterward — and may do it more effectively than a postpartum diet.

But pregnancy is not the time to launch into a strenuous exercise program. The cardiovascular system has enough extra work to do without having to cope with a whole new set of demands. The time to start conditioning yourself is before conception.

Regular exercise three or more times a week is better than less frequent bouts of activity. Competitive sports are out. But casual golf, tennis, or jogging is fine. Working out with light weights can be even better, even for a woman who never used weights before pregnancy. A moderate amount of weight training can reduce low-back pain and help women handle their extra bulk. It will prepare them to tote around a 6- or 7-pound baby after delivery.

The American College of Obstetricians and Gynecologists warns against exercises that require jumping, bouncing, jerky movements, and rapid changes in direction, for these can injure fragile joints. A woman should stretch cautiously and not exercise on her back after the fourth month (when the fetus is large enough to interfere with blood flow). Exercise dangers also include dehydration and high body temperature (it shouldn't exceed 101.3 degrees Fahrenheit), which can trigger premature labor. Drinking plenty of fluids both before and after exercising can help prevent both.

TOXIC PLEASURES — AND PROBLEMS

The latest word on drinking during pregnancy is *no*. Heavy drinking (six drinks or more per day) can cause the severe abnormalities of fetal alcohol syndrome. These include damage to the central nervous system, gross malformation of the head and face, mental retardation, and extremely retarded growth. Just one or two drinks a day at the start of pregnancy can affect the growth of the fetus in more subtle ways. That's what a large-scale study of women in northern California has found. The only hopeful note is that a good number of women who usually drink moderately lose their taste for alcohol during pregnancy.

Smoking is also to be shunned during pregnancy, for nicotine constricts blood vessels leading to the uterus and the placenta and thus can reduce the flow of blood and nutrients to the fetus. Continued use of cigarettes over the course of pregnancy will have enough effect on blood vessels to lower an infant's birth weight.

The moderately good news is that the U.S. Food and Drug Administration has relaxed its recommendation that pregnant women avoid caffeine. The agency still advises caution, however, since caffeine has demonstrated a capacity to cause birth defects in animal studies. If a pregnant woman still wants a cup of coffee (caffeine is another taste that pregnant women often lose), it shouldn't be too strong. Like the nicotine in cigarettes, caffeine can also constrict blood vessels. A recent study of more than 3,000 pregnant women found that caffeine in excess of 150 milligrams a day appears to increase the risk of spontaneous abortion during the first trimes-

---

A GUIDE TO SUPPLEMENTS DURING PREGNANCY

There are a number of vitamin and mineral supplements for pregnant women on the market. In fact, it is now a routine practice for obstetricians to advise or prescribe special vitamin and mineral supplements for their pregnant patients. Women can also get the nutritional insurance they need from a prescription formula or from over-the-counter "maternal" supplements, which are particularly rich in the nutrients they need most.

However it's packaged, though, the dosage of the supplement is critical. It's true that pregnant women need more of every nutrient — but within limits. The need for folacin goes up more than the requirement for anything other than iron, and it only doubles. So even in pregnancy there is no reason to take abnormally high doses of any nutrient. And megadoses of some vitamins may be especially harmful at this time. High doses of vitamins A and D, for example, may harm not only the mother but the development of the fetus as well.

Supplements can also play a role both before and after pregnancy. A woman who's planning to conceive should be careful to build up sufficient reserves of calcium, iron, and other essential nutrients. A balanced supplement with 100 percent of the RDAs provides sufficient insurance. Nursing mothers need to get the same extra nutrients they did during pregnancy until the baby is weaned.

As a guide, this table shows the prepregnancy and pregnancy RDAs, based on the needs of a woman between ages 23 and 50 who weighs 120 pounds before pregnancy and is 5 feet, 4 inches tall.

ter from 1.8 percent to 3.1 percent. Less than 150 milligrams does not seem to increase the danger at all. Tea, cocoa, and colas are safe enough, but a cup of strong coffee, like one of today's home-ground, drip-brewed varieties, can contain as much as 180 milligrams of caffeine.

THE BOTTOM LINE: BASIC CONCERNS

Calories are the number one need. Babies must reach adequate size — 5.5 pounds or more — for the best chance to survive and thrive. For mothers, this means a weight increase of 20 percent during pregnancy (more if they start underweight, less if they start overweight). And weight gain should increase throughout pregnancy, with the most pounds added during the final trimester.

Pregnancy raises the need for *all* nutrients, but women should be particularly certain that they are getting adequate amounts of calcium, iron, zinc, folacin, and vitamin B_6. It is unlikely that diet alone can provide sufficient iron or calcium, and supplements will probably be needed for these minerals and for vitamin B_6 and folacin.

Recommended Dietary Allowances (RDAs) During Pregnancy

Nutrient	Prepregnancy	Pregnancy	Increase	Percent Increase
Protein	44 g	74 g	30 g	68
Vitamin A	800 RE	1,000 RE	200 RE	25
Vitamin D	5 μg	10 μg	5 μg	100
Vitamin E	8 mg	10 mg	2 mg	25
Vitamin C	60 mg	80 mg	20 mg	33
Thiamin	1 mg	1.4 mg	0.4 mg	40
Riboflavin	1.2 mg	1.5 mg	0.3 mg	25
Niacin	13 mg	15 mg	2 mg	15
Vitamin B_6	2.0 mg	2.6 mg	0.6 mg	30
Folacin	400 μg	800 μg	400 μg	100
Vitamin B_{12}	3.0 μg	4.0 μg	1.0 μg	33
Calcium	800 mg	1,200 mg	400 mg	50
Phosphorus	800 mg	1,200 mg	400 mg	50
Magnesium	300 mg	450 mg	150 mg	50
Iron	18 mg	48–78 mg	30–60 mg	167–333
Zinc	15 mg	20 mg	5 mg	33
Iodine	150 μg	175 μg	25 μg	17

Note: RE = Retinol Equivalents (1 retinol equivalent = 1 μg retinol or 6 μg beta-carotene); g = grams; mg = milligrams; μg = micrograms.

Alcohol — even a moderate amount — endangers the fetus. So does cigarette smoking. Both nicotine and caffeine constrict arteries, including those supplying the uterus and placenta. But one cup of medium-strength coffee a day does not appear to pose any danger.

Moderate exercise can reduce problems of pregnancy and help women regain muscle tone and shape more rapidly after delivery.

CHAPTER 24

Feeding Infants and Toddlers

B REAST-FEEDING IS BACK in fashion, and more than half of all babies in the United States now begin life beyond the womb on mother's milk. This not only gets the mother-child relationship off to a psychologically strong start but has physiological benefits for both participants as well.

The hormones that nursing mothers produce help the uterus contract and return to its prepregnancy shape. They may also extend postpartum infertility. And nursing is the natural way for women to employ the surplus fat they pick up during pregnancy. About 10 of those extra pounds are designed to support milk production, and they must be shed in other ways if they are not used to make milk.

For baby, the initial benefits are so great that the American Academy of Pediatrics urges every mother capable of nursing to do so. Even if a woman doesn't want to put up with the hassle of prolonged breast-feeding, she can benefit her baby substantially by nursing for at least the infant's first week or ten days. That's when the breasts produce colostrum, a nutrient-loaded premilk filled with disease-preventing antibodies that give infants the protection their own immune systems aren't yet able to provide.

The immunity-enhancing benefits of breast-feeding are not lost when the breasts stop delivering colostrum and start producing true milk. As long as mothers continue to nurse, they pass on to their babies disease-fighting antibodies and cells that have been programmed by the maternal immune system. And infants on mother's milk have a much better chance of avoiding food allergies.

In addition to protecting infants from disease and allergic reactions, breast-feeding may also help regulate caloric intake, for some studies

287

suggest that formula-fed babies are more likely to be overfed (and result-ingly overweight). Opinion varies on this, however, and so does the clini-cal evidence. But, whatever the case, chubby babies do not necessarily become obese adults (see "Baby Fat and Fats for Baby," pages 294–296).

Far more important are the nutritional advantages of mother's milk. It is the perfect food for infants, designed specifically to meet the needs of the human young, and it cannot be precisely replicated by any kind of infant formula.

Formulas can provide the same amounts of protein and fat as moth-er's milk. But they cannot provide the same kinds of protein, and they generally do not provide quite the same kinds of fat. The proteins in formulas come from cow's milk and are different from those in mother's milk. They are harder for infants to digest, and the amounts of various amino acids they contain (while ideal for calves) are not what's best for babies.

Cow's milk has low levels of cystine, which is abundant in mother's milk, and taurine, a major growth-promoting amino acid. (Neither is essential for older children or adults, but both appear to be necessary in infant diets.) On the other hand, there is far more phenylalanine in cow's milk than in breast milk, and some infants have trouble metabolizing this amino acid. What's more, it is cow's milk protein in formulas that most often triggers allergic reactions in infants.

When it comes to fats, formulas generally do not even attempt to match human milk, which contains a mixture of both saturated and unsaturated fats and a substantial amount of cholesterol. Babies need fat—far more of it than adults do. Fats are a concentrated source of calories (more than twice as calorie-dense as carbohydrates or protein), and it would be just about impossible to pack enough energy into moth-er's milk if fats didn't provide half the calories. Babies must have plenty of the linoleic acid in fats to sustain growth (see "Fatty Acids" section in chapter 3). And development of their brains and central nervous systems also depends upon an adequate intake of fats to produce myelin, the fatty, high-cholesterol substance the body uses to insulate nerve sheaths.

In the United States, most formulas contain few saturated fats and no cholesterol (although cholesterol is added to formulas in certain other countries). They are usually made from vegetable oils high in unsatu-rated fatty acids, which are absorbed more readily than saturated fatty acids. Although there are heavy concentrations of saturates and choles-terol in mother's milk, nutritionists have not been able to learn what benefits (if any) they provide.

The body is capable of producing almost all the fatty substances it needs, as long as it has an adequate supply of essential fatty acids — and these are present in unsaturated fats. But the supply must be adequate. Deficiency of essential fatty acids, which is relatively rare among adults, occurs more frequently among infants and develops much more rapidly.

STARTING TO NURSE

The body is preparing for breast-feeding during pregnancy, not only by laying down a fat reserve for milk production but also by readying the mammary glands to produce and deliver milk. At least nine new mothers out of ten are physically capable of breast-feeding and producing all the milk their infants will need. Breast size has little to do with milk production (bigger breasts have more fat, not larger glands), and normally flat or inverted nipples needn't prove an obstacle. Manipulation during pregnancy will usually promote sufficient protrusion to permit suckling.

The hormone prolactin plays a critical role in bringing the mammary glands into production, and blood levels of this hormone rise during pregnancy (when it is secreted by both the pituitary gland and placenta). But a different hormone, oxytocin, is needed to permit mothers to release or "let down" their milk. This hormone causes smooth muscle all over the body to contract (including the muscles of the uterus). Oxytocin prompts the contraction of muscles surrounding the mammary glands, which squeeze milk out of the ducts. Secretion of both prolactin and oxytocin are stimulated by suckling. Thus, the more an infant suckles, the greater the amount of milk produced and released.

What it takes to get breast-feeding off to a good start is a hungry infant eager to suck vigorously. So infants that are to be breast-fed are generally *not* fed in the nursery and are brought to their mothers frequently. Nursing is much more likely to succeed if it begins on the first day, and the Committee on Nutrition of the American Academy of Pediatrics has strongly recommended that hospitals keep breast-feeding mothers together with their infants during the first 24 hours after delivery.

Mothers needn't become too anxious if it takes several days for breast-feeding to succeed. It is more important for them to work out a nursing pattern during this period than it is for their newborns to get much in the way of sustenance. Infants arrive on the scene with a substantial amount of stored fat and water — more than enough to see them through their first few days. There's little risk in keeping them hungry enough to suckle eagerly and to do their part to get a successful pattern of nursing established.

NUTRITION FOR NURSING

The nutritional demands of nursing aren't all that different from the nutritional demands of pregnancy. Nursing mothers are still "eating for two," and their basic need is for enough extra calories to produce 1–2 pints of milk per day.

But not all those calories need to come from diet. Most nursing mothers start with a surplus of stored fat left over from pregnancy and require no more than an additional 500 dietary calories per day to support lactation. There's also some recent evidence from British studies that maternal metabolism may adapt to the demands of nursing by slowing down, enabling mothers to produce sufficient milk even if they don't get quite that many extra calories.

To provide their fast-growing infants the wherewithal for normal development, nursing mothers need extra amounts of nutrients other than calories. In fact, the need for some is even greater during lactation than during pregnancy. Protein intake, for example, should increase an additional 20 grams per day from the pregnancy level. This makes it equivalent to slightly less than 5 ounces of meat, fish, or poultry (still within the range of what most American women normally consume). Nursing also requires higher levels of vitamins A and C (twice as much C) and several of the B's than does pregnancy (see RDAs for lactating mothers in Appendix Table A1).

The calcium and iron requirements of breast-feeding are just as great as the requirements of pregnancy, and the need for additional zinc, copper, and manganese is greater than during pregnancy. It is unlikely that nursing mothers will get all the calcium and iron they need from dietary sources alone — any more than they did during pregnancy. They will probably have to supplement and should do so as they did during pregnancy (see "Special Nutritional Needs" section in chapter 23 and "A Guide to Supplements During Pregnancy," pages 284–285). Supplementation, however, may not be needed to supply additional amounts of trace elements other than iron, although the requirements for some of these are somewhat higher during lactation than during pregnancy. It is possible to get enough of these other trace elements from the iron-rich foods in which they are also found, even though these foods cannot easily provide all the iron that nursing mothers need.

CAVEATS FOR NURSING MOTHERS

Mothers can pass along a good deal more in their milk than nutrients and protective antibodies. Whatever is in their bloodstreams or stored in their fatty tissues is likely to end up in their infants. Although it is possible for toxic chemicals like PCBs (polychlorinated biphenyls), industrial contaminants, and pesticides to accumulate in fat and invade mother's milk, the risk is relatively small. However, the American Academy of Pediatrics advises women who know they have been exposed to any of these substances to have their milk tested before they start breast-feeding.

Although milk also carries drugs from the mother's body to the child's, the infant's liver and kidneys can usually detoxify and dump the small amounts transmitted before they can accumulate in the bloodstream and reach toxic concentrations. Nevertheless, mothers should discuss the effects of prescription drugs with their doctors and bear in mind that certain over-the-counter drugs, including ordinary aspirin, are also carried by milk to nursing infants.

Among the toxic pleasures, moderate smoking has not been proved to convey dangerous levels of nicotine. There are, however, indications that nicotine has a negative effect on milk production, and nursing mothers who smoke reduce their chances of sustaining an adequate supply of breast milk. In addition, there are concerns about the effects of "passive smoke" on the infant.

The concentration of alcohol in a woman's blood is pretty much the same as the concentration in her milk. But there is no reason to believe that mothers who take a moderate one or two drinks a day are likely to do their babies any harm. As for caffeine, moderation seems to be the rule here too, since caffeine is one of those substances that can build up in a baby's bloodstream. Still, a morning cup of coffee or an afternoon cola seem well within safe limits.

FEEDING PREMATURE INFANTS

Human infants grow faster during the last 10 weeks of gestation than at any other time in their lives. So premature babies come onto the scene with a greater capacity for rapid growth than normal-term babies, but they have substantially lower nutritional reserves. Deficiencies and deficiency diseases, including rickets, are not uncommon among preemies, who have high protein needs and often lack enough sodium, calcium, phosphorus, zinc, and iron.

Nutritionists are not at all certain — and certainly do not all agree — on whether mother's milk or formula is best for premature infants. There are, to be sure, special formulas for the premature. But mothers of premature infants also produce a special milk that is different from the milk of mothers with full-term babies. It is generally richer in protein and sodium. It also comes with the protective antibodies only mother's milk can provide.

Not all pediatricians endorse mother's milk for the premature. First, because children who started off on special formulas grow more rapidly; and second, because there's such great variety in the composition of milk produced by the mothers of preterm infants. This milk often fails to provide suffcient calories and protein and can lack adequate amounts of phosphorus, calcium, sodium, zinc, copper, and the B vitamins. Formulas, however, have shortcomings as well. Not only do they lack the antibodies mother's milk contains and raise the risk of allergic responses but they also contain a combination of amino acids that is more difficult for preemies to metabolize properly.

A possible solution to this dilemma is the bioengineered mother's milk developed at Sweden's celebrated Karolinska Institute. Researchers there focused on nourishing babies who are two and three months premature. The mothers of these children generally produce more milk than their infants can use. The problem is nutrient density: the milk doesn't have as many nutrients to the ounce as it should. What the Karolinska team developed amounts to fortified mother's milk, enriched with protein and antibodies that have been removed from the milk of the mother and mixed with whole mother's milk. In this way, preemies are able to get the nutrients and the immunity they need without having to cope with more fluid than their bodies can handle.

NUTRITIONAL NEEDS OF INFANTS

Full-term infants need a nutrient-dense diet (and relatively high levels of vitamins A and C), but neither breast-fed nor formula-fed babies are likely to require any of the multivitamin, multimineral supplements for infants (although such supplements won't do them any harm). There are, however, three nutrients that pediatricians do worry about babies getting in sufficient quantities. These are vitamin D, fluoride, and iron.

Only small amounts of vitamin D are present in breast milk, but infants are most often born with a supply of this vitamin and can produce all they need when exposed to strong summer sunlight. However, during winter months, nursing babies may need vitamin D supplementation. For babies fed on formula, additional supplementation is unnecessary, since these preparations generally contain all the essential nutrients infants require.

One nutrient that some formulas may lack, however, is fluoride. Ready-to-drink formulas made in areas where water is fluoridated and home-mix concentrates prepared with fluoridated water will usually provide all the fluoride an infant requires. Even in areas where water is unfluoridated, commercially fluoridated water is generally available and should be used to prepare home-mix concentrates. But ready-to-drink formulas that have not been made with fluoridated water or fortified with fluoride will not meet an infant's needs, and neither will breast milk. Doctor-prescribed supplementation is necessary for breast-fed babies and should be given to infants on fluoride-free formula as well.

Although some formulas are also low in iron, babies on iron-enriched formulas will not need iron supplements. Nor are these supplements usually necessary for breast-fed babies, even though some pediatricians recommend them. There is not a great deal of iron in breast milk (or cow's milk, for that matter), but it exists in a unique form that is more readily absorbed than the iron in any other food. While the body can absorb only about 5 percent of the iron in vegetables and 30 percent of the heme iron in red meat, roughly half the iron in mother's milk is absorbable. As a result, breast-fed babies are rarely, if ever, iron-deficient during the first six to nine months of life.

With the exception of vitamin D, fluoride, and eventually iron, breast milk meets all an infant's nutritional needs and will sustain normal growth for the first four to six months. Infant formulas will do this too. But some time after four months (when babies plainly do not need anything more than mother's milk or formula) and before six months (when most babies cannot thrive on these alone), it's time to introduce them to solid foods.

SOLID FOODS

There are no benefits and quite a few potential hazards to introducing solid foods before four months. Not only do younger infants have trouble dealing with spoons and understanding what chewing is all about but they may not even be able to coordinate the swallowing of solids. Their digestive systems and kidneys may not yet be ready to deal with the amounts of protein in solid foods.

If mothers start making the switch to solids prematurely — for whatever reasons, including the discredited theory that eating solid foods makes babies more likely to sleep through the night — they must decide whether or not to cut back the amount of breast milk or formula their infants receive. If they cut back, then they replace breast milk or formula with less nutritionally desirable and appropriate substitutes. If they do not cut back, they provide their children with more calories than they need. Unless infants self-regulate intake, they may then put on weight more rapidly than they should.

While introducing solid foods before four months is not prudent, delaying the introduction much beyond six months is not such a good idea either, for babies then need more to maintain growth than they can get from breast milk or formula. It doesn't much matter what food you start with (single-grain cereals are the traditional first choice). But foods should be introduced one at a time. Giving a beginner a food mixture with several different and equally new ingredients is a poor idea, for the one-by-one rule is designed so that parents can spot an allergic reaction and know for certain what caused it.

Between 6 and 12 months the quantity of solid foods in a child's diet should be gradually increased. But at 12 months, milk should still supply one half to two thirds of total calories. Cow's milk can replace breast milk or formula once a child is getting one third of his or her calories from solids (at least three 4-ounce jars of baby food per day). During this time, solids are meant to supplement, not replace, cow's milk, breast milk, or formula, which remain the sources of most vitamins and minerals.

As infants and toddlers become less dependent on cow's milk, breast milk, or fortified formulas, however, they are at risk of iron deficiency, particularly before they develop a taste for iron-rich meat (at around 18 months). Even marginal deficiencies can cause fatigue and loss of concentration. They will also create learning difficulties and delay development.

Most often, an adequate early diet is all that's needed to prevent deficiency. WIC, the federal nutrition program, has demonstrated how this can reduce anemia among low-income children. From 1975 to 1985 the rate of anemia for children six months to five years who were part of the program dropped from 7.8 percent to 2.9 percent (as measured in six different states). Nevertheless, for children making the transition to solid food, cereals and other foods fortified with iron (as well as B vitamins) provide important nutritional insurance.

As children become more dependent on solid foods, parents have new concerns. Since young children eat relatively little, the nutrient density of their foods is of particular importance. So is salt and sugar content, and adequate variety in their diets.

Most families in the United States use commercial baby foods, but baby's food can also be homemade, and there's a growing tendency today to let infants share what other family members are having for dinner by popping some of it into the blender. The one drawback to this practice is the amount of sodium (in table salt) that may have been added to the food in processing or cooking. Commercially prepared baby foods are now free of added sodium. Responding to the concerns of the National Academy of Sciences that excessive sodium in baby foods might make babies more prone to hypertension later in life, manufacturers ceased adding salt and MSG to baby foods in 1978.

Although babies aren't born with a taste for salt (as they are with a taste for sweets), they do show a preference for moderately salted foods after about four months. But salt cravings are largely acquired, and the amounts most families use in their food are much greater than babies are likely to find appealing.

BABY FAT AND FATS FOR BABY

A number of parents, often eager to spare their children their own struggles with excess weight, are starting youngsters on restrictive diets even before their second birthdays. At North Shore University Hospital outside of New York City, pediatricians find such diets to blame for a quarter of the cases involving failure of very young children to thrive. Typically, these toddlers have been fed lean meats and complex carbohydrates, given skim milk instead of whole, and forbidden to snack between meals.

The connection between excess baby fat and adult obesity is far from direct. Even infants who are substantially overweight during their first six months—well above the 20-percent-over-normal obesity threshold—generally grow into normally proportioned children. The classic British study of the relation between infant obesity and obesity in later life found that nearly nine out of ten obese infants slim down to relatively normal levels by the time they are seven years old. Nevertheless, obese infants are still three times more likely to be overweight at age seven than infants who have grown normally from the start.

Parents are not wrong to be concerned about sustained obesity in children, particularly if there is a genetic tendency toward excess weight. Most babies have little trouble shedding their baby fat. But the more they have and the longer they keep it, the higher the risk of their remaining overweight through life. The risk is greater at two than at one, and increases throughout childhood. If a child remains obese into adolescence, then the odds against ever achieving normal body weight become something on the order of 5 to 1.

The mechanics of obesity aren't fully understood, and the role of excess weight early in life is particularly difficult to explain. Take the question of fat storage, for example. Obese individuals not only have fat cells that are larger than normal but often have a greater number of fat cells as well. Among overweight adults, those with more fat cells tend to have been obese since childhood, while those with a normal number of fat cells have generally put on their excess weight as adults.

Babies rarely add extra fat cells during their first year. It is after the first year that the number of cells begins to increase, and it can keep increasing until adulthood. Nevertheless, when the genetic tendency is strong, babies may start adding extra cells even before their first birthday and can reach an adult fat cell count when they are only a few years old.

The significance of additional fat cells and the roles of diet and exercise in weight control are discussed in chapters 10 and 11. In general, however, the need for babies to get enough food to sustain normal growth — and enough of specific nutrients to meet their developmental needs — makes it difficult for parents to do much dietary restriction before their children reach age two.

It is not a good idea, for example, to substitute skim milk for whole milk much before a child is 18 months old. Replacing whole milk with skim not only takes a good many calories out of the diet but makes milk a more concentrated source of protein and salt. When children are younger than 18 months old, their kidneys may not be up to the job of handling such a rich and concentrated protein source.

There is another reason why babies younger than 18 months should not be put on skim milk: their need for fats. Babies require more fat in their diets than older children or adults. They need the calories in fat for growth and activity, and fat itself is essential to the development of their nervous systems. Even when they are two years old and eating a more or less adult diet, they still may not be able to thrive on a fat-restricting diet appropriate for adults.

For this reason, parents should be wary of acting on the recent recommendation by the National Institutes of Health that *all* children start low-cholesterol diets at age two. Clearly, an overweight two-year-old should be eating differently from a two-year-old of normal body weight, and a child with unusually high blood levels of cholesterol may need a special, physician-prescribed cholesterol-restricting diet. But not all children will benefit from low cholesterol intake. Although dietary cholesterol may pose long-term dangers for children genetically vulnerable to heart disease (see chapter 17), it is not much of a threat for most youngsters. Parents who know there's a genetic risk of heart disease should discuss cholesterol screening for their children with a pediatrician.

In terms of long-term health consequences, weight control is no more important for children two years old and older than is the development of sound nutritional habits. Eating patterns, tastes, and food preferences established in early childhood can have a lifelong beneficial impact on foodstyle.

COPING WITH FOOD FEARS AND FINICKY EATERS

Between ages one and two, just when the world of food is opening up for children, they often become reluctant to experiment with unfamiliar diet items. Even older children resist new foods, imposing bizarre limits on what they are willing to eat and restricting their intake to hamburgers or chicken, peanut butter and jelly, or a particular brand of cereal. Parents can pretty much plan on seeing some pickiness, because most youngsters become distressingly finicky at one time or another. It can provoke considerable parental anxiety, particularly in parents who recognize the importance of variety to sound nutrition. They will worry about their children's getting all the nutrients they need and try any number of ways to overcome or accommodate what they perceive to be unreasonable whims.

But the phenomenon psychologists now call food neophobia, the fear of new foods, is more than just a common piece of behavior. It is prompted by instincts that are universal. Indeed, a fear of unfamiliar foods was probably a potent survival characteristic for small children during most of the past several million years.

There is a wrong way and a right way to cope with food neophobia. The wrong way—and the most common—is to pressure kids to eat. This has more than one drawback. It exacerbates food fears, and, says Leann Lipps Birch, professor of human development at the University of Illinois, Urbana-Champaign, "Kids learn at a very early age that they can control their parents through food."

Birch's research on the food tastes of children has taught her that the worst thing a parent can do is what most try first—bribery. Eat vegetables and you get dessert. "Paradoxically," she says, "when a child is bribed to eat a food, he often ends up liking it less—and liking the food he is bribed with even more." Children quickly come up with the idea that there must indeed be something wrong with broccoli, turnips, or cauliflower, else why would Mommy reward me for eating them?

According to Birch, the best way to help children overcome fear of a new food is simply by exposing them to it. Just letting them watch parents or other children eat the new item — with no pressure to do the same — is the best way to break down resistance. When children see parents or peers obviously enjoying a food, they will make a special effort to learn to like it. Mexican children, for example, are initially no more enthusiastic about hot peppers than are any other youngsters. But they keep trying them, because eating peppers is an adult behavior they want to emulate.

Children are also quick to pick up clues from their parents and often respond to new foods in much the way their parents expect them to respond. So when parents betray their assumption that little Jamie or Jane is going to hate Brussels sprouts, that's just what Jamie or Jane will do.

The reason parents fret about how much or how many different food items their children eat, Birch explains, is because they are worried. "Most parents think their children don't eat enough, especially not enough nourishing foods." But these parental fears are usually unwarranted. Malnourishment is rare among middle-class youngsters in the United States, and children usually get all the nutrients and energy they need over the course of several days, even if these are not properly proportioned at each mealtime.

Parents can fail to recognize this if they don't realize how small proper child-size portions actually are, and if they load their children's plates with servings far larger than the youngsters can or should eat. Children will rightly ignore the excess, for they generally have a much better idea of how much they need to eat than adults do. In fact, children are generally better able to tell when they are full than adults are. "Children can self-regulate their intake very nicely if left alone," says Birch. "But parents can really screw this up if they tell a kid to eat when he's not hungry — to clean his plate."

Although appetite and nutritional needs clearly vary, the rule of thumb for determining child-size portions is one tablespoonful for each year. That's the standard used by the Penn State Nutrition Center. This means a two-year-old shouldn't have to cope with more than two tablespoonfuls each of hamburger, mashed potatoes, and spinach at any one time. But the spoonful-per-year rule changes as children approach school age.

How does this serving-size standard work out in practice? These recommendations from the Penn State Nutrition Center, which agree with the American Academy of Pediatrics, give general daily guidelines for children of different ages. Remember, though, that it's not critical for a child to eat a precisely balanced diet every single day as long as his or her nutrient intake averages out.

Protein (meat, poultry, fish, tofu, peanut butter)

Ages 1–3: two or three 1-ounce servings. Ages 4–6: three 1-ounce servings. Ages 7 and up: four 1-ounce servings.

Vegetables

Ages 1–3: four servings (two or three tablespoonfuls each). Ages 4–6: four servings (four tablespoonfuls each). Ages 7 and up: four servings (five or six tablespoonfuls each).

Fruits

Ages 1–3: four servings (half a fruit each). Ages 4–6: four servings (half a fruit or a whole medium-sized fruit each). Ages 7 and up: four servings (a medium-sized fruit each).

Starches (bread, cereal, rice, pasta)

Ages 1–6: three or four servings per day. (A serving is half a slice of bread, one-quarter cup cooked rice or pasta, one-quarter cup cereal.) Ages 7 and up: four servings per day (a full slice of bread, a half cup of rice, pasta, or cereal each).

Calcium

Young children need the calcium equivalent of about two cups of whole or skim milk per day, or about two ounces of cheese.

THE BOTTOM LINE: BASIC CONCERNS

Breast-feeding is what's nutritionally best for babies, and nursing mothers need to be sure of getting enough extra calories — 500 per day — to produce adequate amounts of milk. For nutrient-dense milk, protein and micronutrient needs also increase during lactation (see Appendix Table A1). Calcium and iron requirements are too great for most nursing mothers to meet without supplementation, although it is possible for them to get enough of other important vitamins and minerals (including the B vitamins, copper, manganese, and zinc) from food alone.

If babies are not breast-fed, then fortified formula should be used. Infants should not be started on solid foods much before they are four months old or long after they are six months old. New foods should be introduced one at a time (usually starting with single-grain cereals). When solid foods supply at least one third of a child's calories, then cow's milk may replace mother's milk or formula. At this point, babies will need iron supplements.

Parents are well advised to watch for early obesity. But it is difficult to restrict infant diets much before age two, and weight control strategies must allow for adequate nutritional intake and the special needs of young children for fats.

CHAPTER 25

Eating
in Adolescence

NUTRITIONAL NEEDS increase through childhood and are highest during the preadolescent and early adolescent growth spurt — when youngsters are shooting up fastest (what nutritionists call the age of peak height velocity). Girls reach this point at about age 12, a bit earlier than boys, whose maximum height gains are usually made between ages 12 and 14.

Anyone who feeds children this age (particularly boys) is familiar with the size of their appetites, which reflect the need for increased energy (to promote growth and fuel high activity levels). Calorie needs of boys rise throughout adolescence and into early adulthood, while calorie needs of girls peak between ages 11 and 14. Although overeating is a danger and obesity a growing risk for adolescents, parents should recognize that adolescent appetites are most often responding to real body needs that can sometimes reach levels of 4,000 calories per day.

Increased food consumption during this high-growth phase should provide all the extra nutrients youngsters require. But this is when the body's need for both calcium and iron (the minerals many American diets provide in inadequate amounts) are highest. The recommended daily allowance (RDA) of calcium for both boys and girls 11–18, which is 1,200 milligrams, is essential to building bones sturdy enough to resist osteoporosis later in life. If youngsters are not getting this much calcium — the amount found in four cups of milk, 7 ounces of processed American cheese, or 1.5 quarts of regular ice cream — then parents should consider supplementation to make up the difference (see "Calcium" section in chapter 21).

The cholesterol-lowering diet recommended by the National Institutes of Health (NIH) for all children over the age of two — high in carbo-

hydrates and low in fat—would make it difficult to supply preadolescents and adolescents with all the calcium they need, even with the use
of low-fat and no-fat dairy products. That's one reason the American
Academy of Pediatrics has objected to the NIH recommendation. A cholesterol-lowering regimen will not benefit most youngsters, although it
should certainly be adopted for those who both are genetically vulnerable
to heart disease and have high serum cholesterol levels.

A low-fat diet, particularly if it reduces fat content by cutting way
back on red meat, can make it all but impossible for youngsters to get
enough iron during this period of maximum growth. While it is possible
and may well be helpful or even necessary for youngsters to use iron
supplements (see "Iron Deficiency" section in chapter 21), this will not
cover the other nutritional losses caused by minimum consumption of
red meat. All the calcium that these children are getting isn't going to do
much efficient bone building if there isn't enough copper, manganese,
and zinc in their diets, and these trace elements, most readily found in
red meat, are hard to find in sufficient quantity anywhere else.

Social changes and new family structures, the number of single
parents, and the number of families with both parents working outside
the home have all affected how Americans eat. Although research from
Cornell University indicates that families of working mothers tend to get
meals that are somewhat heavier on fats and lower in iron than meals
prepared by mothers without outside jobs, commercial surveys of work-
ing-parent families have turned up cheerier news.

Whether or not single mothers or both parents work appears to
make little difference in how often their families sit down to dinner
together, and children of working parents are likely to get more vegetables, less candy, and fewer salted snack foods than children with a parent
at home. Home-alone kids, who take responsibility for more family
chores than other kids, are more likely to know their way around the
kitchen, and the great majority will whip up their own snacks.

INFLUENCES ON ADOLESCENT DIETS

Snacks make up a healthy (or possibly unhealthy) portion of adolescent food intake, for "grazing"—chronic snacking both in the home and
outside it—is endemic among American teenagers. But there's nothing
inherently bad about heavy snacking. It may offend adult notions of
appropriate foodstyle—three square meals (with proper representation
of the basic four food groups) and no eating between meals—but that is
probably not how *most* of the nation does it these days. Nor are teenagers
necessarily grazing on the wrong kinds of food. Researchers at Kent State
University have found snacks to be a significant source of vitamins and
minerals (notably vitamins A and C, magnesium, and calcium) and to
help raise the content of adolescents' diets to RDA levels.

Even allegedly junk foods have nutrients to contribute. The much-maligned Twinkies are made from fortified flour, which has niacin, riboflavin, and other vitamins as well as iron and copper. These micronutrients and the protein the flour contains make Twinkies somewhat more nutrient-dense (and therefore a better caloric bargain) than apples or pears. But when it comes to nutrient density, there's no beating pizza. Just 4 square inches of pizza contain close to the full range of essential nutrients, most of them at nearly one third of RDA levels.

Parents are right to worry about what are considered junk foods if their youngsters snack primarily on high-calorie candy bars, sodas, and other foods of minimal nutrient density. They should be concerned, as well, if grazing patterns involve substantial intake of fast foods, for the heavy concentrations of fats in fast-food burgers, fried chicken, and french fries can throw adolescent diets way off balance (see "Eating Out" section, chapter 9).

Candy bars and french fries are not themselves diet dangers, although a sweet tooth and too many sugary snacks do create dental problems (see "Kids, Candy, and Cavities," page 302). In general, however, it is restricted snacking patterns that cause the most trouble. Variety and moderation, the fail-safe mechanisms of nutrition, provide just as much protection at snack times as at mealtimes. But for any number of reasons, including the heavy influence of advertising, many youngsters limit grazing to a relatively small selection of similar foods. Peer pressure to eat what the other kids eat has a powerful influence on teenage snack food choice.

Concerns about appearance grow in importance throughout adolescence, and they too influence what youngsters choose to graze on. Both boys and girls can become anxious about acne and other skin disorders. There are, however, no dietary solutions to most skin problems. A substantial amount of research has found that neither chocolate nor any other fatty food is likely to cause them. Hormonal changes during adolescence are most likely to blame, and the primary consideration should be hygiene, not diet, in order to avoid infection that could result in scarring.

WEIGHT CONTROL AND EXERCISE

Although weight consciousness is the single greatest adolescent dietary concern, American teenagers are becoming heavier. That's what Dr. William Dietz of the New England Medical Center in Boston and Dr. Steven Gortmaker of the Harvard School of Public Health have determined from the government's periodic Health and Nutrition Examination Survey (HANES). Over the past 15–20 years, the prevalence of obesity has increased 54 percent among children aged 6–11 and 39 percent among children aged 12–17. Meanwhile, evidence is piling up that fat children are more likely to become fat adults than to outgrow obesity, and overweight adolescents have no more than 1 chance in 5 of achieving normal weight later in life.

A major culprit, according to Dr. Dietz, is television. Using data from a series of sequential studies, which included some of the same children, he found that "next to prior obesity, television viewing is the best predictor of subsequent obesity." For children aged 12–17 the correlation was remarkably consistent. Obesity was half as common among children who watched television for less than an hour per day than it was among children who watched for 5 or more hours. Not only does television watching preclude more strenuous activities but, as Dietz explains, "Children eat more while they are watching TV and they eat more of the foods advertised on TV."

Television is not by any means the *sole* influence on youthful or adolescent obesity. Heredity plays a substantial (if not a determining) role. And weight control is not a simple matter at any age (see chapters 10 and 11).

Dieting alone is unlikely to produce weight loss that will be easy to

---

KIDS, CANDY, AND CAVITIES

Children are especially prone to cavities at two points in their lives: around the ages of 6–8 and again in adolescence. Although the reasons aren't certain, it's possible that hormonal changes at those ages alter the saliva and leave teeth especially vulnerable to decay. But while youngsters can't change their hormones, they can reduce their risk of cavities by changing the foods they eat.

Teeth are damaged by acid, which is produced by bacteria in plaque that live off the remnants of carbohydrates on your teeth. The foods that cause cavities most readily seem to be those that stick to the teeth undissolved, without stimulating the flow of cleansing saliva. Raisins therefore are probably worse for teeth than a granola bar.

Sweet snacks may also pose more of a problem than desserts eaten at the end of a meal. The bacteria that cause cavities keep working for 20 or 30 minutes after you finish eating. So if a teenager snacks throughout the day, these bacteria may churn out acid almost continuously. But when sweets are only eaten as desserts, the acid production is limited. In addition, there's a good flow of saliva at the end of a meal, and it can flush out the sucrose the bacteria live on.

Some foods have much less cavity-producing potential than you might expect. Chocolate is relatively safe for teeth; its fat apparently coats sugar molecules so they're less available to the bacteria in plaque. Wheat germ, bran, peanuts, and walnuts also help to buffer bacterial acid.

Some foods and drinks actually block cavity formation. Several kinds of cheese — cheddar, Swiss, and Monterey Jack — seem to prevent acid production, according to research at the University of Minnesota. And tea, particularly oolong, is high in cavity-fighting fluoride. Studies of English schoolchildren have shown that those who drink a cup or two of tea a day have fewer cavities than those who don't.

sustain over time. With exercise, however, dieters can substantially increase their chances of success. Moreover, exercise has significant benefits in addition to weight control, for sound nutrition and exercise together provide the most powerful means we have of preventing such life-threatening diseases as atherosclerosis, hypertension, diabetes, and osteoporosis.

Although the need for exercise is widely recognized today and fitness is the fashion (if not necessarily the common practice) among adults, a 1984 survey by the Office of Disease Prevention and Health Promotion discovered that children now appear to be in worse shape than they were two decades ago. A local study identified typical disease risk factors among children in Jackson County, Michigan. It found the average level of body fat was high, 28 percent had blood pressure above normal, and 41 percent had high levels of serum cholesterol.

The youngsters in the Michigan study were among 24,000 children who took part in the county's "Feelin' Good" fitness program, developed by Dr. Charles Kuntzleman of Spring Arbor College. With regular aerobic exercise — 30 minutes four days a week — body fat declined by 16 percent, blood pressure by 6 percent, and blood cholesterol by 4 percent.

Getting children off their bottoms and out from in front of the television set works best if started early. Make it fun, fitness experts contend, and kids will happily comply. Small children are eager for parental attention and need to learn how to master motor skills. Even older children may desperately want to learn how to play well. What prevents many preadolescents and adolescents from taking part in sports is their insecurity and unwillingness to appear awkward or inept.

To make exercise a habit, children should first learn individual sports like swimming, running, bicycling, or gymnastics — activities they can practice all their lives. Mastering the specialized skills of team sports can wait until they are at least 10 years old and better able to deal with the pressures of team competition. Some experts feel that even a child of 12 is too young to handle this kind of stress. The goal is not to turn kids into athletes, however, but to give them a lifelong habit. Once it is a part of their lives, exercise provides its own rewards — better physical condition, better spirits (mood-enhancing qualities of exercise are real), an improved self-image, and more self-confidence.

EATING DISORDERS

Eating disorders appear to have become far more common in recent years. They now affect a substantial number of adolescents, most of them girls. In a 1985 Gallup survey of teenagers, 40 percent of boys and 34 percent of girls reported episodes of binge eating. More disturbing was the number of youngsters who followed binges with rigid diets and fasts — behavior reported by 12 percent of girls and 4 percent of boys. The difference between boys and girls reflected their perceptions of their own body weight. Nearly 60 percent of girls said they wanted to lose weight, while only 8 percent wanted to gain weight. Among boys, fewer wanted to lose (20 percent) than wanted to gain (28 percent).

Compulsive overeating, the kind that leads to obesity, is the most common eating disorder among American adolescents. However, compulsive undereating has become a growing problem for adolescent girls. It is their perception of themselves as overweight — no matter what they actually weigh — that leads to disorders like bulimia and anorexia nervosa.

Bulimia, which affects far more girls than anorexia does, involves a concern about weight and a fear of not being able to stop eating voluntarily. Periodic secret food binges are its central feature, along with extreme means of controlling weight — vomiting, laxatives, diuretics, radical diets, and fasting. Generally, bulimics are not terribly thin. Their weight is usually in the normal range and may even be somewhat above normal, but it tends to fluctuate. Bulimics realize that their behavior is abnormal and are usually depressed and disgusted with themselves after binging.

Anorexia is based on an intense fear of obesity as well as a wildly inaccurate body image, and it involves significant weight loss. Indeed, for diagnostic purposes, the criteria of anorexia include both a loss amounting to 25 percent of body weight and amenorrhea (the cessation of menstruation characteristic of this disorder). Psychiatrists point out that the name *anorexia* (which means "loss of appetite") is not particularly appropriate, since appetite is not lost until quite late in the illness.

The faulty self-image that anorexics share with a good many bulimics is now very common among young women, even those without eating disorders. In a recent survey of first-year college women, researchers found fear of fatness so widespread that it could not be used to distinguish healthy from anorexic women. Healthy students, as well as anorexic students and students with anorexic attitudes, were equally likely to be "always on a diet," to restrain their eating, and to be disgusted by their hunger.

Body image distortion is now far from unique to anorexics. As a study by Dr. Judith Rodin and her colleagues at Yale notes, "Body size overestimation is characteristic of women in general." The Rodin study suggests that "current sociocultural influences teach women not only what the ideal body looks like but also how to try to attain it." It points to the briefly popular Beverly Hills Diet as having "advocated a form of bulimia," for the book proposed "compensating" for binges by eating lots of raw fruit to induce diarrhea. Bulimic practices, the Rodin study notes, are passed along from one college woman to another as they "teach each other how to diet, and how to binge, purge, and starve."

While estimates of bulimic behavior among women on college campuses reach truly unbelievable heights — 35–60 percent — girls aren't waiting for college to begin. A survey of more than 1,200 high-school girls recently found 21 percent binge-eating at least once each week, and 7 percent vomiting or using laxatives to control weight. A 1986 report on bulimia and anorexia in the *Journal of the American Medical Association* estimates that between 5 and 25 percent of older adolescent and young adult females purge to control weight and warns that many become addicted to the binge-purge cycle.

What the *JAMA* report termed "the self-induced starvation" of true anorexia fortunately remains relatively rare, although a growing number of young women share anorexic attitudes and maintain relatively low body weights. However, adolescents are particularly at risk of this truly life-threatening disorder, which strikes 1 in every 200 teenage girls.

Clearly contributing to the high incidence of these eating disorders is the culturally induced, and often parentally supported, notion of appropriate body size. It seems bizarre, considering the amount of real obesity among adolescents, that so many normal-sized young women come to imagine that they are grotesquely overweight. But the route to bulimia and anorexia is not hard to identify. It shows up in research like a University of California, San Francisco, study which found that nearly 80 percent of 10- and 11-year-old girls have already been on weight-reducing diets.

The message for parents is obvious: push weight control for health only, not for fashion, and watch out for signs of eating disorders. These include the following:

- Sudden or severe weight gain or loss
- Frequent fluctuation of weight
- Food hoarding
- Eating alone
- Skipping meals or fasting
- Frequent nausea, bloating, or constipation
- Exaggerated fear of gaining weight
- Amenorrhea
- Loss of dental enamel (caused by frequent vomiting)

Parents need to keep in mind that even normal adolescent behavior is characterized by rapid shifts and changes. However, if a pattern indicating bulimia or anorexia becomes evident, it needs to be dealt with. These are not simply bad habits. They are serious medical disorders, and there is no quick cure for them. They pose a problem that should be handled, initially at least, by your pediatrician or family physician.

THE BOTTOM LINE: BASIC CONCERNS

The energy demands of preadolescence and adolescence can be exceptionally high. However, calorie needs are linked to activity levels as well as to growth. Parents should keep an eye on both intake and activity, for obesity is common during this period and hard to reverse later in life.

Undereating among adolescent girls is becoming almost as great a concern as overeating. Unrealistic notions of body shape now prompt a growing number of high-school and college women to adopt dangerous bulimic practices and can lead to true anorexia nervosa.

The most important micronutrient needs of preadolescence and adolescence are for adequate calcium and iron. These are peak bone-building years, when the body can make maximum use of calcium and exercise. Extra iron is needed during the growth spurt and continues to be important for girls after the onset of menstruation.

CHAPTER 26

Concerns of
the Adult Years

D URING EARLY ADULTHOOD and the middle years (except for pregnancy and lactation) there are few unusual nutritional needs, the kinds that are so important during infancy, early childhood, adolescence, and later life. Nevertheless, because of dietary influences common today — including diminished consumption of both dairy products and red meat and a high incidence of dieting for weight control — young and middle-aged adults often lack adequate amounts of calcium and iron and can be short of other trace elements (copper, zinc, and manganese) too. Supplemental calcium and iron (see chapter 21) may be necessary for men and most probably are necessary for women whose iron needs are greater than men's during their menstruating years and who run a greater risk of osteoporosis if they deprive themselves of calcium. There are also other special concerns for adults, including foodstyle, weight, exercise, and the risk of major life-threatening diseases.

Early adulthood is a busy, high-pressure period of life. It is when career demands and family responsibilities generally peak. There is rarely time to spare, and it can be difficult to take proper care of yourself. Money constraints limit choices of diet and activity. Hurried meals, missed meals, and snacks can tilt the best-planned diet into imbalance, while emotional stress can upset digestion and raise risk of disease (for stress will boost LDL-cholesterol levels in the blood and release hormones that increase the danger of hypertension). Compulsive overeating and alcohol abuse are health hazards of increasing significance at this time of life.

Foodstyle reflects the two-way pull of regular home-cooked meals designed to meet the needs of young children and the fast-food and desktop-sandwich lunches that, along with richer and more elaborate restaurant meals, often tend to dominate young adult eating patterns outside the home. For single adults and those in their middle years (when family meals are no longer the rule), restaurants provide a substantial portion of nutritional needs, and eating more than one restaurant meal a day tends to increase the chances of throwing diets off balance, with too many calories in protein and fats and too few in carbohydrates.

There are ways to eat sensibly and well in restaurants (see chapter 9) and many more opportunities to make reasonable choices of both restaurants and food today than ever before. A greater variety of ethnic cooking is now available, and awareness of the "fitness" market by both the food industry and restaurateurs has substantially changed many menus.

The average American picks up 15–20 additional pounds between ages 25 and 55, and census data indicate that today's adults are putting on some of this extra weight considerably earlier than their counterparts of 20 years ago. The 1980 census showed that the average weight among Americans aged 25–34 was 6 pounds greater than it was in 1960.

Young adults, however, are not the only Americans at risk of obesity. Average weight of all Americans increased between the mid-1960s and the mid-1970s. What's most surprising about this increase is the fact that it occurred during a period when Americans were eating less, not more, than before. Average caloric intake, a government study reported, dropped a full 10 percent between 1965 and 1977. What that means is that we ate less but had become less active as well — so much so that a substantial reduction in calories could not prevent a net increase in weight.

The obvious answer to weight control for both young and middle-aged adults is at least as much a matter of exercise as diet. Indeed, weight loss without exercise tends generally to be a no-win proposition (see chapters 10 and 11). But the adult years, especially the early ones, are a hard time to sustain the exercise patterns of youth and adolescence. Time constraints make it difficult to invest the two to three hours a week that may be necessary. And if the exercise habit is broken during early adulthood, it is hard to re-establish subsequently.

Nevertheless, exercise pays off handsomely (see chapter 12). It provides a double return in the reduction of disease risks. First, by controlling weight, it helps eliminate obesity as a risk factor. Second, it tends to reduce the influence of just about all other risk factors as well, including even smoking and genetic vulnerability. Aerobic exercise increases oxygen uptake, strengthens muscles (including the heart), lowers pulse rate, reduces LDL cholesterol in the bloodstream, and increases the number of red blood cells. It also tends to lower blood pressure.

Exercise provides specific benefits in the prevention and treatment of several diseases. For diabetics, it will help increase the sensitivity of cells to insulin. To help protect against osteoporosis, exercise (particularly strength exercises that subject bones to stress) causes the body to retain more calcium and strengthen bones.

Dietary interventions can also be a potent means of reducing disease risk. So it's important to determine, as early as possible, what risks you may be running. Screening for early indicators of disease is the vital first step. For some conditions, however, screening may not be endlessly useful. What you should screen for are those conditions you can do something about: hypertension, for instance, and high cholesterol levels, both of which substantially raise the risk of heart disease. And both respond to dietary intervention. Weight loss and (for certain hypertensives) reduced consumption of sodium will often lower blood pressure. Weight loss and reduced consumption of fats will generally lower cholesterol levels (see chapters 17 and 18).

Screening for colon cancer is also a practical move, and one best started at age 40. But while early detection plainly is a benefit, surgery still provides the only possible intervention. As for dietary means of preventing the disease, there are no sure bets, although a number of strategies (discussed in chapter 19) may be useful, including a high-carbohydrate, low-fat diet (particularly low in polyunsaturated fatty acids) and plenty of foods rich in antioxidants, like beta-carotene, and in fiber.

Genetic predisposition plainly plays a significant role in disease, and family histories of hypertension, heart disease, and cancer should encourage screening for these diseases. If there is a family history of non-insulin-dependent diabetes (the form of the disease once called adult-onset), then failure to have blood sugar levels checked periodically seems foolhardy, particularly for those genetically vulnerable adults who are overweight. When diagnosed early, non-insulin-dependent diabetes is easily controlled and almost completely reversible, most often by no more than a relatively modest amount of weight loss.

CHAPTER 27

Nutrition During the Later Years

Let's understand something about the nature of our "aging society." The number of senior citizens is growing larger, but the oldest aren't setting any new records for longevity.

Nevertheless, a radical shift in the nation's demographic profile is under way. Americans over age 65, who made up 11 percent of the population in 1984, will make up 12.7 percent by 1990, at which time they will number 32 million. There will be 35 million by the year 2000, and 50 million by 2030 (17 percent of the population). If we follow demographic projections all the way to 2050, we're looking at 67 million Americans past 65 (21.7 percent of the population), with more than one quarter of them between 75 and 84.

A number of factors can help produce this kind of demographic change. One reason for the predicted growth in the 65-plus category soon after the start of the twenty-first century is simply the number of children born 65 years earlier, during the baby boom that followed World War II. The first members of this outsized generation will turn 65 in 2011.

Population bulges aside, however, declining death rates generally play the most significant role in expanding the ranks of the aging. As death rates fall, life expectancy increases. In the United States, where death rates have dropped sharply since the beginning of this century, life expectancy at birth — the length of time that an average infant will live — is now close to 75 years. This is not the world's highest — it's 77 years in Iceland and 76 years in the Netherlands, Sweden, Norway, and Japan. But throughout most of the Third World, life expectancy today is still well below the 47 years that was the expectation for Americans born in 1900. In Ethiopia and Afghanistan it is now just 40 years, and it's 42 years in Angola and Gambia.

Life expectancy varies considerably from nation to nation and between economic classes because it can be altered in so many different ways. It is influenced by personal hygiene, public sanitation, and other means of controlling environmental hazards, by the availability and capabilities of medical services, and by diet.

Increasing life expectancy generally means that more people will become old but not necessarily that older people will live much longer than they had before. More than 70 percent of the infants born in the United States today should live past age 65, while only 40 percent of the infants born at the turn of century were expected to make it that far. However, for those Americans who reach 65, life expectancy has changed relatively little since 1900. For men, life expectancy at 65 is just two years longer than it was in 1900; for women, just six years longer.

The limited life expectancy gains of older people reflect our inability to extend life beyond its natural limits, no matter how good we get at controlling the factors that tend to shorten it. Preventing disease, resisting infection, and avoiding accidents can take us only so far. There's still the natural wear and tear on body organs and the deterioration of body systems over time. Unless we can control these, human life *span* — the maximum life expectancy possible for our species — isn't going to change much.

Just as the human species has a natural life span, so do individuals — the longevity our genes allow us if we are able to avoid accident and disease. Our potential longevity is no greater now than it ever was — 115 years is about the limit for the species, and the average individual life span falls somewhere around 85. Demographers point out that while the percentage of Americans past 65 has kept growing, the percentage passing the century mark has remained much the same.

Is it likely that medical science will come up with some means of increasing the human life span — a true formula for life extension? So far the answer is a qualified *no*. What qualifies it is how poorly the mechanisms of aging are understood, how little financial support has been given to research on aging in the past, and how much research is presently under way. Among possible nutritional routes to life extension now being explored are undernutrition (not malnutrition) and the use of dietary antioxidants.

The notion that underfeeding can increase life span comes from studies of laboratory rats and mice, which can indeed exceed the characteristic limits of longevity for their kind if they are put on calorie-restricting diets soon after weaning. But although these diets provide adequate amounts of all nutrients, they are so limited in calories that the rats are unable to grow. To have the best chance of setting new life-span records, they must remain on extremely restricted diets (one third of what free-feeding rats and mice eat) until they die. Less extreme diets (70 percent of the free-feeding norm), which retard growth minimally, provide only modest gains in life extension. However, full-grown rodents have shown life-span gains when gradually introduced to restrictive diets in middle age.

Before we assume that what is good for mice is also good for men and women, it's important to note the reservations that many rodent-feeding researchers have about these studies. They point out that laboratory rats and mice are, in general, an overfed and short-lived lot and not necessarily characteristic of their species. So it is possible that underfeeding prolongs life by correcting dietary excesses.

Caloric restriction also lowers the animals' metabolic rates (it's as if they were hibernating while awake), and this metabolic slowdown itself is likely to be the reason for the longer life span of underfed rodents. But its undesirable effects, including physical weakness, make underfeeding an unacceptable life-extension strategy for human beings.

Some researchers have proposed the use of dietary antioxidants — including vitamins A, C, and E, and selenium — as a possible means of life extension. This hypothesis is based on the theory that aging is, in large measure, the result of destructive action by free radicals, those highly reactive molecules (the body's pyromaniacs) that oxidize and destroy tissue. Although dietary antioxidants can indeed help protect vulnerable cells from free radicals, there is no evidence to date that they have any impact on life span.

In fact, micronutrient supplementation, in general, does not appear to provide any longevity gains. Studies of vitamin consumption among a highly selected and nutrition-conscious group of older Americans — readers of *Prevention* magazine — found no relation between mortality and levels of vitamin consumption, except for *increased* mortality rates among those who megadosed on vitamin E (taking more than 100 times the RDA).

In short, there is still no useful way to apply nutrition to the extension of life beyond the natural limits for humans as a species or beyond the individual life-span limits that are our genetic heritage. Still, this reality has not prevented a good many older Americans from seeking rejuvenating regimens. Longevity through diet or supplements sells well.

But the apparent inability of nutrition to break the life-span barrier does not mean the aging can safely ignore basic dietary needs. Although nutrition cannot extend life, nutritional inadequacies clearly can shorten it. Diet can also help limit the impact of disease and permit the elderly to enjoy maximum health and vitality before reaching genetically imposed limits on longevity.

The trouble is that the role of diet among the aging is not one of the better-understood aspects of nutrition. "We have no data concerning how nutrient requirements evolve as people grow older," admits Jean Mayer, the prestigious nutritionist who is president of Tufts University, where the federally sponsored Human Nutrition Research Center on Aging was opened in 1982. Although studies at the center are concerned with sustaining health rather than combating illness, much of its research focuses on degenerative conditions (like osteoporosis, cataracts, and the slowdown of immune responses) that are a part of aging. Indeed, it is difficult to consider the nature and needs of older Americans without taking illness into account.

Americans over 65 generally suffer from several chronic conditions, see their physicians frequently, and consume a great deal of medication. One out of four is hospitalized each year. As a result, they tend to be more health-conscious than the rest of the nation. So it's surprising to find so many ignoring the health consequences of inadequate diets. Government studies of "free-living" older men and women (whose diets can be quite different from those of the institutionalized aging in nursing homes and hospitals) have shown that more than half get less than two thirds of the recommended daily allowances (RDAs), both for calories and for several vitamins and minerals.

But the RDAs these aging Americans fail to meet are not necessarily an appropriate set of allowances for many of them. There is only one set of RDAs for *all* men and women over 50, and there is substantial evidence that nutritional needs change dramatically between the ages of 51 and 65 or 75. As Columbia University's Dr. Myron Winick explains the situation, "Today there is not a single nutrient for which there is a recommended daily allowance for men and women 65 and older. Even worse, there is no data base on which to formulate such recommendations."

Nutritionists are now busy catching up on the special needs and nutritional problems of the aging, not only at the Tufts center and the National Institute on Aging but at universities and research centers across the country. They are investigating physiological changes that alter nutritional needs, aspects of disease prevention that respond to dietary influences, and the roles that foodstyle and other lifestyle changes play in determining food choices and eating patterns of the aging.

EATING PATTERNS OF THE AGING

Eating is generally a more troublesome and less rewarding activity for the aging than for the young. The eating patterns of older people reflect the effects of diminished sensory perception — losses in taste and smell and vision — as well as lost teeth, poor dentures, and limited income.

Appetite is likely to suffer when the ability to taste declines, and a gradual loss of taste appears to be part of the aging process. Taste thresholds for salt, bitter, and sweet start to rise after age 50 — for sour, after age 60 — and 75-year-olds have only half as many taste buds as 30-year-olds. In studies of taste sensitivity, the thresholds for sweetness of aging subjects have been found to be three times greater than those of younger subjects. In other words, the elderly may require three times as much sweetener to experience the same taste sensation as the young. And this taste loss does not appear to be reversible. It is not usually the result of zinc deficiency, even though lack of sufficient zinc (which can cause taste loss in younger people) is fairly common among the aging.

The limited ability of the elderly to appreciate flavor derives not only from loss of taste but from a diminished sense of smell as well. It often also involves poor oral hygiene, for many older persons complain of abnormal tastes that are caused by decay or other dental problems. Teeth or the lack of them clearly contribute to the eating habits of the aging in other ways as well. Roughly half of all Americans over 65 do not have enough natural teeth left to eat a normal diet without difficulty. Loss of teeth makes it difficult to chew meat, fresh fruits, and fresh vegetables. Loss of bone can make dentures hard to fit, and 10 percent of the older Americans who have full sets of dentures find them unsatisfactory.

Social factors also influence how and what older people eat. Diminished income, increased isolation, and the psychological repercussions of retirement, including loss of motivation and self-esteem, all play a role. Apathy extends to lack of interest in preparing meals and eating. This is particularly true of older men who have lost their wives. It is less true of women who have lost husbands.

CHANGING NUTRITIONAL NEEDS

The aging body is plainly a different body from the body of youth or even the body of middle years. It is during the middle years, however, that hormonal changes begin and the body starts to slow down noticeably. As we age, our metabolic rate declines. We become less active. But our energy needs are reduced before our eating habits change, and for a time we are likely to consume more calories than we need and to gain weight as a result.

Lean body mass decreases with age. Our bodies lose muscle and add fat. But relative plumpness among the aging is not necessarily something to be avoided. According to Harold Sandstead, chairman of the department of preventive medicine and community health at the University of Texas Medical Branch at Galveston and former director of the Tufts center, "There is now some evidence that being 10 percent overweight may be beneficial for older people. It apparently has a survival benefit that being 10 percent underweight does not" (see chapter 10).

A clear benefit of extra weight for older women, as Sandstead points out, is the additional stress placed on bone, which stimulates maintenance of bone mass. But if a little extra weight helps, excessive weight hurts, for it can overburden bones already weakened by osteoporosis and cause compression fractures of the vertebrae.

With changes in body composition, age brings changes in the body's systems as well. Everything slows down — circulation, respiration, and heart and kidney function. The immune system also is affected, and one reason adequate nutrition is so important for the aging is to ensure maximum performance by their declining immune systems.

Adequate nutrition, however, is not easily achieved. Loss of muscle and lower activity levels reduce energy requirements. Appetite declines. The elderly need less food and want less.

To ensure enough vitamins and minerals, nutrient density becomes a major consideration in food choice. The aging do not have many spare calories to play with. Many do not have much discretionary income either. And while it is relatively easy to find foods that are rich in micronutrients when price is no concern, it becomes a great deal more difficult when you must work with limited income as well as limited calories.

Getting enough vitamins and minerals into their diets isn't the only nutritional obstacle the aging face. A number of older people, for example, have difficulty converting vitamin D to the hormone that stimulates absorption of calcium.

Absorption in general poses serious problems in later life. As many as 20–30 percent of the aging are unable to produce sufficient stomach acid, a condition called gastrochlorhydria. As a result, their bodies have trouble absorbing calcium, iron, and other trace elements. The stomach may also be unable to produce enough of the intrinsic factor required for vitamin B_{12} absorption, putting the aging at risk of pernicious anemia. When there is too little acid in the stomach to destroy bacteria there, the resulting bacterial invasion of the small intestine can reduce absorption of several vital micronutrients, including folacin.

It's also important to note that alcoholism is common among Americans over 65. Estimates run as high as 10 percent. But, whatever the incidence, the impact of excessive alcohol use on the nutritional status of the aging can be profound. First, alcohol becomes a substitute for more nutrient-dense sources of energy (alcohol's calories rank as low in nutrient density as calories can go). Next, alcohol creates absorption problems and inhibits the movement of folacin, thiamin, and vitamins B_6 and B_{12} into the bloodstream. Finally, alcohol's impact on the liver and pancreas can hamper the body's ability to use all of the fat-soluble vitamins (A, D, E, and K).

FOOD-DRUG INTERACTIONS

The aging are major users of medication. Three out of four Americans over 65 suffer from at least one chronic disease, and 40 percent take at least one drug on a daily basis. Those over 70 average 18 prescriptions a year. So the impact of medication on diet is of no small concern.

Physicians are generally well aware of the nutritional implications of medicines they prescribe. They will take care, for example, that antibiotics will not leave you lacking in vitamins K and B_{12}. But they can't help patients protect themselves from the effects of medications they don't know are being used. And a great many vital nutrients can be waylaid in the digestive tract by common over-the-counter drugs and household remedies.

Take mineral oil — as many aging Americans do — and you may (if you take it often enough) run short of fat-soluble vitamins, which are dissolved in the oil and moved out of the digestive tract before they can be absorbed. Diuretics will deplete bodily stores of calcium, potassium, magnesium, and zinc.

Cimetidine, the primary medication now prescribed for stomach ulcers, affects absorption of certain nutrients in much the same way as does gastrochlorhydria, the disorder that inhibits production of stomach acid. Ordinary antacids can produce these effects as well, inhibiting absorption of iron, calcium, and folacin and limiting production of the B_{12} intrinsic factor.

Heavy-duty vitamin and mineral supplementation, which is hazardous on many levels, can also cause deficiency-creating interactions. Zinc is a popular supplement these days, although there is no reason to believe that doses above RDA levels can relieve colds, cure warts, or do anything else this magical mineral is credited with accomplishing. But large doses of zinc will interfere with absorption of iron and copper. Megadoses of vitamin C can also create copper deficiencies. And an inadequate amount of copper in the bloodstream not only will reduce the body's ability to use iron but can also raise cholesterol levels.

Nutrient-drug interactions work both ways. Iron, zinc, and calcium, for example, will all inhibit absorption of tetracycline and other broad-spectrum antibiotics. Riboflavin interferes with the action of several psychoactive drugs, not by inhibiting absorption but by blocking receptors, the molecules on nerve cells that specially bind those drugs. Alcohol, if it overloads the liver, can increase the potency of some drugs, while protein and cruciferous vegetables (like cabbage and Brussels sprouts) can reduce drug potency by speeding up liver function and rushing drugs out of the bloodstream.

DIET VERSUS DISEASE AND DISABILITY

The major nutritional concern of most older people is likely to be the role of diet in preventing and possibly even arresting the diseases and disabilities of age. What, for example, can be done to reduce the risk of osteoporosis, which threatens almost all women — and a considerable number of aging men as well — with fractures of bones too weak to support body weight?

Like many diseases of age, osteoporosis is most readily prevented earlier in life, when the body is still building bone mass. Loss of bone, due to resorption of bone (as the body draws on its calcium reserves) starts at about age 40. Bone loss accelerates sharply for women after menopause, when they no longer produce the hormone estrogen, which plays an essential role in calcium retention.

Even late in life, however, it is still possible to retard bone loss, but not with calcium alone. Vitamin D, exercise, and prescription estrogen for women are needed. Adequate levels of phosphorus, zinc, copper, and manganese are important, and there is evidence that fluoridation of water will help. (For a more detailed description of osteoporosis and its prevention, see chapter 21.)

Screening for early indicators of those other life-threatening diseases that diet can help prevent should clearly be continued during the later years. Appropriate dietary interventions should be adopted if necessary to lower cholesterol levels in the blood or to reduce blood pressure (see chapters 17 and 18). Weight control remains the most effective means of preventing adult-onset diabetes (see chapter 20) and should be of concern if there is any family history of the disease. It is also prudent to follow the dietary strategies (described in chapter 19) that may minimize the risk of cancer.

For many of the elderly, no disability is more frightening than impaired thought and loss of memory, and there is evidence that at least some reduction in cognitive function is the result of nutritional deficiencies. Nursing home patients with severe deficiencies have suffered substantial losses of cognitive ability and memory.

Even mild deficiencies, it now appears, may cause some diminishment of cognition. A University of New Mexico study of older, well-educated, independent, and financially secure subjects, aged 60–94, found those with the poorest nutritional status scored lowest on tests of memory. In this study, the nutrients that appeared most important to mental acuity were protein, vitamin C, and a number of the B vitamins, including niacin, riboflavin, thiamin, folacin, B_6, and B_{12}.

Like loss of cognition and memory, arthritis is not a life-threatening condition. Yet no disability of age afflicts more older people with as much day-to-day discomfort or so limits their capacity to enjoy life. Much has been made in the press — and there is a whole body of nonprofessional literature — about dietary means of relieving arthritic pain and stiffness. But research has provided little basis for nutritionists to endorse any of these measures, although the use of eicosapentaenoic acid (EPA), a polyunsaturated fish oil, is now being tested.

COMMON DIETARY DEFICIENCIES OF THE AGING

There is some agreement but far from a consensus among nutritionists on just what nutrients the aging are likely to lack and how significant these deficiencies may actually be. Because so many factors can influence their eating habits, modify their nutritional needs, and limit their ability to absorb nutrients, older people can develop deficiencies of virtually any nutrient.

Certain dietary deficiencies merit special concern, however — either because they are so common or because they so threaten the well-being of the elderly. All should be guarded against, both by the aging themselves and by those responsible for their care. Among these deficiencies are shortages of the calcium and vitamin D necessary to combat osteoporosis. Zinc bears watching, for intake is generally well below the RDA, absorption is often compromised, and inadequate levels can reduce immune response and retard healing.

Iron is also a common deficiency of the aging, whose diets are noticeably lacking in rich sources of this mineral. Nevertheless, although anemia among the elderly may sometimes be caused by too little dietary iron, it more often results from infection or inadequate levels of folacin or B_{12}. So folacin and B_{12} belong on the list. Absorption of these two vitamins is frequently impeded by alcohol, drug interactions, and the diminished production of stomach acid. Even though the RDA for these vitamins may be set at levels higher than many older people either need or can use, concentrations in red blood cells are often well below safe levels, particularly among the less affluent elderly.

Folacin and B_{12} are not the only B vitamins the aging are likely to lack. There is also biomedical evidence of marginal thiamin deficiency, found in as many as one quarter of the elderly subjects in some studies. Levels of vitamin B_6 are too low for about one tenth of the aging population, and up to one quarter of the independent elderly in at least one study have been found to have inadequate levels of vitamin C.

REDUCING RISK

What it takes to minimize risk of deficiency and maximize nutritional benefits are sensible regular meals, vitamin-mineral supplements if they are needed, and exercise. That's true for everyone.

But regular meals aren't necessarily the rule for the aging. Older people living alone often tend to eat erratically. The availability of nutritious convenience foods is no guarantee of an adequate diet. For the aging, apathy can be more of an obstacle than problems of preparation or even limitations of income. They tend to pass up meals for snacks that lack the variety and nutrient density their diets require.

Mealtimes have been social occasions for older Americans throughout most of their lives. They are unused to eating alone. Opportunities to share meals with others, which many senior citizen centers now provide, go a long way toward overcoming their lack of interest in eating. Meals-on-Wheels programs for the homebound elderly, while they cannot offer the social opportunities of the centers, do provide a daily visit and ensure that older people get at least one complete meal a day (often meeting half their energy needs).

Since marginal deficiencies of a good many vitamins and minerals are common among the aging, supplementation with a multivitamin, multimineral formula is probably a sensible way to ensure adequate intake. Inappropriate as the current RDAs may be for some of the elderly, they are still the best available guide. So it's reasonable for older people to take a daily multiple supplement with 100 percent of the RDA for most of the micronutrients they are likely to lack.

Although exercise is an important aspect of nutrition at all stages of life, it is plainly not reasonable to start vigorous and demanding activity during the later years without a prolonged period of supervised training and conditioning. Unlike competitive athletes, the aging get no gain from pain. As Dr. Sandstead warns, "When it hurts, that's a signal to stop — that's nature's message."

Exercise is important, however, both for weight control and to lower the risk of osteoporosis. It's even possible that exercise may prove to prevent some physiological changes of aging that had seemed to be inevitable. At the University of California, Davis, Dr. Judith Stern has studied elderly rats exposed to cold for a number of hours. Ordinary rats respond to cold with a 5-degree drop in body temperature called hypothermia, displaying the same inability to sustain bodily warmth that kills many elderly people every winter. But elderly rats who have been exercised for several months can withstand the cold, with a drop in body temperature of less than half a degree.

What kind of exercise is both safe and effective for older individuals? Sandstead recommends walking. "It's probably the best exercise for older people," he says, and certainly best for those who have not taken part in a long-term exercise program. It expends energy and can substantially improve fitness if it involves a gradual increase in the distances covered.

Walking also provides opportunities for sociability, certainly more than jogging does. In some parts of the country, there are now groups that regularly meet for walks through shopping malls. Mall walking is particularly popular in warmer areas, where there are sizable numbers of retired persons and large air-conditioned malls to stroll through.

THE BOTTOM LINE: BASIC CONCERNS

Regular meals are the most important dietary consideration for older men and women, many of whom develop unsound eating habits and casual attitudes about food. Nevertheless, even regular and wholesome meals will not guarantee adequate nutrient intake. Micronutrient needs are high in later life (as body systems become less efficient), and they are made more difficult to meet by increased problems of absorption (including food-drug interactions). Vitamin and mineral deficiencies are common among the elderly, for whom supplementation with multivitamin, multimineral formulas is advisable.

To lower risk of life-threatening disease and to control obesity (which remains a problem for many older people), low-fat, high-carbohydrate diets with substantial amounts of fiber are prudent. Sustaining exercise throughout the later years is vital, both as a means of maintaining health and of extending life to its natural (genetically imposed) limits.

CHAPTER 28

Eating for Health and Pleasure

THAT'S WHAT IT'S ALL ABOUT. Nutrition is knowledge, not rigid rules and prohibitions. Understanding nutrition makes it your servant rather than your master. It doesn't mean that you will necessarily always eat wisely. But it does mean that you can balance your diet and compensate for its inadequacies.

Balance is the goal, and variety the primary means. Variety makes it easy to keep the ratio of carbohydrates, proteins, and fats in your diet within reasonable limits — getting about 50 percent of your calories from carbohydrates, 15 percent from proteins, and no more than 35 percent from fats. And variety can go a long way toward ensuring that all your micronutrient needs are being met.

Just listing the micronutrients you're most likely to lack — vitamins A, B_6, and C, thiamin and riboflavin, calcium, iron, and zinc — underlines the importance of variety. These, the most hard-to-get essentials, are found in milk and meat, legumes and grains, fruits and vegetables. In other words, it takes a little bit of everything to get by.

Still, there's no need to radically alter your foodstyle, even if you're not getting enough red meat to meet the RDA for iron or other trace elements or enough dairy products to keep calcium intake as high as it ought to be. That's what supplementation is for. Supplements not only provide micronutrients you may not choose to get from food, they also provide micronutrients at levels that can't be gotten from food alone.

But supplementation isn't always appropriate — and megadosing is hardly ever the answer. Vitamins and minerals do lots of wonderful things for your body, and they generally do all they can at RDA levels. With very few exceptions (and these therapeutic uses of micronutrients are still mostly experimental), megadosing is ill-advised. Heavy-handed supplementation raises the risk of toxic effects, which exist even for micronutrients like water-soluble vitamin B_6, once considered safe at almost any level. Even well below toxic levels, imprudent supplementation of one micronutrient (taking the wrong amounts at the wrong times) can cause food interactions that deprive you of other vitamins or minerals you need.

Although the potential dangers of oversupplementation are substantial, other nutritional risks are often exaggerated. It is this exaggeration that provides a basis for unreasonable food fears and senseless prohibitions that can diminish the pleasure of eating and create real nutritional problems.

Red meat is undeservedly (and dangerously) labeled bad because of its fats, specifically, the cholesterol and comparatively high levels of saturated fatty acids it contains. But the iron and other trace elements in red meat (impossible to find in such an available form elsewhere) make it sensible to balance fat intake in some way other than by cutting out red meat. Moreover, while saturates should indeed be limited, for they can raise levels of LDL cholesterol, wholesale substitution of polyunsaturates is far from safe, for they are a source of free radicals that increase risk of cancer.

Although salt will not cause hypertension (even though extreme salt restriction can lower blood pressure for some hypertensives), it is not nutritionally blameless either. High salt intake will lower calcium levels in the blood (since the kidneys have trouble reclaiming calcium when they are busy dumping excess sodium), forcing the body to withdraw calcium from bone to replace it.

Sugar does no harm, but complex carbohydrates can do more good. So restricting sugar allows you to take more of your calories in nutrient-rich grains, legumes, and vegetables. These foods also can provide much of the fiber you need to lower serum cholesterol levels and protect the large intestine from diverticulosis and the colon from mutagens that may cause colon cancer.

Alcohol is, on balance, a nutritional asset, for moderate drinking does have health benefits. It raises the ratio of HDL to LDL cholesterol in the bloodstream, thus lowering the risk of atherosclerosis. But at three drinks per day or more, alcohol increases the danger of hypertension. At higher levels of consumption, its impact is disastrous, and no level of drinking is prudent for pregnant women.

The whole notion of good and bad in foods derives, in part, from an an unrealistic expectation of harmlessness. The earth is full of toxic substances, many of them in foods, and our bodies are equipped to handle a substantial amount of toxins. Food additives, in general, are likely to be less harmful than natural toxic substances in food (which require no FDA approval). Some additives even provide inadvertent health benefits. Several preservatives that extend the shelf life of foods contain antioxidants (to prevent spoilage caused by oxidation). In the body, these antioxidants keep right on battling oxidation and help protect body cells from free radicals.

Notions of bad and good are rightly applied to eating habits, and a dangerously unbalanced (high-fat) diet or high-risk foodstyle is plainly not good. But obesity, which is generally perceived as the result of "bad" nutrition, is more closely linked to heredity than to diet. Although excess weight is a risk factor for several life-threatening diseases, it must exceed the ideal level by about 20 percent to be medically significant. But seeking a more slender shape when your excess poundage is either imaginary or substantially less than 20 percent can be nutritionally harmful.

Genetics is not destiny. Excess weight, even when there is a hereditary vulnerability to obesity, can be controlled if not eliminated. However, diet alone is a poor strategy. To take weight off, and keep it off, usually requires both diet and exercise. Moreover, exercise plays a far more significant role in preserving health and lowering risk of disease than weight control alone. It can substantially reduce the risk of just about every disease that can be nutritionally influenced, and it can limit the risk-raising potential of smoking and even heredity.

Best of all, exercise will allow you to consume more calories without gaining weight. If you exercise regularly, not only will you be healthier but you can eat more as well.

Eating, we believe, is one of life's chief pleasures, and you are entitled to enjoy whatever your individual foodstyle dictates. What you have learned should help you to relish the foods of your choice without danger, fear, or guilt. If your tastes are for epicurean fare or plain meat and potatoes, if you are hooked on fast foods, pasta, and beans, or on alfalfa sprouts and brown rice — none of them is inconsistent with sound nutrition. Understanding nutrition should be liberating, for knowledge is the way to expand rather than to restrict the pleasure you find in food.

APPENDIX

Table A1
Recommended Dietary Allowances, 1980

	Age (years)	Weight (kg)	Weight (lbs)	Height (cm)	Height (in)	Protein (g)	Fat-Soluble Vitamins			Water-Soluble Vitamins							Minerals					
							Vitamin A (RE)[a]	Vitamin D (µg)	Vitamin E (mg)	Vitamin C (mg)	Thiamin (mg)	Riboflavin (mg)	Niacin (mg)	Vitamin B6 (mg)	Folacin (µg)	Vitamin B12 (µg)	Calcium (mg)	Phosphorus (mg)	Magnesium (mg)	Iron (mg)	Zinc (mg)	Iodine (µg)
Infants	0.0–0.5	6	13	60	24	kg × 2.2	420	10	3	35	0.3	0.4	6	0.3	30	0.5	360	240	50	10	3	40
	0.5–1.0	9	20	71	28	kg × 2.0	400	10	4	35	0.5	0.6	8	0.6	45	1.5	540	360	70	15	5	50
Children	1–3	13	29	90	35	23	400	10	5	45	0.7	0.8	9	0.9	100	2.0	800	800	150	15	10	70
	4–6	20	44	112	44	30	500	10	6	45	0.9	1.0	11	1.3	200	2.5	800	800	200	10	10	90
	7–10	28	62	132	52	34	700	10	7	45	1.2	1.4	16	1.6	300	3.0	800	800	250	10	10	120
Males	11–14	45	99	157	62	45	1000	10	8	50	1.4	1.6	18	1.8	400	3.0	1200	1200	350	18	15	150
	15–18	66	145	176	69	56	1000	10	10	60	1.4	1.7	18	2.0	400	3.0	1200	1200	400	18	15	150
	19–22	70	154	177	70	56	1000	7.5	10	60	1.5	1.7	19	2.2	400	3.0	800	800	350	10	15	150
	23–50	70	154	178	70	56	1000	5	10	60	1.4	1.6	18	2.2	400	3.0	800	800	350	10	15	150
	51+	70	154	178	70	56	1000	5	10	60	1.2	1.4	16	2.2	400	3.0	800	800	350	10	15	150
Females	11–14	46	101	157	62	46	800	10	8	50	1.1	1.3	15	1.8	400	3.0	1200	1200	300	18	15	150
	15–18	55	120	163	64	46	800	10	8	60	1.1	1.3	14	2.0	400	3.0	1200	1200	300	18	15	150
	19–22	55	120	163	64	44	800	7.5	8	60	1.1	1.3	14	2.0	400	3.0	800	800	300	18	15	150
	23–50	55	120	163	64	44	800	5	8	60	1.0	1.2	13	2.0	400	3.0	800	800	300	18	15	150
	51+	55	120	163	64	44	800	5	8	60	1.0	1.2	13	2.0	400	3.0	800	800	300	10	15	150
Pregnant						+30	+200	+5	+2	+20	+0.4	+0.3	+2	+0.6	+400	+1.0	+400	+400	+150	b	+5	+25
Lactating						+20	+400	+5	+3	+40	+0.5	+0.5	+5	+0.5	+100	+1.0	+400	+400	+150	b	+10	+50

Note: The allowances are intended to provide for individual variations among most normal persons as they live in the United States under usual environmental stresses. Diets should be based on a variety of common foods in order to provide other nutrients for which human requirements have been less well defined.

a Retinol Equivalents (1 retinol equivalent = 1 µg retinol or 6 µg beta-carotene).

b The increased requirement during pregnancy cannot be met by the iron content of habitual American diets nor by the existing iron stores of many women; therefore the use of 30–60 mg of supplemental iron is recommended. Iron needs during lactation are not substantially different from those of non-pregnant women, but continued supplementation of the mother for 2–3 months after parturition is advisable in order to replenish stores depleted by pregnancy.

Table A2

Estimated Safe and Adequate Daily Dietary Intakes of Selected Vitamins and Minerals

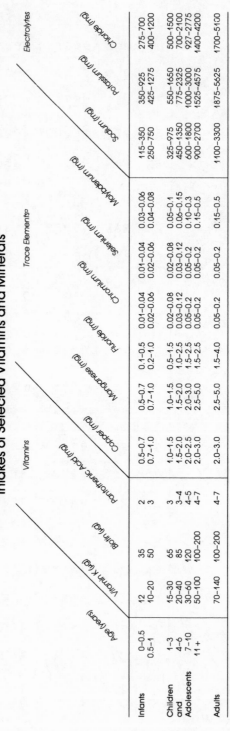

| | Vitamins | | | Trace Elements[a] | | | | | | Electrolytes | | |
Age (Years)	Vitamin K (µg)	Biotin (µg)	Pantothenic Acid (mg)	Copper (mg)	Manganese (mg)	Fluoride (mg)	Chromium (mg)	Selenium (mg)	Molybdenum (mg)	Sodium (mg)	Potassium (mg)	Chloride (mg)
Infants 0–0.5	12	35	2	0.5–0.7	0.5–0.7	0.1–0.5	0.01–0.04	0.01–0.04	0.03–0.06	115–350	350–925	275–700
0.5–1	10–20	50	3	0.7–1.0	0.7–1.0	0.2–1.0	0.02–0.06	0.02–0.06	0.04–0.08	250–750	425–1275	400–1200
Children and Adolescents 1–3	15–30	65	3	1.0–1.5	1.0–1.5	0.5–1.5	0.02–0.08	0.02–0.08	0.05–0.1	325–975	550–1650	500–1500
4–6	20–40	85	3–4	1.5–2.0	1.5–2.0	1.0–2.5	0.03–0.12	0.03–0.12	0.06–0.15	450–1350	775–2325	700–2100
7–10	30–60	120	4–5	2.0–2.5	2.0–3.0	1.5–2.5	0.05–0.2	0.05–0.2	0.10–0.3	600–1800	1000–3000	927–2775
11+	50–100	100–200	4–7	2.0–3.0	2.5–5.0	1.5–2.5	0.05–0.2	0.05–0.2	0.15–0.5	900–2700	1525–4575	1400–4200
Adults	70–140	100–200	4–7	2.0–3.0	2.5–5.0	1.5–4.0	0.05–0.2	0.05–0.2	0.15–0.5	1100–3300	1875–5625	1700–5100

Note: Because there is less information on which to base allowances, these figures are not given in the main table of the RDA and are provided here in the form of ranges of recommended intakes.

[a] Since the toxic levels for many trace elements may be only several times usual intakes, the upper levels for the trace elements given in this table should not be habitually exceeded.

Table A3

Mean Heights and Weights and Recommended Energy Intake

	Age (years)	Weight (kg)	(lb)	Height (cm)	(in)	Energy Needs (with range) (Kcal)
Infants	0.0–0.5	6	13	60	24	kg × 115 kg × (95–145)
	0.5–1.0	9	20	71	28	kg × 105 kg × (80–135)
Children	1–3	13	29	90	35	1300 (900–1800)
	4–6	20	44	112	44	1700 (1300–2300)
	7–10	28	62	132	52	2400 (1650–3300)
Males	11–14	45	99	157	62	2700 (2000–3700)
	15–18	66	145	176	69	2800 (2100–3900)
	19–22	70	154	177	70	2900 (2500–3300)
	23–50	70	154	178	70	2700 (2300–3100)
	51–75	70	154	178	70	2400 (2000–2800)
	76+	70	154	178	70	2050 (1650–2450)
Females	11–14	46	101	157	62	2200 (1500–3000)
	15–18	55	120	163	64	2100 (1200–3000)
	19–22	55	120	163	64	2100 (1700–2500)
	23–50	55	120	163	64	2000 (1600–2400)
	51–75	55	120	163	64	1800 (1400–2200)
	76+	55	120	163	64	1600 (1200–2000)
Pregnant						+300
Lactating						+500

Table A4

Nutritive Value of Foods in
Average Servings or Common Measures

Explanatory Notes:

[a] Symbols used are: tr = trace; u = unknown but thought to be present; 0 = absent or below detection limit.

[b] In bleached asparagus, vitamin A activity is 8 RE.

[c] All canned foods listed, except fruits, have salt added according to commercial practice, unless otherwise noted.

[d] Made with yellow maize-corn meal.

[e] Based on green variety.

[f] If added, approximately 375 RE vitamin A and approximately 15 mg vitamin C per 1 oz portion.

[g] Yellow variety; white products have essentially no Vitamin A activity.

[h] No salt added.

[i] Vitamin A–fortified fluid milk has 140 RE per cup.

[j] Buttermilk has 320 mg sodium per cup.

[k] Zinc content of oysters may vary from 6 to 100 mg/100 gm, probably as a result of environmental conditions. Ascorbic acid content also is variable, from traces to 30 mg/100 gm.

Source: Nutrition and Physical Fitness, 11/e, by George M. Briggs and Doris Howes Calloway. Copyright © 1984 by CBS College Publishing. © 1979 by Saunders College Publishing/Holt, Rinehart & Winston under the title *Bogart's Nutrition and Physical Fitness.* Reprinted by permission of Holt, Rinehart & Winston, Inc.

Food	Weight (gm)	Approximate Measure	Calories (Kcal)	Protein (gm)	Fat (gm)	Total Carbohydrate (gm)	Calcium (mg)	Phosphorus (mg)	Magnesium (mg)	Sodium (mg)
Almonds, chopped	15	12–15 nuts, 2 tbsp	90	3.0	8.0	3	35	75	40	1
Apples, raw with skins	140	1 medium 3/lb	80	0.3	0.5	20	10	10	6	1
Apple juice, canned, no sugar added	125	½ c	60	0.1	tr	15	10	10	4	4
Applesauce, sweetened	125	½ c	100	0.2	0.2	25	5	10	4	4
Apricot										
Fresh	100	2–3 medium	50	1.4	0.4	11	15	20	8	1
Canned, with skin heavy syrup	85	3 halves, 1¾ tbsp juice	70	0.4	0.1	18	5	10	6	3
water pack	85	3 halves, 1¾ tbsp juice	20	0.6	0.1	5	10	10	6	2
Dried, sulfured, raw	30	6–8 medium halves	75	1.2	0.2	20	15	40	15	3
Apricot nectar, canned	125	½ c	70	0.4	0.1	18	10	10	7	4
Artichokes, French, boiled	120	1 large (300 gm as purchased)	30	3.0	0.2	12	60	85	uª	35
Asparagus,										
Fresh, green, cooked	100	½ c cut, 6–7 spears	25	3.0	0.2	4	20	65	15	7
Canned, saltᶜ added	100	½ c cut, 6–7 spears	15	2.0	0.2	3	20	45	9	373
Avocados	100	½ fruit, 4 in long	160	2.0	15	7	10	40	40	10
Baby foods										
Dinners	130	Contents 4½ oz jar								
beef-noodle			70	3.0	2.0	9	12	35	9	35
beef-vegetable			100	7.0	5.5	5	15	62	10	45
vegetable-beef-cereal			60	2.5	1.0	10	20	50	8	60
Fruits and desserts	130	Contents 4¾ oz jar								
apple sauce-pineapple			50	0.1	0.1	13	5	8	4	3
custard pudding			110	2.0	2.5	20	70	60	70	80
fruit pudding			105	1.5	0.4	25	40	40	11	25
Bacon, broiled, drained	25	2 strips, thick	140	6.5	12.5	1	3	55	5	245
Bagels	60	4 in diameter	175	6.5	1.5	34	25	40	12	215
Bamboo shoots	100	¾ c	25	2.5	0.3	5	13	60	45	25
Bananas	115	1 medium	105	1.2	0.6	27	10	20	35	1
Beans										
Canned, with pork and tomato sauce	130	½ c	160	8.0	3.5	25	70	115	35	590
Canned, with pork and sweet sauce	130	½ c	190	8.0	6.0	25	80	145	35	485
Green, snap, fresh or frozen	65	½ c	15	1.0	0.1	3	28	15	13	3
canned	65	½ c	15	0.9	0.1	3	20	15	8	260
Lima, fresh or frozen, boiled	85	½ c	90	5.5	0.3	17	20	60	32	64
Red, canned	125	½ c	120	7.0	0.5	20	35	140	35	4
Refried	120	½ c	230	8.5	12.5	25	50	165	35	340
Soybeans, mature, dry, cooked	90	½ c (1 oz, dry wt.)	120	10.0	5.0	10	65	160	80	2

Po-tas-sium (mg)	Zinc (mg)	Cop-per (mg)	Iron (mg)	Total Vitamin A Activity (RE)	Thia-min (mg)	Ribo-flavin (mg)	Nia-cin (mg)	Vita-min B_6 (mg)	Panto-thenic Acid (mg)	Fola-cin Total (µg)	Vita-min B_{12} (µg)	Vita-min C (mg)	Polyun-saturated Fatty Acids (gm)
115	0.2	0.1	0.7	0ᵃ	0.04	0.1	0.5	0.02	0.07	15	0	trᵃ	1.6
159	0.05	0.01	0.3	7	0.02	0.02	0.1	0.07	0.1	75	0	8	0.1
150	0.04	0.03	0.5	0	0.03	0.02	0.1	0.04	0.07	tr	0	1	0.03
80	0.05	0.06	0.5	1	0.02	0.04	0.2	0.03	0.07	1	0	2	0.07
300	0.3	0.09	0.5	270	0.03	0.04	0.6	0.05	0.2	9	0	10	0.08
120	0.09	0.07	0.3	110	0.02	0.02	0.3	0.05	0.08	1	0	3	0.02
160	0.09	0.07	0.3	110	0.02	0.02	0.3	0.05	0.08	2	0	3	0.03
480	0.3	0.15	1.5	250	tr	0.05	1.0	0.06	0.3	3	0	3	0.03
140	0.1	0.09	0.5	165	0.01	0.02	0.3	0.05	0.08	2	0	1	tr
360	0.4	0.4	1.3	20	0.08	0.05	0.8	0.30	0.60	150	0	10	tr
270	0.6	0.1	0.7	85	0.1	0.1	1.3	0.13	0.2	190	0	30	tr
195	0.5	0.1	0.6	65	0.06	0.1	0.7	0.06	0.2	85	0	18	tr
600	0.4	0.2	1.0	60	0.1	0.1	1.9	0.3	1.0	60	0	8	2.0
60	0.5	0.04	0.5	140	0.05	0.5	0.9	0.06	0.3	65	0.1	2.0	u
180	1.7	0.1	0.9	140	0.04	0.08	2.0	0.10	0.3	7	0.6	2.0	u
100	0.5	0.04	0.5	50	0.06	0.05	1.0	0.07	0.3	2	0.3	1	u
100	0.02	0.04	0.3	3	0.03	0.03	0.1	0.05	u	2.5	0	36	0.
60	0.4	0.06	0.3	8	0.02	0.1	0.1	0.03	0.3	7.5	u	1	u
100	0.2	0.04	0.2	5	0.05	0.06	0.1	0.05	u	u	0.08	35	u
60	1.2	0.1	0.8	0	0.1	0.08	1.0	0.03	0.08	0.5	0.2	0	1.0
45	0.3	0.05	1.6	0	0.2	0.2	2.1	0.03	0.2	14	0	0	u
530	u	u	0.5	2	0.15	0.07	0.6	u	u	u	0	4	u
450	0.2	0.12	0.4	9	0.05	0.1	0.6	0.7	0.3	22	0	10	0.09
270	1.0	0.2	2.3	15	0.10	0.04	0.8	0.4	0.1	30	0	3	u
u	1.0	0.3	3.0	u	0.08	0.05	0.7	0.1	0.1	10	0	3	u
105	0.1	0.03	0.6	30	0.04	0.05	0.2	0.03	0.1	30	0	6	tr
80	0.1	0.06	0.4	30	0.01	0.03	0.2	0.03	0.1	12	0	2	tr
405	0.4	0.5	1.2	20	0.07	0.06	1.0	0.1	0.2	75	0	17	tr
335	1.0	0.2	2.3	tr	0.06	0.05	0.8	0.4	0.1	35	0	0	tr
360	1.0	0.2	2.3	tr	0.30	0.07	0.8	0.2	0.2	20	0	0	u
490	0.6	0.3	2.5	2	0.20	0.08	0.6	u	u	70	0	0	3.0

Food	Weight (gm)	Approximate Measure	Calories (Kcal)	Pro-tein (gm)	Fat (gm)	Total Carbo-hy-drate (gm)	Cal-cium (mg)	Phos-pho-rus (mg)	Mag-ne-sium (mg)	So-dium (mg)
Bean sprouts, See Sprouts										
Beef										
Corned, canned	80	2 slices each, 3 in × 2 in × ¼ in	170	20.0	9.5	0	15	85	20	u
hash, with potatoes	110	½ c	200	10.0	12.5	12	15	75	20	595
Dried, creamed	120	½ c	190	10.0	12.5	9	130	170	40	880
Hamburger, broiled, lean, 21% fat	85	4/lb, raw wt.	240	20.0	16.5	0	10	160	20	50
very lean, 10% fat	85	4/lb, raw wt.	190	23.0	9.5	0	10	195	20	60
Roast, chuck, braised	85	3 oz	240	23.0	16.5	0	10	115	20	40
rib, U.S. choice	85	3 oz	380	17.0	33.5	0	10	160	20	40
Steak, broiled										
round with fat	85	3 oz	220	24.5	13.0	0	10	215	25	60
sirloin with fat	85	3 oz	330	20.0	27.0	0	10	160	20	50
Beef stew, with vegetables	245	1 c	220	15.5	10.5	15	30	185	50	90
Beer	360	12 oz container	150	0.9	0	13	15	50	35	18
Beet greens, boiled	75	½ c	15	1.0	0.2	2	70	20	80	55
Beets, sliced, canned	85	½ c	30	0.8	0.1	7	1	10	10	240
Beverages. See Carbonated beverages, and individual entries.										
Biscuits, from mix, enriched	30	1 of 2 in. diameter	100	2.0	3.6	15	5	120	4	375
Blackberries, boysenberries, etc., raw	70	½ c	35	0.5	0.3	9	25	15	14	0
Blueberries, raw	70	½ c	40	0.5	0.3	10	5	10	4	5
Bok Choy. See Pak Choy.										
Brazil nuts, raw	30	6 large nuts	180	4.0	19.0	3	55	195	65	tr
Bread										
Boston brown, canned	45	1 slice, ½ in thick	95	2.5	0.6	20	40	70	u	115
Corn, from mix	55	2½ in square	180	4.0	6.0	30	135	210	10	265
Cracked wheat	25	1 slice	65	2.3	0.9	12	15	30	9	110
French, Vienna, Italian, enriched	25	1 slice	70	2.4	0.9	13	25	20	5	140
Fry bread, Indian, enriched	60	1 piece, medium	200	4.0	7.5	28	80	80	u	305
Raisin, enriched	25	1 slice	70	2.0	1.0	13	25	20	6	95
Rye, American	25	1 slice	65	2.1	0.9	12	20	40	6	175
White, not enriched	25	1 slice	65	2.1	1.0	12	30	25	5	125
enriched	25	1 slice	65	2.1	1.0	12	30	25	5	125
Whole wheat	25	1 slice	60	2.4	1.1	11	20	65	25	160
Broccoli, fresh or frozen, boiled	85	½ c	25	2.4	0.2	4	45	45	14	2
Brussels sprouts, fresh or frozen, boiled	85	4 large sprouts	30	3.1	0.2	6	25	50	17	12
Burrito, beef, Taco Bell	184	1	465	30.0	21.0	37	85	290	u	325
Butter, salted	5	1 tsp or pat (90/lb)	35	tr	4.0	tr	1	1	tr	40
	15	1 tbsp	100	0.1	11.5	0.1	3	3	tr	120
Cabbage, green, headed										
Raw, shredded	70	1 c	17	0.9	0.1	4	35	20	10	15
Cooked, chopped	70	½ c	15	0.8	0.2	3	30	15	10	10

Po-tas-sium (mg)	Zinc (mg)	Cop-per (mg)	Iron (mg)	Total Vitamin A Activity (RE)	Thia-min (mg)	Ribo-flavin (mg)	Nia-cin (mg)	Vita-min B$_6$ (mg)	Panto-thenic Acid (mg)	Fola-cin Total (µg)	Vita-min B$_{12}$ (µg)	Vita-min C (mg)	Polyun-saturated Fatty Acids (gm)
u	2.5	u	3.4	tr	0.02	0.20	3.0	0.08	0.5	2	1.5	0	0.4
220	1.4	u	2.2	tr	0.01	0.10	2.5	0.08	0.6	u	0.8	0	u
190	1.8	u	1.0	130	0.08	0.20	0.8	0.6	0.7	u	u	1	u
220	3.7	0.07	2.6	10	0.07	0.20	4.5	0.4	0.3	3	1.5	0	0.7
260	4.9	0.09	3.0	7	0.08	0.20	5.0	0.4	0.3	3	1.5	0	0.4
185	3.7	0.07	2.9	10	0.04	0.20	3.5	0.4	0.3	3	1.5	0	0.7
190	3.1	0.07	2.2	20	0.05	0.10	3.0	0.3	0.3	3	1.5	0	1.4
270	5.0	0.09	3.0	7	0.07	0.20	5.0	0.3	0.4	3	2.2	0	0.6
220	3.7	0.07	2.5	15	0.05	0.20	4.0	0.3	0.4	3	1.5	0	1.2
615	2.4	0.05	2.9	250	0.15	0.15	4.7	0.3	0.2	7	1.6	15	u
115	0.2	0.3	0.1	0	0	tr	1.8	0.2	0.2	20	0	0	0
240	0.5	0.1	1.4	370	0.05	0.10	0.2	0.08	0.2	20	0	10	tr
145	0.2	0.1	0.5	tr	0.01	0.03	0.4	0.04	0.1	25	0	2	tr
30	0.1	0.02	0.6	0	0.1	0.1	1.0	0.01	0.1	2	0	0	u
140	0.2	0.1	0.4	12	0.02	0.03	0.3	0.04	0.2	4	0	15	tr
65	0.1	0.04	0.1	7	0.03	0.03	0.3	0.03	0.1	5	0	9	tr
205	1.4	0.4	1.0	tr	0.30	0.03	0.5	0.05	0.1	tr	0	0	7.4
130	u	u	0.9	3	0.05	0.03	0.5	u	u	u	0	0	u
60	0.2	0.02	0.8	15[d]	0.10	0.10	0.8	0.03	0.2	5	0.1	0	u
35	0.4	0.08	0.7	tr	0.09	0.09	0.9	0.02	0.1	u	0	tr	u
20	0.2	0.04	0.8	tr	0.12	0.09	1.0	0.01	0.9	9	0	tr	u
35	u	u	1.0	0	0.10	0.09	1.3	0.02	0.2	10	0	0	u
60	0.2	0.03	0.8	tr	0.08	0.15	1.0	0.01	0.1	9	0	tr	u
50	0.3	0.03	0.7	0	0.1	0.08	0.8	0.02	0.1	10	0	0	u
30	0.2	0.03	0.1	tr	0.03	0.02	0.03	0.01	0.1	9	0	tr	u
30	0.2	0.03	0.7	tr	0.1	0.08	0.9	0.01	0.1	9	0	tr	u
45	0.4	0.09	0.9	tr	0.09	0.05	1.0	0.05	0.2	14	0	tr	u
190	0.2	0.03	0.7	170	0.04	0.09	0.4	0.11	0.2	50	0	50	tr
290	0.3	0.03	0.6	60	0.1	0.1	0.5	0.16	0.3	130	0	60	tr
320	u	u	4.6	335	0.3	0.4	7.0	u	u	u	u	15	u
1	tr	0	tr	40	tr	tr	tr	0	0	0	tr	0	0.1
3	tr	0	tr	115	tr	tr	tr	0	0	0	tr	0	0.3
165	0.3	0.08	0.3	10	0.04	0.04	0.2	0.1	0.1	20	0	35	tr
120	0.3	0.02	0.2	10	0.03	0.03	0.2	0.09	0.1	2	0	25	tr

Food	Weight (gm)	Approximate Measure	Calories (Kcal)	Pro-tein (gm)	Fat (gm)	Total Carbo-hy-drate (gm)	Cal-cium (mg)	Phos-pho-rus (mg)	Mag-ne-sium (mg)	So-dium (mg)
Cakes										
Angel food	40	2 in sector of 10 in cake	105	3.1	0.1	24	5	10	5	110
Cheese cake, frozen	85	1/10 of cake	255	4.6	16.0	24	50	75	8	190
Chocolate with chocolate icing	90	2 in sector of 8 in cake	350	3.9	16.0	51	75	95	30	160
Gingerbread	65	2¾ in square	250	2.8	12.0	32	45	35	14	90
Cupcake, iced	50	1 medium	190	2.0	6.0	30	60	95	10	160
Pound cake	30	3½ in × 3 in × ½ in	140	1.5	9.0	14	6	25	5	35
Yellow with chocolate icing	70	2 in sector of 8 in cake	270	2.9	12.0	41	60	60	13	195
Candy										
Caramels	30	1 oz	120	1.0	3.0	20	40	35	u	65
Chocolate bar										
plain milk chocolate	30	1 oz	150	2.2	9.0	16	65	65	20	25
with almonds	30	1 oz	150	2.5	10.0	14	65	75	u	25
Fudge with nuts	30	1 oz	120	1.0	5.0	20	20	30	u	50
Hard	30	1 oz	110	0	0.3	30	6	2	0	10
Marshmallow	30	1 oz, 4 large	90	0.6	tr	25	5	2	u	10
Peanut brittle	30	1 oz	120	1.5	3.0	25	10	25	u	10
Cantaloupe. See Melons.										
Carbonated beverages sweet, cola type	170	6 oz	70	0	0	19	5	30	2	5
Carrots										
Raw	80	1 carrot 7½ in × 1⅛ in	35	0.9	0.1	7	25	25	10	35
Boiled	70	½ c diced	20	0.5	0.1	4	20	15	8	25
Cashews, roasted	30	1 oz	160	5.0	13.0	8	10	105	80	60
Cauliflower										
Raw	50	½ c whole flower buds	10	2.0	0.1	2	10	20	6	10
Boiled	60	½ c	15	2.0	0.1	3	15	20	7	12
Celery										
Raw	80	2 large stalks	15	0.8	0.1	3	30	20	17	100
Boiled	75	½ c diced	10	0.6	0.1	2	25	15	u	65
Cereals, breakfast										
Ready-to-eat										
bran flakes, 40% enriched	30	1 oz	90	3.5	0.5	22	15	140	50	260
corn flakes, enriched	30	1 oz	110	2.0	0.1	24	1	20	3	350
granola	30	1 oz	150	3.5	7.7	16	20	115	35	3
rice, puffed, enriched	15	½ oz	60	0.9	0.1	13	1	15	3	0
wheat flakes, enriched	30	1 oz	100	3.0	0.5	23	45	100	30	350
wheat, shredded	30	1 oz	100	3.0	0.6	23	10	100	40	3
Cooked (1.3 oz, dry wt, salt added)										
cornmeal and grits, degermed										
unenriched	240	1 c	145	3.5	0.5	31	1	30	10	520
enriched	240	1 c	145	3.5	0.5	31	1	30	10	520
cornmeal, bolted, whole	240	1 c	145	3.5	1.6	29	8	100	u	u
oatmeal	240	1 c	145	6.0	2.4	25	20	180	55	380
wheat, farina light, enriched (e.g., Cream of Wheat)	250	1 c	135	4.0	0.5	28	50	40	10	330
Whole meal (eg., Ralston)	250	1 c	135	5.5	0.8	28	15	150	60	470

Potassium (mg)	Zinc (mg)	Copper (mg)	Iron (mg)	Total Vitamin A Activity (RE)	Thiamin (mg)	Riboflavin (mg)	Niacin (mg)	Vitamin B_6 (mg)	Pantothenic Acid (mg)	Folacin Total (μg)	Vitamin B_{12} (μg)	Vitamin C (mg)	Polyunsaturated Fatty Acids (gm)
40	0.1	0.02	0.3	0	tr	0.1	0.4	tr	0.1	4	tr	tr	0
85	0.4	0.05	0.4	65	0.03	0.1	0.4	0.05	0.5	15	0.4	4	u
130	0.6	0.2	1.3	15	0.08	0.1	0.8	0.03	0.3	6	0.1	tr	u
220	0.3	0.1	2.0	7	0.12	0.1	1.0	0.05	0.3	5	0.1	tr	u
55	0.2	0.06	0.4	25	0.02	0.05	0.1	0.01	0.1	4	0.1	0	u
20	0.2	0.02	0.2	25	0.01	0.03	0.1	0.01	0.09	2	u	0	u
75	0.3	0.08	0.3	15	0.08	0.1	0.7	0.02	0.2	6	0.1	tr	u
55	u	0.01	0.4	tr	0.01	0.05	0.1	tr	0	u	u	0	u
110	0.1	0.3	0.3	20	0.02	0.10	0.1	tr	0.03	2	u	0	u
125	0.1	u	0.5	20	0.02	0.10	0.2	tr	u	1	u	0	u
50	0.1	u	0.3	tr	0.01	0.03	0.1	u	u	u	tr	0	u
1	0	0.03	0.5	0	0	0	0	0	0	0	0	0	0
2	0.01	0.06	0.5	0	0	tr	tr	u	u	0	0	0	0
45	u	u	0.7	0	0.05	0.01	1.0	u	u	u	0	0	u
3	0.01	0.1	0.1	0	0	0	0	0	0	0	0	0	0
155	0.3	0.05	0.6	880	0.03	0.04	0.6	0.04	0.2	24	0	4	0
155	0.2	0.05	0.3	800	0.01	0.02	0.4	0.02	0.1	16	0	3	0
130	1.3	0.2	1.1	3	0.1	0.07	0.5	0.1	0.4	20	0	0	u
100	0.1	0.01	0.3	1	0.02	0.04	0.2	0.06	0.1	30	0	25	0
120	0.1	0.01	0.3	1	0.03	0.04	0.2	0.07	0.1	25	0	30	0
270	u	0.09	0.2	20[e]	0.02	0.02	0.2	0.05	0.3	10	0	8	tr
180	u	0.08	0.2	20[e]	0.02	0.02	0.2	0.05	0.3	u	0	4	tr
180	3.7	0.2	8.1	375	0.4	0.4	5.0	0.5	u	14	1.5	0[f]	tr
25	0.08	0.02	1.8	0[f]	0.3	0.4	3.0	0.02	0.05	3	0	0[f]	tr
140	1.0	0.2	1.1	1	0.17	0.07	0.5	0.10	0.2	14	0	0	u
15	0.2	0.03	0.2	0[f]	0.02	0.01	0.4	0.01	0.04	3	0	0[f]	tr
105	0.7	0.1	4.5	375[f]	0.4	0.4	5.0	0.05	0.2	9	1.5	15[f]	0.24
100	0.9	0.2	1.2	0	0.07	0.08	1.5	0.07	0.2	12	0	0	tr
55	0.2	0.03	0.2	14[g]	0.04	0.02	0.5	0.06	u	1	0	0	tr
55	0.2	0.03	1.5	14[g]	0.24	0.15	2.0	0.06	u	1	0	0	tr
110	0.7	u	0.9	20[g]	0.15	0.04	0.8	u	u	9	0	0	0.8
130	1.2	0.13	1.6	4	0.26	0.05	0.3	0.05	0.5	7	0	0	1.0
45	0.3	0.08	10.3	0	0.2	0.1	1.5	u	0.2	9	0	0	tr
150	1.4	0.2	1.6	0	0.20	0.18	2.0	0.1	0.3	18	0.1	0	tr

Food	Weight (gm)	Approximate Measure	Calories (Kcal)	Pro-tein (gm)	Fat (gm)	Total Carbo-hy-drate (gm)	Cal-cium (mg)	Phos-pho-rus (mg)	Mag-ne-sium (mg)	So-dium (mg)
Chard, Swiss, boiled	70	½ c	15	1.5	0.2	2	55	20	45	60
Cheese										
Natural										
blue or Roquefort	30	1 oz	105	6.0	8.5	0.6	170	110	8	515
cheddar	30	1 oz	115	7.0	9.5	0.4	205	145	8	175
cottage, creamed	110	½ c	120	14.0	5.0	3.0	70	150	6	455
cream	30	2 tbsp	100	2.0	10.0	0.8	25	30	2	85
Parmesan	30	1 oz	130	12.0	8.5	1.0	390	230	15	530
Swiss	30	1 oz	110	8.0	8.0	1.0	270	170	10	75
Pasteurized, processed										
American	30	1 oz	110	6.0	9.0	0.5	175	210	6	405
cheese spread	30	1 oz	80	4.5	6.0	2	160	200	8	380
Cheese fondue	100	⅔ c	260	15.0	18.5	10	320	295	u	540
Cherries										
Raw, sweet	75	10 cherries	50	0.8	0.6	11	10	15	8	0
Red, canned heavy syrup	130	½ c with syrup	110	0.8	0.2	27	10	25	10	3
water pack	125	½ c with juice	55	1.0	0.2	15	15	20	10	2
Chestnuts, water	100		75	1.1	tr	19	4	35	16	95
Chicken										
Canned, boned with broth	150	½ c	165	22.5	8.0	0	14	255	12	500
Creamed	120	½ c	210	17.5	12.0	7	85	140	u	u
Fried										
Breast, meat and skin, flour-coated	100	½ breast	220	31.0	5.0	2	16	230	29	75
Drumstick, meat and skin, flour-coated	50	1 medium	120	13.0	7.0	1	6	85	11	45
Thigh, meat and skin, flour-coated	60	1 medium	160	16.5	9.0	2	8	115	5	55
Kentucky-fried, Col. Sanders										
Drumstick	54	1	135	14.0	8.0	2	20	u	u	u
Thigh	97	1	275	20.0	19.0	12	40	u	u	u
Roasted, light meat without skin	140	5 oz	240	43.5	6.0	0	21	300	40	110
Chicken curry	100		160	9.6	10.0	10	22	85	25	670
Chick peas or garbanzos, cooked without salt	125	½ c (30 gm, dry wt.)	110	6.0	1.0	18	45	106	u	10
Chili con carne, with beans, canned	225	1 c	340	19.0	15.5	30	80	320	65	1355
Chili powder, chilis. See Peppers.										
Chili relleno (stuffed pepper)	110	1 pepper	190	10.5	14.0	6	225	195	u	465
Chocolate, bitter or baking	30	1 oz	140	3.0	15.0	8	20	110	35	1
Sweet, milk. See Candy										
Chow mein, canned, chicken without noodles	250	1 c	95	6.5	0.3	18	45	85	45	725
Clams, canned, with liquid	100	3½ oz, ½ c	50	8.0	0.7	3	55	135	115	u
Cocoa, dry	5	1 tbsp	20	0.6	0.1	4	15	20	4	30
beverage w/milk	250	1 c	220	9.0	9.0	26	300	270	55	125
Coconut, dry unsweetened	30	1 oz	180	2.0	17.5	6	5	50	u	u

Potassium (mg)	Zinc (mg)	Copper (mg)	Iron (mg)	Total Vitamin A Activity (RE)	Thiamin (mg)	Riboflavin (mg)	Niacin (mg)	Vitamin B6 (mg)	Pantothenic Acid (mg)	Folacin Total (μg)	Vitamin B12 (μg)	Vitamin C (mg)	Polyunsaturated Fatty Acids (gm)
230	u	u	1.3	390	0.03	0.08	0.3	u	0.1	u	0	0	tr
25	0.6	0.04	0.2	65	0.01	0.2	0.2	0.04	0.5	14	0.2	0	1.1
30	0.9	0.04	0.2	85	0.01	0.1	tr	0.02	0.1	5	0.2	0	0.27
95	0.4	0.02	0.2	50	0.02	0.2	0.1	0.1	0.25	15	0.7	0	0.12
35	0.2	0.01	0.3	120	tr	0.06	tr	0.01	0.1	4.0	0.1	0	0.36
30	0.9	0.1	0.3	60	0.01	0.1	0.1	0.03	0.1	2.0	u	0	0.19
30	1.1	0.04	0.1	70	tr	0.1	tr	0.02	0.1	2.0	0.5	0	0.28
45	0.8	0.05	0.1	80	0.01	0.1	tr	0.02	0.1	2.0	0.2	0	0.28
70	0.7	u	0.1	60	0.01	0.1	tr	0.03	0.2	2.0	0.1	0	0.18
165	u	0.04	1.2	300	0.06	0.3	0.2	u	u	u	u	0	u
150	tr	0.06	0.3	14	0.03	0.04	0.3	0.02	0.1	6	0	5	0.2
190	0.1	0.2	0.5	20	0.02	0.05	0.5	0.04	0.1	10	0	5	0.1
160	0.1	0.1	0.5	20	0.03	0.05	0.5	0.04	0.1	10	0	3	0.1
380	u	u	2.1	0	0.05	0.04	0.9	u	u	u	u	6	u
140	2	0.2	1.6	75	0.02	0.1	6.3	0.4	0.8	u	0.3	2	1.8
u	u	u	1.1	100	0.04	0.2	4.0	u	u	u	u	tr	u
255	1.1	0.1	1.2	15	0.08	0.1	13.5	0.6	1.0	4	0.3	0	1.9
110	1.4	0.1	0.7	3	0.04	0.1	3.0	0.2	0.6	4	0.2	0	1.6
150	1.5	0.1	0.9	18	0.06	0.2	4.5	0.2	0.7	5	0.2	0	2.1
u	u	u	0.9	10	0.04	0.1	2.7	u	u	u	u	0	u
u	u	u	1.4	20	0.08	0.2	4.9	u	u	u	u	0	u
345	1.7	0.1	1.5	12	0.09	0.2	17.4	0.8	1.4	5	0.5	0	1.4
430	1.7	0.2	1.2	tr	0.02	0.09	0.9	0.1	0.3	5	1.0	5	u
240	2.7	u	2.1	2	0.1	0.03	0.6	0.2	0.4	125	0	0	u
595	4.2	0.8	4.3	30	0.08	0.20	3.3	0.3	0.4	40	u	tr	u
270	u	u	1.3	300	0.08	0.2	0.8	0.1	0.7	15	1.0	55	u
235	0.7	0.8	1.9	2	0.01	0.07	0.4	0.01	0.06	3	0	0	0.5
420	1.2	0.3	1.3	30	0.05	0.10	1.0	0.4	1.2	10	1.6	15	tr
140	1.2	0	4.0	u	0.01	0.1	1.0	0.08	0.3	3	20	0	tr
45	0.1	0.02	0.1	tr	0.01	0.03	tr	0.07	0.6	1	0.1	0	u
480	1.2	0.01	0.8	85	0.10	0.43	0.4	0.11	0.8	12	0.9	2	0.3
160	u	0.2	0.9	0	0.02	0.01	0.2	0.01	0.06	8	0	0	tr

Food	Weight (gm)	Approximate Measure	Calories (Kcal)	Pro- tein (gm)	Fat (gm)	Total Carbo- hy- drate (gm)	Cal- cium (mg)	Phos- pho- rus (mg)	Mag- ne- sium (mg)	So- dium (mg)
Coffee, instant, regular dry powder	2.5	1–2 tsp	4	tr	tr	1	4	10	10	1
Collards, boiled	70	½ c	20	2.0	0.3	3	140	20	20	35
Cookies										
Commercial	35	4 cookies	170	1.5	7.0	25	10	55	5	125
Fig bar	55	4 cookies	200	2.0	3.0	40	45	40	30	175
Oatmeal	50	4 cookies	235	3.0	10.0	35	45	70	20	170
Corn, sweet, yellow										
Fresh or frozen, boiled	80	½ c	70	2.5	0.6	17	4	55	15	3
Canned, whole kernal	80	½ c	50	1.4	0.3	12	2	45	15	200
Cream style	130	½ c	95	2.5	0.5	24	3	80	30	355
Corn fritter	35	1 fritter	130	2.5	8.0	14	20	55	u	165
Corn syrup	20	1 tbsp	60	0	0	15	10	3	u	15
Cowpeas or black-eyed peas										
Immature	80	½ c	90	7.0	0.6	15	20	120	15	1
Mature, dry, cooked	125	½ c (1 oz, dry wt.)	95	6.5	0.4	17	20	120	u	10
Crabmeat	100	½ c, packed	100	18.0	2.0	0.6	45	185	30	550
Crackers										
Butter (eg., Ritz)	15	5 round	75	1.1	3.0	11	25	40	u	180
Graham	15	1 cracker 5 in x 2½ in	55	1.1	1.6	12	5	20	5	70
Rye wafer (eg., Rykrisp)	15	2 wafers	40	1.5	0.2	10	5	50	u	110
Saltines	10	4 each, 2 in square	45	0.9	1.0	7	5	10	3	135
Cranberry jelly, or sauce, canned	35	⅛ c	50	tr	tr	13	1	2	1	10
Cream										
Half-and-half	60	¼ c or tbsp	80	2.0	7.0	3	65	55	8	25
Heavy, whipping	60	¼ c; ½ c whipped volume	210	1.0	22.0	2	45	35	4	20
Light, for coffee	60	¼ c, 4 tbsp	120	1.6	11.6	2	60	50	5	25
Sour	60	¼ c, 4 tbsp	130	1.9	12.6	2	60	50	5	25
Cream substitutes										
Coffee whitener	3	1 tsp or packet	15	0.1	0.8	2	1	12	tr	5
Whipped topping, frozen	10	2 tbsp	30	0.1	2.5	2	1	1	tr	2
Cucumber, raw, peeled	80	½ small	10	0.4	0.1	2	15	15	5	4
Custard, baked	130	½ c	150	7.0	7.5	15	150	155	u	105
Dandelion greens, boiled	50	½ c	20	1.0	0.3	3	75	20	20	25
Dasheen (Japanese taro), raw	100	1⅓ corms	100	2.0	0.2	25	30	60	u	5
Dates, dried	80	10, pitted	230	1.6	0.4	61	25	35	30	2
Doughnuts										
Cake type	40	1 average	170	2.0	9.0	20	15	90	10	225
Yeast, raised	40	1 average	180	2.5	11.0	16	15	30	5	100
Duck, pressed, salted	100		450	9.7	45.0	2	65	150	u	u
Eggnog	250	1 c	340	9.5	19.0	34	330	275	45	140
Eggs, chicken										
Whole, raw or hard cooked	50	1 large	80	6.0	5.5	0.6	30	90	6	70
white	33	1 white	15	3.5	tr	0.4	4	4	3	50
yolk	17	1 yolk	65	3.0	5.0	tr	25	85	3	10
Scrambled	140	2 eggs	190	12.0	14.0	3.0	95	195	15	310
Eggplant, boiled	100	½ c diced	20	1.0	0.2	4	10	20	15	1
Enchiladas, beef										
Frozen, Campbell's	200	7 oz portion	240	15.0	8.5	25	20	190	u	725
Home recipe	190	2 enchiladas	365	32.0	16.7	22	450	480	u	510

Potassium (mg)	Zinc (mg)	Copper (mg)	Iron (mg)	Total Vitamin A Activity (RE)	Thiamin (mg)	Riboflavin (mg)	Niacin (mg)	Vitamin B_6 (mg)	Pantothenic Acid (mg)	Folacin Total (μg)	Vitamin B_{12} (μg)	Vitamin C (mg)	Polyunsaturated Fatty Acids (gm)
90	0.03	0.01	0.1	0	0	tr	0.6	tr	tr	u	0	0	0
175	0.2	0.04	0.7	410	0.04	0.1	0.4	0.08	0.1	35	0	30	tr
25	0.2	0.05	0.2	10	0.01	0.02	0.1	0.02	0.1	1	0	0	u
160	0.4	0.2	1.3	15	0.08	0.07	0.7	0.05	0.2	3	0	tr	u
120	0.5	0.06	1.5	7	0.10	0.07	0.6	0.02	0.3	7	0.05	0	u
160	0.3	0.03	0.4	20	0.06	0.05	1.3	0.13	0.2	40	0	4	tr
135	0.4	0.06	0.3	10	0.03	0.05	0.6	u	u	30	0	5	tr
235	0.8	0.10	0.6	20	0.04	0.08	1.2	u	u	30	0	8	tr
45	u	u	0.6	15	0.06	0.07	0.6	u	u	u	tr	u	u
1	u	0.07	u	0	0	0	0	0	0	0	0	0	0
310	0.6	0.2	1.7	30	0.2	0.09	1.0	0.04	0.2	80	0	15	tr
285	2.0	0.2	1.6	1	0.2	0.05	0.5	0.07	0.3	100	0	0	tr
90	4.5	1.0	0.8	tr	0.2	0.08	3.0	0.3	0.6	2	10	2	0.9
20	u	0.03	0.1	5	tr	tr	0.1	u	u	u	0	0	u
25	0.1	0.02	0.4	tr	0.05	0.04	0.5	0.01	0.1	2	0	0	u
u	u	0.04	0.5	0	0.04	0.03	0.2	u	u	u	0	0	u
15	0.1	0.02	0.3	0	tr	tr	0.6	tr	tr	2	0	0	u
9	tr	tr	tr	1	tr	tr	tr	tr	u	u	0	tr	0
80	0.3	0.07	tr	60	0.02	0.08	0.02	0.02	0.2	1.5	0.2	tr	0.2
45	0.1	0.06	tr	250	0.01	0.08	0.02	0.01	0.2	0.4	0.1	tr	0.8
75	0.2	0.06	tr	110	0.02	0.08	tr	0.02	0.2	1.5	0.1	tr	0.4
80	0.2	0.06	tr	110	0.02	0.09	0.05	0.01	0.2	5	0.1	tr	0.5
20	0.02	u	u	tr	0.	0	0	0	0	0	0	0	tr
2	tr	u	tr	6	0	0	0	0	0	0	0	0	tr
125	0.08	0.04	0.2	tr	0.02	0.03	0.2	0.03	0.2	10	0	8	tr
195	u	0.1	0.6	135	0.06	0.2	0.2	u	u	4	u	0	u
120	u	u	1.0	610	0.07	0.08	u	u	u	u	0	10	tr
515	u	u	1.0	2	0.1	0.04	1.1	u	u	u	0	4	tr
540	0.2	0.2	1.0	4	0.07	0.08	1.8	0.16	0.6	10	0	0	tr
40	0.2	0.05	0.6	7	0.1	0.08	0.7	0.01	0.2	3	0	tr	u
35	0.3	0.04	0.6	8	0.07	0.07	0.6	0.02	0.2	4	0	0	u
u	u	u	2.7	u	u	u	u	u	u	u	u	u	u
420	1.1	u	0.5	200	0.08	0.5	0.3	0.1	1.1	2	1.1	3	0.9
65	0.7	0.05	1.0	80	0.04	0.15	tr	0.06	0.9	25	0.6	0	0.7
45	tr	0.01	tr	0	tr	0.09	tr	tr	0.07	5	0.02	0	0
15	0.6	0.05	0.9	80	0.04	0.07	tr	0.05	0.8	25	0.6	0	0.7
170	1.4	0.07	1.9	160	0.07	0.30	0.1	0.1	1.8	50	1.3	tr	1.4
150	u	0.1	0.6	1	0.05	0.04	0.5	0.08	0.2	2	0	3	tr
155	u	u	2.5	120	0.1	0.2	3.0	u	u	u	u	u	u
585	u	u	5	1200	0.1	0.4	6.0	0.8	0.7	10	2	10	u

Food	Weight (gm)	Approximate Measure	Calories (Kcal)	Pro-tein (gm)	Fat (gm)	Total Carbo-hy-drate (gm)	Cal-cium (mg)	Phos-pho-rus (mg)	Mag-ne-sium (mg)	So-dium (mg)
Fats, shortening,	100	½ c	880	0	100.0	0	0	0	0	0
solid or oil	12	1 tbsp	110	0	12.0	0	0	0	0	0
Figs, fresh	100	2 medium	75	0.8	0.3	20	35	15	15	1
Dried	30	2 small	75	1.0	0.3	20	40	20	20	3
Fish										
Cod, steak, sauteed	110	4 oz	180	30.0	6.0	0	30	285	30	115[h]
Fish sticks, breaded	110	4 sticks	200	19.0	10.0	7	10	190	20	u
Haddock, fried	110	4 oz	180	22.0	7.0	6	45	270	30	195[h]
Mackerel, sauteed	105	3 average	250	23.0	17.0	0	5	295	30	u
Salmon,										
steak, broiled	145	1 average 6 in x 2 in	230	35.0	9.0	0	u	530	60	150[h]
canned, pink	110	½ c	160	23.0	6.0	0	215	315	30	425
red	110	½ c	190	22.0	10.0	0	285	380	30	575
Sardines, canned in oil	85	3 oz drained	170	20.5	9.0	0	370	425	35	700
Sole or flounder, fillet, baked	100	3 oz	200	30.0	8.0	0	25	345	30	235[h]
Swordfish, broiled	100	3 oz	170	26.5	6.0	0	25	260	u	u
Tuna, raw	100	½ c	135	27.5	3.0	0	5	175	30	35[h]
canned in oil	100	½ c	200	28.0	8.0	0	10	230	25	u
in water	100	½ c	130	28.0	0.8	0	15	190	25	865
Flour, wheat										
White, all purpose										
unenriched	115	1 c	420	12.0	1.0	90	20	100	30	2
enriched	115	1 c	420	12.0	1.0	90	20	100	30	2
Whole grain	120	1 c	400	16.0	2.5	85	50	445	135	4
French toast, frozen, Campbell's	65	1 slice	130	5.0	4.3	18	50	85	u	305
Frozen dinners										
Chicken, fried, with potatoes, mixed vegetables	310	11 oz dinner	570	28.0	29.0	48	70	350	60	1075
Meat loaf with tomato sauce, potatoes, peas	310	11 oz dinner	410	25.0	21.0	30	60	365	60	1225
Turkey with gravy, potatoes, peas	310	11 oz dinner	340	25.0	9.0	40	80	260	65	1200
Fruit cocktail, heavy syrup	130	½ c	95	0.5	tr	24	10	15	7	7
Gelatin, dry	8	1 tbsp or packet	30	7.0	0	0	u	u	2	1
Gelatin dessert, plain	120	½ c	71	2.0	0	17	u	u	2	u
Grapefruit, raw	100	½ medium	30	0.6	0.1	8	10	10	8	0
Grapefruit juice, canned										
Unsweetened	250	1 c	95	1.2	0.2	22	20	25	25	3
Sweetened	250	1 c	115	1.4	0.2	28	20	25	25	4
Grapes, raw										
Slip-skin	100	20 grapes	65	0.6	0.3	17	15	10	5	2
Adherent skin	100	20 grapes	70	0.7	0.6	18	10	15	6	2
Grape juice	250	1 c	155	1.4	0.2	38	20	25	25	7
Gravy, canned										
Beef	15	1 tbsp	8	0.5	0.3	0.7	1	5	0	10
Chicken	15	1 tbsp	10	0.3	0.9	0.8	3	4	0	85
Guacamole	120	½ c	140	2.1	12.8	7	15	40	u	165
Ham, baked	85	3 oz	250	18.0	19.0	0	10	145	15	635

Potassium (mg)	Zinc (mg)	Copper (mg)	Iron (mg)	Total Vitamin A Activity (RE)	Thiamin (mg)	Riboflavin (mg)	Niacin (mg)	Vitamin B_6 (mg)	Pantothenic Acid (mg)	Folacin Total (µg)	Vitamin B_{12} (µg)	Vitamin C (mg)	Polyunsaturated Fatty Acids (gm)
0	0	0	0	0	0	0	0	0	0	0	0	0	14.8
0	0	0	0	0	0	0	0	0	0	0	0	0	1.8
230	0.1	0.07	0.4	14	0.06	0.05	0.4	0.11	0.3	u	0	2	0.14
225	0.2	0.1	0.7	4	0.02	0.03	0.2	0.07	0.1	2	0	tr	0.56
420	0.9	0.2	1.0	60	0.08	0.1	3.0	0.3	0.3	10	0.9	0	3.4
u	0.3	0.2	0.4	0	0.04	0.08	2.0	0.06	0.3	10	1.1	0	u
385	1.1	0.2	1.3	tr	0.04	0.08	3.5	0.2	0.1	10	1.4	2	3.2
u	1.0	0.2	1.3	165	0.2	0.3	8.0	0.7	0.9	10	9.4	0	4.6
565	2.4	1.2	1.5	60	0.2	0.08	12.5	1.0	1.9	30	5.8	0	2.4
395	1.0	0.3	0.9	25	0.04	0.2	9.0	0.3	0.6	20	7.6	0	1.6
380	1.0	0.3	1.3	75	0.04	0.2	8.0	0.3	0.6	20	7.6	0	2.6
500	2.4	0.03	2.4	60	0.03	0.2	4.5	0.2	0.7	15	8.5	0	1.8
585	1.0	0.07	1.4	u	0.07	0.08	2.5	0.2	0.8	15	1.2	2	3.8
u	u	u	1.3	600	0.04	0.05	10.5	u	0.2	u	1.0	0	u
180	0.5	0.5	1.3	15	0.02	0.05	6.6	0.9	0.5	u	3.0	7	1.1
u	1.0	0.1	1.9	25	0.05	0.1	12.0	0.4	0.3	15	2.2	0	3.0
275	u	u	1.6	25	0.05	0.1	13.0	0.4	0.3	15	2.2	0	0.3
110	0.8	0.2	0.9	0	0.07	0.06	1.0	0.07	0.5	20	0	0	0.6
110	0.8	0.2	3.3	0	0.5	0.3	4.0	0.07	0.5	20	0	0	0.6
445	2.9	0.6	4.0	0	0.7	0.1	5.0	0.4	1.3	35	0	0	1.6
80	u	u	1.3	75	0.1	0.1	0.7	u	u	u	u	0	u
350	3.0	0.4	3.2	360	0.2	0.6	16.0	0.9	1.6	20	0.7	10	u
360	3.5	0.5	4.0	260	0.3	0.4	5.5	0.7	0.9	20	1.1	10	u
530	3.0	0.4	3.3	80	0.2	0.3	7.0	0.8	1.8	30	0.6	10	u
110	0.1	0.09	0.4	25	0.02	0.02	0.5	0.06	0.1	u	0	2	0.04
u	u	0.1	u	0	0	0	0	0	0	0	0	0	0
u	0.02	0.03	u	0	0	0	0	0	0	0	0	0	0
140	0.1	0.05	0.1	10	0.04	0.02	0.3	0.04	0.3	10	0	35	0.02
380	0.2	0.09	0.5	2	0.1	0.05	0.6	0.05	0.3	25	0	70	0.06
405	0.1	0.12	0.9	0	0.1	0.06	0.8	0.05	0.3	25	0	65	tr
190	tr	0.04	0.3	10	0.09	0.06	0.3	0.11	tr	4	0	4	0.10
185	tr	0.09	0.3	8	0.09	0.06	0.3	0.11	tr	4	0	10	0.17
335	0.1	0.07	0.6	2	0.07	0.09	0.7	0.16	0.1	6	0	tr	0.06
12	0.15	0.01	0.1	0	tr	tr	0.1	tr	u	u	tr	0	0.01
16	0.12	0.01	0.1	2	tr	tr	0.1	tr	u	u	u	0	0.2
565	u	0.3	0.7	55	0.10	0.2	1.6	0.4	0.9	30	0	35	2
200	3.4	0.3	2.2	0	0.4	0.2	3.0	0.3	0.3	1	0.4	0	2

Food	Weight (gm)	Approximate Measure	Calories (Kcal)	Pro- tein (gm)	Fat (gm)	Total Carbo- hy- drate (gm)	Cal- cium (mg)	Phos- pho- rus (mg)	Mag- ne- sium (mg)	So- dium (mg)
Hominy grits. See Cereal, cooked.										
Honey, strained	20	1 tbsp	65	0.1	0	17	1	1	1	1
Ice cream, vanilla										
Plain, 10% fat	65	½ c	135	2.5	7.0	15	90	70	10	60
Rich, 16% fat	75	½ c	175	2.0	12.0	16	75	60	8	50
Ice cream cone, Dairy Queen	142	1 dip, reg.	230	6.0	7.0	35	200	150	u	u
Ice milk, vanilla	65	½ c	90	2.5	3.0	15	90	65	10	50
Ices, water, lime	95	½ c	120	0.4	tr	30	tr	tr	u	tr
Jams and *Jellies*	20	1 tbsp	55	0.1	tr	14	4	2	1	2
Kale, boiled without stems	55	½ c, diced	15	1.4	0.2	3	75	15	10	8
Kidney, braised	100	3½ oz	250	33.0	12.0	0.8	20	240	20	250
Kohlrabi, boiled	80	½ c, diced	20	1.5	0.1	4	25	35	30	5
Kumquat, raw	20	1 medium	10	0.2	tr	3	10	5	2	5
Lamb, choice grade										
Chop, loin, broiled										
lean and fat	95	1 average	340	21.0	28.0	0	10	165	15	50
lean only	65	1 average	120	18.0	5.0	0	10	140	15	45
Leg, roasted, lean only	85	3 oz	160	24.0	6.0	0	10	200	15	60
Shoulder, roasted lean and fat	85	3 oz	280	18.5	23.0	0	10	145	15	45
Lard	12	1 tbsp	110	0	12.0	0	0	0	0	0
Lasagna, frozen, Sara Lee	225	8 oz serving	380	27.0	12.4	43	310	470	55	1100
Lemon juice, fresh	15	1 tsp	5	0.1	tr	1	1	1	1	0
Lemonade, from frozen concentrate	250	1 c	110	0.1	tr	30	2	3	2	1
Lentils, dried, cooked	100	½ c	110	8.0	tr	19	25	120	20	u
Lettuce, raw										
Head, solid (iceberg type)	90	⅙ head	10	0.8	0.1	3	20	20	10	10
Loose leaf, romaine, cos	55	1 c, chopped	10	0.7	0.2	2	35	15	10	5
Liver										
Beef, fried	85	3 oz	200	22.5	9.0	4	10	405	15	155
Calf, fried	85	3 oz	220	25.0	11.2	3	10	455	20	100
Chicken, simmered	70	½ c, chopped	110	18.0	3.5	1	10	110	15	40
Lobster, northern cooked	95	⅔ c meat	90	18.0	1.5	0.3	65	185	20	205
Lychee nuts, raw	150	10 nuts	60	0.8	0.3	15	5	40	u	3
Macaroni and other pasta, cooked										
Unenriched	130	1 c	190	6.5	0.7	40	15	85	25	1'
Enriched	130	1 c	190	6.5	0.7	40	15	85	25	1'
Macaroni with cheese, casserole, baked	200	1 c	430	17.0	22.0	40	360	320	50	1085
Mangoes, raw	165	1 c, diced	110	1.0	0.5	28	20	20	15	3
Margarine	5	1 tsp, 1 pat (90/lb)	35	tr	4	tr	1	1	tr	50
Melons										
Cantaloupe	160	½ small melon or 1 c, cubed	60	1.4	0.4	13	20	25	15	15
Honeydew	170	⅛ melon or 1 c, cubed	60	0.8	0.2	16	10	15	10	15
Watermelon	480	1/16 melon (2 lb with rind)	150	3.0	2.0	35	40	40	50	10

Po-tas-sium (mg)	Zinc (mg)	Cop-per (mg)	Iron (mg)	Total Vitamin A Activity (RE)	Thia-min (mg)	Ribo-flavin (mg)	Nia-cin (mg)	Vita-min B_6 (mg)	Panto-thenic Acid (mg)	Fola-cin Total (µg)	Vita-min B_{12} (µg)	Vita-min C (mg)	Polyun-saturated Fatty Acids (gm)
10	0.02	0.03	0.1	0	tr	0.01	0.1	tr	0.04	0	0	tr	0
130	0.7	0.02	0.05	65	0.02	0.2	0.05	0.03	0.3	1	0.3	0	0.3
110	0.6	0.02	0.05	105	0.02	0.15	0.05	0.03	0.3	1	0.3	0	0.4
u	u	u	u	70	0.09	0.26	u	u	u	u	0.6	u	u
130	0.3	u	0.09	25	0.04	0.2	0.05	0.04	0.3	1	0.4	0	0.1
3	u	u	tr	0	tr	tr	tr	0	0	0	0	0	0
20	0.1	0.02	0.2	tr	tr	0.01	tr	0.01	0.02	1	0	tr	0
185	0.1	0.03	0.5	375	0.03	0.6	0.3	0.05	tr	25	0	20	tr
320	2.4	0.1	13.0	330	0.5	4.8	10.5	0.4	3.8	60	30	u	u
215	u	u	0.2	1	0.05	0.02	0.2	0.1	0.5	u	0	35	tr
35	tr	0.02	0.1	6	0.01	0.02	tr	tr	tr	tr	0	7	0
235	u	0.1	1.2	tr	0.1	0.2	5.0	0.3	0.5	1	2.0	0	1.4
205	3.0	0.1	1.3	tr	0.1	0.2	4.0	0.2	0.4	1	1.4	0	0.25
275	3.6	0.05	1.9	tr	0.1	0.3	5.5	0.2	0.5	1	1.8	0	0.3
205	u	0.1	1.0	tr	0.1	0.2	4.0	0.2	0.5	1	1.8	0	1.1
0	0	0	0	0	0	0	0	0	0	0	0	0	1.1
740	1.4	u	5.6	185	0.4	0.4	4.5	u	u	50	u	15	u
15	tr	tr	tr	tr	tr	tr	tr	tr	tr	1.5	0	5	tr
40	0.02	0.02	0.1	1	0.01	0.02	0.2	0.01	0.03	5	0	15	0
250	1.0	0.3	2.1	2	0.07	0.06	0.6	u	u	36	0	0	0
160	0.4	0.08	0.5	30	0.05	0.05	0.3	0.05	0.2	30	0	5	tr
145	0.2	0.05	0.8	100	0.03	0.04	0.2	0.03	0.1	30	0	10	tr
325	4.3	2.5	7.5	9000	0.2	3.6	14.0	0.7	6.5	70	68.0	25	2.4
385	5.2	6.5	12.1	7000	0.2	3.5	14.0	0.6	6.5	70	51.0	30	3.5
105	3.0	0.2	6.0	3500	0.1	1.9	8.0	0.5	4.2	160	17.5	10	0.67
175	2.1	1.6	0.8	tr	0.1	0.07	u	u	1.4	15	0.5	0	u
155	u	u	0.4	0	u	0.05	u	u	u	u	0	40	tr
105	0.6	0.03	0.7	0	0.03	0.03	0.5	0.03	0.2	5	0	0	tr
105	0.6	0.03	1.4	0	0.2	0.1	2.0	0.03	0.2	5	0	0	tr
240	1.3	0.08	1.8	200	0.2	0.4	2.0	0.09	0.4	10	0.8	0	u
255	0.1	0.18	0.2	640	0.1	0.1	1.0	0.22	0.3	u	0	45	0.11
1	0.01	tr	0	5	0	0	0	0	0	0	0	0	1.2
495	0.2	0.07	0.3	510	0.06	0.03	0.9	0.18	0.2	27	0	65	tr
460	u	0.07	0.1	7	0.13	0.03	1.0	0.1	0.4	u	0	40	tr
560	0.3	0.15	0.8	175	0.4	0.1	1.0	0.7	1.0	10	0	45	tr

Food	Weight (gm)	Approximate Measure	Calories (Kcal)	Protein (gm)	Fat (gm)	Total Carbohydrate (gm)	Calcium (mg)	Phosphorus (mg)	Magnesium (mg)	Sodium (mg)
Milk, cow										
Whole, fluid 3.3% fat	245	1 c	150	8.0	8.2	11	290	225	30	120
2%, low-fat	245	1 c	140	10.0	5.0	14	350	275	40	145
Skim, nonfat, or buttermilk	245	1 c	90	8.5	0.4	12	300	245	30	125
Chocolate, low-fat	250	1 c	180	8.0	5.0	26	285	255	30	150
Dried, instant whole	30	¼ c	160	8.5	8.5	12	290	250	25	120
nonfat	35	½ c	125	12.0	0.2	18	420	345	40	190
Evaporated	250	1 c	340	17.5	20.0	25	660	510	60	265
Condensed, sweetened	40	1 fl oz	120	3.0	3.5	20	105	95	10	50
Milk, human, U.S.	30	1 fl oz	21	0.3	1.3	2.1	10	4	1	5
Milk shakes, commercial	290	10 fl oz	320	10.0	8.0	52	345	265	35	250
Molasses										
Light	20	1 tbsp	50	0	0	13	35	10	9	3
Medium	20	1 tbsp	50	0	0	12	60	15	16	5
Blackstrap	20	1 tbsp	45	tr	0	11	135	15	52	20
Muffins										
Bran	40	1 muffin	110	3.0	5.0	17	55	110	30	170
Cornmeal	40	1 muffin	130	3.0	4.0	19	40	70	20	190
English	55	1 muffin	130	4.0	1.0	18	90	60	10	350
Plain or blueberry	40	1 muffin	125	2.5	4.0	20	15	80	5	200
Mushrooms, raw	35	½ c, sliced	10	1.0	0.1	2	2	40	5	5
Mustard greens, boiled	70	½ c	15	2.0	0.2	2	80	20	10	20
Mustard, prepared, yellow	5	1 tsp	4	0.2	0.2	0.3	4	4	2	65
Noodles, egg, cooked										
Unenriched	105	⅔ c	130	4.5	1.5	25	10	65	25	2
Enriched	105	⅔ c	130	4.5	1.5	25	10	65	25	2
Oils, See Fats.										
Okra, boiled	105	10 pods	30	2.0	0.3	6	100	45	40	2
Olives,										
Green	25	5 large	20	0.2	2.5	0.2	10	4	5	465
Ripe	25	5 large	35	0.2	4.0	0.6	20	4	u	150
Onions										
Green, raw, bulb and top	25	¼ c, chopped, or 3 onions	10	0.4	tr	2	15	10	3	1
Mature, dry	85	½ c, chopped	30	1.5	0.1	7	25	30	10	10
raw	10	1 tbsp, ⅛ onion	4	0.2	tr	0.9	3	4	1	1
boiled	105	½ c, sliced	30	1.0	0.1	7	25	30	10	10
Oranges, raw	130	1 medium	60	1.2	0.2	15	50	20	15	0
Orange juice, fresh or frozen	250	1 c	110	1.7	0.5	26	25	40	25	2
Oysters, raw	120	6 oysters	60	13.0	1.0	tr	220	320	50	610
Pak Choy, raw	100	⅔ c	15	1.0	0.1	3	165	45	u	25
Pancakes, plain	110	4, ea 4 in diameter	240	7.5	9.0	32	145	290	20	650
Papaya, raw	140	½ fruit or 1 c, cubed	55	1.0	0.2	14	35	5	15	4
Parsley, raw	5	1 tbsp, chopped	2	0.1	tr	0.3	5	2	2	2
Peaches, without skin										
Raw, yellow	115	1 medium	45	0.6	0.1	10	5	10	6	0
Canned, heavy syrup	160	2 halves, 3 tbsp syrup	120	0.7	0.2	32	5	20	8	10
water pack	155	2 halves, 3 tbsp juice	35	0.7	0.1	9	5	15	8	6
Dried, sulfured, uncooked	60	½ c (5 halves)	190	3	0.6	48	20	95	35	6

Potassium (mg)	Zinc (mg)	Copper (mg)	Iron (mg)	Total Vitamin A Activity (RE)	Thiamin (mg)	Riboflavin (mg)	Niacin (mg)	Vitamin B_6 (mg)	Pantothenic Acid (mg)	Folacin Total (μg)	Vitamin B_{12} (μg)	Vitamin C (mg)	Polyunsaturated Fatty Acids (gm)
370	1.0	0.08	0.1	75	0.09	0.4	0.2	0.1	0.8	10	0.9	2	0.3
450	1.1	0.08	0.1	140[i]	0.1	0.5	0.2	0.1	0.9	15	1.0	2	0.2
400	1.0	0.08	0.1	140[i]	0.09	0.4	0.2	0.1	0.8	15	1.0	2	tr
420	1.0	u	0.6	140[i]	0.1	0.4	0.3	0.1	0.7	10	0.8	2	0.2
425	1.0	0.06	0.1	90	0.09	0.4	0.2	0.09	0.7	10	1.0	2	0.2
600	1.5	0.1	0.1	2	0.1	0.5	0.3	0.1	1.1	15	1.4	2	tr
765	1.9	0.2	0.4	140	0.1	0.8	0.5	0.1	1.6	20	0.4	3	0.6
140	0.4	0.08	0.1	30	0.03	0.2	0.1	0.02	0.3	4	0.2	tr	0.1
16	0.05	0.01	0.01	20	0.004	0.01	0.1	0.003	0.07	2	0.02	2	0.2
500	1.0	0.06	0.2	100	0.12	0.66	0.6	0.12	u	u	0.9	tr	u
185	u	u	0.9	0	0.01	0.01	u	u	u	u	0	0	0
215	0.9	0.3	1.2	0	0.01	0.02	0.2	0.04	0.07	2	0	0	0
585	u	u	3.2	0	0.02	0.04	0.4	u	u	u	0	0	0
90	0.9	0.08	1.1	40	0.1	0.1	1.1	0.11	0.2	16	0.1	2	u
55	u	u	0.7	20[d]	0.08	0.09	0.6	u	u	u	u	0	u
310	0.4	0.17	1.6	0	0.25	0.18	2.0	0.02	0.3	18	0	0	u
50	0.2	0.03	0.5	8	0.1	0.1	1.0	u	u	u	u	tr	u
145	0.1	0.04	0.3	tr	0.04	0.2	1.5	0.04	0.8	7	0	1	tr
120	0.2	0.05	0.9	360	0.03	0.04	0.2	0.11	tr	u	0	20	tr
5	0.03	0.02	0.1	0	u	u	u	u	u	u	0	0	0
45	0.6	0.02	0.6	20	0.03	0.02	0.4	0.02	0.2	2	tr	0	u
45	0.6	0.02	0.9	20	0.10	0.09	1.5	0.02	0.2	2	tr	0	u
185	u	0.1	0.5	50	0.1	0.2	1.0	0.08	0.2	10	0	20	tr
10	0.02	0.09	0.3	6	tr	tr	tr	0.01	0	3	0	0	0.3
5	0.07	0.09	0.4	2	tr	tr	tr	tr	tr	3	0	0	0.5
60	0.07	0.01	0.3	50	0.01	0.01	0.1	u	0.4	10	0	8	0
135	0.3	0.1	0.4	4[g]	0.02	0.04	0.2	0.1	0.1	8	0	8	tr
15	0.03	0.01	0.1	tr	tr	tr	tr	0.01	0.01	1	0	1	0
115	0.6	0.08	0.4	4[g]	0.03	0.03	0.2	0.1	0.1	10	0	8	tr
235	0.1	0.06	0.1	25	0.11	0.05	0.4	0.08	0.3	40	0	70	0.03
495	0.1	0.11	0.5	50	0.22	0.07	1.0	0.10	0.5	110	0	125	tr
310	25[k]	9.0	7.2	75	0.1	0.2	1.6	0.04	0.6	12	17	10[k]	1.0
305	u	u	0.8	300	0.05	0.1	0.8	u	u	u	0	25	tr
175	0.8	0.07	1.1	30	0.15	0.24	1.0	0.23	0.4	12	1.3	tr	u
360	0.1	0.02	0.1	280	0.04	0.04	0.5	0.03	0.3	u	0	85	0.04
25	tr	0.02	0.2	30	tr	0.01	tr	0.01	0.02	2	0	6	tr
170	0.1	0.06	0.1	45	0.01	0.04	0.9	0.02	0.1	3	0	6	0.04
150	0.1	0.08	0.4	55	0.02	0.04	1.0	0.03	0.1	5	0	4	0.04
150	0.1	0.08	0.5	80	0.01	0.03	0.8	0.03	0.1	5	0	4	0.04
785	0.4	0.29	3.2	80	0.02	0.06	2.8	0.09	0.3	4	0	6	0.29

Food	Weight (gm)	Approximate Measure	Calories (Kcal)	Pro-tein (gm)	Fat (gm)	Total Carbo-hy-drate (gm)	Cal-cium (mg)	Phos-pho-rus (mg)	Mag-ne-sium (mg)	So-dium (mg)
Peanuts, roasted, salted	30	1 oz, 30 nuts	165	7.5	14.0	5	20	115	50	120
Peanut butter	15	1 tbsp	95	4.0	8.0	3	10	60	25	95
Pears										
Raw, with skin	165	1 3½ in × 2½ in	100	1.0	0.7	25	20	20	10	1
Canned, syrup	160	2 halves and 3 tbsp juice	115	0.3	0.2	30	10	10	6	8
water pack	155	2 halves and 3 tbsp juice	45	0.3	tr	12	5	10	6	4
Peas										
Green, frozen boiled	80	½ c	65	4.0	0.4	11	20	70	20	80
Canned, drained	85	½ c	75	4.0	0.4	14	20	65	10	200
Split, dry, cooked	100	½ c (1 oz, dry wt.)	115	8.0	0.3	20	10	90	8	15
Peas and carrots, frozen, boiled	80	½ c	50	2.5	0.3	9	20	50	15	65
Pecans	30	1 oz, 20 halves	200	2.5	20.0	4	20	80	40	tr
Peppers, hot (chili)										
Green, canned, sauce	15	1 tbsp	3	0.1	tr	1	1	2	u	u
Red, dry, chili powder	3	1 tsp	10	0.3	0.4	1	5	10	4	25
Peppers, sweet										
Green, raw	75	½ c, chopped	15	0.9	0.1	4	5	15	15	10
Red, raw	90	1 medium	25	1.0	0.2	5	10	20	u	u
Pickles, cucumber										
Dill	135	1 large	15	0.9	0.3	3	35	30	1	1930
Sweet	35	1 medium	50	0.2	0.1	13	4	5	tr	u
Relish, sweet	15	1 tbsp	20	0.1	0.1	5	3	2	u	105
Pies										
Apple, berry, rhubarb	160	⅙ of 9 in pie	400	3.5	17.5	60	15	35	5	475
Cherry, peach	160	⅙ of 9 in pie	410	4.0	18.0	60	20	40	u	480
Cream, pudding type with meringue	150	⅙ of 9 in pie	380	7.5	18.0	50	105	150	u	390
Custard	150	⅙ of 9 in pie	330	9.5	17.0	35	145	170	u	u
Lemon meringue	140	⅙ of 9 in pie	360	5.0	14.5	55	20	70	u	395
Mince	160	⅙ of 9 in pie	430	4.0	18.0	65	45	60	u	710
Pecan	140	⅙ of 9 in pie	580	7.0	31.5	70	65	140	u	305
Pumpkin	150	⅙ of 9 in pie	320	6.0	17.0	35	80	105	10	325
Sweet potato	150	⅙ of 9 in pie	325	7.0	17.0	36	105	130	u	330
Pineapple, diced or crushed										
Raw	155	1 c	75	0.6	0.7	19	10	10	20	1
Canned, in heavy syrup	155	½ c solids and liquid	100	0.5	0.1	26	20	10	20	1
in juice	125	½ c solids and liquid	75	0.5	0.1	20	20	10	20	2
water pack	125	½ c solids and liquid	40	0.5	0.1	10	29	5	20	2
Pineapple juice	250	1 c	140	0.8	0.2	34	40	20	35	2
Pinenuts, pinon	30	1 oz, 4 tbsp	180	3.5	17.0	6	3	170	u	u
Pizza, cheese	65	⅛ of 14 in pizza	150	8.0	5.5	18	145	125	20	455
Sausage	65	⅛ of 14 in pizza	160	5.0	6.0	20	10	60	u	490
Plantain	275	1 banana 11 in × 2 in	220	2	0.7	57	5	60	65	7
Plums, raw	70	1 medium	35	0.5	0.4	9	2	5	4	0
Canned, purple, in heavy syrup	140	3 and 3 tbsp syrup	120	0.5	0.1	31	10	15	7	25
Popcorn with oil and salt	10	1 c	40	0.9	2.0	5	1	20	10	175

Potassium (mg)	Zinc (mg)	Copper (mg)	Iron (mg)	Total Vitamin A Activity (RE)	Thiamin (mg)	Riboflavin (mg)	Niacin (mg)	Vitamin B₆ (mg)	Pantothenic Acid (mg)	Folacin Total (µg)	Vitamin B₁₂ (µg)	Vitamin C (mg)	Polyunsaturated Fatty Acids (gm)
190	0.9	0.1	0.6	0	0.09	0.04	4.9	0.1	0.6	8	0	0	4.1
100	0.4	0.09	0.3	0	0.02	0.02	2.4	0.05	0.3	3	0	0	2.1
210	0.2	0.19	0.4	3	0.03	0.07	0.2	0.03	0.1	12	0	7	0.16
100	0.1	0.08	0.3	0	0.02	0.03	0.4	0.02	tr	2	0	2	0.05
80	0.1	0.08	0.3	0	0.01	0.02	0.1	0.02	tr	2	0	2	0.01
120	0.6	0.09	1.2	55	0.2	0.1	1.6	0.1	u	70	0	8	0.06
80	0.7	0.1	1.6	50	0.08	0.05	0.7	0.04	0.1	20	0	7	0.06
295	1.1	0.07	1.7	4	0.2	0.09	0.9	0.04	0.6	5	0	0	0.05
155	0.4	0.07	0.8	80	0.13	0.1	1.1	0.09	0.2	10	0	10	tr
170	u	0.3	0.7	4	0.2	0.04	0.3	0.05	0.5	4	0	1	u
u	u	u	0.1	10	tr	tr	0.1	u	u	u	0	10	0
50	0.1	u	0.4	90	tr	tr	0.2	u	u	u	0	2	tr
155	0.2	0.07	0.5	30	0.06	0.06	0.4	0.2	0.2	15	0	95	tr
u	u	u	0.4	330	0.06	0.06	0.4	u	0.2	20	0	150	tr
270	0.4	0.03	1.4	15	tr	0.03	tr	0.01	0.3	4	0	8	tr
u	0.05	0.07	0.4	3	tr	0.01	tr	tr	0.07	1	0	2	0
u	0.01	0.05	0.1	u	0	0	0	u	u	0	0	tr	0
125	0.1	0.1	0.5	5	0.03	0.03	0.6	0.06	0.2	8	0	2	u
165	0.06	0.1	0.5	70	0.03	0.03	0.8	u	u	u	0	tr	u
210	u	u	1.1	75	0.05	0.2	0.3	u	1.4	14	u	tr	u
u	u	u	0.9	85	0.08	0.3	0.5	u	u	u	tr	0	u
70	u	u	0.7	60	0.04	0.1	0.3	u	u	14	u	4	u
280	u	0.1	1.6	tr	0.10	0.06	0.6	u	u	u	u	2	u
170	u	u	3.9	20	0.20	0.1	0.4	u	u	u	0	tr	u
245	0.6	0.08	0.8	380	0.05	0.2	0.8	0.06	0.8	5	u	tr	u
250	u	u	0.8	360	0.08	0.2	0.5	u	u	u	u	6	u
175	0.1	0.17	0.6	3	0.1	0.1	0.7	0.13	0.2	16	0	24	0.23
130	0.1	0.13	0.5	2	0.1	0.03	0.4	0.10	0.1	6	0	9	0.05
150	0.1	0.12	0.4	4	0.1	0.02	0.4	u	u	u	0	12	0.04
155	0.1	0.13	0.5	2	0.1	0.03	0.4	0.09	0.1	6	0	9	0.04
335	0.3	0.22	0.6	6	0.1	0.05	0.6	0.24	0.2	58	0	27	0.07
u	u	u	1.5	1	0.4	0.07	1.3	u	u	u	u	u	u
85	0.8	0.2	0.7	100	0.04	0.1	0.7	u	u	24	u	5	u
115	0.8	u	0.8	100	0.06	0.08	1.0	u	u	23	u	6	u
895	0.2	0.14	1.1	200	0.1	0.1	1.2	0.53	0.5	39	0	33	tr
115	0.1	0.03	0.1	20	0.03	0.06	0.3	0.05	0.1	1	0	6	0.09
120	0.1	0.05	1.1	35	0.02	0.05	0.4	0.04	0.1	3	0	1	0.03
u	0.2	0.03	0.2	u	u	0.01	0.2	0.02	0.04	0	0	0	u

Food	Weight (gm)	Approximate Measure	Calories (Kcal)	Protein (gm)	Fat (gm)	Total Carbohydrate (gm)	Calcium (mg)	Phosphorus (mg)	Magnesium (mg)	Sodium (mg)
Pork										
Chop, broiled, lean and fat	80	1 medium	300	19.5	24.5	0	10	210	15	45
lean only	50	1 medium	110	13.0	6.5	0	5	135	10	30
Loin, roasted, lean and fat	85	2½ in × 2¼ in × ½ in	310	21.0	24.0	0	10	220	20	50
Spareribs, braised	90	yield from 6½ oz as purchased	400	18.5	35.0	0	15	220	u	65
Potatoes										
Baked	200	1 large	140	4.0	0.2	35	15	100	45	5¹
Boiled, pared	135	1 medium	90	2.5	0.1	20	10	55	30	3¹
French-fried, McDonald's	70	1 "order"	220	3.0	10.2	28	9	70	20	120
frozen, reheated	100	20 strips	140	2.0	5.0	23	5	65	15	30¹
Mashed with milk	100	½ c	100	2.0	4.5	13	25	50	15	350
Potato chips	20	10 chips, 2 in diameter each	115	1.0	8.0	10	10	30	10	200
Potato salad. See Salads.										
Pretzels	30	10 3-ring pretzels	120	3.0	1.0	24	10	25	7	480
Prunes, dried, raw	50	5–6	120	1.3	0.2	30	25	35	20	2
Cooked without sugar	110	½ c	115	1.2	0.2	30	25	40	20	2
Prune juice, canned	255	1 c	180	1.5	0.1	45	30	65	35	10
Puddings										
Almendrado	65	⅓ c and 2 tbsp sauce	100	2.7	4.3	14	35	50	u	35
Apple Brown Betty	110	½ c	160	1.5	4.0	30	20	25	5	165
Capirotada	155	½ c	385	10.8	14.0	58	230	200	u	335
Chocolate, instant, packaged	130	½ c	160	5.0	3.0	30	185	120	u	160
Custard	130	½ c	150	7.0	7.5	15	150	155	u	105
Rice with raisins	130	½ c	200	5.0	4.0	35	130	125	u	95
Tapioca	80	½ c	110	4.0	4.0	14	85	90	u	130
Vanilla, home recipe	130	½ c	140	4.5	5.0	20	150	115	u	85
Pumpkin, canned	245	1 c	80	2.0	0.7	19	45	90	60	10
Radishes, raw	45	5 large	7	0.4	tr	1	10	10	7	10
Raisins	35	¼ c	105	1.0	0.2	28	15	35	10	4
Rhubarb, cooked with sugar	120	½ c	140	0.5	0.1	37	175	10	15	2
Rice, cooked, salt added										
Brown	130	⅔ c	160	3.5	0.8	35	15	95	40	370
White, enriched	135	⅔ c	150	3.0	0.1	35	15	85	10	515
Precooked, instant	110	⅔ c	120	2.5	tr	25	3	20	u	300
Rolls and buns										
Danish pastry	65	1, of 4 in diameter	250	4.0	14.0	29	70	65	10	250
Hamburger or frankfurter bun, enriched	40	1 average	115	3.4	2.0	20	55	30	10	240
Hard rolls, enriched	50	1 large	135	4.3	1	28	10	40	12	285
Plain pan rolls, white, enriched	30	1 small	85	2.5	1.5	15	20	25	10	140
Rutabagas, boiled	85	½ c, cubed	30	0.8	0.1	7	50	25	12	4
Salads										
Chef's (lettuce w / ham, cheese, dressing, Red Barn)		1 serving	285	13.0	24.0	3	150	185	u	u
Potato, home recipe	125	½ c	120	3.5	3.5	20	40	80	u	650
Tuna fish	100	½ c	170	15.0	10.0	4	20	145	u	u

Po-tas-sium (mg)	Zinc (mg)	Cop-per (mg)	Iron (mg)	Total Vitamin A Activity (RE)	Thia-min (mg)	Ribo-flavin (mg)	Nia-cin (mg)	Vita-min B₆ (mg)	Panto-thenic Acid (mg)	Fola-cin Total (µg)	Vita-min B₁₂ (µg)	Vita-min C (mg)	Polyun-saturated Fatty Acids (gm)
215	2.3	0.13	2.7	0	0.8	0.2	4.5	0.3	0.5	3	0.4	0	2.0
145	1.5	0.04	1.6	0	0.5	0.1	2.9	0.1	0.2	2	0.2	0	0.5
235	2.2	0.05	2.7	0	0.8	0.2	4.8	0.3	0.5	4	0.5	0	2.0
300	u	u	4.7	0	0.8	0.4	6.1	u	u	u	0.6	0	2.2
780	0.4	0.3	1.1	tr	0.2	0.07	2.7	0.3	0.4	20	0	30	tr
385	0.4	0.1	0.7	tr	0.1	0.05	1.6	0.2	0.3	15	0	20	tr
250	0.2	0.1	0.4	tr	0.1	0.04	2.4	0.2	0.1	15	0	9	u
365	0.3	0.11	0.6	0	0.07	0.02	1.1	u	u	15	0	11	u
260	0.1	0.1	0.4	45	0.08	0.05	1.0	0.2	0.2	10	0	10	u
225	0.2	0.04	0.4	tr	0.04	0.01	1.0	0.04	0.1	2	0	5	u
30	0.3	0.05	0.6	u	0.1	0.1	1.2	0.01	0.1	5	0	0	tr
370	0.2	0.20	1.2	100	0.04	0.07	0.8	0.13	0.2	2	0	2	0.05
355	0.2	0.20	1.2	30	0.01	0.11	0.8	0.23	0.1	tr	0	3	0.05
705	0.5	0.17	3.0	1	0.04	0.18	2.0	u	u	1	0	10	0.02
50	u	u	0.3	60	0.02	0.08	0.03	0.02	0.3	8	0.4	tr	u
110	u	u	0.6	20	0.06	0.04	0.4	u	u	u	u	1	u
355	u	u	2.5	50	0.1	0.20	3.0	0.1	0.4	6	0.3	0	u
170	u	u	0.4	40	0.04	0.20	0.2	u	u	u	u	0	u
195	u	0.1	0.6	135	0.06	0.2	0.2	u	u	4	u	tr	u
235	0.4	0.04	0.6	30	0.04	0.2	0.2	u	u	5	u	tr	u
110	u	0.04	0.4	60	0.04	0.2	0.1	u	u	2	u	0	u
175	u	0.05	tr	45	0.04	0.2	0.2	u	u	u	u	0	u
535	0.4	0.26	1.8	8300	0.05	0.15	1.0	0.13	1.0	35	0	11	tr
130	0.1	0.04	0.4	tr	0.01	0.01	0.1	0.03	0.08	10	0	10	0
265	0.1	0.10	0.7	tr	tr	tr	0.3	0.08	tr	1	0	1	0
115	0.1	0.03	0.2	15	0.02	0.03	u	0.02	0.1	6	0	4	0
90	0.8	0.1	0.7	0	0.1	0.03	1.8	0.2	0.5	20	0	0	0.3
40	0.5	0.07	1.2	0	0.2	0.01	1.4	0.05	0.3	12	0	0	tr
u	0.2	u	0.9	0	0.1	u	1.1	u	u	3	0	0	0
60	0.6	u	1.2	15	0.16	0.16	1.5	u	u	u	u	tr	u
35	0.2	0.07	1.2	tr	0.20	0.13	1.6	0.01	0.2	15	0	tr	u
50	0.3	0.05	0.6	tr	0.05	0.06	0.6	0.03	0.2	30	0	0	u
25	0.4	u	0.5	tr	0.08	0.05	0.6	0.01	0.1	15	0	0	u
140	u	u	0.2	50	0.05	0.05	0.7	0.08	0.1	15	0	20	0
u	u	u	2.2	125	0.2	0.2	1.2	u	u	u	u	13	u
400	0.3	u	0.8	20	0.1	0.09	1.4	u	u	u	u	14	u
u	u	u	1.3	50	0.04	0.1	5.1	u	u	u	u	1	u

Food	Weight (gm)	Approximate Measure	Calories (Kcal)	Pro- tein (gm)	Fat (gm)	Total Carbo- hy- drate (gm)	Cal- cium (mg)	Phos- pho- rus (mg)	Mag- ne- sium (mg)	So- dium (mg)
Salad dressings										
Blue cheese	15	1 tbsp	75	0.7	8.0	1.0	10	10	u	165
French, regular	15	1 tbsp	65	0.1	6.0	3.0	2	2	2	220
low-calorie	15	1 tbsp	20	0	0.9	3.0	2	2	u	125
Italian, regular	15	1 tbsp	70	tr	7.0	1.0	1	1	2	115
low-calorie	15	1 tbsp	15	tr	1.5	0.7	tr	1	u	120
Mayonnaise	15	1 tbsp	100	0.2	11.0	0.3	3	4	tr	80
Salad dressing	15	1 tbsp	65	0.2	6.5	2.0	2	4	tr	90
Thousand Island	15	1 tbsp	60	0.1	6.0	2.5	2	3	u	110
Salmon. See Fish.										
Sandwiches										
Bacon, lettuce, tomato on white bread	150	1 average	280	7.0	15.5	30	55	90	u	u
Egg salad on white bread	140	1 average	280	10.5	12.5	30	70	155	u	u
Fish fillet, fried, on bun, McDonald's	135	1 average	410	15.0	21.5	37	95	235	20	760
Ham and cheese on white bread, Red Barn		1 average	350	20.0	19.0	30	215	240	u	u
Hamburger on bun, "Big Mac,"	95	1 regular	250	13.0	9.6	28	50	120	15	540
McDonald's	185	1 large	560	26.0	32.0	40	160	290	30	1060
Roast beef, Arby's	141	1 regular	350	22.0	15.0	32	200	u	u	1220
Tuna salad on white bread	105	1 average	280	11.0	14.0	25	50	135	u	u
Sashimi. See Fish, tuna, raw.										
Sardines. See Fish.										
Sauces										
Butterscotch	45	2 tbsp	200	0.5	7.0	35	40	25	u	u
Cheese	40	2 tbsp	65	3.0	5.0	2	90	65	u	u
Chocolate										
thin syrup	40	2 tbsp	100	0.9	0.8	25	7	35	u	u
fudge type	40	2 tbsp	125	2.0	5.0	20	50	60	u	35
Custard	70	¼ c	85	3.5	4.0	10	80	80	u	u
Hard sauce	20	2 tbsp	95	0.1	5.5	12	2	1	u	u
Hollandaise	50	¼ c scant	180	2.0	18.5	0.4	25	80	u	u
Soy	35	2 tbsp	25	2.0	0.5	4	30	40	u	2665
Tartar	15	1 tbsp	75	0.2	8.0	0.6	3	4	u	100
Tomato catsup	15	1 tbsp	15	0.3	0.1	4	3	10	3	155
White, medium	125	½ c	200	5.0	15.5	11	145	115	20	475
Sauerkraut, canned	120	½ c	25	1	0.3	6	40	25	20	800
Sausages										
Bologna	30	1 slice, 4¼ in x ⅓ in	90	3	8	0.5	3	25	5	285
Frankfurter (all meat)	45	1 average	145	5	13	1.0	5	40	5	505
Liverwurst	30	1 oz	95	4	8	0.6	5	65	u	u
Luncheon meat, pork, cured	30	1 oz	100	3.5	9	0.7	5	25	5	370
Pork sausage links	50	3 links	185	11	15	1.0	15	80	10	720
Salami, dry	30	3 small slices	125	7	10	0.8	5	40	6	560
Vienna, canned	50	3 sausages	135	5	12	1.0	5	25	5	450
Scallops										
Breaded, fried	95	3½ oz	180	17.0	8.0	10	u	u	u	u
Steamed	95	3½ oz	105	22.0	1.5	3	110	320	u	250
Sesame seeds, hulled	40	¼ c	220	7.0	20.0	7	40	220	7	u
Sherbet, orange	95	½ c	135	1.0	2.0	29	50	35	7	45
Shrimp, canned	85	3 oz.	100	20.5	0.9	0.6	100	225	45	835
French-fried	85	3 oz	190	17.5	9.5	8	60	160	40	160

Potassium (mg)	Zinc (mg)	Copper (mg)	Iron (mg)	Total Vitamin A Activity (RE)	Thiamin (mg)	Riboflavin (mg)	Niacin (mg)	Vitamin B_6 (mg)	Pantothenic Acid (mg)	Folacin Total (µg)	Vitamin B_{12} (µg)	Vitamin C (mg)	Polyunsaturated Fatty Acids (gm)
5	0.04	u	tr	6	tr	0.02	tr	u	u	u	tr	tr	4.3
15	0.01	u	0.1	u	u	u	u	u	u	u	0	u	3.4
15	u	u	0.1	u	u	u	u	u	u	u	0	u	0.5
2	0.02	0.1	tr	tr	tr	tr	tr	0	0	0	0	0	4.1
2	u	u	tr	tr	tr	tr	tr	0	0	0	0	0	0.9
5	0.02	0.04	0.1	10	tr	0.01	tr	u	0.02	0	0	0	5.7
1	0.08	u	tr	6	tr	tr	tr	0	0.02	0	0	0	3.1
20	0.02	u	0.1	10	tr	tr	tr	u	u	u	u	tr	u
u	u	u	1.5	85	0.2	0.1	1.5	u	u	u	u	15	u
u	u	u	2.4	100	0.2	0.02	1.0	u	u	u	u	2	u
u	u	u	1.6	20	0.2	0.4	2.9	0.1	u	20	0.8	2	u
u	u	u	3.1	60	0.4	0.3	2.5	u	u	u	u	0	u
u	u	u	2.6	30	0.2	0.4	3.7	0.1	u	20	0.8	4	u
u	u	u	3.8	40	0.8	0.6	6.5	0.2	u	30	1.5	5	u
u	u	u	4.5	u	0.3	0.3	5.0	u	u	u	u	u	u
u	u	u	1.2	50	0.1	0.1	4.0	u	u	u	u	1	u
u	u	u	1.4	60	tr	tr	tr	u	u	u	0	0	u
u	u	u	0.1	45	0.01	0.08	0.1	u	u	u	u	tr	u
u	u	0.2	0.6	tr	0.01	0.03	0.2	u	u	u	0	0	u
105	u	u	0.5	6	0.02	0.08	0.2	u	u	u	tr	0	u
u	u	u	0.4	60	0.04	0.2	0.1	u	u	u	u	tr	u
u	u	u	tr	60	tr	tr	tr	0	0	0	0	0	u
u	u	u	0.9	300	0.03	0.04	tr	u	u	u	u	tr	u
135	u	u	1.7	0	0.01	0.09	0.1	u	u	u	0	0	0
10	u	u	0.1	3	tr	tr	tr	u	u	u	u	tr	u
55	0.04	0.09	0.1	20	0.01	0.01	0.2	0.02	u	tr	0	2	u
175	0.5	0.05	0.2	140	0.05	0.2	0.2	0.06	0.8	1	0.2	1	u
235	0.2	0.12	1.9	3	0.02	0.02	0.3	0.16	0.1	u	0	18	0
45	0.6	0.01	0.4	0	0.02	0.04	0.7	0.05	0.1	1	0.4	5	0.3
75	0.8	0.04	0.5	0	0.09	0.05	1.2	0.06	0.2	2	0.6	12	1.2
u	u	u	1.8	1200	0.08	0.29	u	u	0.8	8	24.3	0	0.7
60	0.5	0.01	0.2	0	0.09	0.04	0.8	0.06	0.2	2	0.4	4	1.1
160	1.4	0.03	0.6	0	0.3	0.1	2.2	0.2	0.4	7	0.7	tr	0.6
115	1.0	0.03	0.4	0	0.2	0.09	1.5	0.2	0.3	u	0.6	tr	1.0
50	0.8	0	0.4	0	0.04	0.05	0.8	0.06	u	u	0.5	0	0.8
u	u	0.1	u	0	u	u	u	u	0.1	15	u	0	u
455	u	0.1	2.8	0	u	0.06	1.3	u	u	18	1.1	u	0.4
u	u	0.6	0.9	0	0.07	0.05	2.0	u	u	25	0	0	u
100	0.7	u	0.2	20	0.02	0.04	0.1	0.01	0.03	7	0.08	2	0.07
105	1.8	0.1	2.7	tr	0.01	0.03	1.5	0.05	0.2	10	u	0	0.4
195	0.8	0.3	1.8	u	0.03	0.06	2.5	0.05	0.3	5	0.6	u	u

Food	Weight (gm)	Approximate Measure	Calories (Kcal)	Protein (gm)	Fat (gm)	Total Carbohydrate (gm)	Calcium (mg)	Phosphorus (mg)	Magnesium (mg)	Sodium (mg)
Soups										
Albondiga (meatballs in tomato broth)	240	1 c with 4 meatballs	340	18.5	21.4	17	25	175	u	180
Bean with bacon	250	1 c	170	8.0	6.0	22	80	130	45	950
Bouillon, broth, consomme	240	1 c	15	3.0	0.5	0.1	15	30	u	780
Cream soups canned										
Chicken diluted with water	245	1 c	115	3.5	7.5	9	35	40	5	990
Chicken diluted with milk	250	1 c	190	7.5	11.5	15	180	150	20	1050
Mushroom diluted with water	245	1 c	130	2.5	9.0	9	45	50	5	1030
Mushroom diluted with milk	250	1 c	200	6.0	13.5	15	180	160	20	1075
Chicken noodle, from dry mix	250	1 c	55	3.0	1.0	7	30	30	5	1285
Clam chowder, Manhattan	245	1 c	80	4.0	2.5	12	35	60	10	1810
Onion	240	1 c	55	4.0	1.5	8	25	10	2	1050
Split pea with ham	250	1 c	190	10.0	4.5	28	20	210	48	1010
Tomato	265	1 c	100	2.5	2.5	19	50	65	15	945
Vegetable beef	245	1 c	80	5.5	2.0	10	15	40	6	955
Soybeans, mature, dry, cooked	90	½ c (1 oz, dry wt.)	120	10.0	5.0	10	65	160	80	2
Spaghetti										
Canned, with tomato sauce and meatballs, Franco American	210	1 can, 7½ oz	250	10.4	12.8	23	20	120	u	1035
Home recipe, with tomato sauce										
with cheese	250	1 c	260	9.0	9.0	35	80	135	30	955
with meatballs	250	1 c	330	18.5	11.5	40	125	235	40	1010
Spinach, fresh or frozen, boiled	90	½ c	20	2.5	0.2	3	90	40	60	50
Sprouts, raw										
Alfalfa	100	1 c, packed	40	5.0	0.6	5	30	u	u	u
Mung bean	100	1 c, packed	35	4.0	0.2	7	20	65	u	5
Soybean	100	1 c	50	6.5	1.5	6	50	70	u	u
Squash										
Summer, boiled	90	½ c	10	0.8	0.1	3	20	20	15	1
Winter										
baked	100	½ c	65	2.0	0.4	15	30	50	17	1
boiled	120	½ c	45	1.5	0.4	10	25	40	17	1
Strawberries										
Fresh	150	1 c, whole	45	1.0	0.5	10	20	30	15	2
Frozen, sweetened	255	1 c	245	1.4	0.3	66	30	30	20	8
Sugar										
Brown	220	1 c, packed	820	0.	0.	210	185	40	u	65
White										
granulated	200	1 c	770	0.	0.	200	0	0	0	2
	4	1 tsp	15	0	0	4	0	0	0	tr
powdered	8	1 tbsp	30	0	0	8	0	0	0	tr
Sundaes, ice cream w / topping										
Hot fudge, McDonald's	164	1 regular	310	7.0	11.0	46	215	236	35	175
Banana split, Dairy Queen	383	1 regular	540	10.0	15.0	91	350	250	u	u

Potassium (mg)	Zinc (mg)	Copper (mg)	Iron (mg)	Total Vitamin A Activity (RE)	Thiamin (mg)	Riboflavin (mg)	Niacin (mg)	Vitamin B_6 (mg)	Pantothenic Acid (mg)	Folacin Total (µg)	Vitamin B_{12} (µg)	Vitamin C (mg)	Polyunsaturated Fatty Acids (gm)
460	u	u	3.6	50	0.2	0.2	5.0	0.6	0.7	10	1.2	8	u
400	1.0	0.4	2.0	90	0.1	0.03	0.6	tr	u	32	u	2	1.8
130	u	u	0.4	u	tr	0.05	1.8	u	u	u	u	0	tr
90	0.6	0.1	0.6	55	0.03	0.06	0.8	tr	u	2	u	0.2	1.5
275	0.7	0.1	0.7	95	0.07	0.26	0.9	0.06	u	8	u	1	1.6
100	0.6	0.1	0.5	0	0.05	0.09	0.7	0.01	0.3	7	0.1	1	4.2
270	0.6	0.1	0.6	40	0.08	0.28	0.9	0.06	u	u	u	2	4.6
30	0.2	0.03	0.5	6	0.07	0.06	0.9	tr	u	1	u	0.3	0.3
260	0.9	0.15	1.9	90	0.06	0.05	1.3	0.08	0.1	10	2.1	3.0	1.3
70	0.6	0.12	0.7	0	0.03	0.02	0.06	0.05	u	15	0	1.0	0.6
400	1.3	0.37	2.3	45	0.15	0.08	1.5	0.07	u	2	u	1.0	0.6
295	0.2	0.09	0.4	80	0.06	0.05	0.8	0.1	u	7	u	5.0	0.2
175	1.5	0.18	1.1	190	0.04	0.05	1.0	0.07	u	10	0.3	2.0	0.1
490	0.6	0.3	2.5	2	0.20	0.08	0.6	u	u	70	0	0	3.0
375	u	0.3	2.2	100	0.15	0.2	3.4	u	u	u	u	u	u
410	0.2	0.3	2.3	250	0.2	0.2	2.5	0.1	0.8	2	0.6	15	u
665	3.5	0.4	3.7	300	0.2	0.3	4.0	0.4	0.5	15	0.6	20	u
300	0.5	0.1	2.0	750	0.06	0.1	0.4	0.2	0.2	60	0	20	tr
u	1.0	u	1.4	u	0.1	0.2	1.5	u	u	u	0	15	tr
235	0.9	u	1.4	2	0.1	0.1	0.8	u	u	u	0	20.	tr
u	1.6	u	1.1	8	0.2	0.2	0.8	u	u	u	0	15	tr
125	0.2	0.07	0.4	35	0.04	0.07	0.7	0.2	0.1	10	0	9	tr
470	u	u	0.8	350	0.05	0.1	0.7	0.09	0.3	u	0	15	tr
315	u	u	0.6	350	0.05	0.1	0.5	0.1	0.3	u	0	10	tr
245	0.2	0.07	0.6	25	0.03	0.1	0.3	0.09	0.5	26	0	85	0.28
250	0.1	0.05	1.5	6	0.04	0.1	1.0	0.08	0.3	38	0	105	0.16
755	u	0.7	7.5	0	0.02	0.07	0.4	u	u	u	0	0	0
5	0.1	0.04	0.2	0	0	0	0	0	0	0	0	0	0
tr	tr	tr	tr	0	0	0	0	0	0	0	0	0	0
tr	tr	tr	tr	0	0	0	0	0	0	0	0	0	0
410	1.0	0.13	0.6	50	0.07	0.3	1.1	0.1	u	u	0.7	2	u
u	u	u	1.8	150	0.6	0.6	0.8	u	u	u	0.9	18	u

Food	Weight (gm)	Approximate Measure	Calories (Kcal)	Pro-tein (gm)	Fat (gm)	Total Carbo-hy-drate (gm)	Cal-cium (mg)	Phos-pho-rus (mg)	Mag-ne-sium (mg)	So-dium (mg)
Sunflower seeds, raw	35	¼ c	200	8.5	17.0	7	45	305	13	10
Sweet potatoes										
Baked in skin	145	1 potato, 5 in × 2 in	160	2.5	0.6	35	45	65	45	15
Boiled in skin	130	½ c mashed	150	2.0	0.5	35	40	60	u	15
Candied	105	½ medium	180	1.5	3.5	35	40	45	u	45
Syrup, maple-flavored, artificial	20	1 tbsp	50	0	0	13	20	2	u	2
Tacos, beef	80	1 taco	160	11.0	8.5	9	135	160	u	200
Tamales, canned	100	3½ oz	140	4.5	7.0	14	20	40	10	665
Home recipe, chicken	130	2 tamales	275	8.3	23.7	8	100	60	u	60
Tea, instant	1	½ tsp	0	0	tr	tr	0	5	3	1
Tofu, soybean curd	120	1 piece, 2½ in × 2¾ in × 1 in	85	9.5	5.0	3	155	150	130	10
Tomatoes, raw	135	1 medium	25	1.5	0.2	6	15	35	20	4
Canned	120	½ c	25	1.0	0.2	5	30	25	15	190
Tomato juice, canned	180	¾ c	30	1.4	0.2	7	15	35	20	500
Tomato paste	130	½ c	110	4.4	0.5	26	45	115	75	40
Tongue, beef, braised	100	3½ oz	250	21.5	17.0	0.4	5	120	16	60
Tortillas										
Corn, lime-treated	30	1, of 6 in diameter	65	1.5	0.6	14	60	40	30	u
White flour	30	1, of 6 in diameter	110	3.0	1.0	20	4	50	15	250
Tostada, with beans and small portion of cheese	210	1 tostada	335	11.6	17.6	35	195	245	u	350
Tuna. See Fish										
Turkey, roasted										
Light meat	85	2 slices, each 4 in × 2 in × ¼ in	170	25	7	0	20	175	20	55
Dark meat	85	4 slices, each 2½ in × 1½ in × ¼ in	185	25	10 0	0	30	165	20	65
Turnips, boiled	80	½ c, cubed	20	0.6	0.2	4	25	20	10	25
Turnips greens, boiled	70	½ c	15	1.5	0.2	3	135	25	20	10
Veal cutlet, broiled	85	3 oz	180	23.0	9.5	0	10	195	20	55
Vinegar, cider	15	1 tbsp	2	tr	0	1	1	1	u	tr
Waffles										
Made from mix	75	1, of 7 in diameter	210	6.5	8.0	25	180	260	20	515
Frozen, Aunt Jemina	45	2 sections	125	2.6	4.0	19	35	170	10	310
Walnuts, English	100	1 c halves	650	15.0	64.0	16	100	380	135	2
	15	2 tbsp, chopped	100	2.5	10.0	3	15	60	20	tr
Watercress, raw	35	10 sprigs	5	0.8	0.1	1	55	20	5	20
Wheat bran, crude	30	1 oz	60	4.5	1.0	17	35	355	135	3
Wheat germ, raw	30	1 oz	100	7.5	3.0	13	20	315	90	tr
Toasted	30	1 oz	110	8	3.0	14	15	325	90	1
Wine, dessert (18.8%)	105	3½ fl oz	140	0.1	0	8	10	u	4	7
Table (12.2%)	100	3½ fl oz	90	0.2	0	4	10	15	10	10
Yeast										
Dry, active	5	1 tbsp	20	2.5	0.1	3	3	90	3	4
Brewer's, debittered	5	1 tbsp	25	3.0	0.1	3	15	140	10	10
Yogurt										
Low-fat, plain	230	8 fl oz carton	145	12.0	3.5	16	415	325	40	160
Fruit, sweetened	230	8 fl oz carton	225	9.0	2.6	42	315	245	30	120
Regular, plain	230	8 fl oz carton	140	8.0	7.5	11	275	215	25	105

Potassium (mg)	Zinc (mg)	Copper (mg)	Iron (mg)	Total Vitamin A Activity (RE)	Thiamin (mg)	Riboflavin (mg)	Niacin (mg)	Vitamin B6 (mg)	Pantothenic Acid (mg)	Folacin Total (µg)	Vitamin B12 (µg)	Vitamin C (mg)	Polyunsaturated Fatty Acids (gm)
335	u	0.6	2.6	2	0.7	0.08	2.0	0.4	0.5	80	0	0	8.9
340	1.0	0.2	1.0	920	0.1	0.08	0.08	0.05	1.0	10	0	25	tr
620	u	0.2	0.9	900	0.1	0.08	0.8	0.3	1.0	9	0	20	tr
200	u	0.06	0.9	660	0.06	0.04	0.4	u	u	7	0	10	u
35	tr	0.08	0.2	0	0	0	0	0	0	0	0	0	0
210	u	u	2.0	60	0.07	0.1	2.3	0.3	0.3	25	0.7	3	u
u	0.9	0.05	1.2	u	u	u	u	u	u	u	u	u	u
90	u	u	0.9	300	0.05	0.1	2.7	0.2	0.3	1	0.1	7	u
50	tr	0.01	tr	0	0	0.02	0.1	u	u	u	0	0	0
50	u	u	2.3	0	0.07	0.04	0.1	u	u	u	0	0	3.0
300	0.3	0.10	0.6	110	0.07	0.05	0.9	0.1	0.4	25	0	30	tr
350	0.2	0.12	0.6	70	0.06	0.04	0.8	0.1	0.3	25	0	22	tr
445	0.3	0.27	1.2	70	0.07	0.05	1.3	0.35	0.5	u	0	75	0
1340	1.0	0.77	3.2	215	0.3	0.2	4.0	0.49	0.6	u	0	70	0
165	u	0.07	2.2	0	0.05	0.3	3.5	0.1	2.0	u	u	0	u
u.	0.03	0.06	0.9	tr	0.04	0.02	0.3	0.02	0.03	tr	0	0	0.3
30	u	u	1.0	0	0.08	0.04	0.5	0.02	0.03	5	0	0	0.6
425	u	u	3.2	170	0.3	0.2	1.3	0.2	0.4	10	0.2	10	u
240	1.7	0.04	1.2	0	0.05	0.1	5.3	0.4	0.5	5	0.3	0	1.7
235	3.5·	0.1	1.9	0	0.05	0.2	3.0	0.3	1.0	8	0.3	0	2.6
145	0.07	0.03	0.3	tr	0.03	0.04	0.2	0.06	0.08	13	0	15	tr
125	0.1	0.04	0.8	460	0.1	0.2	0.4	0.1	0.1	40	0	50	tr
260	4.1	0.04	2.7	0	0.06	0.2	4.5	0.3	0.8	15	1.6	0	tr
15	0.02	0.01	0.1	0	0	0	0	0	0	0	0	0	0
145	u	u	1.0	60	0.1	0.2	u	u	0.5	u	u	0	u
95	0.4	0.03	2.2	120	0.2	0.2	2.3	0.12	0.2	2	tr	tr	u
450	2.8	0.9	3.1	3	0.3	0.1	0.9	0.7	0.9	45	0	2	45.0
70	0.4	0.1	0.4	1	0.06	0.02	0.2	0.1	0.1	5	0	tr	7.0
100	u	0.03	0.6	170	0.03	0.06	0.3	0.04	0.1	70	0	30	tr
315	2.7	0.4	4.2	0	0.2	0.1	0.6	0.2	0.1	80	0	0	0.6
230	4.7	0.7	2.6	u	0.6	0.2	1.0	0.3	0.9	80	0	0	1.5
270	4.7	0.18	2.6	0	0.5	0.2	1.6	0.28	0.4	100	0	0	1.84
100	0.1	0.06	1.6	0	0.02	0.02	0.2	0.05	0.02	2	0	0	0
115	0.1	0.03	0.1	0	0.01	0.03	0.1	0.04	1	0	0	0	0
140	u	0.2	1.1	tr	0.2	0.4	2.5	0.1	0.6	7	0	0	0
150	u	u	1.4	tr	1.2	0.3	3.0	0.1	0.6	9	0	0	0
530	2.0	u	0.2	35	0.1	0.5	0.3	0.1	1.3	25	1.3	2	0.1
400	1.5	u	0.1	25	0.08	0.4	0.2	0.1	1.0	20	1.0	1	0.1
305	1.3	u	0.1	70	0.07	0.3	0.2	0.1	0.9	20	0.8	2	0.15

INDEX

A, vitamin. *See* vitamin A
abdominal pain. *See* pain
acetaminophen, 199
acetoacetic acid, acetone, acetyl-coA, 33
acetylcholine levels, 188, 189
acid-alkaline balance, 73, 74, 77, 78, 80;
  and excess acid or alkaline, 80, 83, 172
acne. *See* skin
activity: athletic performance, *see* athletes; and bone-building, 4, 76; calories
  burned by, *see* calories; hard physical
  work, 82; and inactivity, 77, 155–156,
  158, 162, 163, 220, 268, 308; intellectual, *see* intellectual performance;
  physical, decline in, 85–86, 260–261.
  See also exercise
additives. *See* food processing
adenosine, 199; triphosphate (ATP), 160–
  161
adolescents, 108, 131, 138; athletic, 163;
  diabetic, 247; diet favored by, 105, 119,
  130, 300–301; eating disorders of, 303–
  305, 306; nutrient needs of, 10, 53, 74,
  79, 90, 200, 257, 261–265 *passim*, 269,
  299, 306; weight/obesity of, 131, 158,
  295, 299, 301–306. *See also* children
adoption studies (of body type), 139
adrenal glands, 41, 187
adrenaline, 135, 198, 200; excitement/
  anxiety/stress and, 168, 187, 212, 225,
  231. *See also* hormone(s); stress
adults: diet and exercise concerns of, 307–
  309. *See also* elderly, the
aerobic energy, 161, 166
aerobic exercises, 157, 160–163 *passim*,
219, 230, 231, 303, 308. *See also* exercise
Aerobics (Cooper), 164
affluence and diet. *See* diet(s)
aflatoxin, 233–234
Africa, 35, 234, 240
age: and heart disease, 205; and weight
  gain, 120, 141, 158. *See also* adolescents; adults; children; elderly, the;
  infants
Agriculture, U.S. Department of, 107,
  121, 177
alcohol: AHA limit on, 213; beer, wine,
  spirits, 94, 170, 173, 177, 183, 195, 196,
  197; benefits of, 3, 193–194, 196, 208,
  213, 218, 219, 322; blood alcohol level
  (BAL), 194–195; calories in, 197, 315;
  depletion of nutrients by, 116, 171, 265,
  318; and mortality rate, 196–197; during pregnancy and lactation, 194, 283,
  286, 291, 322; and stomach disorders,
  171, 172, 173; toxic effect of, 194, 197,
  218, 230, 231, 284, 286, 316, 322 (*see
  also* alcoholism)
alcoholism, 194, 307; and cancer, 194,
  236, 243, 244, 246; in elderly, 315; and
  hypoglycemia, 186; iron overload in, 88;
  and medication, 273, 316; nutritional
  deficiencies, 44, 53, 56, 79, 82, 90, 197,
  315; nutritional needs, 36, 89
aldosterone, 227. *See also* hormone(s)
alfalfa sprouts, 122, 235
alkaline imbalance. *See* acid-alkaline
  balance
allergies: and allergens, 178, 179, 180; and
361

allergies (*continued*)
asthma, arthritis, 182–183; child-
hood/infant, 179, 181–182, 287, 288,
291, 293; exercise heightening reaction, 181; food intolerance distin-
guished from, 174, 179; to gluten,
175; and headaches, 178, 182, 183,
184; histamine and, 37, 180, 181, 183;
and inflammation (sulfur and), 75;
and mood changes, 185; to MSG,
127, 183–184; supplements and, 52,
60, 168; tests for, 180, 181, 182. *See
also* toxicity
aluminum, 78, 265
Alzheimer's disease, 188, 189
amenorrhea. *See* menstruation
American Academy of Pediatrics, 287,
289, 290, 297, 300
American Cancer Society, 154, 242, 244
American College of Obstetricians and
Gynecologists, 283
American Diabetes Association, 244
American Heart Association (AHA), 110–
111, 213–214, 244, 252
American Medical Association (AMA),
226; *Journal*, 259, 305
Ames, Bruce, 235
amino acids: absorption of, 173;
bioamines, 37, 183; and brain function,
187–190; and cholesterol, 40; deficiency of, 35, 37, 54; eight essential, 36;
as energy source, 32, 34, 51, 53, 102,
165, 166; interaction of, with other
elements, 52, 170, 171; produced (metabolized) in body, 26, 36, 46, 59, 61;
toxicity of, 37. *See also* protein
amitriptyline, 273
ammonia buildup. *See* blood
amnesia, 89
amniotic fluid, 102
amphetamines: fake, 199; and hunger/
weight loss, 135, 147, 148, 193. *See also*
drug use
anaphylaxis, 178, 181, 183. *See also* allergies
Anderson, James, 218, 252
Andres, Reubin, 141
anemia: diet deficiency and, 37, 49, 51–58
passim, 70, 282; different types of, 260;
in elderly, 318; food sensitivity and,
183; infant, 257, 261, 281, 294; iron-
deficiency, 60, 85, 86, 256–263, 281;
pernicious, 57, 58, 255, 315; in pregnancy, 282; sickle-cell, 6, 63, 260;
"sports" or "runners'," 165; as toxicity
effect, 89, 91, 101
anesthetics, 149
ANF (atrial natriuretic factor), 223

anorexia, 136, 179, 264, 305; anorexia
nervosa, 168, 304, 306
antacids, antibiotics. *See* medication
antibodies, 35, 53, 90, 178; lactation and,
287, 291, 292; reduced protection by, 50
anticoagulants, anticonvulsants. *See*
medication
antioxidants: and cancer, 235, 237–239,
246, 309, 323; and life extension, 312;
vitamins as, 59, 60, 61, 64, 65, 69, 70,
238. *See also* oxidation and reduction
anus, inflammation around, 89
anxiety, *See* stress
apathy, 57, 78, 80, 82, 89; and foodstyle,
120, 314, 318. *See also* mental problems
appetite loss: appetite suppressants and,
135, 148, 149, 152; as deficiency symptom, 47, 55, 77–82 *passim*, 86, 89, 90,
256, 258; drugs, alcohol, smoking and,
193, 197, 201; fever or post-surgery,
270, 273, 274; as toxicity symptom, 68,
69, 75, 77. *See also* anorexia; hunger
apples. *See* fruits
apricots, 190, 239
arachidonic acid, 41. *See also* fatty acids
arginine, 36. *See also* amino acids
arms, inflamed areas on, 89
Army, U.S.: records of twins, 139
arsenic, 28, 29, 74, 95–96. *See also* trace
elements
arteries, "hardening of," 60. *See also*
atherosclerosis
arthritis, 41, 60, 178, 317; allergies and,
183; medication for, 172; rheumatoid,
183
artificial foods. *See* food processing
ascorbic acid. *See* vitamin C
aspirin. *See* medication
asthma, 53, 178, 271; allergies and, 182–
183; medication for, 172, 273
astronauts, 26, 164, 268
atherosclerosis, 94, 125, 128, 230, 245,
252; cholesterol and, 60, 162, 206–210,
211, 214, 220, 221, 322; exercise and,
208, 220, 303. *See also* heart disease
athletes: ATP reserves of, 160–161; competitive, 166–168; exercise habits and,
162–163; iron deficiency in, 87, 165,
166, 261; nutritional needs of, 164–166;
osteoporosis in, 264; potassium depletion in, 82; supplements and diets for,
52, 70, 165–166, 168; water needs of,
166. *See also* activity; exercise
Atkins Diet, 150. *See also* diet(s)
ATP. *See* adenosine
atrial natriuretic factor (ANF), 223
Australian health studies, 225, 230, 231
autism, 191

avocados, 39, 112, 183, 214

B, vitamins, *See* vitamin B group
baby boom, 310
baby foods. *See* infants
back pain. *See* pain
bacteria: intestinal, 71, 175, 177; iron
    overload and, 88; mouth, 302; salmo-
    nella, mutagenesis test using, 235
bad breath, 33, 34, 250
balanced diet. *See* dietary balance
bananas. *See* fruits
Banting, William, 152
barley. *See* grains
basal metabolism. *See* metabolism
"basic four" food groups, 108
beans, 105, 108, 120, 214; as digestive
    blockers, 149; dried, 76, 87, 88, 110;
    fava, 183, 260; as fiber source, 109, 110,
    177, 265; and flatulence, 177; as nutri-
    ent source, 49, 57, 70, 76, 78, 88, 177.
    See also soybeans and soybean prod-
    ucts; vegetables
bed rest, prolonged, 77, 162, 268. *See also*
    activity (and inactivity)
beef. *See* meat
bee pollen, 168
beer. *See* alcohol
beets, 235. *See also* vegetables
behavioral modification, 146
benzocaine, 149
beriberi, 44, 45, 47, 48, 255
berries. *See* fruits
beta-carotene. *See* carotenoids
beta-thalassemia, 63, 260
Beverly Hills Diet, 149, 150, 153, 304. *See
    also* diet(s)
bicycling, 156, 157, 163, 166, 167, 261. *See
    also* athletes; exercise
bile and bile acids, 39, 71, 110, 173, 174,
    240; cholesterol converted to, 90, 207,
    208
bioamines. *See* amino acids
biotin. *See* vitamin B group
Birch, Leann Lipps, 296–297
birth weight. *See* infants
Björntorp, Per, 144
bladder, 65, 66
bleeding. *See* blood (loss of)
blindness. *See* vision problems
bloating, 174; as toxicity effect, 89, 91,
    110
blood: acidity of, 33; ammonia buildup in,
    33, 34, 167; clotting (coagulation) of, 38,
    41, 64, 69, 71, 75, 76, 207, 217, 218, 272;
    fat/cholesterol levels in, 71, 94 (*see also*
    cholesterol); fatty acids in, 41, 138;
    glucose in bloodstream, *see* glucose

(blood sugar); loss of, 56, (as toxic effect)
    89, 91 (*see also* menstruation); oxygen
    in bloodstream, *see* hemoglobin; oxy-
    gen; plaque formation in, 206–207, 217,
    221; platelets, 78, 207, 217, 221; vita-
    mins and, 47, 50, 56. *See also* blood cells
blood alcohol level (BAL), 194–195. *See
    also* alcohol
blood cells: nutrient deficiency and, 56,
    57, 58, 62, 69, 70, 78, 272; red, replac-
    ment of, 257–258; vitamin toxicity and,
    60, 63, 71
"blood doping," 261
blood pressure: alcohol and, 193, 194, 197;
    caffeine and, 198; diet and, 76, 136, 145,
    206, 225, 309, 317; exercise and, 155,
    161, 162, 230, 231, 303, 308; food sensi-
    tivity and, 183; high, 205, 219, 220 (*see
    also* hypertension); measurement of,
    222–223, 224; nicotine and, 200; sodium
    and potassium (salt) consumption and,
    5, 10, 81, 82; systolic and diastolic, 223,
    225, 229, 230
blood sugar. *See* glucose
blood transfusions, 88
body consciousness, 8
body fat, 20, 38, 131–145; dietary fat
    stored as, 155; distribution of, 142–144,
    157; fat cells, 137–139, 144, 158; "set-
    point" for, 137. *See also* fats; obesity;
    weight; weight gain; weight loss
body mass index (weight-for-height), 16–
    17
bok choy, 239. *See also* vegetables
bone damage or loss, 61, 65, 77, 78, 88;
    fractures, 75, 84, 263, 314; osteomala-
    cia, 68, 69, 78; rickets, 45, 68–69, 76,
    255, 291. *See also* osteoporosis
bone formation, 4, 64–71 *passim,* 75–79
    passim, 84, 88–95 *passim,* 162. *See also
    entries for individual minerals*
bone marrow, 57, 60, 86, 95, 258, 259, 260
bone meal, 265
bone pain. *See* pain (joint or bone)
bone spurs or deformities, 93
Boston vitamin D study, 267
brain/brain cells: damage to, 54, 70, 71,
    194; diet and, 187–190; glucose needed
    by, 31, 33, 34, 134; hypothalamus, and
    hunger, 134, 135, 136; vitamins and, 47,
    54
bran. *See* grains
Brazil, 67
bread, 105, 110; fortified, 49, 50, 87, 108,
    261, 262, 266; muffins, 129; whole
    grain, 90, 108, 253–254, 271. *See also*
    grains
breast cancer. *See* cancer

breast cysts, 70
breast-feeding. *See* lactation
breathing. *See* respiration
brewer's yeast. *See* yeast
Briggs, George, 123
Britain. *See* England
broccoli, 76, 87, 93, 111, 153, 154, 239, 262. *See also* vegatables
bronchitis, 271
Brown, Michael S., 211
bruising, superficial, 60, 215
brussels sprouts, 125, 239, 246, 273, 316. *See also* vegetables
BSA (protein), 180–181
bulimia, 304–305, 306
Burger King, 119, 129
Burkitt, Denis, 240
burns. *See* injury
burnt toast, 235
butter and butterfat. *See* dairy products

C, vitamin. *See* vitamin C
cabbage, 93, 125, 171, 177, 239, 246, 273, 316. *See also* vegetables
caffeine. *See* coffee
calcidiol, calcitriol, calcitonin, 266–267. *See also* vitamin D
calcium, 75–77, 256; for adults/elderly, 10, 307, 315, 316, 318; alcohol and, 171; in arteries, 207; for athletes, 165, 166; and blood pressure, 228–229, 231; and cancer, 243; child/adolescent needs, 10, 200, 291, 298, 299, 306; as electrolyte, 75, 76; excess of (hypercalcemia), 68, 77, 79, 84, 171 (*see also* kidney stones); in "fad" diets, 151; fiber interference with, 170, 265; interaction of, with other minerals, 4, 77, 78, 79, 84–85, 92, 170–171, 192, 265, 266, 322; interaction of, with vitamin D, 4, 10, 64, 68, 69, 76, 77; measurement of, 258–259; -medication reaction, 273, 316; and osteoporosis, 263–269 (*see also* osteoporosis); in pregnancy/nursing diet, 75, 280–281, 290; in processed or restaurant foods, 123, 129; protein interference with, 152; RDA for, *see* RDAs (Recommended Dietary Allowances); sources of, 77, 102–115 *passim*, 122, 128, 299, 300 (*see also* dairy products; milk); and stomach acid, 172; supplemental, need for, 266, 269, 281, 285, 290, 298, 299, 307; toxicity of, 75, 77, 116
calcium carbonate, 77, 265, 269, 281
calcium hydroxide, 77
California Bureau of Chronic Diseases, 219
"California cuisine," 121

calories: in alcohol, 197, 315; athletes' needs, 164, 165, 167; burned by activity, 18–20, 30, 134, 156–157, 159–160, 161, 164, 219–220 (*see also* metabolism); and cancer, 240–242, 246; children's needs, 299; consumption of, decrease in, 154, 308; counting, 146; defined, 30; in dietary balance, 16, 112, 127; in "fast foods," 119; fats as source of *see* fats; infant/nursing mother needs, 288, 289–290, 298; kilocalories (Kcal), 30; labeling of content, 106, 107; low-calorie diets, *see* diet(s); low-calorie food products, 122; protein as source of, *see* protein; in sample foods lists, 113, 114–115, 116; in vitamins, 45; and weight or weight loss, 17–20, 109, 110, 133–139. *See also* energy
Cameron, Ewan, 245
Campbell's Soup, 122
cancer: alcohol and, 194, 236, 243, 244, 246; breast, 10, 41, 234–238 *passim*, 241, 242, 243; caffeine and, 198; carcinogens producing, 233–243 *passim*; cervical, 236; colon, 10, 41, 63, 76, 109, 110, 234–246 *passim*, 322, (screening for) 309; diet and, 6, 232–246, 309, 317; DNA changes and, 233–237 *passim*, 241; endometrial, 236; esophageal, 236, 242; exercise and, 243, 246; fat intake and, 41, 220–221, 237, 241–242, 244, 245, 309, 322; free radicals and, *see* free radicals; gastrointestinal, 236; heredity and, 234, 309; liver, 236, 243; lung, 233–239 *passim*; nose, 234; pancreatic, 243; prostate, 236, 242; rectal, 244; skin, 233; smoking and, 233–239 *passim*; spleen, 237; stomach, 105, 128, 236, 242–243, 244; supplements in treatment or prevention of, 5, 56, 60, 67, 70, 76, 94, 109, 237–238, 243, 244, 245; uterine, 41, 242, 243; vulnerability to, 234, 266; weight and, 144, 160, 242, 246
candy, 301, 302. *See also* chocolate; sugar
Cannon, Walter, 134
cantaloupes, 239. *See also* fruits
carbohydrates: chemical composition of, 32; in dietary balance, 16, 111; as energy source, 30–31, 49, 51, 78, 88, 89, 109, 110, 150, 213; and high-, low-, or no-carbohydrate diets, *see* diet(s); "loading" of, 167; metabolism of, 46, 81, 82, 88, 91, 171, 173; in processed food, labeling information, 106, 107; simple and complex (sugars and starch), 32, 109, 153, 177, 218, (in ethnic food) 127, 128, 130, (in diabetic diet) 252, 254. *See also* fiber; sugar

carbonated beverages. *See* soft drinks
carbon atoms, 31, 39, 46, 214
carbon dioxide, 31, 33, 83, 161, 177
carcinogens. *See* cancer
cardiopulmonary resuscitation (CPR)
    procedures, 205
cardiovascular problems. *See* heart dis-
    ease
carotenoids, 66, 67, 238–239, 244, 246;
    beta-carotene, 64, 66, 238–239, 309. *See
    also* vitamin A
carpal tunnel syndrome, 53
carrots, 67, 176, 181. *See also* vegetables
casein, 107, 200
cassava (as fiber source), 240
cataracts. *See* vision problems
cauliflower, 93, 239. *See also* vegetables
cavities. *See* teeth and gums
celery, 235. *See also* vegetables
celiac disease, 175
cell membrane structure, 73
cell reproduction, 78. *See also* nucleic
    acids (DNA and RNA)
cells, blood. *See* blood cells
cells, nerve. *See* nerve tissue/cells
celluloses, 109, 110; methylcellulose,
    149. *See also* fiber
central nervous system: and blood pres-
    sure, 223; deficiencies and, 41, 79, 89;
    and hunger, 134, 135; nutrients needed
    by, 31, 33, 34, 47, 53, 288; toxicity and,
    80, 283
cereals, 108, 170, 244; as fiber source, 110;
    fortified, 49, 50, 87, 113, 261, 262, 266;
    high-cereal diet, 265; for infants, 293,
    294, 298; as mineral source, 79, 81. *See
    also* grains
cerebral palsy, 54
"challenge" test for allergies, 180
charcoal-broiling. *See* cooking
cheese, 71, 108, 124, 129, 214, 302; allergy
    to, 182, 183; as calcium source, 76, 264,
    299; imitation, 107, 123. *See also* dairy
    products
Chemistry of Love, The (Liebowitz), 192
Chicago exercise study, 230
chicken, chicken nuggets, chicken soup.
    See poultry
children: allergies of, 179, 181–182; atti-
    tude of, to new foods, 119, 296–297;
    autistic, 190; blindness in, 67; calcium-
    magnesium needs of, 10, 69, 75, 79, 108;
    cavities of, 302, (and fluoride needs) 93;
    celiac disease in, 175; and cholesterol,
    295–296; copper needs of (and Menkes'
    disease), 89; diabetes in, 247; disease
    risk among, 303; exercise habits for,
    163, 303; growth of, *see* growth, growth
    retardation; hyperactive, 189–191;
    hypercholesterolemia in, 211; ill, spe-
    cial needs of, 271; and imitation foods,
    123; iodine needs of, 92; iron needs of,
    10, 70, 73, 85, 86, 87, 261, 262, 272; and
    iron toxicity, 88; in low-income or
    Third World families, 35–36, 65, 66–67,
    89; obese, 138–139, 294–295, 298; salt
    tolerance of, 103; selenium supple-
    ments for, 74; of working mothers, 120,
    300. *See also* adolescents; infants
Chilean manganese miners, 92
China, 74, 92, 234, 242
Chinese food, 121, 127, 172; MSG in, 127,
    183–184
chloride, 73, 74, 80, 83
chlorpromazine, 273
chocolate, 119, 171, 182, 183, 214, 265,
    301, 302; for lovers, 192
cholecystokinin (CCK), 135, 149
cholesterol, 38, 50, 316; accumulation of,
    33, 40, 41, 94, 145, 207, 208; alcohol
    and, 193, 208, 213; amounts of (sample
    foods lists), 216–217; "bad" vs. "good,"
    40, 216–217; chemical structure and
    function, 39–40, 207, 214; coffee and,
    199–200; diet and, 125, 208–211, 213–
    218, 252, 309, 317, 322, (fiber in) 109,
    110, 170, (children's diet) 295–296, 299–
    300; exercise and, 155, 162, 208, 303,
    308; and gallstones, 174; and heart
    disease, 10, 205–206, 207–221; HDL
    and LDL, 196, 207–208, 211–220 *pas-
    sim*, 225, 307, 308, 322; measurement/
    limitation of, 111, 208, 213; for nursing
    infants, 41, 288; serum, 208–221, 300;
    stress and, 212, 307; vitamin claims
    and, 60, 70; and vitamin D, 40, 207. *See
    also* fats, saturated
cholestyramine, 209
choline, 188, 189
Christmas Carol, A (Dickens), 185
chromium, 72, 73, 74, 94
cimetidine, 172, 316. *See also* medication
circulatory failure, 81
cirrhosis of the liver. *See* liver (body or-
    gan)
citric acid (Krebs) cycle, 33
citrus fruits. *See* fruits, citrus
clay, eating of (pica or geophagy), 77, 90,
    100–101, 280
cobalamin. *See* vitamin B_{12}
cobalt, 95
cocaine. *See* drug use
cocoa, 285
coconut oil. *See* oils
cod-liver oil, 65, 68
coenzymes, bound and detachable, 48. *See*

coenzymes (continued)
   also enzyme(s)
coffee, 243, 262; and caffeine, 167–168,
   193, 198–200, 230, 265, 284, 286, 291
   (see also soft drinks); decaffeinated,
   172, 173
Coindet, J. R., 92
cola drinks. See soft drinks
cold, clammy feeling, 86, 249
cold, extreme. See temperatures
colds: vitamin C in treatment of, 5, 60,
   271, 273
collagen, 35, 50, 207, 256; nutrient deficiencies and, 59, 61, 84. See also protein
colon, 174, 175–177; cancer of, see cancer;
   irritable, 176
colostrum, 287
Columbia University, 104, 192, 278, 313
coma, 78, 80, 81; diabetic, 248, 249–250
concentration, loss of; confusion, disorientation. See mental problems
constipation, 47, 75, 77, 82; fiber and, 109,
   110, 176, 240, 322
contraceptives, oral, 56, 60, 62. See also
   medication
convenience foods, 119; frozen, 62, 108,
   124, 126–127
convulsions, 53, 54, 75–81 passim, 256
Cook, Captain James, 60–61
cooking: charcoal-broiling, 234, 235, 243,
   246, 273; and cookbooks, 228; and
   cookware, 27, 94, 121, 262, (nonstick)
   125; to eliminate oligosaccharides, 177;
   frying, see fried foods; and glucose
   release time, 254; home, 124–127, 228;
   importance of, 125; nutrients destroyed
   by, 47, 49, 50, 53, 54, 56, 62, 125, 127,
   128; vitamin-destroying enzyme destroyed by, 49, 125. See also food processing
Cooper, Kenneth, 164
coordination loss, 50
copper, 73, 290, 298; as bone- or blood-
   builder, 4, 63, 84, 88, 91, 264, 269, 272,
   274, 300; deficiency of, 85, 88–89, 90,
   95, 130, 218, 260, 266, 267, 291, 316; for
   elderly, 317; sources of, 89, 116, 267,
   301; supplemental, need for, 88, 262;
   toxicity of, 88, 89, 237
corn, 175; -based diet, 51–52, 255; as fiber
   source, 240
Cornell University, 50, 120, 165, 300
cornmeal, 77. See also grains
corn oil. See oils
corn syrup, 107, 124. See also sugar
cortisol, 212. See also hormone(s)
CPPT (Coronary Primary Prevention
   Trial), 209–210

cramps. See muscle cramps or spasms
Crapo, Phyllis, 253
cretinism, 92
cucumbers, 128. See also vegetables
cultural ideas. See foodstyle
cystic fibrosis, 94
cystine, 36, 288. See also amino acids
cytotoxic test for allergies, 180

D, vitamin. See vitamin D
dairy products, 49, 52, 64, 105, 245; allergy to, 181, 182, 183; butter/butterfat,
   58, 65, 105, 124–129 passim, 214; buttermilk, 175; as calcium source, 76, 78,
   105, 107, 269; consumption of, 124; fats
   in, 37, 105; ice cream, 42, 109, 122, 247,
   252, 253, 299; imitation, 58, 107, 123;
   sour cream, 126, 175; yogurt, 108, 124,
   126, 127, 129, 175, 266, 280. See also
   cheese; eggs; milk
dancers, 165, 168, 264. See also athletes
Davis, Clara, 104
death, causes of: diabetes, 248; iron deficiency or overload, 86, 87; magnesium
   toxicity, 80; pernicious anemia, 57;
   riboflavin deficiency (in aminals), 50;
   scurvy, 61; sodium loss (extreme), 81.
   See also mortality rate
debilitation. See weakness, listlessness
deep frying. See fried foods
dehydration, 81, 166, 283. See also water
delirium, dementia. See mental problems
Denmark: research in, 71, 139, 215
Denny's, 129
dental problems. See teeth and gums
depression: and antidepressants, 190;
   blood sugar and, 186, 187; exercise and,
   162; as deficiency symptom, 47, 51, 55,
   78, 80, 82, 89; as toxicity symptom, 65.
   See also mental problems
dermatitis, 51. See also skin
developing nations. See Third World
dextrose, 107. See also sugar
DHEA (steroid hormone). See hormone(s)
DHS (docosahexaeonic acid), 215
diabetes, 34, 60, 219; deficiency symptoms resembling, 94; and diet, 247–254;
   diet pills and, 148; exercise and, 155,
   160, 162, 186, 247–251 passim, 303,
   308; fiber and, 110, 171, 252; glucose
   levels and, 63, 72; and heart disease,
   205, 206, 248, 252; heredity and, 9–10,
   234, 247, 249, 250, 254, 309, 317; and
   insulin, 186, 247, 249, 250, 251, 254;
   insulin-dependent, 247–248, 254; and
   ketosis, 33; and mineral deficiency, 79,
   82; non–insulin dependent, 160, 248–
   249, 250, 254, 309, 317; symptoms of,

diabetes, (*continued*)
248, 249; as toxicity effect, 51;
weight/obesity and, 72, 144, 247,
250–251, 254, 317
diarrhea: bloody, 51; clay eating as
relief of, 100; as deficiency cause,
79, 81, 83; as deficiency symptom,
51, 56, 65, 82, 83; food intolerance/
allergy and, 174, 175, 176, 182; supplement toxicity and, 60, 62, 65, 68,
81, 89, 91, 110
diary. *See* food diary
diet(s): affluence and, 105, 131, 236, 241;
"anti-arthritis," 183; astronaut, 26;
baseline, 109–114, 123; "basic four,"
108; bland, 172; and brain function,
187–190; and cancer, *see* cancer; for
competitive athletes, 168; corn-based,
51–52, 255; and diet pills, diet candies
and gum, 145, 148, 149; elimination (in
allergy test), 180, 181, 182; fashions and
fads in, 7, 118, 120–123, 132, 139, 145,
146, 147–154, 304; food-combining,
152–153; high-carbohydrate, 35, 120,
153–154, 155, 167, 168, 188, 251–252,
254; high-carbohydrate, low-fat, 104,
145, 147, 153, 299–300, 309, 320; high-
cereal, 265; high-fat, 41–42, 105, 155,
174; high-fiber, 3, 176, 240, 245, 246,
251–252, 254; high-protein, 187, 188;
illness, 270–274; liquid protein, 79, 144,
151; low-calorie, 82, 87, 115, 144, 150,
151, 241; low-cholesterol, 209–210,
213–214, 295–296, 299–300; low- or no-
carbohydrate, 31, 145, 149–150, 151,
152, 187, 251; low-fat, 105, 171, 187,
209, 245 (*see also* high-carbohydrate,
low-fat, *above*); low-sodium, 83, 223–
224, 226–228; macrobiotic, 245; and
malnutrition, 44; pregnancy, 277–286;
prehistoric, 101–102, 155; rice, 226–
227; sodium-free, 81 (*see also* low-
sodium, *above*); supplementation of,
see supplements; synthetic, 27 (*see also*
TPN [total parenteral nutrition]); variety in, 8, 103–104, 108–111; vegetarian/
vegan, 58, 81, 84, 91, 115–116, 257; "yo-
yo" pattern of, 136, 145. *See also* food;
hunger; weight gain; weight loss
Diet Analysis Chart, 12, 14–15
dietary balance, 16, 20, 111, 112, 116, 321;
eating out and, 127, 129; minerals and,
74, 85
Dietary Guidelines for Americans, 107,
252
Diet Free (Kuntzleman), 19
diethylpropion, 148
"diet-induced thermogenesis," 155, 156

diet pills, candies, gum. *See* diet(s)
Dietz, William, 158, 301, 302
digestion, 169–177; allergic reactions of,
178; disorders of, 56, 88, 109 (*see also*
intestine[s]; stomach); fiber and, 109.
See also enzyme(s); fiber; metabolism
digestive blockers, 149
dinitrophenol, 148
disaccharides, 32. *See also* lactose; sucrose
disease: vulnerability to, *see* heredity. *See
also* illness; *entries for individual
ailments*
disease prevention: exercise, 155, 159,
160, 162, 205, 208, 218–220, 243, 246;
nutrition, 6, 9–10. *See also* heart disease; osteoporosis
Disease Prevention and Health Promotion, U.S. Office of, 303
disorientation. *See* mental problems
diuretics, 79, 81, 82, 149, 168, 316; caffeine, 167–168, 269; and diuretic effect
(water loss), 150, 151, 152; thiazide,
dangers of, 224
diverticulosis, 109, 110, 176, 240, 322;
and diverticulitis, 176
dizziness, 37, 53, 187; and vertigo, 78, 79
DNA. *See* nucleic acids
docosahexaeonic acid (DHA), 215
dolomite pills, 265
dopamine levels, 188, 189
Drewnowski, Adam, 154
drinking. *See* alcohol; alcoholism
drowsiness, 249. *See also* lethargy, sluggishness; sleep
drug use: cocaine, 189–191, 193; in suppressing appetite, 135, 148; and vitamin
deficiency, 44. *See also* amphetamines;
medication
Duke University, 181
duodenum, 173; ulcers of, 172. *See also*
ulcers
Dutch East Indian Medical Service, 48
dwarfism, 90. *See also* growth retardation

E, vitamin. *See* vitamin E
eating disorders, 303–305, 306. *See also*
anorexia
eating out, 119, 121, 127–130, 183, 308.
See also "fast foods"; takeout meals
eating patterns. *See* foodstyle
eating when ill, 270–274
eczema, 181, 182. *See also* skin
edema, 36, 70, 95
EFA. *See* fatty acids (essential)
eggs, 245; allergy to, 181, 182; and cholesterol, 209, 213, 214; consumption of,
124; imitation, 123; as protein source,

eggs, (continued)
36, 108; raw, and biotin, 170; as vitamin/mineral source, 49, 58, 65, 69, 76, 87
Egypt, early, 185
eicosapentaenoic acid (EPA), 41, 215, 218, 317. See also fatty acids
elderly, the: the aging process, 59, 70, 310–320; eating patterns of, 313–314, 318–319; excess calcium in, 69; and exercise, 163, 317, 319, 320; malnutrition among, 44, 120; nutrient needs of, 10–11, 53, 68, 69, 89, 90, 91, 267, 312–320; weight of, 314
electrolytes, 74, 75, 76, 79, 80–83; imbalance or loss of, 145, 151, 224; ions, 79, 80, 81, 82, 83
electron exchange, 30. See also oxidation and reduction
elimination diet. See diet(s)
Emory University, 101–102
emotional disturbance, emotional stress. See mental problems; stress
endocrine, 242
endorphins: and hunger, 135
enemas, 78, 82
energy: aerobic, 161, 166; burst of, ATP and, 160–161; loss of, diet deficiency and, 37, 60, 89, 258, 259 (see also weakness, listlessness); sources of, 30–34, 45, 111, 257 (see also amino acids; carbohydrates; fats); supplement release of, 47–55 passim, 77, 78, 79, 86, 89, 91. See also calories; glucose (blood sugar); oxidation and reduction
England: allergy studies, 179, 182; cancer studies, 241; diet fad, 152; diet studies, 58, 68, 90, 186, 268, 282; metabolic studies, 135, 290; obesity studies, 294; incidence of rickets, 255
environmental toxicity. See toxicity
enzyme(s): and coenzymes (vitamins B and C, trace elements), 47, 48, 50, 51, 53, 57, 64, 85; digestive blockers and, 149; functions of, 34–35, 91, 94, 173–175, 239; interactions of, 73, 76, 78, 79, 95, 171, 227; kidney (renin), 227–228, 229; metalloenzymes, 85, 89, 90; vitamins destroyed by, 49, 63, 125, 171
EPA. See eicosapentanoic acid
epinephrine, 190, 192
Epsom salts, 79
erythromycin (antibiotic). See medication
ESA (Estimated Safe and Adequate amount): biotin, 55; minerals, 73, 81, 82, 83, 88, 91; pantothenic acid, 50; vitamin K, 71. See also RDAs (Recommended Dietary Allowances)

Eskimos, 37, 215–216
esophagus/esophageal sphincter, 170–172
essential nutrients. See nutrients, essential
Estimated Safe and Adequate amount. See ESA
estrogen, 40; and calcium/bone loss, 4, 76, 164, 165, 168, 264–269 passim, 317; excess, and cancer risk, 242, 266. See also hormone(s)
ethnic food. See foodstyle
exercise, 159–168; and allergic reaction, 181; and cancer, 243, 246; dangers of, 164, 186, 283; for disease prevention, 155, 159, 323 (see also entries for individual disorders); for elderly, 163, 317, 319, 320; habitual, need for, 162–164, 308; and heart rate, see heart rate; and injuries, 164; during pregnancy, 283–285, 286; for weight loss, 133, 137, 139, 144, 145, 147, 156–158, 160–164, 303, 308, 323. See also activity; athletes; calories; weight loss
exhaustion, 256. See also fatigue; stress
extremities. See hands and feet
eyes: and eyelids, 66; red or light-sensitive, 49; sores around, 53; vitamin A and, 64, 65, 66, 67. See also vision problems

facial sores, 49
fashions and fads. See diet(s)
"fast foods," 7, 108, 121, 129–130, 307; chicken nuggets, 119, 129; fats in, 119, 129, 130, 301; hamburgers, 119, 130, 213, 234, 235, 301, (Big Mac), 112–113; pizza, 119, 121, 130, 301. See also eating out
fasting, 151, 152
fat and fat cells, body. See body fat
fatigue: as diabetes symptom, 248; as deficiency symptom, 47, 50, 57, 61, 81, 82, 86, 258, 293; as drug side effect, 224; in "hypoglycemia," 187
fats: and alcohol absorption, 195; animal, 70, 125–126, 128, 173 (see also dairy products; meat); chemical structure of, 39; dietary, and body fat, 155; dietary, and cancer, 240–242; in dietary balance, 16; different kinds of, 39; in digestive (metabolic) process, 38, 46, 50, 64, 78, 79, 89, 109, 153, 173–174; as energy (calorie) source, 30, 31–32, 38, 102, 133, 144, 150, 155, 166, 200, (infant need of) 288; in "fast foods," 119, 129, 130, 301; flavor and satiety value of, 37–38, 102, 154,155; high-fat, low-fat diets, see diet(s); and infant fat cells, 138, 295;

fats (*continued*)
  low-fat food products, 122, 127; in
    processed food, labeling informa-
    tion, 106, 107; purified (potassium
    lack in), 82; rancid, 237; saturated/
    unsaturated, *see* fats, saturated; fats,
    unsaturated
fats, saturated: and cholesterol, 4, 125,
    210–216 *passim*, 220–221, 288, 322;
    defined, 39; dietary limit on, 110, 113,
    125, 213, 245, 252, 322; in processed or
    restaurant foods, 123, 128, 129; sources
    of, 214–216
fats, unsaturated, 213, 230, 288; and
    cancer risk, *see* cancer; and cholesterol,
    215–217; defined, 39; in home cooking
    and restaurant food, 125–126, 128;
    hydrogenated, 39, 126, 214
fat-soluble vitamins. *See* vitamin(s)
fatty acids, 37–42; amounts of (sample
    foods list), 216–217; in bloodstream, 41,
    138; in chemical structure of fats, 39,
    166; conversion of fats to, in digestive
    (metabolic) process, 29, 32, 38, 53, 55,
    78, 94, 167–168, 174; essential (EFA),
    and deficiency of, 40, 41, 288; ketone
    production from, 33; omega-3, 215, 221;
    vitamin protection of, 49, 61; "waste"
    of, without glucose, 32, 34. *See also* fats,
    saturated; fats, unsaturated
fava bean and favism, 183, 260
FDA (Food and Drug Administration,
    U.S.), 54, 148, 149, 182, 190, 199, 226,
    284; food labeling requirements, 106,
    107, 228, 244
feet. *See* hands and feet
Feingold, Ben F., 189, 190
feminism: and weight control, 132. *See
    also* women
ferritin, 86, 258, 259. *See also* iron
ferrous sulphate, 262. *See also* iron
fetal alcohol syndrome, 194, 283
fetal growth, 90, 194. *See also* pregnancy
fever: demand for vitamin C in, 61; as
    exercise danger, 284; as toxicity effect,
    75, 77, 81, 89, 91, 186; treatment of,
    270–271, 273
fiber, 87; and cancer, 239–240, 244, 309;
    and cholesterol, 110, 170, 322; and
    constipation or diverticulosis, 109, 176,
    240, 322; defined, and different kinds of,
    111; glucose/mineral absorption im-
    peded by, 32, 90, 110, 170, 171, 252, 262,
    265; high-fiber diet, *see* diet(s); overdose
    problems, 110, 154; soluble and insolu-
    ble, 110, 111, 240, 246; sources of, 90,
    110, 111, 177, 218, 239, 240, 246; in
    weight-loss/obesity treatment, 135, 149

"fight or flight" reaction, 223. *See also*
    stress
fillers (in weight-loss treatment), 135,
    149. *See also* fiber
Finland: osteoporosis studies in, 94
Finn Crisp crackers, 122
fish and shellfish: in "basic four" group,
    108; and cholesterol, 216; fatty acids in,
    41; increased consumption of, 105, 122,
    124; in macrobiotic diet, 245; as protein
    source, 101, 128; raw, vitamin B_1 de-
    stroyed by, 49, 171; as vitamin/mineral
    source, 52, 58, 64, 69, 78, 87, 88, 94, 238,
    (bone-building) 262, 265, 267, 268
fish oil. *See* oils
Fit for Life (Diamond and Diamond), 153
flatulence. *See* gas
flavor and aroma, 37, 102, 154, 155; artifi-
    cial flavorings, 191; and loss of sense of
    smell or taste, 89, 90, 120, 313–314; and
    taste for sweets and salt, *see* salt (so-
    dium); sugar
fluid loss. *See* water
fluoride, 73, 93–94, 302; and osteoporosis,
    267–268, 269; supplemental, need for,
    292, 317
flushing of skin. *See* skin
folacin (folic acid), 46, 63, 272; B_{12} defi-
    ciency masked by, 57, 58; deficiency of,
    53, 56, 57, 130, 171, 259, 260, 282, 316;
    elderly need for, 11, 315, 316, 317, 318;
    in pregnancy, 56, 282–284; sources of,
    57, 112, 114, 282; supplemental, need
    for, 282, 285. *See also* vitamin B group
food: allergic reactions to, *see* allergies;
    "basic four" groups, 108; and choice of
    diet, 103–117, 176 (*see also* diet(s));
    content of, 108–110; and drugs, interac-
    tion with, *see* medication; ethnic, and
    cultural ideas about, *see* foodstyle;
    interaction of, 3–4, 170–171; intoler-
    ance for, 174–175, 177, 178, 179, 265;
    "junk," 3, 301; "lite," 122; and mood,
    185–192; multi-ingredient, 112; raw,
    49, 125, 170, 171, 177; sensitivity to,
    178, 179–180, 182–183; substitute
    (artificial), *see* food processing; taste of,
    see flavor and aroma; toxicity of, *see*
    toxicity. *See also* convenience foods;
    eating out; fried foods; nutrients, essen-
    tial; nutrition; snack foods
Food and Drug Administration, U.S. *See*
    FDA
food diary, 11–13, 109, 116, 146, 181, 258
food industry, 121–122, 265–266
food neophobia, 296–297
food processing: additives in, 81, 107, 322,
    (preservatives) 121, 182–183, 235, 237,

food processing (*continued*)
323; artificial or imitation foods and flavorings in, 58, 107, 123, 154, 190, 214 (*see also* margarine); baby food, 113, 294; fortified foods, 44, 47, 113, 130, 294, 301 (*see also* bread; cereals; milk); and glucose release time, 254; and labeling of packaged products, 106, 107, 228; nutrients destroyed by, 47, 49, 50, 53, 54, 56, 62, 79, 125; nutrients unharmed by, 65; salting, smoking, pickling, 105, 128, 242–243, 244, 246
food processor, 121. *See also* cooking
food stamp program, 107
foodstyle, 108, 109, 118–130, 307–308, 323; adolescent, 105, 119, 130, 301; childhood habits and, 296; and cultural ideas, 99–101, 104, 131–132, 139, 280; of elderly, 313–314, 318–319; ethnic food, 121, 127–128, 130, 172, 183–184; gourmet dining and products, 120–121, 127; supplementation of, *see* supplements
Food Values of Portions Commonly Used (Pennington and Church), 112, 113, 116, 198
fractures. *See* bone damage or loss
Framingham Heart Study, 199, 208, 217, 220
free radicals, 65, 69, 207; and cancer, 59, 125, 237, 245, 246, 322, 323; vitamin/mineral destruction of, 70, 94, 245, 312
fried foods, 62, 105, 119, 124, 125, 301; deep frying, 125, 129; stir frying, 125, 127, 128
Friedman, Meyer, 212
frozen foods. *See* convenience foods
fructose, 32, 107, 173, 252, 253. *See also* sugar
fruit juice, 124, 166, 177, 271; essential nutrients in, 112; lemon juice as salt substitute, 228; orange juice, 62, 82, 113, 152, 266; processed, 107, 113
fruits, 70, 92, 105, 108, 154, 214; apples, 111, 129, 170, 176, 177; in anti-cancer diet, 239, 244, 246; bananas, 82, 83, 177, 183; berries, 125, 170, 177, 183; children's needs, 298; consumption of, 124; fibrous, 110; pineapples, 183; pears, 181; in prehistoric diet, 101, 155; raw, 125, 177; sensitivity to, 182, 183; vitamin B$_{12}$ deficiency in, 58. *See also* fruit juice; fruits, citrus
fruits, citrus, 94, 271; allergic reactions to, 182, 183; lemons and limes, 28, 60, 238; oranges, 57, 60, 176, 182; pectin (fiber) in, 110, 170, 176; as potassium source, 82; and scurvy, 28, 60, 255; vitamin C

in, 239. *See also* fruit juice
Funk, Casimir, 45

galactose, 32. *See also* carbohydrates
gallbladder, 110; and gallstones, 174
Gallup survey (1985), 303
gangrene, 248
Garland, Cedric, 243
garlic, 218, 271
gas, 110; food intolerance and, 174, 175, 177
gastrin, gastritis, 172. *See also* stomach
gastrochlorhydria, 315, 316
gastrointestinal problems. *See* intestine(s)
genetic disorders, genetic potential for disease. *See* heredity
genetic material in cells. *See* nucleic acids (DNA and RNA)
genitals, 89, 90
geophagy. *See* clay, eating of
Geriatric Medicine (Andres et al.), 143
Ghana: kwashiorkor in, 35–36
ghee (clarified butter), 127. *See also* dairy products
ginseng root, 168
glands. *See* adrenal glands; mammary glands; reproductive glands; thryroid gland
globin (protein), 37. *See also* hemoglobin
glucomannan, 149. *See also* fiber
glucose (blood sugar), 30–34, 40, 53, 162, 177, 212; absorption of, 32, 110, 171, 173, 251–252, 253; and ATP, 160–161; cooking and, 254; deprivation effects, 30, 33, 186–187; and glycemic index, 252–254; and hunger, 134; infant craving for, 102; insulin regulation of, 247, 248, 249, 250; minerals and, 72, 79, 91, 94; and muscles, 32, 33, 34, 166; test for, vitamin C and, 63; in TPN formula, 29, 34, 72. *See also* hypoglycemia
gluten. *See* grains
glycemic index, 252–254. *See also* glucose (blood sugar)
glycerol molecule, 39, 138, 174
glycogen, 155, 160; loss of (in fasting or exercise), 151, 166–167
goiter, 92–93, 95, 255
Goldberger, Joseph, 51
Goldstein, Joseph L., 211
Gortmaker, Steven, 301
gourmet dining. *See* foodstyle
gout, 152, 224
grains, 214; allergy to, 175, 181, 182; barley, 110, 154, 218; bran, 109, 111, 176, 240, 246, 265, 302; cornmeal, 77; fiber in, 90, 109, 111, 218, 240; gluten in, 175, 210; and grain group in "basic

grains (*continued*)
four," 108; millet, 175, 240; minerals
in, 77, 78, 79, 84, 87, 90–94 *passim*;
protein in, 105, 175; vitamins in, 45, 48,
57, 58; wheat flour, 105, 182; wheat
germ, 238, 302; whole, 91, 94, 109, 120,
176, 244, 245, 246; whole wheat, 57,
110, 154. *See also* bread; cereals; rice
Grandjean, Ann C., 164
grapes, 177, 271. *See also* fruits
"grazing." *See* snack foods
Greece, 73, 215
Greenland. *See* Eskimos
greens (turnip, mustard, collard), 239, 262.
See also vegetables
grits, 108. *See also* grains
growth, 90, 261
growth retardation: alcohol and, 194, 285;
as deficiency effect, 41, 69, 75, 76, 89,
90, 256; as toxicity effect, 68, 101
Grundy, Scott M., 215
guacamole, 128
gum (glutinous substance), 110. *See also*
fiber
gums (mouth tissue). *See* teeth and gums
Gurewich, Victor, 218
gymnasts, 165, 166, 168, 264. *See also*
athletes

hair, 38, 47; analysis of, 259; loss of, 55, 61
hallucinations, 51. *See also* mental problems
hallucinogens, 185
hamburgers. *See* "fast foods"
hands and feet: cold, 86; foot infection (in
diabetes), 248; numb/tingling/stiff, 50,
53, 54, 75, 76, 83, 184, 249
HANES (Health and Nutrition Examination Survey), 301
Harvard University, 219, 239, 301; alumni
exercise patterns studied, 163–164,
219–220; genetic potential
of students, 6
Harvey, William, 152
headaches, 50, 65, 67, 68, 95, 187, 249;
allergies and, 178, 182, 183, 184; caffeine withdrawal and, 198; migraine,
178, 182, 183
healing process, 35, 256; scurvy and, 61;
and slow healing, 41, 217, 249; trace
elements and, 84–85, 90, 260, 318;
vitamins and, 56, 59, 60, 62, 71, 272,
274
Health and Human Services, U.S. Department of, 107
Health and Nutrition Examination Survey
(HANES), 301
health clubs, 163

heart, the, 94; B₁ (thiamin) concentration
in, 49; damage to, *see also* heart disease;
regulation of, 78, 79, 80, 82, 88, (*see also*
heart rate); strengthened by exercise,
161, 162
heartburn, 171–172
heart disease, 6, 61, 70, 145; alcohol and,
193, 194, 196, 208, 213, 218, 219, 246;
altered rhythm, 78, 80, 82, 83, 95,224,
258; caffeine and, 199; cardiovascular
problems, 52, 88, 205, 218; cholesterol
and, 10, 205–206, 207–221, 296; coronary, 144, 196, 205, 212, 219, 220;
diabetes and, 205, 206, 248, 252; diet
and, 105, 125, 128, 206, 210, 213; diet
pills and, 148; enlargement, 41, 282;
exercise and, 162, 205, 208, 218–220;
fatty acid deficiency and, 41; heredity
and, 10, 212, 219, 220, 234, 296, 300,
309; ischemic, 206; Keshan disease, 74,
94, 95; magnesium in treatment of, 79;
mineral deficiencies and, 82, 89; prevention of, 110, 205–221; saturated fats
and, 39; smoking and, 205–206, 230–
231; Type A, 212; and weak pulse, 82;
weight/obesity and, 160, 162, 220, 225.
See also atherosclerosis; hypertension
heart rate: caffeine, nicotine and, 198,
200; exercise and, 157, 160, 161, 162,
308
heat: extreme, *see* temperatures; nutrients destroyed by, *see* cooking
heavy metal toxicity, 60. *See also* toxicity
hemicelluloses, 110. *See also* fiber
hemoglobin, 37, 56, 57; iron and, 85, 86,
88, 165, 257, (drop in) 87, 258, 260–261;
toxic buildup of, 95, 248. *See also* oxygen
hemorrhoids, 240
Hennekens, Charles, 239
Herbert, Victor, 56
heredity: and alcoholism, 197; and cholesterol, 211, 213; and genetic disorders, 6,
37, 58, 63, 88, 89, 260; and genetic
potential (vulnerability to disease), 6, 9–
10, 35, 37, 55, 189, 282, 308, 309 (*see
also entries for individual disorders*);
and genetic programming differences, 7,
34; and iron overload, 237, 263; and
weight, 10, 137, 138–139, 157, (*see also*
obesity)
hip fracture, 75, 263. *See also* osteoporosis
Hippocrates, 65
Hirsch, Jules, 137
histamine, 37, 172, 180–181, 183
histidine, 36; and toxicity (histidinemia),
37. *See also* amino acids

hives, 178, 183
honey, 107. *See also* sugar
Honolulu Heart Study, 217, 220
hormone(s), 186, 227; ANF, 223; calcium and, 76, 77; cholesterol and, 39, 40, 207, 212, 307; fatty acids and, 38; and hunger, 135; and mammary glands, 289; parathyroid, 77, 79, 229; sex, 39, 40; steroid (DHEA), 39, 149; thyroid, 92, 93, 148, 149; toxic effects on, 69, 77; vitamins B and D in formation of, 50, 53, 64, 69, 266–267. *See also* adrenaline; estrogen; insulin
"hot dog headache," 183. *See also* allergies; headaches
hot flashes, 70. *See also* menopause
Howard Johnson's, 129
Human Nutrition Research Center on Aging, 312
hunger, 133, 134–135, 136, 137; as diabetes or hypoglycemia symptom, 248, 249; food or alcohol increasing, 153, 154, 197; and satiety, 38, 135, 153; and taste for sweets, *see* sugar. *See also* appetite loss; flavor and aroma
Huntington's chorea, 6
hydrocarbons (in charcoal-broiling). *See* cooking
hydrochloric acid. *See* stomach acid
hydrogen, 177; atoms, 31, 39, 214; handling enzymes, 50; ions, 80, (*see also* electrolytes)
hydrogenation. *See* fats, unsaturated
hyperacidity, 172
hyperactivity, 189–190
hypercalcemia. *See* calcium (excess of)
hypercholestrolemia, 211
hyperglycemia, 249, 250–251
hypertension, 206, 222–231; alcohol/smoking and, 197, 213, 230–231, 322; diet and, 6, 228–230 (*see also* salt [sodium]); diet pills and, 145, 148; heredity and, 224, 309; medication for, 172, 205, 224, 228; mineral deficiency and, 94, 95; stress and, 223, 230, 231, 307; weight and, 144, 160, 225. *See also* blood pressure; stroke
hypoglycemia, 186–187, 249. *See also* glucose (blood sugar)
hypothalamus. *See* brain/brain cells
hypothermia, 319. *See also* temperatures

ice cream. *See* dairy products
Iceland, 242
IgE. *See* immunoglobulin E
illness: diet during, 270–274. *See also* disease

imipramine, 273
imitation (artificial) foods. *See* food processing
immune system: and allergies, 178, 179, 183; in diabetes, 248; infant, 287; minerals needed by, 5, 85, 90–91, 271, 272, 282; vitamins needed by, 47, 50, 57, 62, 272
immunoglobulin E (IgE), 178, 179, 183
impotence. *See* sexual potency
inactivity. *See* activity
Indian food, 127–128
indigestion. *See* digestion
indoles (chemicals), 239, 273
infant mortality, 277. *See also* mortality rate
infants: baby fat of, 138, 294–296; and baby foods, 113, 294; birth weight of, 261, 277–278, 279, 285, 286; breast-feeding of, *see* lactation; chloride deficiency and, 83; choice of diet by, 104; formulas for, 41, 288, 291, 292, 293, 298; iron deficiency/anemia in 257, 261, 281, 291, 293–294; and Menkes' disease, 89; premature, 69, 70, 88, 278, 291–292; scurvy in, 61, 63; solid foods for, 293–294, 298; special needs of, 36, 38, 41, 288, 292—293, (supplemental) 53, 54, 55, 68, 71, 85, 89, 261; and taste for sweets and salt, 102–103, 119, 294. *See also* children
infections, 5; genetic disorder and, 37; nutrient deficiency and, 35, 41, 61, 65, 256, 260; nutrients in resisting, 46, 59, 60, 62, 66, 89, 90, 272; toxicity effect and, 86, 88
inflammation, 89
ingredients: artificial, 123; labels listing, 107; and multi-ingredient foods, 112. *See also* food processing
injury: burns, 56, 62, 82, 89; exercise and, 164; and mineral deficiency, 79, 82. *See also* bone damage or loss; healing process; infections
insomnia. *See* sleep
insulin: as appetite stimulant, 135, 153, 154; -dependent diabetes, 247–248, 254; exercise and, 155, 162, 251, 308; and hypoglycemia, 186, 187; sensitivity to, 94, 162, 308; and tryptophan, 188. *See also* diabetes; hormone(s)
insulin shock. *See* hypoglycemia
intellectual performance: impaired learning, 86, 261, 293; memory loss, 317. *See also* mental problems
intermittent claudication, 70. *See also* pain (muscle)

intestine(s): bacteria in, 71, 175, 177; disorders of, 55, 56, 65, 82, 109, 110, 176, 240 (see also constipation); large, see colon; small, 173–175. See also stomach
intolerance for food. See food
intrinsic factor, 58, 316
invertase, 175. See also enzyme(s)
iodine, 73, 92–93, 108, 128, 255
ions. See electrolytes
Iranian research team, 90
iron: absorption of, 87, 88, 90, 101, 263, 272 (see also vitamin C); for adults/elderly, 10, 11, 315, 318; for athletes, 87, 165, 166; child/adolescent need for, 10, 70, 73, 85–87 passim, 261, 262, 291–294, 299, 306; deficiency of, 5, 9, 85–88, 120, 130, 165–166, 170, 200, 266, (infant) 291, 293–294 (see also anemia); in healing, 274; heme, 87, 260; -medication reaction, 273, 316; during menstruating years, see menstruation; in pregnancy/nursing diet, 85, 117, 261, 262, 263, 280, 281, 282, 290; sources of, 87, 115, 122, 197, 262, 268, 301, 322; storage of, 86, 88, 237, 270; supplemental, need for, 85, 262, 268, 281, 282, 285, 290, 292, 298, 300, 307; toxicity of, 20, 86, 87–88, 237, 262–263
irritability, 37, 51, 61, 186, 248
isoleucine, 36. See also amino acids
isometric, isotonic exercise, 230, 268. See also exercise
isothyiocyanates (chemicals), 239
Italian food, 121, 127, 128
Italy: food studies in, 105, 210, 215
itching, 249; allergy and, 181

Jamaica, 105
Japan and Japanese, 6, 226, 238, 245; Japanese food, 121, 127, 128; stomach cancer, 105, 242–243
Jason and the Argonauts, 73
jaundice, 51, 71
Java, 48
Jeejeebhoy, K. N., 27, 72
Jenkins, David, 253
Jewish tradition, 100
jogging, 156, 157, 158; and injuries, 164. See also exercise
Johns Hopkins University, 103, 199, 238–239
Journal of Clinical Oncology, 245
Journal of the American Medical Association (JAMA), 259, 305
judo, 165. See also athletes
"junk food," 3, 301

K, vitamin. See vitamin K
Kaiser-Permanente Health Maintenance Organization, 157, 196, 218
kale, 239, 262. See also vegetables
Karolinska Institute (Sweden), 291
Kempner, Walter, 226–227
Kent State University, 300
Kentucky Fried Chicken, 129
Keshan disease, 74, 94, 95
ketoacidosis, 249–250
ketones and ketosis. See toxicity
Keys, Ancel, 104–105, 210
kidneys (body organ), 94, 200; and blood pressure, 222–223, 226, 227, 229, 230; body fat and, 38; and calcium, 265, 268, 322; diabetes and, 248; diet deficiency and, 41, 82; diet or diet pill damage to, 40, 148, 152; disorders of, as cause of mineral deficiency or excess, 78–83 passim, 226; and electrolyte balance, 80; infant, 290, 295; vitamin damage to, 49, 67. See also kidney stones; uremia
kidneys (food), 49
kidney stones, 53, 60, 62, 68, 79, 256, 265
Kies, Constance, 92
kilocalories (Kcal), 30. See also calories
Kissebah, Ahmed, 144
kiwi fruit, 122
Klatsky, Arthur, 196, 197
konjac root, 149. See also fiber
K rations, 104
Krebs (citric acid) cycle, 33
Kritchevsky, David, 205, 210, 218, 241–242
!Kung Bushmen, 103, 104
Kuntzleman, Charles, 303
kwashiorkor, 35–36, 37

labeling of packaged food. See food processing
LaChance, Paul, 149, 150
lactase, 174, 175
lactation, 144, 261; benefits of, 287–288, 291–293, 298; nutrient needs of, 10, 34, 41, 44, 53, 279, 283, 289–290, 298; and prostaglandins, 38; and toxicity, 290–291
lactic acid, 161
lactose (milk sugar), 32, 176, 188; intolerance for, 174–175, 177, 265. See also sugar
lamb. See meat
Langley Porter Psychiatric Institute, 180
Laragh, John, 227
lard. See shortenings, solid
laxatives. See medication
lead toxicity, 260, 265. See also toxicity
learning difficulties. See intellectual performance

lecithin, 38, 39, 40, 188
legs, inflamed areas on, 89
legumes, 111, 127, 171, 153. *See also*
   beans; peas
lemons and limes. *See* fruits, citrus
lentils, 253
lethargy, sluggishness, 55, 186, 258. *See
   also* apathy; weakness, listlessness
*Letter on Corpulence Addressed to the
   Public* (Banting), 152
lettuce, 177, 181, 182, 235, 239. *See also*
   vegetables
leucine, 36. *See also* amino acids
licorice, 82. *See also* candy
Liebowitz, Michael, 192
life expectancy. *See* mortality rate
light: vitamins destroyed by exposure
   to, 47, 50, 53
lignin, 110. *See also* fiber
Lind, James, 28, 60
linoleic acid, 41, 173, 288
linolenic acid, 41. *See also* fatty acids
lipase, 175. *See also* enzyme(s)
lipids, 39. *See also* fats
lipoproteins, 174, 207; low- and high-
   density (LDL and HDL), *see* cholesterol
liposuction, 147
liquid protein diet. *See* diet(s)
"lite" foods, 122
liver (body organ): alcohol and, 88, 94,
   194, 195–196, 243, 273, 315; bile produced by, 39, 71; cholesterol in, 40, 41,
   94, 208, 211, 212; cirrhosis of, 88, 94,
   243; enlargement of, 282; "fatty," 36,
   37; glucose stored in, 31, 53, 173, 186,
   212, 253; glycogen stored in, 155; hypoglycemia caused by disorder of, 186;
   minerals stored in, 86, 88, 237, 270;
   nutrient deficiency and, 70, 78; toxicity
   effect on, 49, 51, 65, 67, 69, 86, 88, 234;
   toxicity inactivation by, 239, 273, 290;
   tryptophan and, 189; vitamin A stored
   in, 66–67
liver (food): as iron source, 262, 268; as
   vitamin source, 49, 51–52, 57, 58, 65,
   69, 70, 71
livestock: dietary needs of, 28
longshoremen: study of, 219–220
lungs: cholesterol deposited in, 41; nutrient protection of, 59, 65, 66, 70, 83, 94;
   smoking damage to, 200. *See also* cancer
Lunin, Nikoli, 45
lysine, 36, 37. *See also* amino acids

McCarran, David, 229
McDonald's, 129; Big Mac, 112–113
macrobiotic diet, 245. *See also* diet(s)

macrominerals, 72–83, 85, 116. *See also*
   minerals
magnesium, 82; as bone-builder, 4, 73, 74,
   75, 78, 79; -calcium balance, 79, 192,
   265; deficiency of, 78, 79–80, 230, 266,
   316; sources of, 79, 128, 300; toxicity of,
   78–79, 80, 116
magnesium sulfate, 79
malnutrition, 44, 120, 175, 193; hospital
   food and, 272
malt and maltose, 32, 175. *See also* sugar
mammary glands, 38, 289. *See also*
   lactation
manganese, 73, 290, 298; as bone-builder,
   4, 84–85, 91, 264, 269, 300; deficiency
   of, 91, 130, 267; for elderly, 317; sources
   of, 92, 200, 267; supplemental, need for,
   91, 116, 262; toxicity of, 91, 92
mangoes, 122, 239
maple syrup, 107. *See also* sugar
margarine, 39, 126, 129, 214. *See also*
   shortenings, solid
Massachusetts Institute of Technology
   (MIT), 188
Mattson, Fred H., 215
Mayer, Jean, 312
Mayo Clinic, 245, 267
mayonnaise, 214. *See also* salad dressing
mazindol, 148
Meals-on-Wheels programs, 318
measles, 56
measuring intake, 11. *See also* food diary
meat: allergy or sensitivity to, 181, 183;
   avoidance of, in low-cholesterol diet,
   214; beef consumption, 105, 121, 124,
   128; hamburgers, *see* "fast foods";
   lamb, 181, 182; lean, 102, 126; and meat
   group in "basic four," 108; as nutrient
   source, 52, 58, 64, 78, 92, 94, 267, (organ
   meats) 49, 87, 88, 262 (*see also* kidneys
   [food]; liver [food]; pork, 100, 210; in
   prehistoric diet, 101, 102; processed,
   107 (*see also* food processing); red, 3, 92,
   124, 126, 262, 322, (diets eliminating) 4,
   87, 88, 91, 108, 300; substitutes for, 107,
   123; veal, 124, 126, 128
mediators (chemical agents), in allergic
   response, 178–180
Medical College of Wisconsin, 144
Medical Research Council (England), 186,
   282
medication: antacids, 78, 172, 265, 316;
   antibiotics (tetracycline, erythromycin), 60, 62, 71, 82, 265, 273, 316; anticoagulant, 63; anticonvulsant, 79, 80;
   antidepressant, antipsychotic, 273;
   aspirin, 60, 62, 172, 173, 181, 199, 291;
   carcinogenic, 233; cholesterol-lower-

medication (*continued*)
ing, 208, 209, 218; for diabetes, 251
(*see also* insulin); diet pills, 145, 148,
149; food interaction with or interaction of, 272–273, 315–316, 318; for
hypertension, 172, 205, 224, 228; laxatives, 78, 176; nursing mothers' use of,
290–291; and nutritional needs, 44, 56,
60, 62, 116; stomach irritation by, 172;
supplements blocked by or interfering
with, 56, 63, 78, 265. *See also* amphetamines; contraceptives, oral; diuretics
megadoses: danger, ineffectiveness, or
interference of, 44, 47, 63. *See also*
supplements; toxicity
Mellanby, Edward, 68
memory, 38, 188; loss of, 317. *See also*
mental problems
Menkes' disease, 89
menopause: hot flashes of, 70; and postmenopausal estrogen or bone loss, 242,
264, 266, 267, 269, 317
menstruation, 136, 194, 264; and amenorrhea, 164, 304, 305; iron needs during,
10, 87, 261, 306, 307; and PMS (premenstrual syndrome), 53, 54, 70, 191–192
mental problems: confusion, disorientation, 51, 53; delirium, 30, 51, 78, 80;
dementia, 51; emotional disturbance,
57, 95, 180–181; loss of concentration,
47, 293; paranoia, 89; personality
change, 50; psychiatric disorders,
179–180, 190. *See also* depression;
intellectual performance; memory;
schizophrenia
mental retardation, 37, 89, 101, 194, 283
metabolism: basal, 92, 134–136, 137;
"crossroads of," 51; defined, 30; diet
pills and, 148; exercise and, 156, 157,
158, 160, 162–164; faulty, 33, 44, 59, 78;
maternal, 290; mineral role in, 77–78,
81, 82, 90, 91; premature infant, 291;
smoking and, 201; vitamin role in, 44,
46, 48, 53, 59, 61, 68; weight loss and,
225. *See also* carbohydrates; digestion;
fats; fatty acids; protein
metalloenzymes. *See* enzyme(s)
methane, 177
methionine, 36, 37. *See also* amino acids
methylcellulose. *See* celluloses
Metropolitan Life Insurance Company
weight-for-height tables, 16, 17, 140–
141, 142, 143, 213
Mexican food, 121, 127, 128, 130, 172
Michigan State University, 153
microminerals. *See* trace elements
microwave oven, 121, 125
migraine. *See* headaches

milk: and cancer, 243; and cholesterol,
214; cow's, for babies, 288, 293, 298;
exposed to light, 50; fortified, 69, 113,
122, 255, 261, 262, 266, 267; intolerance
for or allergy to, 174–175, 181, 182; low-
and no-fat, 122; and milk group in
"basic four," 108; milk shakes, 271; as
mineral source, 76, 79, 264–265, 267,
280, 299; mother's, 261, 287–293, 298
(*see also* lactation); skim vs. whole, for
infants, 294, 295; stomach acid stimulated by, 172–173; in tea, effect of, 200;
as vitamin source, 45, 62, 66, 67, 69,
113, 122. *See also* dairy products; soybeans and soybean products
milk of magnesia, 79. *See also* magnesium
milk sugar. *See* lactose
millet. *See* grains
mineral oil. *See* oils
minerals: "big seven" (macrominerals),
72–83, 85, 116; deficiency of, 5, 66, 74–
83 *passim*, 84–96 *passim*, 151, 269, 316;
essential, 28–29, 72–74; importance of
balance of, 74, 85; medication effects
on, 78, 265; in soil, *see* soil; sources of
(sample foods list), 115–116; supplemental, need for, 271, 284 (*see also*
supplements); synthetic, 52; vegetables
as source of, *see* vegetables. *See also*
trace elements; *entries for individual
minerals*
mints, 171, 191
miso, 105. *See also* soybeans and soybean
products
Mississippi State University, 128
molybdenum, 73, 74, 94, 95. *See also* trace
elements
Monell Chemical Senses Center (Philadelphia), 103
monosaccharides, 32. *See also* fructose;
galactose; glucose (blood sugar)
monosodium glutamate. *See* MSG
monounsaturated fatty acids, 39. *See also*
fats, unsaturated
mood: food effect on, 185–192
Mormons, 236
mortality rate: alcohol and, 196–197;
exercise and, 219–220; infant, 277; and
life expectancy, 140–141, 310–312. *See
also* death, causes of
Moscone, George, 185
mother's milk. *See* milk
Mount Zion Medical Center (San Francisco), 212
mouth: cracks at corners of, 49; dry, 61,
250; reddened, 49, 51; sore, 51, 54; sores
or inflammation around, 53, 89. *See
also* saliva; teeth and gums; tongue

MSG (monosodium glutamate), 127, 183–184, 294

mucous membranes: dry and sticky (in sodium excess), 81; vitamin A and , 59, 65, 66, 67

muffins. *See* bread

multimineral, multivitamin supplements. *See* supplements

Multiple Risk Factor Intervention Trial, 208

multiple sclerosis, 54

muscle(s), 82; contraction of (including heart), 38, 74–75, 80, 176, 206, 289; glucose and, 32, 33, 34, 166; mineral aid to, 91; myoglobin in cells of, 85, 86; pain in, *see* pain; vitamin E and, 69, 70

muscle cramps or spasms: as deficiency symptom, 47, 50, 75, 76, 78, 79, 81; exercise causing, 161; stomach cramps, 174, 176; as toxicity effect, 89, 91

muscle loss or weakness: as deficiency symptom, 34, 35, 37, 61, 68, 69, 70; as toxicity effect, 75, 77, 82, 83; weight loss and, 150, 151, 157

muscular dystrophy, 70, 94

mushrooms, 235

Muslim tradition, 100

mutagens, 235, 237, 240, 246, 322. *See also* cancer

myelin, 288

myocardium, 206. *See also* muscle(s)

myoglobin, 85, 86, 165

NASA (National Aeronautics and Space Administration), 26

nasal congestion, 182; and runny nose, 178. *See also* colds

National Academy of Sciences, 62, 243, 244, 245, 294

National Cancer Institute (NCI), 109, 244, 252

National Center for Health Statistics, 120

National Heart, Lung, and Blood Institute (NHLBI), 209

National Institute on Aging, 141

National Institutes of Health (NIH), 190, 192; cholesterol/blood pressure studies and diet, 209, 212, 224, 229, 295, 299–300; weight studies, 16, 17, 141

National Jewish Center for Immunology and Respiratory Medicine, 179

National Research Council of the National Academy of Sciences, 11, 28 73, 106

nausea and vomiting: as allergic reaction, 182; clay eating in relief of, 100; as deficiency symptom, 37, 50–55 *passim*, 78, 81, 82, 83, 95; as diabetes symptom,

248, 249, 250; in diverticulitis, 176; low-carbohydrate diet and, 152; as toxicity effect, 60–67 *passim*, 75, 77, 81, 89, 91. *See also* bulimia

Nautilus machines, 157, 163, 219. *See also* exercise

nerves and nerve tissue/cells, 91, 288; mineral deficiency and, 89, 94; minerals and nerve impulses, 73, 74, 75, 76, 80, 81, 82, 83; neurotransmitters and, 37, 54, 162, 185, 187–190, 192, 199; vitamins (A and B) and, 50, 54, 57, 65, 66

nervousness, 249

nervous system. *See* central nervous system

neurological disorders: as toxicity effect, 91, 92

neurotransmitters. *See* nerves and nerve tissue/cells

New England Journal of Medicine, 183

New England Medical Center, 301

New York Hospital–Cornell Medical Center, 227

New York State Attorney General, 62

New Zealand, 74, 238

niacin. *See* vitamin B₃

nickel, 29, 95, 260. *See also* trace elements

nicotine. *See* smoking

nicotinic acid, nicotinamide, 52, 190. *See also* vitamin B₃ (niacin)

nitrites and nitrosamines, 235, 238. *See also* food processing

Nobel Prize for Medicine, 211

noradrenaline, 225. *See also* adrenaline

norepinephrine levels, 188, 189, 192

North Shore University Hospital, 294

Norwegian diet research, 28, 45, 46, 61, 158

"nouvelle cuisine," 120

nucleic acids (DNA and RNA), 34, 55, 56, 57, 78, 90, 260; changes in DNA, and cancer, *see* cancer; trace elements in, 85

numbness. *See* hands and feet

nursing mothers. *See* lactation

nutrients, essential, 26–42, 46, 72–74, 255; fats as, 154; food conversion to, 26; in McDonald's Big Mac, 112–113; major (in sample foods list), 113; measurement of deficiency, 258–259; and nutrient density, 111, 280, 288, 292, 294, 315, 318, (in snack, convenience, or restaurant food) 119, 127, 128, 129–130, 301; Recommended Dietary Allowances, *see* RDAs; recording intake, *see* food diary; "safe and adequate" amounts, *see* ESA (Estimated Safe and Adequate amount); water as, *see* water; working

nutrients (*continued*)
together, 4, 170
nutrition: and disease prevention, 6, 9–
10; fashions in, 7; and genetic potential, *see* heredity; "nonsense" of, 3–5;
special needs, *see* adolescents; athletes;
children; elderly, the; infants; illness;
total parenteral, *see* TPN. *See also*
diet(s); food; malnutrition; nutrients,
essential
Nutrition and Physical Fitness (Briggs and
Callaway), 14, 113, 116
Nutritive Value of Foods (Gebhardt and
Matthews), 216
nuts, 49, 76, 78, 88, 214, 245, 265, 302;
allergy to, 181, 182; peanuts and peanut
butter, 52, 108, 119, 233–234, 235, 297,
302; salicylates in, 191

oats, oatmeal, 111, 218. *See also* grains
obesity, 86; adult, 308, 320; alcohol and,
197; body mass index (weight-for-
height) and, 16; and cancer, 144, 160,
242, 246; carbohydrates and, 34, 42,
111; childhood/adolescent, 138–139,
158, 294–295, 298–306 *passim*; and
cholesterol levels, 208, 213; and diabetes, 72, 144, 250, 254; fats and, 41-42,
154; as health risk, 131, 132, 141, 145,
205, 219; and heart disease, 144, 160,
162, 206, 220; heredity and, 10, 138–
139, 254, 295, 302, 323; and hyperten-
sion/blood pressure, 144, 160, 225, 231;
inactivity/exercise and, 155–156, 308,
(TV watching) 158, 163, 302, 303; pre-
vention/treatment of, 6, 110, 135, 146,
147, 151. *See also* exercise; weight
oils, 171, 245; coconut, 125, 127–128,
214–215; cod-liver, 65, 68; corn, 125,
216; fish, 39, 215, 216, 221, 317; mineral, 176, 316; olive, 39, 125, 128, 215,
221; palm, 129, 214, 215; peanut, 215;
safflower, 125, 215; seed, 221; vegetable, 39, 64, 70, 125, 129, 173, 214, 221;
wheat germ, 70. *See also* fats, saturated;
fats, unsaturated
Olefsky, Jerrold, 169, 253
oligosaccharides, 177. *See also* carbohydrates
olive oil. *See* oils
Olson, Alfred, 177
Olympic Committee, U.S., and Olympics,
164–165, 257
omega-3 fatty acids. *See* fatty acids
onions, 177, 183, 218. *See also* vegetables
oranges, orange juice. *See* fruit juice;
fruits, citrus
Oregon Health Sciences University, 229

organic solvents and anemia, 260. *See also*
toxicity
orthomolecular psychiatry, 191
osmosis, 80, 176, 226
osteomalacia. *See* bone damage or loss
osteoporosis, 84, 192, 256, 263–269; as
deficiency symptom, 68, 69, 75, 76, 91–
92, 93, 264, 307; exercise and, 76, 162,
264, 268, 269, 303, 308–309, 319, (as
risk) 164, 165; heredity and, 10, 264;
male, 76, 263–264; prevention of, 4, 6,
94, 318, (in early years) 264, 281, 299,
316–317 (*see also* exercise and, *above*);
weight and, 268, 314. *See also* bone
damage or loss
Overeaters Anonymous, 136
overweight. *See* weight
oxalic acid, 170, 265
oxaloacetic acid, 33
oxidation and reduction, 31, 49, 51, 73, 85.
See also antioxidants
oxygen: in bloodstream, 59, 73, 78, 160,
161, 237, (failure of) 206, 219 (*see also*
hemoglobin); in burning process, 31,
134; premature infants given, 70
oxytocin, 289
oysters, 171. *See also* fish and shellfish

Paffenbarger, Ralph S., 163, 219–220
pain: back, 53, 54, 57; gallbladder, 174;
heart, 79; joint or bone, 60, 61, 67, 77,
78; muscle, 55, 70, 75, 76, 78, 79; stom-
ach/abdominal, 170–172, 182, 183, 250
Paleolithic era, 101–102
pallor. *See* skin
palm oil. *See* oils
palpitations, 187
pancreas, 91, 173, 174, 175, 315; insulin
produced by, 248, 249, 250; tumors/
cancer of, 186, 243
pantothenic acid. *See* vitamin B group
papayas, 239. *See also* fruits
paralysis, 47, 48, 50, 57, 58, 82
paranoia, 89. *See also* mental problems
parathyroid hormone. *See* hormone(s)
parenteral: defined, 27. *See also* TPN
(total parenteral nutrition)
Pariza, Michael, 242
Parkinson's disease, 92
parsnips, 253. *See also* vegetables
pasta, 105, 108, 120, 128, 175. *See also*
grains
pasteurization, 62, 121. *See also* food
processing
Pauling, Linus, 60, 190, 245, 271
PCBs (polychlorinated biphenyls), 290.
See also toxicity
PEA (phenylethylamine), 192

peaches, 239. *See also* fruits

peanuts, peanut butter, peanut oil. *See* nuts; oils

pears, 181. *See also* fruits

Pearson, Thomas, 199

peas, 108, 110, 171, 181. *See also* vegetables

pectin, 110, 170. *See also* fiber

pellagra, 45, 51–52, 191, 255; alcoholism and, 197

Pennsylvania State University, 50, 297

Pentagon cholesterol study, 212

pepper. *See* spices

peppers, red, 239. *See also* vegetables

pepsin, 170

peptides, 135, 149

performance, physical and intellectual. *See* activity; athletes; intellectual performance

personality change. *See* mental problems

perspiration. *See* sweating

pesticides, 290. *See also* toxicity

phentermine, 148

phenylalanine, 36, 37, 288. *See also* amino acids

phenylethylamine (PEA), 192

phenylketonuria (PKU), 37

phenylpropanolamine (PPA), 148

phospholipids, 39. *See also* fats

phosphorus, 68; as bone-builder, 4, 69, 73–78 *passim*; deficiency of, 76, 77, 78, 291; for elderly, 317; sources of, 78, 115; toxicity of, 76, 77, 78, 116

photosynthesis, 25, 238

physical development or retardation. *See* growth; growth retardation

phytic acid, 90, 170, 262, 265

pica. *See* clay, eating of

pickling. *See* food processing

pineapples, 183. *See also* fruits

pizza. *See* "fast foods"

PKU (phenylketonuria), 37

Plant Fiber in Foods (Anderson), 110

plaque, blood. *See* blood

plaque, dental, 302. *See also* teeth and gums

platelets. *See* blood

PMS (premenstrual syndrome). *See* menstruation

polyphenols, 200

polyunsaturated fatty acids, 39. *See also* fats, unsaturated

pork. *See* meat

potassium, 73, 74, 80, 83; and blood pressure, 229, 231; deficiency, 79, 82, 151, 229, 316; sources, 82, 112, 115, 271; toxicity, 82, 83

potatoes, 175, 181, 247, 252; consumption of, 124; french-fried, 125, 129, 301; sweet, 239; wild, 100–101. *See also* vegetables

pot belly (in children), 37, 175

poultry, 154, 214; allergy to, 181; chicken nuggets, 119, 129; chicken soup, 270, 271; consumption of, 124; cooking methods (and fat), 126; fried chicken, 125, 301; as iron source, 87, 262, 268; as protein source, 105, 108, 210, 297

PPA (phenylpropanolamine), 148

Prasad, A. S., 90

pregnancy, 10, 44; diet for, 277–286; diet supplements needed for, 281, 282, 283, 286; exercise during, 283–285, 286; and heartburn, 171; and Keshan disease, 74; mineral needs during, 75, 85–93 *passim*, 117, 261, 262, 263, 280–282; protein needs during, 280; RDAs for (table), 285; toxic pleasures during, 194, 199, 285, 286, 322; vitamin needs during, 47, 53, 56, 282–283; and vitamin toxicity, 63, 284; and weight, 144, 148, 278–279, 286, 287

premature infants. *See* infants

premenstrual syndrome (PMS). *See* menstruation

preservatives. *See* food processing (additives)

Prevention magazine, 312

Pritikin diet, 154. *See also* diet(s)

processed food. *See* food processing

progesterone, 267. *See also* hormone(s)

prolactin, 289

prostaglandins, 38, 41, 173, 223

protein: allergy to (gluten), 175; animal/milk, 102, 105, 107, 130, 288, 295 (*see also* dairy products; fish and shellfish; meat; poultry); athletes' need for, 164–165; beer and wine as source of, 197; BSA, 180–181; as calorie/energy source, 79, 110, 213 (*see also* fats); cholesterol differences in, 210; complete, 36; deficiency of, 35, 37, 58, 66–67, 260; in dietary balance, 16, 112; in digestive (metabolic) process, 35–36, 55, 78–82 *passim*, 90, 94, 171, 172, 173, (and liver function) 273; and electrolyte action, 80; excess, toxicity of, 152; ferritin and transferrin, 86, 258, 259; globin, 37 (*see also* hemoglobin); in healing process, 35; high- or liquid protein diet, *see* diet(s); infant/child needs, 288, 291, 297–298; in Japanese diet, 105; as magnesium source, 79; and mental acuity, 317; in pregnancy or lactation diet, 280, 290; in prehistoric diet, 102; in processed food, labeling information, 106, 107; supple-

protein (continued)
  mental, need for, 168, 271; trace
  elements in, 85; vegetable, 107, 122,
  128, 177; and vitamin A deficiency,
  66–67; See also amino acids; collagen;
  enzyme(s); lipoproteins
protein-sparing modified fast (PSMF), 151
prunes, 183. See also fruits
psoralen derivatives, 235
psoriasis, 67. See also skin
psychiatric disorders. See mental problems
psychiatry, orthomolecular, 190
psychosomatic reactions, 179
Public Health Service, U.S., 51, 93
Puerto Rico Heart Health Program, 217,
  220
pulse, weak, 82. See also heart disease
pulse rate. See heart rate
pumpkins, 239. See also vegetables
pyridoxine. See vitamin B$_6$

radiation, 233, 260. See also toxicity
radishes, 177, 235. See also vegetables
raisins, 177. See also fruits
Ramazzini, Bernardino, 220
rancidity, 237
rashes. See skin
raw food. See food
RDAs (Recommended Dietary Allowances), 11, 12–13, 17, 20, 28, 73, 106–
  107, 109, 116, 117, 130; for athletes,
  165, 166; calcium, 75, 76, 116, 229,
  264–265, 269, 299; for elderly, 313,318,
  319; iodine, 92; iron, 85, 281; in Mc-
  Donald's Big Mac, 112; magnesium, 78,
  116; phosphorus, 77, 116; of popular
  diets, studied, 150; pregnancy, 285;
  protein, 165; vitamin A, 65, 106, 239;
  vitamin B, 47, 49, 51, 53, 57; vitamin C,
  60, 106, 271, 273; vitamin D, 68; vitamin E, 69; zinc, 89, 273. See also ESA
  (Estimated Safe and Adequate amount)
Reagan, Ronald, 234
recording intake. See food diary
red meat. See meat
reduction. See oxidation and reduction
red wine, 170, 183. See also alcohol
refrigeration, effect or lack of, 105, 136
renin. See enzyme(s)
reproductive glands, 65, 66
respiration: depressed, 79, 80, 81; rapid,
  95, 198; shortness of breath, 86, 183,
  258; sulfite sensitivity and, 183; wheezing, 182, 183
restaurant food. See eating out
restlessness, 60, 61
retinoblastoma (eye tumor), 234

retinol, 66, 67
Retinol Equivalents (REs), 12, 66, 116
retrolental fibroplasia, 70. See also vision
  problems
rhubarb, 265
riboflavin. See vitamin B$_2$
rice, 111, 128, 153; as nonallergenic food,
  175, 181, 182; parboiled, 254; polished,
  48; "stone powder" added to, 77; as
  vitamin/mineral source, 45, 84, 108. See
  also grains
rice diet, 226–227. See also diet(s)
rickets. See bone damage or loss
RNA. See nucleic acids
Rockefeller University, 126, 137, 211, 273
Rodin, Judith, 154, 304
Rolls, Barbara, 103–104
Rose, William C., 36
Rosenman, Ray, 212
roughage. See fiber
running, 156; marathon, 164, 165, 166,
  167, 264. See also athletes; exercise
runny nose. See nasal congestion
Russian cholesterol research, 210
Rutgers University, 149
rye: allergy to, 181, 182. See also grains

"safe and adequate" amounts. See ESA
  (Estimated Safe and Adequate amount)
safflower oil. See oils
St. Elizabeth's Hospital (Boston), 218
salad bars, 119, 122, 128–129, 183
salad dressing, 109, 126, 129; mayonnaise,
  214
Salazar, Alberto, 257
salicylates, 190
saliva, 173, 235, 302. See also mouth
salt (sodium), 73; -calcium reaction, 77,
  265, 322; craving for, 103, 294, 313;
  "danger" of, 3, 5, 81, 226; deficiency of,
  81, 83, 166, 291; as electrolyte, 74, 80,
  81, 82, 83; and hypertension, 10, 103,
  127, 129, 213–214, 223–228, 231, 294,
  309, 322; iodized and noniodized, 92,
  93; and PMS, 192; in processed or restaurant food, 103–107 passim, 123, 127,
  128, 129, 228, 294; sources of, 81, 116;
  toxicity of, 81–82
Saltman, Paul, 130
San Diego Clippers, 84
Sandstead, Harold, 314, 319
satiety. See hunger
saturated-unsaturated fats. See fats, saturated; fats, unsaturated
sauerkraut, 61
sausages, 183, 262. See also meat
schizophrenia: niacin and, 43, 52, 190–
  191; symptoms resembling, 88, 89.

schizophrenia (*continued*)
    See also mental problems
school lunch program, 107
Schwarz, Klaus, 28–29, 74, 95
Scott, Captain Robert, 61
scurvy, 44; alcoholism and, 197; citrus
    fruits/vitamin C and, 28, 45, 46, 56, 60–
    61, 63, 255, 260
seafood. *See* fish and shellfish
seasonings, 191. *See also* salt (sodium);
    spices
seaweed, 92, 128, 245
seeds and seed oils, 221, 265
seizures, 77, 78
selenium, 73, 237–238, 312; deficiency
    and toxicity, 74, 94, 95, 238, 244
serotonin, 37, 188, 189, 190
"setpoint," 137. *See also* body fat
Seventh Day Adventists, 236
sexual maturity delayed, 90, 101
sexual potency, 43, 70, 73, 159; and impo-
    tence, 224
shellfish. *See* fish and shellfish
shortenings, solid, 214; Crisco, 155; lard,
    128, 216. *See also* dairy products; fats;
    margarine
shortness of breath. *See* respiration
sickle-cell anemia. *See* anemia
silicon, 29, 95. *See also* trace elements
sinuses, 66, 271
skiing, skating, 157, 164, 165. *See also*
    athletes; exercise
skin, 41, 47, 90; acne, 65, 67, 301; cancer,
    233; dermatitis, 51; dry, scaly, rough,
    37, 61, 65, 67; eczema, 181, 182;
    flushed, 81, 184; healthy, 38, 65, 66;
    pale, 83, 86, 249; rashes, 55, 178, 181;
    yellow, in carotenoid overdose, 67
skin test for allergies, 180, 182
sleep, 186, 188–189; and sleep distur-
    bance, 50, 55
smell, loss of sense of. *See* flavor and
    aroma
smoked foods. *See* food processing
smoking, 141, 171, 172, 193, 200–201; and
    cancer, 233–239 *passim*, 243; exercise
    and, 308; and heart disease, 208, 213,
    219, 220, 230–231; and need for vita-
    mins, 10, 44, 60, 62, 116, 200; during
    pregnancy and lactation, 284, 286, 291
snack foods, 103, 119, 300–301, 302, 307,
    318
sodium. *See* salt
soft drinks, 113, 124, 172; caffeine in, 200,
    291; carbonated, 171, 177; cola, 182,
    266, 285, 291; diet, 122, 124
soil: trace elements in, 58, 74, 92–93, 94.
    See also trace elements

sorghum, 170
South Africa, 240
soybeans and soybean products, 52, 107,
    128, 175, 210, 245, 253; allergy to, 181,
    183; miso, 105; soy milk, 58 tofu, 105,
    122, 128, 297
speech defects, 37
spices: black pepper, 235, 271; no-sodium,
    228; and spicy foods, 172, 271
spina bifida, 282
spinach, 87, 170, 235, 239, 262, 265. *See
    also* vegetables
spinal cord degeneration, 57, 58
spinal pain. *See* pain (back)
spleen: cancer of, 237; enlargement of,
    282; iron and copper stored in, 86, 88,
    237, 258, 259
spontaneous abortion: caffeine and, 199,
    284
sports. *See* athletes
"spot reducing" exercises, 157. *See also*
    exercise
Spring Arbor College, 303
sprue, 175, 176
squamous-cell carcinoma (lung cancer).
    See cancer
squash, 67, 170, 238, 239. *See also* vegeta-
    bles
Stanford University, 196, 212, 218, 219
"starch blockers," 149
starches: children's needs, as complex
    carbohydrates, major sources and diges-
    tion of, 32. *See also* carbohydrates
starvation, 260. *See also* anorexia
steatorrhea, 79
sterility, 41
Stern, Judith S., 156–159 *passim*, 162,
    163, 165, 168, 319
steroid hormone DHEA. *See* hormone(s)
sterols, 40. *See also* cholesterol
stiffness. *See* hands and feet
Stillman Diet, 149. *See also* diet(s)
stir frying. *See* fried foods
stomach, 66; cancer of, *see* cancer; cramps
    in, 174, 176; in digestive process, 170–
    173; vitamin or drug irritation of, 51,
    172. *See also* digestion; intestine(s);
    ulcers
stomach acid, 170, 172–173, 199, 316, 318
"stone powder," 77
stress: anxiety, 51, 145, 156, 162, 172,
    187, 212; and blood pressure/heart
    disease, 219, 223, 230, 231, 307; and
    cholesterol, 212, 307, and hyperacidity,
    172; nutrient deficiencies and, 256, 260;
    physical, 62, 260 (*see also* injury; sur-
    gery); vitamin C and, 60, 62

stress hormone. *See* adrenaline
stroke, 77, 105, 128, 222, 225, 230, 231
Stunkard, Albert, 139
sublingual test for allergies, 180
substitute (artificial) foods. *See* food processing
sucrose, 32, 107, 175, 252–253. *See also* sugar
sugar, 3, 32, 42, 82, 110, 247, 322; as additive, different forms of, 107; artificial sweeteners substituted for, 123, 154; blood, *see* glucose; calorie content of, 152; consumption of, 124; hunger increased by, 153, 154; and mineral absorption, 88, 170, 171, 262; and taste for sweets, 102, 119, 154, 201, 294, 301, 313–314; and violent behavior or hyperactivity, 185, 187, 190. *See also* carbohydrates
sulfa drugs, 56. *See also* medication
sulfites, sensitivity to, 182–183
sulfur, 73, 75, 80, 95
sunlight, 69, 76, 77, 267, 292; and cancer, 233. *See also* vitamin D
supplements: guidelines for choosing, 115–117, 284, multimineral, 85, 117, 166, 262, 292, 319, 320; multivitamin, 44, 117, 165, 282, 292, 319, 329; need for 44, 168, 238, 271, 273, 312, 321–322, (during pregnancy) 281, 282, 284, 286; unbalanced, dangers of, 171, 262 (*see also* toxicity). *See also entries for individual minerals and vitamins*
surgery: diet and, 272, 273–274; recovery from, 60, 62, 71, 79 (*see also* healing process); weight-loss, 147
Swanson Center for Nutrition, 164, 165, 166, 167
sweating, 83, 187; and sodium or potassium loss, 81, 82, 166
Sweden: carbohydrate loading in, 167
sweets. *See* candy; sugar
swelling. *See* edema
swimming, 157, 160, 161, 268. *See also* exercise
synthetic (artificial) foods. *See* food processing
synthetic vitamins and minerals, 44, 52, 54, 69, 71

Taco Bell, 130
takeout meals, 119, 122. *See also* eating out
tannin, 170, 200, 262
taste. *See* flavor and aroma
taurine, 36, 288. *See also* amino acids
Taylor, Judy, 27, 72
Tay-Sachs disease, 6

T cells, 90. *See also* immune system
tea, 170, 200, 262, 285, 302
teeth and gums: dental problems of elderly, 314; swollen or bleeding gums, 60, 61; tooth decay (cavities), 65, 68, 93, 302, 305, 314; tooth discoloration, 93, 94; vitamins/minerals and, 65, 66, 68, 75, 77, 93–94. *See also* mouth
temperature, body. *See* cold, clammy feeling; fever
temperatures: extreme heat or cold, 60, 62, 82, 256, 260, 319
testosterone, 40
tetracycline (antibiotic). *See* medication
thalassemia. *See* beta-thalassemia
theophylline, 273
thiamin. *See* vitamin B₁
Third world: culturally acceptable foods in, 100–101, 280; dietary changes in, 251; dietary deficiencies in, 104, 255–256, 279, (protein) 35, (vitamin/mineral) 49, 58, 65, 66, 67, 76, 93; infant mortality in, 277, life expectancy in, 310
thirst, 81, 166, 248, 249, 250
threonine, 36. *See also* amino acids
thyroid gland, 92, 93, 255; diet pills and, 148, 149. *See also* hormone(s)
"tiger piss," 84
Time magazine, 209
tin, 29. *See also* trace elements
tingling. *See* hands and feet
tobacco. *See* smoking
tofu. *See* soybeans and soybean products
tomatoes, 82, 94, 101, 177, 182, 183, 239. *See also* vegetables
tongue: sore or swollen, 49, 51, 55, 56, 57; smooth, 53, 54, 56. *See also* mouth
total parenteral nutrition. *See* TPN
toxicity: amino acid, 37; caffeine, 199; carcinogenic, 233–234; environmental, 233, 260, 290; excess protein, 152; food (natural), 100, 101, 102, 109, 168, 235, 322; food additives and, 113, 322; heavy metal, 60; hemoglobin buildup, 95, 248; inactivated by liver, 239; ketone (ketosis), 33–34, 151, 152, 167, 248, 250; lead, 260, 265; megadose or buildup, 20, 44, 93, 94, 95, 321–322 (*see also entries for individual minerals and vitamins*); and toxic pleasures, 193–201, 230, 285–286, 291 (*see also* alcohol; coffee; smoking). *See also* allergies
TPN (total parenteral nutrition), 36; lack of small intestine and, 27, 173; nutrients contained in, 28–42 *passim*, 49, 71, 73, 99, (and deficiencies) 41, 46, 55, 56, 72, 89, 94; before surgery, 272
trace elements, 73, 84–96, 116; absorp-

trace elements (*continued*)
   tion, 90, 110, 170–171; deficiency, 74,
   84, 197, 315; sources, 29, 130, 261,
   300, 322; supplemental, need for,
   74, 85, 290, 307
transferrin, 258, 259.   *See also* protein
tremors, 78, 79, 187
triglycerides, 39, 138, 166,174, 207, 214,
   215
trypsin, 171
tryptophan, 36, 54; effect of, 37, 52, 188–
   189. *See also* amino acids
Tufts University, 158, 218, 314
tumors, 186, 234. *See also* cancer
TV watching: and obesity, 158, 163, 302,
   303
Twiggy, 132
Twinkies and "Twinkie defense," 185,
   301
twin studies, 139, 250
twitching, 79
Tylenol, 199
tyrosine, 188, 189. *See also* amino acids

Uganda, 240
ulcers, 172–173, 199, 316; as vitamin
   toxicity effect, 51
underweight. *See* weight
UNICEF, 67
University of: Alabama, 153, 227, 272;
   California, (Berkeley) 40, 123, 157, 228,
   235, (Davis) 103, 156, 159, 319, (Irvine)
   173, (San Diego) 90, 91, 169, 172, 215,
   243, 253, (San Francisco) 132, 180, 305;
   Colorado, 90; Illinois, 36, 296; Iowa,
   167; Kentucky, 218, 252; Michigan,
   154; Minnesota, 103, 104, 210, 302;
   Mississippi, 225; Nebraska, 92; New
   Mexico, 317; North Carolina, 268;
   Pennsylvania, 148, 205; Southern California, 208, 266; Sussex (England), 186;
   Texas, 172, 211, 215, 314; Toronto, 27,
   253; Wisconsin, 45, 46, 52, 68, 242
unsaturated fats. *See* fats, unsaturated
uremia, 33, 151, 152
uric acid, 59
urination, frequent, 248
uterus, 66; cancer of, 41, 242, 243; muscle
   contraction of, 38, 289

vagina, 66
valine, 36. *See also* amino acids
vanadium, 29, 74, 95. *See also* trace
   elements
variety. *See* diet(s)
veal. *See* meat
vegetable oil, vegetable protein. *See* oils;
   protein

vegetables, 58, 70, 105, 108, 214; children's needs, 298; cruciferous, 239, 244,
   246, 273, 316; as fiber source, 109, 111,
   240, 246; frozen, 62, 124; green, yellow,
   and orange, 57, 64, 66, 72, 84, 110, 238,
   244, 262, 282; as mineral source, 76, 79,
   92, 93, 102, 268; mutagen-blocking,
   237; in prehistoric diet, 102; raw, 125,
   171; in restaurant food, 127, 128. *See
   also entries for individual vegetables*
vegetarians and vegans, 54, 58, 84, 116,
   237, 245; and mineral deficiencies, 81,
   84, 88, 91, 257; and pregnancy diet, 280
vertebrae fracture, 75. *See also*
   osteoporosis
vertigo. *See* dizziness
Veterans Administration Hospital: Long
   Beach, California, 28; San Antonio,
   Texas, 227
villi and microvilli, 173, 174, 175
violent behavior: sugar and, 185, 187
vision problems, 49; blindness, 248;
   blurring, 41, 65, 249; cataracts, 50, 148;
   childhood blindness, 67; night blindness, 65, 66, 95. *See also* eyes
vitamin(s): caloric content of, 45; defined,
   45–46; destroyed by food processing,
   light, enzyme, or alcohol, 47–56 *passim*, 62, 63, 125, 127, 128, 171; discovery of, 45; essential, 28, 46; expiration
   date of, 117; fat-soluble, 45, 46, 64–71,
   122, 171, (how they work) 64; -medica-
   tion interaction, 56, 63; megadoses,
   danger, ineffectiveness, or interference
   of, 44, 47, 63 (*see also* toxicity); RDAs
   for, *see* RDAs (Recommended Dietary
   Allowances); sources of (sample foods
   list) 114–115; supplemental, need for,
   271, 273, 284, 286, 292, 312 (*see also*
   supplements); synthetic, 44, 47, 49, 50,
   54, 69, 71; water-soluble, 45, 46–63, 64,
   65, 68, 71, 177, (how they work) 48. *See
   also entries for individual vitamins*
vitamin A, 5, 68, 106, 171, 239; as antioxidant, 59, 64, 65, 238, 312; deficiency of,
   65, 66–67, 123, 166, 256, 315; during
   fever, 270; in healing, 272, 274; infant
   need of, 292, named, 45; for nursing
   mother, 290; sources of, 64, 65–67, 107,
   108, 112, 114, 122, 238, 300; supplemental, need for, 65; toxicity of, 20, 44,
   65, 67, 244, 271, 283
vitamin B group: biotin, 46, 55, 170; as
   coenzymes, 47, 48, 50, 51, 53, 57, 64;
   deficiency of, 43, 47–59 *passim*, 108,
   123, 283, 291; family of, 46–59; in
   healing, 272, 274, named, 45, 65; for
   nursing mothers, 290, 298; pantothenic

vitamin B group (continued)
  acid, 46, 50, 51; phosphorus and, 78;
  in physical stress, 62; sources of,
  49–58 passim, 107, 114–115, 197;
  supplemental, need for, 55, 56, 57, 273,
  282, 294. See also folacin (folic acid);
  entries for individual B vitamins
vitamin B₁ (thiamin), 46, 50, 51, 272;
  deficiency, 47–48, 125, 166, 256, (in
  elderly) 11, 315, 317, 318; destroyed by
  enzyme, 49, 125, 171; sources, 49, 112,
  114, 125; toxicity, 49
vitamin B₂ (riboflavin), 46, 47, 51, 272,
  316; deficiency, 49–50, 165, 166, 256,
  259, 260; destroyed by heat or light, 50,
  125; and mental acuity, 317; sources,
  49–50, 114, 301; supplemental, need
  for, 273
vitamin B₃ (niacin), 46, 272; and cholesterol, 218; deficiency, 43, 51–52, 54,
  166, 190–191; and mental acuity, 317;
  and schizophrenia, 43, 52, 189, 191;
  sources, 52, 112, 114, 301; toxicity, 51,
  52
vitamin B₆ (pyridoxine), 46, 272; and
  autism, 190; deficiency, 53–54, 130,
  190, 256, 259, 260, 282, (in elderly) 11,
  315, 317, 318; and PMS, 191–192; in
  pregnancy, 53, 282–283; sources, 54,
  114; supplemental, need for, 53, 286;
  toxicity, 44, 47, 53, 54, 168, 192, 322
vitamin B₁₂ (cobalamin), 46, 47, 95, 170,
  272; deficiency, 57–59, 108, 171, 189,
  259, 260, (in elderly) 315, 316, 318; and
  mental acuity, 317; sources, 58, 114;
  supplemental, need for, 58; vitamin C
  and, 63
vitamin C (ascorbic acid), 44, 48, 64, 106;
  as antioxidant, 59, 61, 238, 312; for
  athletes, 165, 168; caloric content of,
  45; and cancer, 5, 60, 245, 246; as cold
  cure, 5, 60, 271, 273; deficiency of, 189,
  256, (in elderly) 11, 317, 318 (and
  scurvy) 28, 45, 46, 56, 60–61, 63, 260;
  destroyed by heat, 56, 62, 125, 128;
  discovery of, 46; in healing, 272, 274;
  and iron absorption, 59, 61, 63, 152, 171,
  260, 262, (inhibited) 63; for nursing
  mothers and infants, 290, 292; in prehistoric diet, 102; for smokers, 10, 60,
  62, 200; sources of, 61–62, 108, 112,
  115, 239, 262, 300; supplemental, need
  for, 60, 273; toxicity of, 60, 62–63, 316
Vitamin C and the Common Cold
  (Pauling), 271
vitamin D, 171: and calcium loss/absorp-
  tion, 4, 10, 64, 68, 69, 76, 77, 264, 266–
  267, 269, 315; and cancer, 243; cholesterol and, 40, 207; deficiency of, 68, 76,
  78, 171, 255, 260, 267, 315; discovery of,
  68; for elderly, 11, 69, 315, 317, 318; for
  infants, 292; milk fortified with, 69,
  113, 122, 255, 267; sources of, 64, 68–
  69; supplemental, need for, 68, 267,
  292; toxicity of, 20, 68, 69, 77, 283
vitamin E, 171; as antioxidant, 59, 64, 69,
  70, 238, 312; claims for, 43, 70, 165,
  168, 191; deficiency of, 69, 70, 239, 315;
  sources of, 64, 70; supplemental, need
  for, 69; toxicity of, 69, 70–71, 312
vitamin K, 171; deficiency of, 71, 315,
  316; in healing, 272, 274; sources of, 64,
  71; supplemental, need for, 71,
vomiting. See nausea and vomiting

walking: difficulty in, 53, 54; as exercise,
  157, 219, 268, 319 (see also exercise)
Walton, Bill, 84–85, 88, 91, 267
water: content of, in food, 108; in digestive tract (and diarrhea), 176; fluoridation of, 93–94, 268, 269, 292, 317; need
  for, 29–30, 104, 166, 271, 273. See also
  dehydration
water pills. See diuretics
water retention. See edema
water-soluble vitamins. See vitamin(s)
Wayne State University, 90
weakness, listlessness: as deficiency
  symptom, 50, 57, 68, 77, 78, 258; as
  diabetes or hypoglycemia symptom,
  248, 249; as toxic effect, 75, 82. See also
  apathy; energy (loss of); fatigue; lethargy, sluggishness; muscle loss or weakness
weak pulse, 82. See also heart disease
weariness. See fatigue
weight: calories and, 17–20, 111, 133–139;
  and cancer, 144, 160, 242, 243, 246;
  control of, 146, 246; and diabetes, 144,
  247, 250–251, 254, 317; distribution of,
  142–144; foodstyle and, 120; and heart
  disease, 220, 225; -for-height tables, 16–
  17, 140–143, 213; heredity and, 10, 137,
  138–139, 157; and hypertension, 144,
  160, 225; and life expectancy, 140–141;
  "normal" or "setpoint," 137, 141, 158;
  and osteoporosis, 268, 314; overweight,
  17, 20, 278, 286, 295, (and risk) 242, 268,
  272, 314 (see also obesity); pregnancy,
  278, 286; underweight, 278, 286, (and
  risk) 20, 141, 242, 246, 272, 314 (see also
  anorexia); women and, 131–132, 168.
  See also body fat
weight gain: diets for, 20, 111; fat intake
  and, 42; inactivity and, 156; in middle
  age group, 120, 141, 158; during preg-

weight (*continued*)
nancy, 278–279, 285; over setpoint
rate, 137; smoking as limit on, 201.
See also weight
weight loss: athletes and, 164, 165; and
blood pressure, 136, 225, 231, 309; as
deficiency symptom, 57; as diabetes
symptom, 248; in diabetes treatment,
251, 254, 309; diets/strategies for, 7, 20,
111, 132–137, 144–145, 146–158, 160–
164, 226, 323; in fever, 273; speed of,
150; after surgery, 274; as toxicity
symptom, 68, 75, 77. *See also* weight
weight training, 157, 230, 283–284. *See
also* exercise
Wendy's, 129
wheat flour. *See* grains
wheat germ, wheat germ oil. *See* grains;
oils
wheezing. *See* respiration
whole wheat, whole grain. *See* grains
Why Your Child Is Hyperactive (Feingold),
190
WIC (Women, Infants and Children)
program, 277, 294
"widow's hump," 263. *See also*
osteoporosis
Wilson's disease, 89
wine, red, 70, 183. *See also* alcohol
Winick, Myron, 278, 313

Wistar Institute, 205, 241
women: anemia in, 257, HDL levels of,
208; and weight control, 131–132, 168;
special needs of, *see* lactation; menopause; menstruation; osteoporosis;
pregnancy
Worcestershire sauce, 190, 228
World War II, 28, 105, 144, 278
wounds. *See* injury
wrestlers, 164, 165, 166, 168, 230. *See also*
athletes
Wurtman, Richard and Judith, 188, 189

xerophthalmia, 66

Yale University, 154, 304
yeast, 49, 52, 57, 94; brewer's, 58, 197
yogurt. *See* dairy products

zinc, 73, 96, 101, 270; as bone-builder, 4,
84, 91, 264, 269, 300; as cold cure, 271,
273; deficiency of, 5, 66, 84, 89–91, 123,
130, 256, 266, 267, 271, 291, (for elderly)
314, 316, 317, 318; and immune system,
5, 85, 90–91, 271, 272, 282; -medication
reaction, 273, 316; in pregnancy/nurs-
ing diet, 89, 262, 281–282, 290, 298;
sources of, 90, 91, 107, 115, 220, 267;
supplemental, need for, 89, 262, 273,
282, 316; toxicity of, 89, 91, 260